The Pre-Raphaelite
Illustrators

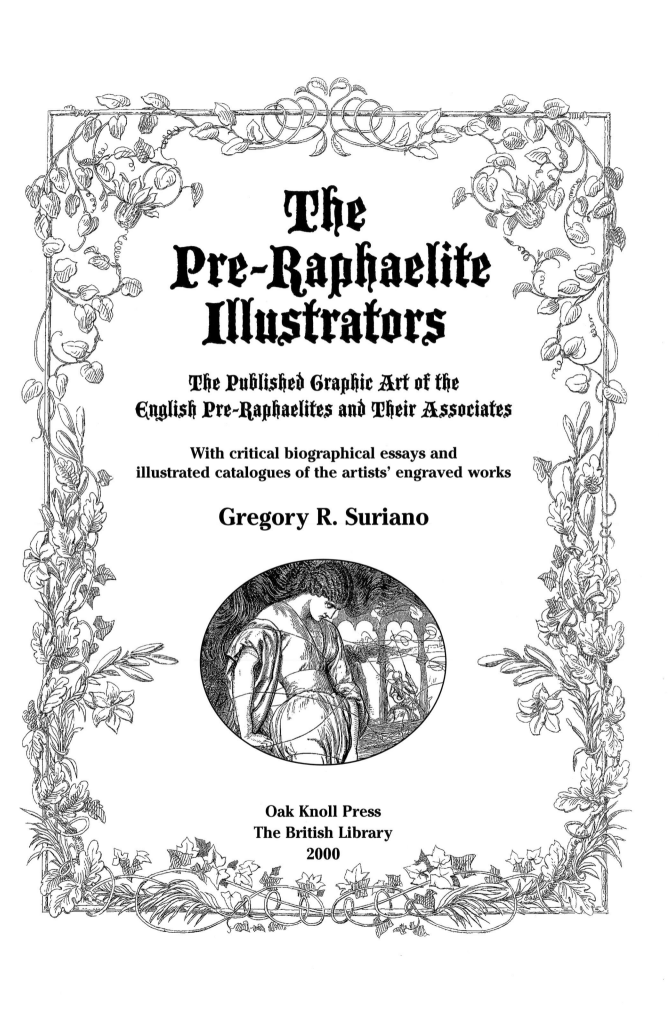

The Pre-Raphaelite Illustrators

The Published Graphic Art of the English Pre-Raphaelites and Their Associates

With critical biographical essays and
illustrated catalogues of the artists' engraved works

Gregory R. Suriano

Oak Knoll Press
The British Library
2000

First Edition

Copyright © 2000 by Gregory R. Suriano

Title: **The Pre-Raphaelite Illustrators**
Author: Gregory R. Suriano
Designer/Typographer: Gregory R. Suriano
Copyeditor: Susan B. Rotondo
Indexer: Nanette Cardon
Director of Publishing: J. von Hoelle

Published by **Oak Knoll Press**, 310 Delaware Street, New Castle, DE 19720, USA, and
The British Library, 96 Euston Road, London, NW1 2DB, UK

ISBN: 1-58456-021-5 [USA]
ISBN: 0-7123-4681-3 [UK]

Library of Congress Cataloging-in-Publication Data
Suriano, Gregory R., 1951–
    The Pre-Raphaelite illustrators: the published graphic art of the English Pre-Raphaelites and their associates; with critical biographical essays and illustrated catalogues of the artists' engraved works / Gregory R. Suriano.
        p. cm.
    Includes bibliographical references and index.
    ISBN: 1-58456-021-5
    1. Illustration of books—19th century—England. 2. Pre-Raphaelites—England—Biography. 3. Pre-Raphaelitism—England.
    I. Title.

NC978.S87 2000
760´.0942´09034—dc21   99-087847

British Library Cataloging-in-Publication Data available from The British Library

Ford Madox Brown

Ford Madox Brown

Details from the following illustrations appear as spot art throughout the book:
• *Frontispiece* for *The Brown Owl* (Ford Madox Brown), p. 1 • **The Lady of Shalott** for *Poems by Alfred Tennyson* (William Holman Hunt), p. 3 • **Abraham** and **The Sower** for *Lyra Germanica* (Ford Madox Brown), p. 4 • **Bhanavar Among the Serpents of Lake Karatis** for *The Shaving of Shagpat* (Frederick Sandys), p. 6 • **About Toys** for *Good Words* (Arthur Boyd Houghton), p. 13 • *Titlepage illustration:* **The Grass upon My Grave** for *Byron's Poetical Works* (Ford Madox Brown), p. 14 • **Oenone** for *Lays of the Scottish Cavaliers* (Joseph Noel Paton), p. 54 • **Until the Day Break and the Shadows Flee Away** in *King Solomon and the Fair Shulamite* (Simeon Solomon), p. 246 • **The Wishing Well** for *London Society* (Frederick R. Pickersgill), p. 272 • **Morgan-le-Fay** in *Reproductions of Woodcuts by F. Sandys* (Frederick Sandys), p. 318 • **The Father's Leave-Taking** in *Twenty-one Etchings Published by the Etching Club* (William Holman Hunt), p. 325 • **The Spirit of the Storm** in the *Quarto* (Frederick Sandys), p. 326 • **Una and the Lion** [#2] for *Gems of Literature* (Joseph Noel Paton), p. 336

Contents

Frederick Sandys

First Appearances of Important Books
in the Artist Catalogues

For information on editions and reprints of a repeated
multiartist volume, see the artist section in which it first appears:

The Book of British Ballads: Paton • *The Cornhill Gallery:* Leighton
Dalziels' Bible Gallery and *Art Pictures from the Old Testament:* Armstead
Dalziels' Illustrated Arabian Nights' Entertainments: Millais
The *Germ:* Brown • *The Home Affections:* Millais • *Idyllic Pictures:* Sandys
Lyra Germanica: Brown • *The Music Master:* Hughes
National Nursery Rhymes: Hughes • *Parables from Nature:* Burne-Jones
Pictures of Society: Lawless • *Poems by Alfred Tennyson:* Hunt
Rural England: Hughes • *Touches of Nature:* Armstead

Preface

My enthusiasm for the graphic art of the Pre-Raphaelites is boundless, even after nearly two decades of research and collecting. These unforgettable images were produced for books and periodicals by such nineteenth-century English artists as Dante Gabriel Rossetti, William Holman Hunt, John Everett Millais, Arthur Hughes, and Ford Madox Brown. Each little engraved masterpiece remains as rewarding to me today as the first time I discovered it in a library or bookshop.

The need to share my love of this wonderful material—to *do* something with a personal passion—has been the impetus behind my seemingly endless research and the writing of this book. To say to an audience, "Isn't this stuff terrific? Look, let me show you" gives meaning to years of study and self-pleasing acquisitiveness.

For me, the Pre-Raphaelites are poetic painters of ideas whose works speak in a visual language that can be widely appreciated; illustrators in all their art, from paintings to wood-engravings; virtuosic comic-strip artists; and in a league with the great story-tellers and stylists of twentieth-century American illustration, printmaking, and painting—Howard Pyle, John Sloan, N. C. Wyeth, Lynd Ward, Rockwell Kent, Maxfield Parrish, Thomas Hart Benton, Grant Wood, Winsor McCay, Jack Kirby, Hal Foster, Milton Caniff, Will Eisner, and a host of others in both the "commercial" and "fine-art" fields. The work of the Pre-Raphaelites is nonacademic, exciting, stylized, personal, offbeat, and immediately appealing—and in painting, so colorful as to make art before them and for decades after them shamefully dull by comparison. But this is the superficial appeal; behind the dazzle is an intensity of feeling both poetical and polemical, integrity in the pursuit of historical and natural accuracy, and a dedication to emotional and visual realism that demands the use of human models for the largest paintings as well as the tiniest illustrations.

This is why Pre-Raphaelite art in general, despite its narrative basis, is *more* than illustration, stating more than Pyle, or Wyeth, or even Kent. Further, it is the contention of this book (and for the purposes of categorizing the illustrations as Pre-Raphaelite here) that the Aesthetic movement—its art devolved of meaning and its elements superficially dedicated to conveying a beautiful arrangement of forms and colors, parodied by Du Maurier in *Punch* and by Gilbert and Sullivan in *Patience* and by Oscar Wilde in himself—may have drawn inspiration from some aspects of Rossettian Pre-Raphaelitism; but that the true Pre-Raphaelites and their associates, and Rossetti himself, always retained that mysterious, poetic, idea-based essence that barely touched the Aesthetic movement. The early drawings of such Aestheticians as Walter Crane and Frederic Leighton are here considered as Pre-Raphaelite illustration because they are substantial and evocative, not yet having become merely decorative.

At its heart, this book is the work of a collector, or perhaps a librarian, who must research, pursue, discover, assess, accumulate, list, annotate, categorize, and organize.

This massive effort—the years of following artistic heroes through the musty volumes of libraries and book dealers—has been aimed at achieving the daunting goal of finding every Pre-Raphaelite etching, every engraving on steel and wood, every original print ever published by the major Pre-Raphaelites from Hunt and Millais to Hughes and Brown—as well as unearthing the exceptional Pre-Raphaelite work of illustrators like George Du Maurier, Arthur Boyd Houghton, and Matthew Lawless. One has to know, however, when to call a halt to the process, or the knowledge and fun of the "search experience" cannot be shared—something that must be the goal of good research and good writing. That I have probably stopped short of a catalogue raisonné of these works goes without saying, and there is no claim that this book qualifies as such; but I think, and it is hoped, that it is pretty close to being one. I do claim, though, to have seen the originals of almost all the illustrations in the book's artist catalogues.

I trust that I have prepared a book that is conscientious and comprehensive, with substantial critical insight that adds to the literature of the subject, and that may become an important reference work for collectors, aficionados, students, and scholars. I have sought to accomplish this not only by providing reproductions of nearly five hundred artworks but also through the sources consulted in researching and through the book's organizational principles.

As a collector and a scholar it has made the most sense to me to concentrate on sources contemporary with the works being discussed. Since the vagaries of art criticism over the course of the last century have kept moving the Pre-Raphaelites around a chessboard of Symbolist, formalist, literary, Marxist, and other momentary associations, there seemed to be no substitute for the stories told by, and opinions of, these artists themselves, and for the essays and reviews that appeared during the lifetimes of the Pre-

Raphaelite illustrators. Nevertheless, I have been happy to consult some of the twentieth century's seminal books on the subject, beginning with Forrest Reid's *Illustrators of the Sixties* and William Fredeman's *Pre-Raphaelitism: A Bibliocritical Study*—followed by Gordon Ray's *The Illustrator and the Book in England from 1790 to 1914*; dictionaries by Rodney Engen, Simon Houfe, and Basil Hunnisett; and finally Paul Goldman's two books on Victorian illustration and Leonard Roberts's extraordinary Arthur Hughes catalogue raisonné. But these were simply starting points or supplementary sources. What the period itself had to say seemed to me the most pertinent, and in my text I have primarily incorporated the "eyewitness" accounts of Dante Gabriel and William Michael Rossetti, William Holman Hunt, John Everett Millais, William Bell Scott, Edward Burne-Jones, Ford Madox Brown, Frederic Shields, the Dalziel Brothers, and various critics, engravers, publishers, artists, and literary figures of the Victorian era.

The many books containing such letters and accounts have been of great importance in the research, as have original letters in several library manuscript collections. Most of all, there could be no substitute for seeing and examining the works of art themselves. Much of the published material is contained in my own collection of books, periodicals, and prints. I have also had the opportunity to examine these images firsthand in numerous library rare-book and print departments, and in special collections such as the British Museum's Dalziel Brothers scrapbooks and the Hartley Collection of proof wood-engravings and wood-blocks at the Museum of Fine Arts, Boston.

Aside from beginning, as is customary in the field, with Reid's and Fredeman's essential guidebooks, I have relied upon years of independent research in compiling the artists' catalogues, which I believe are the most extensive and complete ever published. I have tried not to set too many restrictions for myself: this book covers not merely the general 1860s era of illustration but all the graphic works of the major and associated Pre-Raphaelites (the exception being "influenced" artists like Du Maurier and Houghton). Similarly, the critical essays not only note illustrative accomplishments but discuss the entire career of each artist and his relationship with the Pre-Raphaelite movement. The Bibliography serves as a list of recommended material and contains primarily the works consulted in researching this book; full references to works cited in the text and captions are also contained in the Bibliography.

This brings me to the organization of the book, beginning with the treatment of notes. My basic principle has been that the use of primary voices is an important part of telling a story, and the use of numbered footnotes is a real annoyance. Therefore, the note is contained within the text: any quoted material is referenced by an indication of the writer, book or collection, date (which speaks volumes), and page number—sometimes in parentheses, sometimes within the flow of the text. This type of "conversational note" is, I think, a reader-friendly approach. For short forms of the sources, a title rather than the author's name is repeated, since the writer quoted is usually referred to in the text. The idea of notes, it seems to me, should be to bring the sources into the discussion, not to provide references that can only be deciphered through back and forth checking against a bibliography. Also toward that antideciphering end, *p.* is always used for page numbers, *vol.* for volumes, and there are no streams of multipunctuated numerals.

The Pre-Raphaelite Illustrators is divided into four sections, the plan of which has been the guiding factor behind my research for at least ten years. The Introduction paints a broad picture of the publishers, engravers, and early illustrators of the Victorian era and discusses the contributions of the Pre-Raphaelites in both painting and published graphics. The three remaining parts are divided thus: "1. The Artists and Their Works: Illustrations of the Major Pre-Raphaelites"; "2. The Artists and Their Works: Illustrations of the Pre-Raphaelite Associates"; and "3. The Artists and Their Works: Illustrations in the Pre-Raphaelite Style." All of these sections are composed of chapters devoted to individual artists; each chapter contains an essay, a catalogue, and a picture gallery. Every essay discusses the general career of the artist and his contributions to published graphics, critiquing and listing the most important Pre-Raphaelite images. Immediately following is a complete catalogue of that artist's known works for publication, accompanied by a gallery of Pre-Raphaelite black-and-white graphics—many of which have never been printed beyond their first appearances. While not every image I would have liked to reproduce (that is, every Pre-Raphaelite–style work in existence) was able to be included, I can proudly say that this book contains the largest collection of strictly Pre-Raphaelite illustrations ever assembled—including artists' complete contributions to such important books as the Moxon *Tennyson*, *The Parables of Our Lord*, and the Dalziel *Bible Gallery*.

The organization of the artist catalogues requires a quick guide. A catalogue's focus is upon those artworks created specifically by the artist for the purpose of illustrating a book or periodical or producing an original print. This book is not concerned with the steel-engraved prints that were made from existing paintings, which appeared in the *Art Journal* and other periodicals or which were sold to the public individually (and lucratively) by print publishers like Gambart and Agnew. In all cases, the illustration or print is the main focus of the catalogue, and these are always in boldface. From that standpoint, it has seemed important to track each piece's progress as it made its way through various publications during its Victorian-era life; there is, therefore, almost always a section in a catalogue called "Books Containing Reprints" for many works that appeared first in periodicals like *Good Words* and *Once a Week* and then ended up in books that collected these images in more congenial form, often taken from the original wood-blocks impressed onto (mounted) india paper.

The "Periodicals" section appears first in a catalogue, giving the periodical title, volume, date, and all the works by an artist in that volume; each illustration title is followed by the page number, engraver, and (if applicable) the destination for its reprint.

"Books" comes next, and these are works that contain first appearances of the graphics; only the images by the chapter's artist are listed. Because the titles of these works are often better known than their authors, and these are catalogues of art and not "official" bibliographies, it has made sense to alphabetically list the books by *title*—followed by author, publisher (London is understood; other places noted), and date. Any reprinted pieces included in these books are also indicated.

Following these is "Books Containing Reprints," which lists only the engravings that previously appeared elsewhere; these works' original sources are given for easy cross-referencing.

Finally, in the "Individual Prints" section are the artist's graphics that are often found in galleries or collections as single prints, whether or not they were intended as such or are contained in literary/print volumes like the poetry books of the Etching and Junior Etching clubs. These artist-created prints are listed by the print title, with publishing information secondary.

At the end of each of these headings there is occasionally an additional, separated bit of information on a book or print that is "questionable"; these may refer to works that have sometimes been mentioned in connection with an artist but that I have been unable to locate (or just could not examine), or to works that may not strictly belong in the catalogue (as it is constituted) but contain noteworthy artwork.

Because of the much smaller amount of listed and pictorial material in the "Associates" and "Style" parts, their catalogues are organized as a whole, alphabetically, and their graphic designs maintain a two-column format throughout.

Some other stylistic points should be noted. All punctuation, spellings, and capitalization in quotations from both manuscripts and published sources have been retained (except for necessary changes, like capitalizing a quote's first letter for clarification). Titles of novels that were serialized in periodicals are given in the text in italics; in the artists' catalogues and captions, however, to better distinguish them as sources for a series of illustrations in a specific periodical, they are in boldface and quotes (that is, all literary works in periodicals are presented in quotes). Noteworthy binding designs by an artist, as well as book reissues or alternate editions, are frequently included as addendum-type information (the lists are by no means exhaustive). For many graphics in the catalogues, second titles (designated *a.k.a.*) are also provided, to help clarify a century-plus of conflicting names found in reference books, biographies, museum collections, and reprint volumes.

Given the mass of information in this book, it would seem that layers of overwrought distinctions would clutter the landscape unnecessarily; thus, things have been simplified in the catalogues. A titlepage is a *titlepage*, whether preliminary or not. A picture designated *titlepage illustration* describes any art, from a small vignette to a full-page design, on a titlepage. Page numbers for periodical illustrations may indicate the actual or facing page. Full information on major books (*Dalziels' Bible Gallery*, *Touches of Nature*,

Poems by Alfred Tennyson, et al.) is given *only* in the artist catalogue in which the book is first mentioned (see the listing of initial catalogue appearances of these books, following the Contents page). Similarly, full information for prints is given only one time (for each publication) in each entry. Bibliographic references to publishers have uniformly been shortened to last or single names. If a few, usually untitled, works illustrate a poem or short story, they are often designated by an order number ("#2"), particularly in the captions.

Most of the reproductions have been taken from my personal collection, using original printings (or wood-block–printed versions). The engravings are reproduced primarily in black line rather than halftone, to emphasize as well as possible the linear qualities of the artistic techniques. Captions always give dimensions (in inches) of the illustrated image, but catalogues include such information, along with plate/block descriptions, only for "Individual Prints." The captions also contain published source works for the images (as well as the most significant reprint appearances) and/or credit public collections that have provided photographs. All illustrations reproduced in each separate artist section (text and catalogue) are understood to be by that artist.

The artists have been chosen by some basic criteria. The "Major Pre-Raphaelites" and "Associates" sections include every artist who either painted or illustrated in a primarily Pre-Raphaelite style—or simply, those artists who were personally connected to the movement and managed to produce even a few illustrations. These artists have been the focus of a serious attempt to track down every published graphic each one produced, whether Pre-Raphaelite in character (in the catalogues, only these images are marked by asterisks) or not.

"Illustrations in the Pre-Raphaelite Style" features men who were primarily illustrators, whose personal relationships with the main Pre-Raphaelite painters were insignificant but who clearly were influenced in style and content by the Pre-Raphaelites—and who produced many (but never all) of their graphic works in that style. Their catalogues feature only those works in the style (and therefore no asterisk designations are necessary), and are not divided into sections like "Periodicals" and "Books"; only the most important reprint appearances are mentioned.

The choice of artists has been based on standard classifications of their works by many historians, as well as on subjective decisions. Certainly among the Pre-Raphaelites and their associates would be any artist who came into contact on a continuing basis with the Rossetti/Burne-Jones/Hunt/Millais circle and drew illustrations, and any artist who basically was a Pre-Raphaelite in graphic art, if not necessarily in other spheres (e.g., Frederic Leighton). The influenced artists, being primarily illustrators, are a more subjective group. I've included those well-known illustrators who, it seems to me, produced at least a handful of engraved pieces that may be considered Pre-Raphaelite—regardless of whether their general style belongs in another category. Thus, J. R. Clayton, Walter Crane, George Du Maurier, Arthur Boyd Houghton, George Pinwell, and John Tenniel all end up with surprising contributions to Pre-Raphaelite illustration.

Let me now gratefully acknowledge the help given me at the following institutions since the early 1980s and the debt owed to those persons who have proven gracious and invaluable to my efforts: the Boston Public Library, especially Karen Shafts of the Print Department and Roberta Zongi of Rare Books; the New York Public Library, especially the Print Room and Berg Collection; Shelley Langdale of the Department of Prints, Drawings, and Photographs, Museum of Fine Arts, Boston; Iris Snyder of the Delaware Art Museum Library; the Alexander Library,

Rutgers University, New Brunswick; the Department of Prints and Drawings, and Joan Friedman, curator of Rare Books, Yale Center for British Art, New Haven; the Pierpont Morgan Library, New York, especially the Print Room; Stephen Ferguson, curator, Rare Books Division, Princeton University Libraries; Joe Bourneuf of the Widener Library and Brenda Breed and Melanie Wisner of the Houghton Library, Harvard University, Cambridge, Massachusetts; the Fogg Art Museum, Harvard University, Rare Books, and especially Miriam Stewart and Wendy Topkins of the Prints and Drawings departments; the British Museum, London, Department of Prints and Drawings, Dalziel Collection; the Victoria and Albert Museum, London, Department of Prints, Drawings, and Paintings, especially Lionel Lambourne; and the Library of Congress, Washington, D.C., Rare Book Collection and Prints and Photographs Division.

Thanks is also due to the many people who, within the past two years, have aided me in tying up loose ends of research (often providing some of the most valuable information in this book) and obtaining photographs: Katrina Thomson, assistant keeper, Prints and Drawings, National Gallery of Scotland, Edinburgh, and Tessa Sidey, Art Department curator, Birmingham Museums and Art Gallery—for assistance well beyond expectations; Robin Rodgher, principal officer of Fine and Applied Art, Perth Museum and Art Gallery; Colin Harrison, assistant keeper, Department of Western Art, Ashmolean Museum, Oxford; Hugh Stevenson, curator, Department of Art, and Winnie Tyrrell of the Photolibrary, Glasgow Museums; J. Bennett, assistant curator, and Joseph Sharples, assistant curator, Walker Art Gallery, Liverpool; Margaret Timmers, curator of prints, Department of Prints, Drawings, and Paintings, Victoria and Albert Museum; Norma Watt, assistant keeper of art, Castle Museum, Norwich; David Morris, curator of prints, Whitworth Art Gallery, University of Manchester; Annie Dulau, curator, Hunterian Museum and Art Gallery, University of Glasgow; Kathryn Pryor, assistant librarian, Norfolk Studies, Norfolk and Norwich Central Library; Tim Wilcox, curator of exhibitions, Melva Croal, curator of art, and Ruth Greenbaum, Gallery Services, Manchester City Art Galleries; Craig Hartley, senior assistant keeper, Prints, Fitzwilliam Museum, Cambridge; Norah Gillow, keeper, William Morris Gallery, London Borough of Waltham Forest; Susan Reed, Department of Prints, Drawings, and Photographs, and Karen Otis, Photographic Services, Museum of Fine Arts, Boston; Janice Chadbourne, curator of fine arts, Boston Public Library; A. V. Griffiths, keeper, Department of Prints and Drawings, British Museum, for invaluable research and counsel, who also procured the very welcome help of Paul Goldman and Robin de Beaumont; and David Schenck, author of *Directory of the Lithographic Printers of Scotland, 1820–70*, for his exceptional dedication in unearthing several significant pieces of information on Joseph Noel Paton's works (and obtaining important input from Mr. Griffiths and Professor Michael Twynam).

On a personal level, I wish to thank: the professors in my graduate program at Rutgers University who years ago inspired (and accepted) my unconventional interests in art history—Dr. Matthew Baigell and Dr. Gerald Needham; William Dane, supervising librarian, Special Collections, and Barry Redlich, principal librarian, Art and Humanities, at the Newark (New Jersey) Public Library—whose exceptional collections of nineteenth-century periodicals and books have always been essential to my research; Simon Weager and his colleagues at Ian Hodgkins and Company in Gloucestershire, for their superb catalogues and helpful correspondence over the years; John Lewis von Hoelle, my congenial editor at Oak Knoll Press; Susan B. Rotondo, for her copyediting, and Nanette Cardon, for her indexing; Jeanette Toohey of the Delaware Art Museum, Wilmington, for her interest in my collection; my editorial colleague, Susanne Jaffe, whose support in navigating the waters of publishing has helped me in editing wonderful art books and writing this and other demanding books; another publishing colleague, Frank Finamore, whose advice in editing and design has been essential; Marilyn Campbell, who as managing editor at Rutgers University Press steered many challenging art-history manuscripts of a Victorian nature my way for scholarly copyediting; my friends Jerry Pocius, who introduced me to the world of rare-book sales, and Donald Maxton, a companion of many years in the haunting of used-book shops and the scouring of antiquarian book fairs; and finally, those to whom this book is dedicated . . .

To my wife, Sandy, for her love and understanding patience in enduring outrageous book purchases, marathon computer sessions, reams of photocopies, and solitary trips to libraries and museums . . . and to my sons: Daniel, an artistic little boy fascinated with language, books, and heroes, and Michael, a toddling boy of joyous and energetic disposition. I am proudest of the fact that the actual writing and design of this book has only rarely infringed on the important time spent with them all.

Arthur Boyd Houghton

Ford Madox Brown

Introduction:
The Pre-Raphaelites and Published Graphic Art in Victorian England

The Pre-Raphaelites who practiced the fine art of illustration for engraving began to change the course of graphic art in England in the mid-1850s, with the publication of *The Music Master* (1855), *Poems by Alfred Tennyson* (1857), and *The Poets of the Nineteenth Century* (1857). These books contain the earliest wood-engraved art by Dante Gabriel Rossetti, William Holman Hunt, Arthur Hughes, Ford Madox Brown, and John Everett Millais. For the previous five decades, publishing and engraving had been marching steadily on, improving technologically, gaining in popular consumption and appeal, and in general contributing to an explosion of universally accessible printed material.

Eighteenth-century copper-engravings were created as book illustrations and as prints—often with a political or moralizing purpose, as in the case of the medium's most famous practitioners, William Hogarth, Thomas Rowlandson, and James Gillray, all of whom engraved or etched their own work. Proliferating at the same time were individual "art prints," engraved after the paintings of old masters and well-known English artists like Hogarth, Thomas Gainsborough, Joshua Reynolds, Richard Wilson, and Benjamin West. In the years 1774–78, the monthly *Copper-Plate Magazine* was published by J. Walker and H. D. Symonds, with portrait, landscape, and historical plates.

In the early decades of the nineteenth century, metal-engraved art increasingly graced books: Rowlandson's hand-colored etchings for William Combe's *Doctor Syntax* series (1812, 1820, 1821); Richard Westall's designs for Thomas Campbell's *The Pleasures of Hope* (1820); John Constable's paintings engraved by David Lucas (*Various Subjects of Landscape, Characteristic of English Scenery*, 1833); J.M.W. Turner's hundreds of highly influential landscape illustrations for such books (often issued in series parts) as *Picturesque Views in England and Wales* (1832), *The Rivers of England* (parts, 1823–27), and Samuel Rogers's *Italy* (1830) and *Poems* (1834). Thomas Stothard, who contributed to the Rogers books, produced thousands of illustrations for steel- and wood-engravings; and the equally ubiquitous W. H. Bartlett's topographical views filled such

*Samuel Prout: **Venice** (steel-engraving, Freebairn; 3 5/8 x 5 3/8; The Keepsake for 1830)*

books as *The Scenery and Antiquities of Ireland* (1842). Annuals (Christmas gift books) like the publisher Smith, Elder's *Friendship's Offering* were popular for about two decades beginning in the 1820s and featured steel-engraved or mezzotint plates of landscapes, domestic scenes, and beautiful women to go with senti-mental stories and poems. The most famous of these annuals is *The Keepsake* (published by Hurst, Chance, and R. Jennings); the 1830 edition, despite broad-appeal intentions, includes contributors of major stature, with writings by Mary Shelley, Lord Byron, Sir Walter Scott, and Lady Caroline Lamb, and art by Stothard, Turner, Samuel Prout, R. P. Bonnington, and David Wilkie.

John Martin: **Paradise Lost, Book 9, Line 780: Satan Tempting Eve** *(mezzotint proof, Martin; 5 5/8 x 7 7/8;* Paradise Lost *[Part 9], 1826)*

Important metal-engraved prints were also produced as regional etchings of topography and architecture. Among the most significant are George Cuitt's plates for *Picturesque Buildings at Chester* (1810–11) and *A History of Chester* (1815) and John Sell Cotman's series of books chronicling his native Norfolk's antiquities (e.g., *Specimens of Northern and Gothic Architecture in the County of Norfolk, 1816–1818*). John Crome, who produced more than forty landscape etchings, was also part of this Norwich school of artists—an environ-ment from which the ultimate Pre-Raphaelite illustrator, Frederick Sandys, sprung. David Wilkie and Andrew Geddes were among the other artists who both designed and executed etchings.

Three artists whose engravings were very influential on the next generation of draughts-men were John Flaxman, John Martin, and William Blake. Flaxman was a sculptor who worked for the pottery firm of Josiah Wedgwood (which to this day uses Flaxman designs on its wares). While in Rome he was commissioned by other English citizens to

illustrate *The Iliad, The Odyssey,* and subjects from Dante and Aeschylus. These spare, clas-sical outline drawings (engraved by Thomas Piroli and published in Rome in 1793, the *Iliad* and *Odyssey* published in England in 1805) were frequently reprinted for decades there-after and influenced artists in every medium. John Martin's huge canvases of biblical scenes—vast panoramas with titles like *The Fall of Ninevah* and *Belshazzar's Feast*—attracted public and critical acclaim. For his two most famous books (issued in parts), Milton's *Paradise Lost* (1825–27) and *Illustrations of the Bible* (1831–35), Martin designed and engraved his mezzotints of sub-jects in this same transcendental spirit. The *Paradise Lost* appeared in several formats and subsequent editions, which alone assured that Martin's imaginative illustrations contin-ued to be admired in England for much of the century.

William Blake, the poet and visionary painter/printmaker/illustrator (who would become so favored by the Pre-Raphaelites, especially Rossetti and Frederic Shields), was a commercial metal-plate–engraver; among his jobs was the engraving of his friend Flaxman's illustrations for *The Theogony* (1817). Blake engraved his own designs for a number of books, including John Gay's *Fables* (1793) and his patron William Hayley's *Ballads* (1805). He developed unique methods of printmaking, notably "relief etch-

*William Blake: **The Ravens, the Sexton, and the Earthworm** (steel-engraving, Blake; 3 1/8 x 3 5/8; Gay's* Fables, *1793)*

ing" (*Songs of Innocence*, 1789, and *Jerusalem*, 1804–20); his mature line-engraving technique produced a masterpiece in the 1825 print set, *The Book of Job*.

Blake was a beacon of inspiration for several other "pastoral" artist-engravers during the second quarter of the century. His small, bucolic wood-engravings (the only ones he ever did) for Robert Thornton's *The Pastorals of Virgil* (1821) clearly inspired similar prints by Edward Calvert and Samuel Palmer. In the 1820s, Calvert engraved, on both wood and copper, arcadian scenes in a sturdy style that prefigured the bold-lined woodcuts of William Morris's Kelmscott Press in the 1890s. Palmer, noted for his transcendent watercolors, was perhaps the finest of all Victorian painter-etchers. His prints are exquisite rus-

tic miniatures, masterpieces of finely wrought detail and lofty, spiritual ideas; these were created and published primarily in Etching Club collections from the 1850s through the 1870s.

This artist-etcher tradition was strong throughout the nineteenth century, reaching fruition in books published by organizations like the Etching Club and Junior Etching Club, in the preeminent etcher James Abbott McNeill Whistler's hundreds of etchings—such as the sixteen of the *Thames Set* of 1871—and at the end of the period in the more personal printmaking of William Strang, Seymour Haden, Philip Gilbert Hamerton, Alphonse Legros, D. Y. Cameron, Frank Short, and Frank Brangwyn. The Etching Club—although it was founded in 1838 by such "old school" artists as Richard Redgrave, John Horsley, Charles West Cope, and Thomas Creswick—would become an important impetus to Pre-Raphaelite etching beginning in the late 1850s.

As will be seen, there was little original art produced for wood- or steel-engraving that was not linked to illustration of poetry or prose in the Victorian era. Not surprisingly, the self-proclaimed serious etchers of the Club, in the words of James Laver (*A History of British and American Etching*, 1929, p. 50), "seemed all to have regarded etching as a

*Edward Calvert: **The Brook** (wood-engraving, Calvert, 1829; 2 x 3 1/2; as published in Samuel Calvert's* A Memoir of Edward Calvert, *1893)*

Samuel Palmer: **The Herdsman's Cottage: Sunset** *(etching, Palmer, 1850; 3 3/4 x 3; Portfolio, vol. 3, 1872 [as* **Sunrise***])*

method of illustration. . . . [The typical question at each meeting was] 'What shall we illustrate next?'" Basil Gray (*The English Print*, 1937, p. 105) agreed: "The Etching Club and the Junior Etching Club were as much dining clubs as anything else, and when they addressed themselves to etching, the members required a set subject: as with the contemporary school of wood engravers, they were illustrators." These two groups (among the founders of the Junior Etching Club in 1857 was noted *Punch* illustrator Charles Keene, soon joined by Millais, Whistler, John Tenniel, and Fred Walker) offered the period's major venues for original Pre-Raphaelite etchings: *Etchings for the Art Union of London* (1857), *Passages from the Poems of Thomas Hood* (1858), *Passages from Modern English Poets* (1862), *A Selection of Etchings by the*

Etching Club (1865), and other volumes.

Steel-engraving developed from the limitations of the low-production copper plates and the need to produce metal plates capable of printing the hundreds or thousands of impressions required by the ever-growing public thirst for printed material beginning in the 1830s. One of the first of these steel-engraved book illustrations was created for an 1822 edition of Milton's *Paradise Lost*; soon followed the famous woman-oriented *Keepsake*-style annuals and book collections of the landscapes of Turner, Creswick, Prout, and Bartlett. Throughout the century, steel-engraving was the preferred method for the reproduction of existing paintings, whether as illustrations for books, as fine-art–quality prints of Royal Academy–exhibited works published in the *Art Journal* and other periodicals, or as single prints sold as art to the public and based on famous paintings whose rights had been purchased directly from the artists. Both Holman Hunt and Millais derived considerable incomes from the sales of rights to their paintings to print publishers like Agnew and Gambart.

The steel-engraved interpretation was essentially tonal, so if an illustration was especially prepared for a publication, it was often done in wash or watercolor or some nonlinear method. (The fact that an illustration was a new work of art, created specifically for use in a new publication, is the criterion upon which steel-engravings are included in this book.) There are many examples of Pre-Raphaelite steel-engraved frontispieces and titlepage art (the medium's chief uses in the Victorian era for original illustrations) for publishers like Macmillan and Hurst and Blackett. These always beautiful, even precious, illustrations by Millais, Hunt, Hughes, Paton, and other Pre-Raphaelites were usually engraved by Charles Henry Jeens or John Saddler, two of the most respected of the "small-plate" steel-engravers. Jeens engraved from the late 1840s for, among others, the *Art*

Journal and the Macmillan Golden Treasury Series. Saddler, active from the late 1820s, engraved Millais's frontispieces for the novels *John Halifax, Gentleman* (1861) and *Mistress and Maid* (1863), as well as illustrations by Turner, Tenniel, Gustave Doré, and Edward Poynter.

The most notable of the early illustrators in the period of the great expansion of publishing produced much of their work in the old method of drawing on metal: George Cruikshank, John Leech, Hablot Browne (Phiz), William Makepeace Thackeray, and the Pre-Raphaelite William Bell Scott all etched their own illustrations (Leech and Browne specializing in Dickens's works) from the 1830s and for several decades thereafter. Their sketchy style, and the desire of the

William Holman Hunt: **Titlepage illustration** *for* The Story of the Christians and Moors of Spain, *1878 (steel-engraving, C. H. Jeens; 2 7/8 x 2 1/4)*

Victorian reproductive wood-engravers to emulate the linear qualities of the etching/engraving tradition in the very different medium of wood-engraving, guided the work of the newer generation of artists and commercial engravers on wood—who needed to supply an endless stream of artwork for the increasingly large numbers of periodicals and books. This far-reaching revolution in illustration, which characterized most of the century's printed art, can be directly ascribed to the pioneering work of Thomas Bewick—who in biblical manner begat those who begat others in the family of professional wood-engravers and illustrators.

Thomas Bewick was born in 1753 in Northumberland, the son of a farmer. He was trained as a commercial metal engraver. In the 1770s and '80s he engraved some of his work on wood (including Gay's *Fables* and *Select Fables*) and formed a partnership with Thomas Beilby and, for a while, his brother, John Bewick. Some of the most prized and collected of all books of this period are these early Bewick-illustrated-and-engraved books: *A General History of Quadrupeds* (1790), *The History of British Birds* (vol. 1, 1797; vol. 2, 1804), and *The Fables of Aesop and Others* (1818).

Bewick's revolution in reproductive illustration involved the use of metal-engraving tools, such as a burin, to incise lines on the surface of a boxwood block by cutting across the (end) grain; traditional woodcuts were cruder because they used a knife to cut along the grain, usually of woods softer than the durable boxwood. Bewick engraved his own nature-observed drawings in a "white-line" method that built up tone and delineated lines by inscribing into the "dark" surface like a metal-engraving—the lines thus engraved did not print and all that was *left* (the raised surface) received the ink. Bewick's works were continually reissued during the Victorian era and were held in high respect by, among others, John Ruskin.

Bewick "begat" a whole school of illustrators and engravers, beginning a relationship that wood-engravers and artists would enjoy for much of the century as masters, apprentices, and coproducers of the contents of books and periodicals for publishers. Luke Clennel was Bewick's first successful apprentice and did much purely reproductive engraving—such as Samuel Rogers's *The Pleasures of Memory* (1810), after Thomas Stothard. William Harvey, an engraver and artist for Bewick, became the first renowned illustrator for wood-engravings; after his apprenticeship with Bewick ended in 1817, he studied drawing in London. He is said to have made about three thousand illustrations during the 1830s. Harvey's style (and high productivity) influenced John Gilbert and George Cruikshank, and in the 1840s and 1850s he expanded his audience with work for the popular *Penny Magazine* and the *Illustrated London News*. With the help of Harvey, Bewick illustrated/engraved the *Aesop* of 1818 and James Northcote illustrated his own *One Hundred Fables* (1828) with vignettes similar to Bewick's.

Thomas Bewick: **The Fox and the Stork** *(woodengraving, Bewick; 3 3/8 x 2 3/8;* The Fables of Aesop, *1818)*

Thomas Bolton was one of the engravers influenced by Harvey, and he is considered a pioneer in the use of photography on woodblocks. G. W. Bonner, as a commercial engraver in the 1820s and 1830s, cut Harvey's artwork and taught the profession to two giants of Victorian wood-engraving, W. J. Linton and Henry Vizetelly. John Jackson apprenticed to Bewick in the 1820s, worked for Harvey, and engraved illustrations for the *Penny Magazine* and Knight's *Pictorial Edition of the Works of Shakespeare* (8 vols., 1839–43), mainly illustrated by Kenny Meadows and Harvey. Jackson collaborated with William Andrew Chatto to produce the magnum opus on the craft, *A Treatise on Wood Engraving* (1839; revised, 1861).

Publishing pathfinder Charles Knight was responsible for the proliferation of popular and cheap books and periodicals from the 1830s on. His *Penny Magazine* (1832–45) was the seminal "mass-market" journal that brought wood-engraved illustrations to the public. He first issued his major publishing projects of Shakespeare's *Works* and illustrated titles like E. W. Lane's *The Arabian Nights* (1838–40), with Harvey's art, in parts so as to be more affordable. A second important publishing entrepreneur of this foundation period for wood-block–illustrated publications was Herbert Ingram, who, advised by Henry Vizetelly, founded the *Illustrated London News* in 1842. Throughout the rest of the century, this illustrated periodical and the groundbreaking, energetically illustrated humor magazine *Punch* (established in 1841 by the wood-engraver and Bewick pupil Ebenezer Landells) were the repositories of work by the greatest of Victorian (though not necessarily Pre-Raphaelite) illustrators, from Charles Keene and Birket Foster to George Du Maurier and John Tenniel.

John Orrin Smith was also employed by William Harvey and worked on the first critically acclaimed wood-engraved book of the Victorian era, Samuel Carter Hall's *The Book of British Ballads* (1842, 1844)—which contains early artwork by soon-to-be–Pre-Raphaelites

Joseph Noel Paton and William Bell Scott. Harvey Orrin Smith (later Orrinsmith), John's son, engraved much work of the transitional 1850s period (and beyond), including the art of Richard Doyle, C. W. Cope, John Gilbert, and John Leech. Horace Harral, a pupil of John Orrin Smith, formed a wood-engraving partnership with Harvey Orrin Smith and W. J. Linton, and engraved for many of the periodicals of the 1850s–'70s: *London Society*, the *Illustrated London News*, the *Cornhill Magazine*, and the *Graphic*. Josiah Whymper was a watercolorist and self-taught wood-engraver, whose prominent London firm worked for Charles Knight, the *Illustrated London News*, and *Sunday at Home* and engraved John Gilbert's drawings for *The Lady of the Lake* (1853) and *The Lay of the Last Minstrel* (1854). Among his apprentices were some of the era's finest illustrators: Fred Walker, Charles Keene, J. W. North, Charles Green, and George Pinwell.

Henry Vizetelly, son of the printer-engraver James Henry Vizetelly, was apprenticed to G. W. Bonner and John Orrin Smith in the 1830s and helped engrave Knight's *Arabian Nights*. With his brother James he formed Vizetelly Brothers in 1841 and produced successful works like Lockhart's *Ancient Spanish Ballads* (1842). In the 1850s Henry became well known for his color blocks and was favorably compared with George Baxter, the era's premier engraver of color prints. Vizetelly commissioned many of Birket Foster's illustration projects in both color and black and white, including *Christmas with the Poets* (1851) and Tupper's *Proverbial Philosophy* (1854), one of the nicest of the 1850s books, with contributions also by John Gilbert and John Tenniel. Vizetelly founded rival papers to the *Illustrated London News* in 1843 (*Pictorial Times*) and 1855 (*Illustrated Times*).

John R. Thompson's engravings spanned a long period, from his early cuts after Harvey, Prout, John Thurston, and Edward Corbould to plates after Stothard and Edwin Landseer

for Rogers's *Italy* and after William Mulready for Goldsmith's *The Vicar of Wakefield* (1843). Some of Thompson's most notable work was for the Pre-Raphaelites in publisher Edward Moxon's *Poems by Alfred Tennyson* and in Aytoun's *Lays of the Scottish Cavaliers* (1863), after Joseph Noel Paton. William Thomas worked with his illustrator brother George H. Thomas in New York, Paris, and Rome. In the early 1850s he set up as a wood-engraver in London, working with Harral and then with Linton on the *Illustrated London News*. He engraved Daniel Maclise's fine designs for Tennyson's *The Princess* (1860), illustrations in the periodical *London Society*, and a great Pre-Raphaelite piece, Frederick Sandys's "The Waiting Time," for *Churchman's Family Magazine* in 1863. In December 1869 Thomas founded one of the most important illustrated periodicals of the nineteenth century: the *Graphic*, whose artists included Fred Walker, Hubert Herkomer, Luke Fildes, William Small, and George Pinwell.

James D. Cooper's engraved work spanned many fashions of the period: he began cutting blocks for the *Illustrated London News* (1850s through 1870s), then for books by artists Birket Foster, Harrison Weir, Robert Barnes, and Thomas Morten. From 1883 he produced more "tonal" engravings in the Aesthetic-oriented *English Illustrated Magazine*, including those after Du Maurier and Rossetti. Through the last quarter of the century, he specialized in color wood-engravings interpreting the art of Randolph Caldecott and Kate Greenaway. Edmund Evans had a similar journey. He apprenticed as a wood-engraver to Ebenezer Landells in 1840 and worked for the *Illustrated London News* and *Punch*. In the 1860s his own business began specializing in color wood-engravings, producing the famous yellow-backs, cheap editions of books for various publishers that had color art printed on yellow paper covers. He engraved Birket Foster and Richard Doyle designs in color for gift books, created a series of sixpenny color "toy" books—whose artist was Walter Crane—and also worked with Greenaway and Caldecott.

William H. Hooper brought the progress of Victorian wood-engraving full circle, back to the "artistic" wood-engravings favored by Bewick. Apprenticed to Thomas Bolton, he engraved the designs of John Gilbert and then became manager of Joseph Swain's firm, which engraved the wood-blocks of the best Pre-Raphaelite artists of the era. From the 1870s he returned to basics, adopting a more open-spaced, thicker-lined style derived from the great early woodcut masters, thus becoming an important force in the woodcut revival of the Arts-and-Crafts movement. In this style Hooper worked with Walter Crane, Selwyn Image (at the *Century Guild Hobby Horse*), and William Morris (at the Kelmscott Press, helping Burne-Jones illustrate the famous Kelmscott *Chaucer* of 1896).

Many of the above engravers will be seen in the artist catalogues that follow to have worked on the illustrations of the Pre-Raphaelites from the 1850s through the 1880s. John Thompson, Horace Harral, Thomas Bolton, Butterworth and Heath, James D. Cooper, Edmund Evans, W. H. Hooper, H. Orrinsmith, W. Thomas, W. J. Linton, Joseph Swain, and the Dalziel Brothers all collaborated with the Pre-Raphaelite artists, with varying degrees of success. Of these engravers, Linton was the most influential and aggressive in promoting his political and artistic beliefs and creating an environment receptive to the art of wood-engraving.

William James Linton was born in 1812 and apprenticed with Bewick's disciple G. W. Bonner. The wood-engravers who followed Bewick within a few decades gradually evolved their techniques from the artist-engraver method of building a picture from darkness to light (through the incising of white lines) to imagining an artist's black lines as needing to be left in relief, in order to pro-duce a direct facsimile of another's drawing. Linton combined both methods, working with Thompson and John Orrin Smith and engraving art by Harvey and Meadows from the 1830s and for the *Illustrated London News* from its founding in the 1840s, when he also worked on the influential *Book of British Ballads*. Linton, a social activist, exhibiting painter, and poet with serious ideas about the artistry and importance of wood-engraving, founded or edited many periodicals over the years (*Illuminated Magazine, Illustrated Family Journal, People's Journal, English Republic*).

Kenny Meadows: **My Mother Tarries Long** *for "Gil Morrice" (wood-engraving, W. J. Linton; 6 x 1 7/8;* The Book of British Ballads, *ser. 1, 1842)*

In the 1850s Linton joined with his old partner's son, Harvey Orrin Smith. The firm engraved the work of distinguished artists, including Frederic Leighton (for *Romola* in the *Cornhill Magazine*, 1862–63), Walter Crane (their up-and-coming apprentice), and Rossetti (for the Moxon *Tennyson*). In 1866, by the time of his emigration to America (where he revitalized the entire illustration/engraving environment, was art director for *Frank Leslie's Illustrated Newspaper*, and wrote important books on the subject), Linton was one of the most respected men in British publishing. Rossetti preferred his workmanship to the Dalziels'; and when it came time to illustrate his sister's *Goblin Market* (1862) and *The Prince's Progress* (1866), the artist specifically sought out Linton. In writing to the publisher, Macmillan, about changes to the second edition of *Goblin Market* (April 21, 1866), Rossetti emphasized: "Linton has taken great pains—the large block especially giving him I am sure a great deal of trouble—and I would like his name to appear on the title-page (if not already printed) thus: *With 2 designs by D. G. Rossetti / Engraved by W. J. Linton*" (Lona Mosk Packer, *The Rossetti-Macmillan Letters*, 1963, p. 63). Nevertheless, in reality Linton's engravings were pretty lifeless, linearly vapid, and actually among the least appealing of Sixties products.

The two most important engraving firms began their commercial enterprises in the 1840s and for forty years were almost exclusively responsible for the artistic excellence of English periodicals and books in that golden age: Joseph Swain and the Dalziel Brothers. Swain was born in 1820, worked in his father's printing firm in London from 1829, and apprenticed with the wood-engraver Thomas Williams in the 1830s. His own wood-engraving business was started in the mid-1840s. *Punch* quickly grew so pleased with his work that he became head of its engraving department, with numerous assistants, forming an enduring partnership with the chief *Punch* cartoonist, John Tenniel. But Swain also produced a massive amount of high-quality work for books and the great magazines that often featured Pre-Raphaelite art: the *Cornhill Magazine*, *Once a Week*, *Good Words*, the *Argosy*. Among his protégés were the fine illustrator Fred Walker and the engraver W. H. Hooper.

Swain showed a number of prints at the Royal Academy in the 1860s, notably his cuts of Sandys's "Harald Harfagr" and "Danae in the Brazen Chamber" and Leighton's illustrations for *Romola*. Swain was held in high esteem (above the Dalziels) by critics and most of the Pre-Raphaelite artists, as perhaps the finest interpreter of their drawings; Tenniel, Millais, Sandys, and Rossetti all preferred his work. There is no better engraver

Edward J. Poynter: **Ducie of the Dale** *(wood-engraving, Swain; 6 1/8 x 4 1/2; Once a Week, vol. 8, 1863, p. 476)*

of the period insofar as the faithful, facsimile reproduction of an artist's original intentions, well-balanced thicknesses of lines, a clean, crisp technique that honors white areas, and a result that approaches the influential German styles of Albrecht Dürer and Alfred Rethel.

But it was the firm founded by the brothers Dalziel that had the greatest effect on English illustration. One procedure of the period was that the engravers commissioned artists to work on book projects for publishers; this the Dalziels did with a vengeance, and with integrity and the determination to create outstanding, artistic volumes. George and Edward Dalziel were in business together as wood-engravers in London by 1840. They did work for the earliest issues of *Punch*, engraving Leech's designs. One of their first books was the set of *Waverley Novels* known as the Abbotsford edition, in the mid-1840s, which includes engravings after Paton and Harvey. At the same time they engraved designs of the leading but pedestrian illustrators of the day: Corbould and Meadows for *Punch* and the *Illustrated London News*; Cruikshank for the multiedition *Ingoldsby Legends*; and Richard Doyle for *Jack the Giant Killer* (1851). In the 1850s the firm expanded with the addition of several more family members, and the Dalziels began to produce what they called their Fine Art Books—volumes entirely engraved and supervised by them, and published by Smith, Elder,

Chapman and Hall, and in most cases, George Routledge.

The first wave of artists they favored and sponsored included Birket Foster, John R. Clayton, John Tenniel, Frederick Pickersgill, and John Gilbert. All of these were transitional figures at the time—producing not quite as ephemeral and sketchy work as Harvey and Meadows, but not yet ready to make the same commitment to fine-art illustration as would the Pre-Raphaelites later in the decade and through the 1860s. John Gilbert especially became a wealthy and successful illustrator, easily churning out hundreds of decent but cursory drawings for *The Salamandrine* (1852), *Poems by Henry Wadsworth Longfellow* (1856), and his magnum opus, *The Works of Shakespeare* (1858–61, 3 vols.; a.k.a. *The Gilbert Shakespeare*). Pickersgill too was well regarded by the Dalziels, and when they felt inspired by Rethel's Dürerish wood-engravings for a modern "Dance of Death" published in 1848, they thought of Pickersgill, for an 1850 *Life of Christ* project. Other protégés who flourished in the 1860s were George Pinwell, who designed a hundred pictures for *Dalziels' Illustrated Goldsmith* (1865), and John D. Watson, who did 110 drawings for Routledge's well-received edition of *Pilgrim's Progress* (1861).

The publisher Alexander Strahan asked the brothers to be art directors for his new magazine, *Good Words*, which certainly owes the high caliber of its art and its roster of prestigious illustrators to the Dalziels. Some of the titles for which they were totally responsible were the major books of the era: *The Poets of the Nineteenth Century* (1857), *The Home Affections by the Poets* (1858), *Poems by Eliza Cook* (1861), *Orley Farm* (1861), *Lalla Rookh* (1861), *English Sacred Poetry* (1862), Millais's *Parables of Our Lord* (1864), *Dalziels' Illustrated Arabian Nights' Entertainments* (1865), *Alice's*

George Dalziel, left, *and Edward Dalziel, c. 1842 (paintings by Robert Dalziel; photo-engravings, as published in* The Brothers Dalziel: A Record of Fifty Years' Work, 1840–1890, *1901)*

Adventures in Wonderland (1865), *Ballad Stories of the Affections* (1866), *Golden Thoughts from Golden Fountains* (1867), *Poems by Jean Ingelow* (1867), *North Coast* (1868), *Through the Looking Glass* (1871), *Sing-Song* (1872), and *Dalziels' Bible Gallery* (1881)—an ongoing project begun in the early 1860s, after the English publication of the Nazarene woodcut masterpiece, *Schnorr's Bible Pictures.*

When the Dalziels engraved some of the Pre-Raphaelites' designs for *The Music Master*, *Poems by Alfred Tennyson*, and *The Poets of the Nineteenth Century* in the mid-1850s, the artistic quality of illustrative art was again undergoing a change. John Tenniel, one of the stars of the era and stylistically akin to Pre-Raphaelite art in his finer work, was nevertheless not quite of the new school; Lewis Carroll commented, "Mr. Tenniel is the only artist, who has drawn for me, who has resolutely refused to use a model, and declared he no more needed one than I should need a multiplication table to work a mathematical problem" (quoted in Martin Gardner, *The Annotated Alice*, 1960, p. 25, n. 1). According to the memoir *The Brothers Dalziel: A Record of Fifty Years' Work, 1840–1890* (1901, pp. 41–42), "In Kenny Meadows' days, the artists in black and white had not thought of the advantages of drawing from the living model; neither William Harvey nor Sir John Gilbert ever drew from Nature, and George Thomas was one of the first . . . to draw on wood direct from life. . . . It created something of a sensation at the time, for the idea of an illustration being drawn from the life had not before been heard of except in special cases. No doubt Mulready had life models for his *Vicar of Wakefield* drawings, and later on Millais never drew without life, nor did any of the pre-Raphaelite School. . . ."

The Dalziels perfected the art of facsimile wood-engraving—that is, cutting away everything, even in the most minute area of cross-hatched lines, that the artist did not draw. The planed and polished surface of a hard boxwood block, using the end grain (blocks were seldom over five inches square and larger images were made up of several blocks bolted together), was first covered with a thin coating of "Chinese" white. The artist drew right on the block—preferably in pen/brush and ink—in reverse, and the original drawing was thus cut away by engravers using burins/gravers for incising lines. The artist would then review and correct hand-pulled proofs (often made by rubbing a spoon against the back of the paper pressed against the inked block) for further work by the engraver. For large-circulation magazines and most books, the life of the block was greatly extended by taking a wax mold from the block and then making a metal electrotype (stereotype) version from which to print.

The destruction of the artist's drawing by cutting became a concern as soon as the pres-

John Gilbert: **His Mother She Prepared a Feast** (*wood-engraving, Dalziels; 5 x 4; The Salamandrine, 1852*)

tigious illustrator-painters of the Pre-Raphaelite school began their publishing careers. Photography seemed to be the answer. First the practice was to make photos of the block drawings before cutting. In *Some Practical Hints on Wood-Engraving* (1879), W. J. Linton relates that photographing the original drawing had been used since the late 1850s for reference. "I have before me at this writing photographs [of Leighton's drawings on wood-blocks to *Romola* for the *Cornhill Magazine*], with which, I doubt not, he compared my engravings, although the blocks were never delivered. I have similar photographs of the drawings of Noel Paton, Rossetti, and others, sent to me in those days, by men who chose my work, to prevent me from cutting the whole soul out of them" (p. 72). The publisher George Smith claimed that he initiated the idea of photographing the *Romola* illustrations before they were cut to help soothe the fastidious Leighton's ire over perceived problems with the engraving of his drawings (Leonard Huxley, *The House of Smith, Elder*, 1923, p. 140).

It is generally acknowledged that the first successful example of photography used on a wood-block was Thomas Bolton's engraving (actually, there are several) of a Flaxman relief sculpture in Catherine Winkworth's *Lyra Germanica* of 1861. The Dalziels, of course, were concerned with saving the valuable original drawings from destruction and were thrilled when technical advances allowed for the photographing of the paper artwork onto the wood, rather than having the artist draw directly on the block. The brothers claimed that their first such use of photography was with the early-'60s *Bible Gallery* illustrations (*Brothers Dalziel*, p. 42). When the *Bible Gallery* was finally published in 1881 in a limited edition of india-paper proofs printed from the original blocks, the heyday of engraved illustrations was practically over. Since the 1840s, lithographic, graphotype, and anastatic reproduction had all been used to cut out the

middleman and reproduce drawings exactly. For the perfectly faithful reproduction of paintings on special paper in periodicals and books, or as sold by print publishers such as Goupil, the photogravure, a continuous-tone intaglio (etching) process, was increasingly used from the 1880s. So too was photo-engraving, also called halftones (if tonal black and white) and line blocks (for linear drawings), whereby art was photographed onto a metal plate and etching left a relief "block"—a wood-engraving without the wood-engraver. The artists' catalogues in the present book would not be complete without listing the fine late works containing original illustrations reproduced by this method: Holman Hunt's in *The Light of the World* (1893); *Dramas in Miniature* (1891), *The Brown Owl* (1892), and *The Feather* (1892), all illustrated by Ford Madox Brown; and the superb Greville/George MacDonald children's books with late-career pen drawings by Arthur Hughes, such as *Phantastes* (1905) and *The Magic Crook* (1911).

In February 1855, Dante Gabriel Rossetti wrote to fellow poet-artist William Bell Scott: "[William] Allingham is shortly to be out with a new or demi-seminew vol. for which I have not yet ceased to be astounded at having drawn an illustration. . . . Hughes has done several for the same purpose, and the great Millais thus engaged for one. . . . I have been asked by Moxon to do some for the Tennyson you have seen advertized, and said I would, but I don't know whether I shall, as all the most practicable subjects have been given away already,—my own fault, however, as Millais had asked me . . . long ago" (Princeton University Library, Troxell Collection). The books referred to are, of course, *The Music Master* and the Moxon *Tennyson*. Thus entered the Pre-Raphaelites into the world of the Dalziels, Swain, Linton, and the great Victorian publishers.

The art of engraved illustration until the mid-1850s was in a bustling, developed, and well-respected but creatively stagnant stage.

Waiting to be born was a revolution—against styleless, slapdash illustrations—akin to that of the Pre-Raphaelites' late-1840s rebellion against the brown-soup, classical-formula, emotionless paintings of the Royal Academy and its established artistic heroes past and present, such as Joshua Reynolds, Benjamin West, Benjamin Robert Haydon, and William Etty.

William Michael Rossetti, eminent Victorian writer and art critic and one of the seven original Pre-Raphaelite brethren, in 1881 wrote a succinct and personal explanation of the origins and aims of the Pre-Raphaelite Brotherhood at the time of its creation in 1848 ("The Pre-Raphaelite Brotherhood," *Magazine of Art*, vol. 4, p. 435):

"These four young men [Dante Gabriel Rossetti, William Holman Hunt, John Everett Millais, and Thomas Woolner] came together, interchanged ideas, found that there were several things which they agreed in liking, and several others which they agreed in greatly disliking. . . . One thing which they much liked was the serious, earnest simplicity of the earlier Italian art; its reverent and chastened spirit; its freedom from trick and convention—or I should rather say from that species of convention which has been transmitted with authoritative or pedantic pomposity to the existing schools of art; its diligent attention to detail—sometimes of decorative patterning, at other times of object-painting, at others of expression and action; its sweet unloaded flavouring of personal predilection, without the taint of personal self-display. And, on the other hand, one thing which they much disliked was the weak half-heartedness of the prevalent modes of contemporary art; its affectation of ease and sufficiency, lapsing into shallowness and pretence; its meagre generalising, the cloak of ignorance, or precision of presentment; its genteel lack of backbone, and limp creed of cleverness; its indifference to a firm grasp of facts, whether in the subject-matter of the work of art, or in its constituent portions. With a feeling compounded of enthusiasm and iconoclasm these young artists rallied to the mediaeval Pre-Raphaelite painters; and, as their tendencies fixed and developed, and their scheme of work matured, they called themselves the Pre-raphaelite Brotherhood. . . .

"Hunt and Woolner were probably the most provoked and scornful at the shortcomings and evasions of the popular English art of their day: they imported into the movement its chief spice of bitterness and antagonism. To this they both united very superior powers of thought, strenuous working faculty, and a keen desire for actual demonstrable attainment in realisation and execution. Rossetti was from the first a poet in words, no less than a painter; the only one of the four who had at the time a considerable foundation of literary culture, joined with an original, ideal, or (as

John Everett Millais: **Lorenzo and Isabella** *(oil, 1849; 40 1/2 x 56 1/4; Walker Art Gallery, Liverpool; photogravure, as published in William Holman Hunt's* Pre-Raphaelitism and the Pre-Raphaelite Brotherhood, *vol. 1, 1905)*

some might call it) Romantic turn of mind, much in sympathy with chivalric mediaevalism. He was the chief starter of projects, suggester of novel ideas or combinations, artificer of designations, inciter to intellectual enterprise. Millais was essentially the pictorial eye and hand, with much less spontaneous tendency than Hunt and Woolner to a drastic reform in modes of work, and still less of the mental outlook and imaginative resilience of Rossetti."

On this basis, Pre-Raphaelitism developed, taking along with it the most important English artists of the century in all media, and refining its influences (such as early-Italian/Germanic art), its tastes and themes (literary above all, and Arthurian, and religious and social), and its techniques (direct recourse to nature and human models, the use of bright, luminous colors). In the formative 1840s, the simplified, religious, essentially "pre-*Raphael*ite" art of the German Nazarenes in Rome (Johann Friedrich Overbeck, Peter Cornelius, and others), as well as the engravings of Dürer and Holbein, were much appreciated in England. So when the time came to apply a new style of fresco painting to the rebuilt Houses of Parliament, a committee sponsored a series of competitions for cartoons/paintings of English history and literature. Prince Albert, head of the committee, admired the Nazarenes and in fact sought out Peter Cornelius when he was in London to work on, or at least advise on, the intended frescoes. The competitions of the 1840s opened up opportunities for new artists, many working in the Nazarene style. Ford Madox Brown, the Pre-Raphaelite godfather, had visited the Nazarenes in Rome, and his competition entry was *The Body of Harold Brought Before William the Conqueror*—a work that prefigured the Pre-Raphaelite emphasis on shallow space, contorted poses, and the use of living models. Among the winners were William Dyce, Charles West Cope, Henry Townsend, Daniel Maclise, and George Frederick Watts.

Dante Gabriel Rossetti: **The Girlhood of Mary Virgin** *(oil, 1849; 32 3/4 x 25; Tate Gallery, London; photogravure, as published in Elisabeth Luther Cary's* Poems of Dante Gabriel Rossetti, *vol. 1, 1903)*

From the prize-winning, clear-colored, Nazarene-inspired work it was merely a short skip in logic to appreciation of the new style of hyper-realistic, brilliantly colored, imaginative paintings of Millais, Brown, Hunt, Hughes, Paton, and others in the late 1840s and throughout the heyday of Pre-Raphaelitism in the 1850s. For in 1849, when Millais, Hunt, and Collinson showed their first "P.R.B." paintings —*Lorenzo and Isabella, Rienzi*, and *Italian Image-Makers*—in the Royal Academy Exhibition, and Rossetti presented *The Girlhood of Mary Virgin* at the Free Exhibition, they were well received, as works in the Nazarene tradition. But with the following year's exhibited paintings, the "secret" of the *P.R.B.* initials attached to the works became known and the critical uproar, based upon the *impudence* of these young artists, was intense. Rossetti, thin skinned as far as criticism went, was prone to exhibit gingerly from then on; Millais feared for his budding establishment career; and Hunt kept on fighting the good fight and seeking buyers for his works.

Suddenly, John Ruskin, the admired author of *Modern Painters*, set things straight with his defense of the movement in two letters to the *Times* in 1851 and his subsequent personal championing of (and often financial assistance to) Millais, Rossetti, Shields, Burne-Jones, Thomas Seddon, John Inchbold, James Smetham, and many others. For the rest of the decade, the critics remained somewhat hostile but divided, as the artists' personal styles and reputations changed and they acquired patrons and won prizes at exhibitions.

The Brotherhood drifted apart and reformed in various circles of friends and literary/artistic groups. Often with Ruskin's help, patrons bought their works. Rossetti's privately presented drawings and watercolors spread his reputation in the best "reclusive-legendary artist" marketing manner. The prodigy Millais became an A.R.A. (Royal Academy Associate) in 1853, with fame balancing on his new popular themes in such paintings as *The Proscribed Royalist* (1853) and *The Rescue* (1855). Hunt traveled to the Middle East (1853–56) to paint extraordinary works of symbolism, of intense clarity and color. Arthur Hughes, fired up by the Brotherhood's 1850 journal, the *Germ*, started exhibiting Pre-Raphaelite pictures at the Royal Academy (1852's *Ophelia*), became friends with Hunt, Rossetti, and Brown, and even posed for Millais's *The Proscribed Royalist*. Edward Burne-Jones and William Morris rhapsodized over the *Germ* and created their *Oxford and Cambridge Magazine* (monthly issues in 1856);

Rossetti contributed—and wrote to his good friend, William Bell Scott, in February 1857: "Two young men proprietors of that [*Oxford and Cambridge*] Magazine, recently come from Oxford, are very intimate friends of mine— their names are Morris and Jones. They have turned artists, . . . and both are men of real genius. Ruskin has the most unbounded hopes of them both" (Princeton University Library, Troxell Collection).

The year 1857 was a momentous one for the Pre-Raphaelites. Rossetti and his two Oxford friends (together with Val Prinsep,

Ford Madox Brown: ***Jesus Washing Peter's Feet*** *(oil, 1852–56; 46 x 52 1/2; Tate Gallery, London; autotype, as published in Ford Madox Hueffer's* Ford Madox Brown: A Record of His Life and Work, *1896)*

John R. Spencer-Stanhope, John H. Pollen, and Arthur Hughes) embarked on the famous wall-decoration project at the Oxford Union Debating Hall, all their artwork based on Arthurian themes—thus inaugurating a second, Rossetti-led Pre-Raphaelite phase that emphasized medievalism, symbolism, decorative elements, poetic inspiration, beautiful forms, heightened emotion, and themes of love and death.

Meanwhile, one of the original brothers, Thomas Woolner, had emigrated to Australia in 1852 to prospect for gold—sparking Ford Madox Brown's poignant masterpiece of contemporary realism, *The Last of England* (1855; Brown used himself and his family as models). Woolner returned to resume his sculptor's career in 1854 and produced a medallion of his friend Alfred Tennyson that eventually was engraved as the frontispiece to Moxon's *Poems by Alfred Tennyson*. Ford Madox Brown had painted one of his finest works, *Jesus Washing Peter's Feet*, exhibited in various stages in 1852 (Royal Academy) and 1856 (Liverpool). This painting was among the Pre-Raphaelite works (the others were by Hunt, Millais, and Hughes) that inflamed the imagination of Frederic Shields in 1857, at the Manchester Art Treasures Exhibition.

Brown in these years of renewed activity among the growing circle (including the beginning of their work in illustration) was a mover and shaker in the promotion of his friends' talents. Rossetti and Ruskin had taught at F. D. Maurice's Working Men's College, where Brown, in 1857, replaced Rossetti. The next year Brown helped found the Hogarth Club (an exhibiting alternative to the Royal Academy), which included Burne-Jones, Rossetti, Hughes, Morris, Woolner, Spencer-Stanhope, Scott, John R. Clayton, John W. Inchbold, and others; it was dissolved in 1861, just as Brown joined Morris in the creation of his decorative-arts firm, Morris, Marshall, Faulkner, and Co. Perhaps most importantly, Brown organized, and showed at, 1857's Free Exhibition of Pre-Raphaelite works at Russell Place, which included just about anyone who was associated with the movement—even Rossetti, who sent, in addition to watercolors, photographs of his Moxon *Tennyson* designs (Hunt sent his as well), and whose *Dante Drawing an Angel on the First Anniversary of the Death of Beatrice* (1853) and *Dante's Dream at the Time of the Death of Beatrice* (1856) won

over the critic of the *Saturday Review*: "The drawings really give the solemn, mysterious, spiritual, and yet most simple pathos which the words convey. . . . To show how far Mr. Rossetti is from being a servile imitator of the facts and phenomena of external nature—which is the popular notion of a pre-Raphaelite—we need only mention that 'Love' in the picture [*Dante's Dream*] is personified, as in Dante's *Vita*, and appears as a grown youth with red wings and blue robe, and a bow and arrows in his hand" ("A Pre-Raphaelite Exhibition," vol. 4, 1857, p. 11).

Hunt and Millais, among others, were on their way to wealth and popular success through the publication of engraved prints based on their successful exhibited paintings. Hunt's *Light of the World*, issued by Gambart in 1860, with over a thousand impressions was very successful and assured his popularity, especially as a painter of religious works. In the 1860s, Gambart also brought out *Isabella, or the Pot of Basil* and *Claudio and Isabella* and Hunt's best-received engraving, *Finding the Saviour in the Temple*, with over three thousand impressions. Noel Paton did well with Hill's issuing of his *Hesperus* in 1863 and *The Pursuit of Pleasure* in 1864. But it was Millais whose paintings were assiduously purchased by such print publishers as Agnew, McLean, Graves, and Gambart and published to great acclaim and financial remuneration, from the mid-1850s (*The Huguenot*, *The Order of Release*) through the 1890s.

Despite the permutations of the Pre-Raphaelite movement through the last five decades of the nineteenth century, its *spirit* remained essential, unchanged, and vital, especially for the artists of the original Brotherhood and their early associates. There are a few basic elements, in combination with other graphic influences (see below), that characterize Pre-Raphaelite painting, and illustration as well. Holman Hunt remained true to the founding aims of the Brotherhood, up until his last paintings and majestic two-volume history/autobiography, *Pre-Raphaelitism and the Pre-Raphaelite Brotherhood* of 1905–06. The nature of their art, he felt, was to paint serious, great ideas (in his case, social and religious) with the utmost dedication to re-creating reality in every colorful detail. That attitude encompassed the symbolism and allegorical elements that comment on and shore up the points of Pre-Raphaelite paintings, derived from the great Flemish/German masters before Raphael, like Memling, van Eyck, and Dürer—whose colors were the jewel-like models for the Pre-Raphaelites'. "All our circle knew," says Hunt, by the

Arthur Hughes: **Home from the Sea** *(oil, 1863; 20 x 25 3/4; Ashmolean Museum, Oxford; photo-engraving, as published in William Holman Hunt's* Pre-Raphaelitism and the Pre-Raphaelite Brotherhood, *vol. 2, 1906)*

formation of the P.R.B. in September 1848, "that deeper devotion to Nature's teaching was the real point at which we were aiming. . . . The first principle of Pre-Raphaelitism was to eschew all that was conventional in contemporary art" (*Pre-Raphaelitism and the Pre-Raphaelite Brotherhood*, 1905, vol. 1, pp. 134, 125). True Pre-Raphaelite work—not the later crowd-pleasing, figure-oriented paintings of Millais, not the dreamlike Botticellian arrangements or Kelmscott woodcuts of Burne-Jones, not the perfectly painted historical-scene re-creations of Frederic Leighton and Lawrence Alma-Tadema, not the theatrical stage-plays with mock Pre-Raphaelite themes of John W. Waterhouse—has the elements Hunt felt were essential and expands upon them. These works invest with meaning all the parts of a carefully observed and painted landscape, the

faces and poses of figures painted directly from models, and numerous symbolic ingredients; they are paintings of ideas, not form. Even the pure landscapes of the Pre-Raphaelite nature artists John Brett, Thomas Seddon, and John Inchbold are essentially moral propositions defined by the integrity of the keenest, Ruskinian observation of God's work in nature, and the artistic and social importance of hard work in the very act of painting.

Certainly, these artists' ideas could be social, and there was much in the air of social realism, social consciousness, and just plain socialism. William Morris, Walter Crane, and W. J. Linton were seriously involved in the socialist political movement. Brown was unstinting in his concern and help for the poor and working people, constantly raising money for widows—along with his artist friend, the very religious Frederic Shields. In his monumental paean to labor in all its forms, *Work* (1852–65), Brown includes the portraits of reformers Thomas Carlyle and F. D. Maurice. Brown, Ruskin, and Rossetti all taught at Maurice's Working Men's College. But most of the Pre-Raphaelite contemporary "social realism" pictures were not so political, concentrating on untimely deaths (Arthur Hughes's *Home from the Sea*, 1863) or concerned with what was called "fallen women" (Hunt's *The Awakening* [a.k.a. *Awakened*] *Conscience*, 1853, and Rossetti's unfinished *Found*, 1853–81).

That their picture ideas, however, were

primarily literature derived is undeniable. Literature and narrative in general were favored in paintings at the popular exhibitions at the English and Scottish Royal academies and other galleries, and in the engraved wall-prints and book/periodical illustrations that spread the fame of all talented Victorian artists. As Sidney Colvin wrote in 1870, "Englishmen love best the picture that possesses the most narrative or literary interest, quite apart from its pictorial value" ("English Painters of the Present Day: E. J. Poynter, A.R.A.," *Portfolio*, vol. 1, p. 2). But for the Pre-Raphaelites, painting and decorative design and illustration and poetry and criticism and literature (whether their own or their favored writers') were all essential links in the chain of visual art, and no great Pre-Raphaelite illustration ever fails to interpret intelligently or add significantly to the written word with which it is associated.

Nearly every Pre-Raphaelite painting and work of graphic art is related to literature. Rossetti, Brown, Hunt, Hughes, and others usually designed their own picture frames and had the poetic lines that inspired a painting lettered right onto the frame. Some art actually inspired poems (Algernon Charles Swinburne based poetry on a Simeon Solomon drawing and on Sandys's earliest drawing for his "Cleopatra" wood-engraving). The interchangeability of sources between paintings and illustrations was so obvious that most Victorian artists had no hesitation about basing important canvases upon previously published illustrations. Brown's paintings *The Coat of Many Colours* (1866), *The Corsair's Return* (1870–71), and *The Traveller* (1884) are color replicas of three illustrations; Hunt's exceptional late Pre-Raphaelite painting *The Lady of Shalott* (1886–1905) is the same composition as his famous illustration in the Moxon *Tennyson* of 1857; one of Hughes's loveliest and most radiant paintings, *The Door of Mercy* (1893), is based on a wood-engraving that appeared in *Good Words for the*

Young in 1871; Millais derived watercolor works from most of his *Parables* engravings; and Poynter's painting *Feeding the Sacred Ibis in the Halls of Karnac* (1871) duplicates his 1867 *Once a Week* illustration.

Thematically, Rossetti, Hunt, Millais, Hughes, Walter Deverell, and Charles Allston Collins began their careers with religious and Shakespearean subjects: *Ecce Ancilla Domini* (Rossetti, 1850); *Christ in the House of His Parents* (Millais, 1850; a.k.a. *The Carpenter's Shop*); *A Converted British Family Sheltering a Christian Priest from the Persecution of the Druids* (Hunt, 1850); *Twelfth Night* (Deverell, 1850); *Convent Thoughts* (Collins, 1851); *Claudio and Isabella* (Hunt, 1850 / R.A., 1853); *The Annunciation* (Hughes, 1858); and two *Ophelia*s (Millais and Hughes; both 1852).

William Holman Hunt: Design for the 1850 painting **Claudio and Isabella** *(photo-engraving, as published in William Holman Hunt's* Pre-Raphaelitism and the Pre-Raphaelite Brotherhood, *vol. 1, 1905)*

Rossetti of course, proceeded in a Dante-inspired haze of wildly personal and attractive watercolors, also invoking Malory and Tennyson and his own overheated sonnets. Hunt increasingly emphasized personal and complex religious symbolism (*The Hireling Shepherd*, 1851; *The Light of the World*, 1853; *The Scapegoat*, 1854). Millais's brilliantly odd takes on literature, love, and genre in drawings (some inspired by his romance and marriage with Ruskin's wife, Effie) and paintings (*Ophelia* and *The Vale of Rest*, 1859) soon gave way to prosaic Victorian anticipations of Norman Rockwell paintings (without the wit and playfulness). Hughes painted contemporary themes of love and loss, and Arthurian legends galore. Brown's subjects were genre, sunlit nature, history, religion, and Byron. Paton painted Shakespeare and Scottish history and the fairy world (a whole subgenre of Victorian art). Burne-Jones concentrated on things Arthurian and mythological.

When it came to literature and the printed word, the worlds of Victorian visual and written arts were intertwined both inspirationally and personally. It is important to realize, in any discussion of the paintings of the Pre-Raphaelites, and in talking of the literary/publishing and art worlds, that these creative, talented Victorians were one big social club. They dined together and talked of art and life and literature late into the night. They rented houses together and overstayed lodging welcomes. They shared studios and travels. They illustrated each other's works. They posed for each other's paintings. They embarked on decorative group projects. They entered the same exhibitions and drew on the wood-block and etched for the same engravers and publishers and clubs. They wrote letters that were unabashedly polite, complimentary, and supportive of each other's work, and raised money or found patrons for one another.

The associations were intricate and serpentine (in addition to the obvious closeness of the Brotherhood members and like painters in the first five years of Pre-Raphaelitism). Various enterprises such as the Morris design firm, the Hogarth Club, the Oxford murals adventure, the Moxon *Tennyson*, the Dalziels' bible-illustration project, and the two etching clubs kept everyone in touch in a working relationship, inclusive of the original Brotherhood and second-phase Pre-Raphaelites and almost any artist working in a Pre-Raphaelite manner. Hunt painted in the Middle East with Seddon, a good friend of Brown. Rossetti was friendly with Ruskin and James Smetham, and his "circle" included, in the 1860s and 1870s, Shields, Solomon, Burne-Jones, and Swinburne. Sandys lived at Rossetti's for a while in the 1860s, as did Swinburne and the writer George Meredith. Frederic Shields was a faithful lifelong friend to both Brown and Rossetti, often staying at their homes. Ruskin tried to instruct and support his various favorites, from Millais to Rossetti, and traveled to the continent with Burne-Jones, Inchbold, and Brett—sometimes paying for their trips and buying their works. William Bell Scott maintained a steady friendship and correspondence with Rossetti up until the latter's death and was a friend of the wood-engraver W. J. Linton, whose apprentice was Walter Crane.

Between artist and wood-engraver, illustrators Fred Walker, George Pinwell, J. W. North, John Watson, Frederick Pickersgill, John

William Bell Scott, left, *John Ruskin,* middle, *and Dante Gabriel Rossetti, 1864 (photograph; photo-engraving, as published in* Some Reminiscences of William Michael Rossetti, *vol. 1, 1906)*

Clayton, Matthew Lawless, and Charles Keene all had special working relationships with the Dalziels, as did Rossetti with Linton and Walter Crane with Evans. Burne-Jones worked closely with Hooper, the chief engraver at Morris's Kelmscott Press; Keene, North, Pinwell, and Fred Walker all apprenticed with Whymper.

Henry Holiday was a friend of Hunt and Burne-Jones. Rossetti lived for a while in the early 1870s under joint tenancy with the Morris family at Kelmscott Manor; Morris's collaboration in book design at his Kelmscott Press with lifelong friend and creative partner Burne-Jones is renowned. Noel Paton had known Millais since their student days at the Royal Academy, and they remained friends until Millais's death; Paton also maintained friendships with Ruskin and Shields. Val Prinsep studied in Paris with George Du Maurier (in whose novel *Trilby* he turns up). Burne-Jones went to Italy with Prinsep, and for a while stayed at his family's Little Holland House in the painterly company of perennial house guest George F. Watts. John Inchbold and Thomas Woolner were friends of Rossetti, the poet Coventry Patmore, and literary giants Tennyson and Browning—the latter two often socializing with many of the Pre-Raphaelites. Arthur Hughes had good relationships with the writers William Allingham (an early Rossetti friend), George MacDonald, and even Lewis Carroll, as did Millais with Anthony Trollope.

On even more personal levels, Collinson was engaged (twice) to Christina Rossetti. John Ruskin's wife, Effie Gray, had their marriage annulled and married her savior, John Everett Millais—who had up until then been Ruskin's chief protégé. Brown's daughter (with his first wife, who had died in 1846 from consumption) Emma Lucy married William Michael Rossetti. Holman Hunt's two wives were Waugh sisters—as was Thomas Woolner's wife, Alice. And a sister of Burne-Jones's wife, Georgiana, was married to Edward Poynter. Small world—and just the tip of the relationship-iceberg in the arts community of Victorian England. That this big, interdependent group of artists and writers would not be drinking from the same fountain of inspiration, especially in the area of book and periodical publication, would have been an impossibility.

It was at the point—in the mid-1850s—when the original Brotherhood members had decidedly gone their separate ways that their artistic aims found significant and renewed fulfillment in their published graphic art. Aside from the immature illustrative work of William Bell Scott and Joseph Noel Paton, a few things by Millais, and some etchings by H. J. Townsend for the Etching Club, Pre-Raphaelite illustration can be said to have officially begun with one of the most famous of all nineteenth-century English books, *Poems by Alfred Tennyson*, published by Edward Moxon in 1857—and usually known as the Moxon *Tennyson*.

There were two Pre-Raphaelite prologues to this important book. The first, of course, was the *Germ*, the four volumes of which were published in 1850 and were more liter-

John Everett Millais: **St. Agnes of Intercession** *(etching proof, Millais, 1850; 4 1/2 x 7 3/8; courtesy Birmingham Museums and Art Gallery)*

ary than pictorial, chiefly concerned with proclaiming the movement's art theories and poetic inspirations. Its contents included poetry by Thomas Woolner ("My Beautiful Lady," "Of My Lady in Death"), Coventry Patmore, Dante Rossetti ("Hand and Soul," "The Blessed Damozel"), William Bell Scott, and Walter Deverell, as well as essays on art by Ford Madox Brown and J. L. Tupper and book reviews by William Rossetti. Of chief graphic interest are the four etchings, one in each of the volumes: Hunt's for the two named poems by Woolner (two images on one plate in the fine-line, angular early-Italian style); Brown's *Cordelia*, based on an earlier drawing series and in the Nazarene-historical style of his *Chaucer at the Court of King Edward III* (1845–51); *The Child Jesus* by Collinson, almost a perfect representation of the style of the early-Renaissance frescoes engraved by Lasinio that fired up the Brotherhood in 1848; and Deverell's *Viola and Olivia*, whose prominent figures would not seem out of place among Millais's later, more prosaic, wood-engravings.

The second ground-breaking "prologue" was 1855's *The Music Master* by William Allingham, containing Millais's "The Fireside Story"; eight main pieces by Arthur Hughes, somewhat unrefined drawings in the sparse, elongated, angular early-P.R.B. style; and the influential "Maids of Elfen-Mere" by Rossetti. In a letter to William Bell Scott (February 23, 1855), Allingham notes that Arthur Hughes had "originated the plan" for the book's illustrations (Princeton University Library, Troxell Collection).

By 1856 Holman Hunt was back from the Holy Land and Europe, where he had already begun work on his illustrations for Moxon's

Poems by Alfred Tennyson. Millais, always an exceptional and highly original draughtsman, entered enthusiastically into the project and eventually produced eighteen illustrations. Rossetti dawdled, and finally tackled his illustration task—thereby working with the literary, fine-detailed, small-scale approach he favored, and thus able to get his art before the public without the risk of exhibiting. All of this was in the service of one of the trio's favorite poets.

The Pre-Raphaelites' work, in connection with that of Thomas Creswick, John C. Horsley, William Mulready, and others of the "old school," produced a revolutionary—if uneven and unsatisfying—volume. As professional as was Millais (who brought his fellow Pre-

John Everett Millais: **The Fireside Story** *(wood-engraving proof, Dalziels; 3 x 5; for the illustration in* The Music Master, *1855)*

Raphaelites into the project through talks with Tennyson, who admired him) in readying his work in a timely fashion, Rossetti was dilatory and petulant, complaining of the best subjects having been taken by the others and causing Moxon to miss publication during the lucrative Christmas (1856) season. Nevertheless, the Moxon *Tennyson* contains some of the grandest illustrations of the nineteenth century, especially Millais's "A Dream of Fair Women" duo, "St. Agnes' Eve," "The Death of the Old Year," and "The Lord of Burleigh"; Hunt's "Godiva" and his and Rossetti's for "The Lady of Shalott"; and Rossetti's two for "The Palace of Art." The disconcerting mixture of artists was not helped by an equally odd collection of

William Holman Hunt: **The Lady of Shalott** *(photograph of the drawing on the wood-block for the illustration in* Poems by Alfred Tennyson, *1857; photogravure, 4 x 3 1/2; as published in Joseph Pennell's* Some Poems by Alfred, Lord Tennyson, *1901)*

wood-engravers, older and newer: the Dalziels (by far the best results, despite Rossetti's denigrations of their work), J. Thompson, W. J. Linton, C. T. Thompson, and T. Williams.

In the same year, 1857, a more stunning volume appeared, the Rev. Robert Aris Willmott's *The Poets of the Nineteenth Century*, wherein Ford Madox Brown instantly joins the ranks of the Pre-Raphaelite illustrators with his superb effort, "The Prisoner of Chillon" from Byron, and Millais contributes two amazing pieces, "Love" and "The Dream." Hughes has one minor fairy drawing, and there's

some nice work by Tenniel and Clayton.

The rest is, shall we say, history—the history of what some call the golden age of English illustration, the Sixties school. Following shortly on the heels of these works were volumes that contain major wood-engraved images by the Pre-Raphaelites and their associates, and by many other artists whose work is included in this book because they often produced illustrations clearly dependent on elements of the Pre-Raphaelite style. Among these books are: Willmott's *English Sacred Poetry*, perhaps the best collection of original book work of Sixties artists, with illustrations by Hunt, Sandys, H. H. Armstead, J. D. Watson, and Henry Stacy Marks—arguably the latter two artists' finest work; *Dalziels' Illustrated Arabian Nights' Entertainments*, with contributions by Houghton, Millais, Tenniel, and Pinwell; Millais's masterpiece, *The Parables of Our Lord and Saviour Jesus Christ*, containing twenty absolutely perfect Pre-Raphaelite works expertly cut by the Dalziels; *Home Thoughts and Home Scenes*, with Houghton's eccentric and charming art; *Lalla Rookh*, graced with Tenniel's Germanic, uncharacteristically serious engravings; the Arthur Hughes–illustrated edition of Tennyson's *Enoch Arden*; and Christina Rossetti's *Goblin Market* and *The Prince's Progress*, for which her brother Gabriel created four extraordinary illustrations. All of these were published in the 1860s, except for the ultimate Sixties Pre-Raphaelite work (finally seeing print in 1881), *Dalziels' Bible Gallery*—with its large-format proof wood-engravings designed with obvious care and full artistic commitment by everyone who was anyone: Armstead, Sandys, Poynter, Leighton, Solomon, Houghton, Pickersgill, Burne-Jones, Hunt, and Brown. It is no coincidence that all of these great books (other than *Enoch Arden*) are Dalziel-commissioned Fine Art Books.

At the same time, the art for the illustrated, quality magazines that began to appear in 1859 with *Once a Week* was no less significant.

Indeed, the publishers and engravers for these journals and the beautifully bound gift books were usually the same. Illustrations that first appeared in periodicals like the *Cornhill Magazine* and *Good Words* frequently found their way—especially if by a "name" artist like Leighton, Millais, Du Maurier, or Fred Walker—into compilations of illustrations often printed in deluxe editions from the original wood-blocks. The publisher Smith, Elder produced the Thackeray-edited *Cornhill Magazine*, where Millais's illustrations for several Trollope novels (*Framley Parsonage, The Small House at Allington*, et al.) first appeared, as did Frederic Leighton's for George Eliot's *Romola*. Millais's art also graced the book versions of Trollope's novels, and Leighton's Eliot illustrations kept resurfacing, courtesy of Smith, Elder—in *Twenty-five Illustrations by Frederic Leighton from the Cornhill Magazine* (1867); in a deluxe two-volume *Romola*, with the blocks printed on india paper, in 1880; and in *The Cornhill Gallery* (1864), one of the most desirable of Sixties books, since it contains, printed from the original blocks, Leighton's *Romola* engravings, much Millais art, and wonderful works by Sandys, Du Maurier, Paton, and others. Smith, Elder (never one to miss a recycling, repackaging, or repricing opportunity) also issued single books devoted to *Cornhill* art by Millais and the chief illustrator of the "idyllic" (naturalistic) school, Fred Walker.

Strahan, a publisher dedicated to serving a large public through quality and low-priced books and periodicals, produced *Sunday Magazine*, the *Argosy*, and *Good Words*—the latter probably the most successful of these illustrated monthlies in the early 1860s and boasting some of the finest illustrations. In the pages of its sister publication, *Good Words for the Young*, in the early 1870s, the novels of George MacDonald (*At the Back of the North Wind, The Princess and the Goblin*), with their timeless Arthur Hughes illustrations, were triumphant—most making it into book form, writer and artist intact, soon thereafter.

John Everett Millais: **Christmas at Noningsby— Morning** *(wood-engraving, Dalziels; 6 3/4 x 4 1/4;* Orley Farm, *vol. 1, 1862;* Millais's Illustrations*)*

Strahan published a wonderful collection of eighty (mostly) previously printed works in *Millais's Illustrations* of 1866, as well as one of the best of the compilations, *Touches of Nature* (1867), with illustrations from their periodicals by Millais, Armstead, Houghton, Sandys, Hunt, Lawless, Watson, and many other luminaries.

Sampson Low, whose periodicals *Churchman's Family Magazine* and *London Society* showcased work—often lifelessly engraved by the second tier of commercial wood-engravers—by Armstead, Lawless, Sandys, Poynter, Millais, and Thomas Morten, reprinted their best illustrations in *Pictures of*

Society, another of the must-have books of the period. Cassell, the proprietors of the *Quiver*, reissued that magazine's illustrations—including Sandys's "The Advent of Winter," rechristened "October"—in their *Idyllic Pictures* of 1867.

By far the finest periodical for illustrations, just nosing out *Good Words*, was *Once a Week*, its first volume out of the gate in 1859 with eight still–Pre-Raphaelite–tinged drawings by Millais. The publication's major illustrators—Walker, Sandys, Pinwell, Morten, Lawless, Tenniel, Watson, Small, even Whistler—ended up (far from their original poetical inspirations) in Walter Thornbury's *Historical and Legendary Ballads and Songs* of 1876. This book and the Dalziel *Bible Gallery* represent the swan song of Sixties and Pre-Raphaelite illustration.

In addition to the elements based on the stylistic requirements of engraved line drawings, the Pre-Raphaelites' graphic art is energized by the same themes, visual techniques, and influences that characterize their paintings. How are the style and character of Pre-Raphaelite art defined?

The basic elements of Pre-Raphaelite painting are a finely detailed realism based on direct observation of nature and life models; hyper-realistic colors that glow with vitality and sunlit strength; compositions that emphasize figures in shallow space and details and background so significant that they act as an equal partner, forming an overall decorative scheme, with the main figures of the picture; literary and poetic themes, especially medieval, religious, mystical, romantic (in both senses), and tragic; nods to the Nazarenes and early/pre-Renaissance German/Flemish/Italian schools of painting with their crisp contours, nonformalized naturalism, and bright colors; an emphasis on quirky poses and the visualization of strong emotions, to the point of making all players in a pictorial drama readable personalities; and

a reliance on, and accumulation of, symbolic/allegorical details to bring home a concept or idea. This "idea" importance cannot be stressed enough, for the Pre-Raphaelites knew it was what set them apart from other painters, including those Academy-bound conventional artists who came before them and those artists who thought they were following the Pre-Raphaelite (and especially Rossettian) traditions by creating "beautiful" canvases of artfully arranged females and pseudo-medieval scenes.

Rossetti, the supposed symbol of change in the movement, is himself the best example of unchanging Pre-Raphaelitism (despite Holman Hunt's criticisms to the contrary)—because what he wrought is not essentially what he was. He remained a Pre-Raphaelite, not a formalist or an Aesthete. As his work in oils increased in the 1860s and 1870s, his powers of realistic depiction of life models, objects, and plant life also increased: he wouldn't think of creating his works of ideals and ideas, of poetry made flesh, of allegorical fables of love and yearning and loss and sensuality, of literary criticism—without making it *real* to the viewer through application of the original Pre-Raphaelite ideals.

As Rossetti guided the artists working on the Oxford Union murals in 1857, his enthusiasm was tempered by the need to impart true Pre-Raphaelite principles to his charges. According to one of them, Val Prinsep, during the decoration of the Debating Society's walls that inaugurated the second phase of Pre-Raphaelitism, "Gabriel [Rossetti], as we called him, praised our work with the greatest generosity, and he also criticised freely. Of all the work on those walls the most wonderful was undoubtedly that of Morris. Artistically it was not unpleasing, for Morris had a decided genius for decoration; but the details were most monstrous. . . . [Rossetti said to Morris:] 'Top, . . . you must do that woman's head again! . . . It's not human—you must get some nature. Now . . . like a good chap, you get your sketch-book and go down and make a sketch of Stunner Lipscombe, and you'll get it all right" ("A Chapter from a Painter's Reminiscence," *Magazine of Art*, new ser., vol. 2, 1904, pp. 169–70).

These elements were the firm basis upon which Pre-Raphaelite painting and illustration worked their magic—whether by Rossetti and

William Holman Hunt: Chairs and sideboard (c. 1855; made by Messrs. Crace; photo-engraving, as published in William Holman Hunt's Pre-Raphaelitism and the Pre-Raphaelite Brotherhood, *vol. 2, 1906)*

Hunt and Brown or by those that adopted their spirit and methods at least some of the time, like Poynter and Hughes. In Pre-Raphaelite graphic art, there were additional factors at work.

1. *The Pre-Raphaelites placed their illustrations on a level with their paintings.* These artists emphasized creative integrity and hard work in all areas, from decorated furniture to Royal Academy–worthy canvases. The most salient example of this emphasis is, of course, the guild of decorative artists that William Morris formed in 1861 to bring fine art into people's daily lives. The original members of "Morris, Marshall, Faulkner & Co., Fine Art Workmen in Painting, Carving, Furniture, and the Metals" were Morris, Brown, Rossetti, Hughes, Burne-Jones, Philip Webb, Charles

Faulkner, and Peter Paul Marshall. The prospectus (reprinted in William Michael Rossetti's *Ruskin: Rossetti: PreRaphaelitism*, 1899, pp. 268–71) reads in part: "The Growth of Decorative Art in this Country owing to the efforts of English Architects, has now reached a point at which it seems desirable that Artists of reputation should devote their time to it. . . . The artists whose names appear above . . . will be able to undertake any species of decoration, mural or otherwise, from pictures, properly so called, down to the consideration of the smallest work susceptible of art beauty. . . . These artists, having for many years been deeply attached to the study of the Decorative Arts of all times and countries, have felt more than most people the want of some one place where they could either obtain or get produced work of a genuine and beautiful character. They have therefore now established themselves as a firm, for the production, by themselves and under their supervision, of: I. Mural Decoration, either in Pictures or in Pattern Work, or merely in the arrangement of Colours, as applied to dwelling-houses, churches, or public buildings. II. Carving generally, as applied to Architecture. III. Stained Glass, especially with reference to its harmony with Mural Decoration. IV. Metal Work in all its branches, including Jewellery. V. Furniture, either depending for its beauty on its own design, on the application of material hitherto overlooked, or on its conjunction with Figure and Pattern. VI. Painting. Under this head is included Embroidery of all kinds, Stamped Leather, and ornamental work in other such materials, besides every article necessary for domestic use."

In the decorative area, no small credit should be afforded Rossetti, Morris, Burne-Jones, Hughes, Brown, Shields, Henry Holiday, Walter Crane, and a host of other artistic giants of the period for their creation of some of the finest stained-glass window designs since the Middle Ages—as well as furniture, tapestries, tilework, and other decorative items. But certainly, among all the "nonexhibition" arts, the *illustrations* of these men were their most influential accomplishments. Rossetti, who exhibited little, came to the attention of a larger public chiefly through articles on his art in periodicals (especially by the *Athenaeum*'s art critic, former P.R.B. member F. G. Stephens) and through publication of a few famous drawings—drawings so startlingly original and so powerful that they enhanced his legendary status as the shadowy leader of the Pre-Raphaelites and practically built his artistic reputation until the major retrospectives immediately following his death in 1882. His "Maids of Elfen-Mere"—arguably the first printed truly Pre-Raphaelite illustration—in *The Music Master* was, in fact,

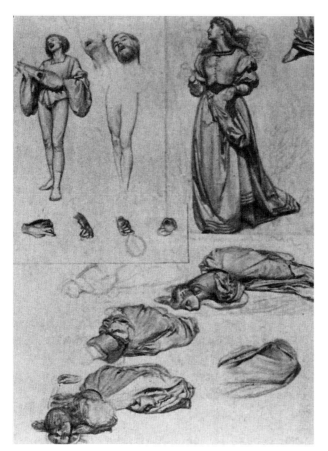

Frederick Sandys: Studies for the illustration **Amor Mundi** *in the* Shilling Magazine, *1865 (photo-engraving, as published in* Print-Collector's Quarterly, *vol. 7, no. 2, 1917)*

the chief impetus to Burne-Jones's interest in both Rossetti and the practice of Pre-Raphaelite art. Georgiana Burne-Jones, in her *Memorials of Edward Burne-Jones* (1904, vol. 1, pp. 119–20) quotes her late husband as stating in 1855 on seeing "Maids": "It is I think the most beautiful drawing for an illustration that I have ever seen; the weirdness of the Maids of Elfenmere, the musical timed movement of their arms together as they sing, the face of the man, above all, are such as only a great artist could conceive."

A letter from Rossetti to William Allingham (March 22, 1855) about the Dalziels' cutting of "Maids" reflects how significant all of these tiny works of art became to Rossetti, and how he anguished over their treatment: "I have been looking at the mangled remains of my drawing again by the light of your friendly letter, but really can only see it, in its present state, as a conceited-looking failure. . . .

"I showed the proof yesterday to Woolner, who saw the original drawing, and he was as shocked as myself. . . . It would be possible to improve it a good deal, I believe . . . by cutting out lines, by which means the human character might be partially substituted for the oyster and goldfish cast of features, and other desirable changes effected. On getting your letter I marked parts of the proof with white, and find something might probably be done. But first I would like to show the whitened proof to one or two friends, and take their opinion as to whether, even if the changes were properly made, the thing could possibly be allowed to come out. . . . At any rate I cannot at present conceive of its being brought to any state in which my name could be put to it, much as I should like my name to appear in your book" (George Birbeck Hill, ed., *Letters of Dante Gabriel Rossetti to William Allingham*, 1897, pp. 113–15).

Hunt, Millais, Brown, and the others may have been somewhat less transcendent but no less inspired and dedicated in their illustrations. They all worked exceedingly hard in preparing their wood-engravings (and steel-engravings, and the occasional etching)—treating them, in terms of creativity, composition, and labor, exactly as they would a major painting. Brown's diary gives a log of the hours he devoted to his illustration, "The Prisoner of Chillon," for *The Poets of the Nineteenth Century.* His 1856 diary entries show that he worked on the drawing almost daily for three weeks—including two days spent (at University Hospital) searching for and sketching a corpse (Virginia Surtees, ed., *The Diary of Ford Madox Brown,* 1981, pp. 166–68). Millais's marked-up proofs of his illustrations (where the engravers gave the artists an opportunity to correct any "mistakes" in their execution) are endless examples of his fastidious attention to the smallest detour from his intended effects. On Saddler's steel-engraved proof, for example, of his "The Convalescent" (for Dinah Mulock Craik's *Nothing New,* 1861), Millais draws a small eye and nose and points to the brow, writing: "This line . . . a little too dark," adding, "Soften black hair . . . still more." He then draws an outline of a shape edge and writes, "Increase the throat a shade more on front as I have done in pencil, one faint line will do it" (Museum of Fine Arts, Boston, Hartley Collection).

Frederick Sandys in particular exemplified the Pre-Raphaelite ideal of making detailed studies from models and nature for paintings and for the smallest illustration. Although his illustra-

tive work basically ended in the 1860s, his reputation as a wood-block artist remained so great that George Du Maurier described the main character of Barty in his 1896 novel *The Martian* as an artist who "made most elaborate studies of drapery, in pen and ink . . . in the manner of Sandys and Albert Dürer!" (p. 326).

John Everett Millais: **The Unmerciful Servant** *for* **"The Parables Read in the Light of the Present Day"** *(wood-engraving proof, Dalziels; 5 1/2 x 4 1/4 [paper: 8 1/4 x 7]; with Millais's notations for corrections; for the illustration in* Good Words, *1863; courtesy Museum of Fine Arts, Boston, John H. and Ernestine A. Payne Fund [Hartley Collection])*

This attitude and approach was passed on to a whole school of illustrators, who would never consider creating a drawing for the wood-engraver without making detailed sketches from nature and using live models. In Victorian England, all illustration may not have been Pre-Raphaelite, but the period's graphic art can be divided clearly into two eras: that of the caricaturist-draughtsmen, prolific and unrealistic, whose careers were in full swing before 1855; and everything after that, all of which in some way derived from the spirit, styles, themes, or technique of Pre-Raphaelite illustration. The fin-de-siècle writer and illustrator Laurence Housman recognized this, emphasizing in his monograph on Arthur Boyd Houghton in 1896:

"The main difference between their [Hunt's, Millais's, and Rossetti's] work and that of the others [in the Moxon *Tennyson*] was that the pre-Raphaelites had something to say very pertinent to the subject in hand, the rest nothing. . . .

"The illustrations of the pre-Raphaelites were personal and intellectual readings of the poems to which they belonged, were not merely echoes in line of the words of the text. Often they were the successful summing up of the drift of an entire poem within the space of a single picture. . . ." Housman continues, indicating how Houghton and other illustrators not usually linked with the Pre-Raphaelites were, indeed, much influenced by them, and stating that Pre-Raphaelitism results everywhere in illustration derived from a "personal outlook . . . [a] means of expression acquired at first hand and not by tradition" (pp. 13–16).

2. *The relationship between literature and visual art was heightened.* Favorite poets of the Pre-Raphaelites included Keats, Poe, Dante, Shakespeare, Byron, Shelley, Malory, and Tennyson. Keats, one of the heroes of the original Brotherhood, especially kept the fires of inspiration going. Artworks based on Keats's and Tennyson's poetry include: Hughes's paintings *La Belle Dame sans Merci* (1861–63), *The Knight of the Sun* (c. 1859–60), *The Eve of St. Agnes* (two triptychs, 1855–56

*William Holman Hunt: **Isabella and the Pot of Basil** (oil, 1867; 72 3/4 x 44 1/2; Laing Art Gallery, Newcastle; photogravure, as published in William Holman Hunt's* Pre-Raphaelitism and the Pre-Raphaelite Brotherhood, *vol. 2, 1906)*

and 1858), *Sir Galahad* (1865–70), and *The Lady of Shalott* (1863–64); *Endymion* (1873), a book of engravings by Poynter; Hunt's *The Eve of St. Agnes* (1848; a.k.a. *The Flight of Madeline and Porphyro*), *Isabella and the Pot of Basil* (1867), and *The Lady of Shalott* paintings; another *Eve of St. Agnes*, an 1858 drawing by James Smetham; Hughes's contemporary genre painting *April Love* (1855–56); *Mnemosyne*, a Rossetti canvas of 1881; and of course Millais's seminal P.R.B. work, *Lorenzo and Isabella*. Tennyson was an ideal choice

Dante Gabriel Rossetti: **Mythic Uther's Deeply Wounded Son** *for "The Palace of Art" (photograph of the drawing on the wood-block for the illustration in* Poems by Alfred Tennyson*, 1857; photogravure, 3 1/4 x 3 5/8; as published in Joseph Pennell's* Some Poems by Alfred, Lord Tennyson*, 1901)*

for the group's plunge into wood-engraved illustration, the three original Pre-Raphaelites together providing thirty drawings for Moxon's *Poems*. Their own circle widened to include and influence writers, such as William Allingham, George MacDonald, Coventry Patmore, Robert Browning, Algernon Charles Swinburne, George Meredith, Christina Rossetti, Anthony Trollope, William Makepeace Thackeray (the editor of the *Cornhill Magazine*), and Tennyson himself.

The projects of the Dalziels, with a variety of artists represented, in particular governed the books in which the Pre-Raphaelites' illustrations appeared, especially the engraving firm's own magazine, *Good Words*. Although commercial periodical assignments were often not dependent on the artists' whims and preferences, it was still obvious to "pack-

agers" like the Dalziels *who* did *what* best. Certainly books with rustic/pastoral/slice-of-life themes might be given to Walker, Pinwell, or J. W. North; themes medieval and historical seemed to suggest Sandys, Hunt, and Lawless; Du Maurier came to be known for his realistic interpretations of Victorian society—both serious and satirical; Millais seemed to shine in all subjects but eventually settled down to do contemporary scenes for Trollope and other novelists.

It is obvious from the concurrent literary/artistic origins of the movement—the Brotherhood's four issues of the *Germ* in 1850 and Burne-Jones's and William Morris's *Oxford and Cambridge Magazine* of 1856—that those involved, or wishing to be involved, with these new cultural directions could be both writers and artists, often at the same time. While the *Germ* featured only four etchings over as many issues, and the *Oxford and Cambridge Magazine* no illustrations at all, there were in these publications poetry, stories, and articles on art by those who were artists, or wished to be artists, or cared passionately about art, or wrote sympathetically on the new artistic aims.

Of the early Pre-Raphaelites, F. G. Stephens began as an artist but eventually had a distinguished career as an art critic. Thomas Woolner was a sculptor who wrote five books of poetry, published by Macmillan and George Bell. William Michael Rossetti was a prodigious writer, editor, and critic of both literary and artistic subjects. Charles Allston Collins wrote *A Cruise upon Wheels* and other travel books. William Morris, producing only

William Bell Scott: **Frontispiece** *for* Poems by a Painter, *1854 (etching, Scott; 4 1/2 x 2 7/8)*

one easel painting and joining in the Oxford Union project, was one of the great artist-craftsmen and poets of the Victorian era.

Of the major painters/illustrators, Noel Paton's *Poems by a Painter* was published by Blackwood in 1861; Hunt produced a monumental memoir in *Pre-Raphaelitism and the Pre-Raphaelite Brotherhood* of 1905–06; Val Prinsep wrote several books and essays, the most famous being *Imperial India*. Henry Wallis, a fine but unproductive Pre-Raphaelite painter, devoted much of his later career to volumes about ceramics. Walter Crane, a powerful voice for socialism and the art of the book, counted among many writings his famous *Of the Decorative Illustration of Books* (1896). George Du Maurier late in life became a respected novelist with his self-illustrated *Peter Ibbetson*, *Trilby*, and *The Martian*. William Bell Scott was an art historian and the prolific if uninspired poet of *Hades* (1838), *Poems by a Painter* (1854), *Poems, Ballads, Studies from Nature, Sonnets, Etc.* (1875), and *A Poet's Harvest Home* (1882). John Ruskin, the ultimate Victorian art critic, made architectural and nature drawings in order to illustrate his theories of art in dozens of influential works, including *Modern Painters* (1843–60) and *The Stones of Venice* (1853); he even wrote one of the period's best-known children's books, *The King of the Golden River* (1851). Simeon Solomon composed poems, notably "A Vision of Love Revealed in Sleep," over-the-top hallucinations twisted from Swinburne and Rossetti. Dante Gabriel Rossetti, of course, was the premier poet of the movement, whose substantial writings were better known by the public and critics during his lifetime than were his paintings.

3. *Pre-Raphaelite illustrated*

work emphasizes themes of love and loss and death. Certainly the Pre-Raphaelites in all their art were obsessed with such themes. In their paintings, the tragic death is treated in Henry Wallis's *The Death of Chatterton* (1856) and *The Stonebreaker* (1857) and W. L. Windus's *Too Late* (1858); Hughes's *Home from the Sea* and *The Woodman's Child* (1860); Paton's *The Bluidie Tryst* (1855); and Millais's *Ophelia*. Rossetti's obsession with the tragic deaths of loved ones is both pathetic and mystical: *Dante's Dream at the Time of the Death of Beatrice* (watercolor, 1856, and oil, 1871); *Beata Beatrix* (1864–70); and his phenomenal pen-and-ink drawing *How They Met Themselves*—completed while honeymooning with the sickly Elizabeth Siddal in 1860—which depicts two lovers meeting their doubles in a premonition of death.

The poetry and stories in the Sixties periodicals reek of tragic loss in romantic love, and motherless children and childrenless mothers. Everybody seemed to be dying young in literature—and in the real Victorian world. Among the Pre-Raphaelites, Brown experienced the death of his first wife, Elizabeth, in 1846 (in childbirth) and the

Dante Gabriel Rossetti: **Dante's Dream at the Time of the Death of Beatrice** *(oil, 1871; 83 x 125; Walker Art Gallery, Liverpool; photogravure, as published in Elisabeth Luther Cary's* Poems of Dante Gabriel Rossetti, *vol. 1, 1903)*

Frederick Sandys: **Manoli** *(wood-engraving, Swain;
7 x 3 7/8;* Cornhill Magazine, *vol. 6, 1862, p. 346;* The
Cornhill Gallery; Reproductions of Woodcuts by
F. Sandys)*

death of his young, talented son Oliver in
1874. Holman Hunt's first wife, Fanny, died
shortly after their 1865 marriage, in Florence
of cholera. Burne-Jones's mother had died
shortly after his birth, and his son
Christopher died at the age of three weeks;
William Michael Rossetti's young daughter
died in 1883. Frederic Shields, stricken by
poverty during his early career, lost both of
his younger brothers to fatal diseases. Illness

claimed the lives of youthful Pre-Raphaelite
painters Walter Deverell and Thomas Seddon
in 1854 and 1856 respectively, as it also did
Charles Allston Collins at age forty-five.
Talented illustrators Morten, Lawless,
Pinwell, and Walker all died young, at the
peak of their powers.

Rossetti mourned the tragedy of Dante's
loss of Beatrice incessantly in drawings and
watercolors, and then experienced his own
love's tragedy with the laudanum overdose of
his young wife Elizabeth Siddal in 1862; he
later resided for months at a time under the
same roof with his passionate love, Jane
Morris, wife of his good friend William
"Topsy" Morris—although Morris looked the
other way, the lovers were discreet, and they
eventually cooled their passions into a warm
platonic affection. Rossetti's own early death,
in 1882, deeply affected all his friends. Ruskin,
to no one's dismay, found himself without his
wife, Effie Gray, when she fell in love with the
stern critic's protégé, Millais, in 1853 and finally obtained an annulment due to "nonconsum-
mation" of the marriage. Millais's drawings of
the period are often of lovers betrayed,
opportunities lost, and lovers married to
other people (*The Man with Two Wives*, 1854,
and his "When I First Met Thee" engraving in
Thomas Moore's *Irish Melodies* of 1856). Let us
not forget that one of the central events of the
Victorian age was the untimely death of the
Queen's beloved Prince Albert in 1861.

The Pre-Raphaelite illustrators, no
strangers to death and lost love, yet
Romantics in their elevation of such losses to
tragic proportions, added mystical, allegorical, and very human emotions to their
Romanticism. The grandness of previous
Romantic art and literature became the partic-
ulars of real people with modern emotions—
especially given that these artists' pictures,
from largest canvas to smallest wood-block,
were usually "assembled" from images taken
directly from nature, from models who might
also be their friends. This is what makes Pre-

Raphaelite illustrations so powerful, and not of the rhetorical or theatrical type that might employ the standard dramatic gestures of the art of David or Ingres or even Fuseli and Blake; neither were they decorative arrangements impressive in

*William Holman Hunt: Design for the illustration **At Night** in* Once a Week, *1860 (photo-engraving, as published in William Holman Hunt's* Pre-Raphaelitism and the Pre-Raphaelite Brotherhood, *vol. 2, 1906)*

technique but lacking in ideas and emotions, like those of the artists of the 1880s and 1890s. The Pre-Raphaelite response to love and death was intense, poetic, sensual, and often somewhat morbid. Lawless's "Dead Love" (*Once a Week*, 1862) interprets Swinburne's story of a woman's love for a dead hero—whose coffin she keeps in her room. The grisly poem "Rosamund, Queen of the Lombards" (*Once a Week*, 1861) gave birth to one of Sandys's greatest wood-engravings, and verses by Christina Rossetti, "Amor Mundi" (*Shilling Magazine*, 1865), produced an oppressive—and impressive—Sandys compo-

sition filled with images of *decomposition*, as lovers see the tragedy of their mortal actions in the future.

The poetic particularization of life's tragedies produced many other great Pre-Raphaelite illustrations on death and love; these include: Sandys's "The Sailor's Bride" (*Once a Week*, 1861), "Manoli" (*Cornhill Magazine*, 1862), and "If" (*Argosy*, 1866); Hunt's *Of My Lady in Death* etching for the *Germ*, "At Night" in an 1860 *Once a Week*, and his "The Ballad of Oriana" sepulchre scene and Rossetti's "Lady of Shalott" Lancelot picture in the Moxon *Tennyson*; Arthur Hughes's "The Farewell Valentine" for *Good Words* (1862), "Blessing in Disguise" for *Sunday Magazine* (1869), and graveyard illustrations in *The Music Master*; Lawless's "Rung into Heaven" (*Good Words*, 1862) and "The Betrayed," "King Dyring," "Twilight," and "Broken Toys," all for *Once a Week* (1861–63); Du Maurier's "A Time to Dance" for *Good Words* (1861); Watson's "A Mother's Grief" (*English Sacred Poetry*); Millais's "The Border Widow" (*The Home Affections*); Shields's "An Hour with the Dead" and Poynter's "The Broken Vow" for *Once a Week* (1861 and 1862, respectively); and many, many more.

4. *Pre-Raphaelite illustration took inspiration from a distinct group of artists who were especially concerned with linear art: Albrecht Dürer, Hans Holbein, William Blake, Alfred Rethel, Ludwig Richter, and Julius Schnorr von Carolsfeld, among others.* Following the example of their own revolt in painting against the Royal Academy, Rossetti, Hunt, Millais, Brown, Sandys, and the rest set out to revitalize illustration, according to the methods of

*Matthew J. Lawless: **The Betrayed** (wood-engraving, Swain; 3 3/4 x 4 3/8; Once a Week, vol. 3, 1860, p. 155)*

their own graphic gods. They aimed to break the stylistic monopoly of "sketch artists" like John Leech, Richard Doyle, Kenny Meadows, and John Gilbert, while building upon the progress made in the 1850s by kindred spirits like Townsend, Clayton, Pickersgill, and Tenniel.

The daringly personal graphic art of William Blake was philosophical and stylistic fuel for many of the Pre-Raphaelites. Rossetti, while still a student, enthusiastically purchased an original Blake notebook, which included severe criticisms of such Royal Academy favorites as Titian, Rubens, Rembrandt, and Sir Joshua Reynolds—thus providing one of the sparks for the Brotherhood's revolution. Rossetti later helped finish the Gilchrist *Life of Blake* (published in 1863), and his Pre-Raphaelite friends James Smetham and Frederic Shields contributed to the revised edition of 1880. William Bell Scott, too, was a Blake enthusiast, creating a volume of his own etchings after sketches by Blake. Along with Frederick Sandys (with his Dürer-like monograms) and almost every Pre-Raphaelite artist, Scott revered Dürer; his *Albert Dürer: His Life and Works* was published in 1869.

The influence of past masters of engraving on wood and steel, and of present German artists reviving their styles, was a major ingredient of the stew that gives Pre-Raphaelite illustration its essential character. No doubt the best wood-engravers, the Dalziels and Swain, understood the importance of line and its gradations in this tradition—more than did other engravers, from Linton to Thompson—and their "look" contributed much to the Pre-Raphaelite works' Germanic quality. The Dalziels knew of, and were impressed by, two important books recently published with woodcut illustrations by German artists, who reworked and "improved" the approach of Dürer and Holbein, expanding the cuts' tonal

qualities; the Dalziels, as of 1850 creators of their Fine Art Books for other publishers, wished to emulate and share in this artistic revival. Their own *Bible Gallery* was a

William Blake: **The Nativity** *(etching, W. B. Scott, 1875; 5 1/4 x 7 3/4;* William Blake: Etchings from His Works by William Bell Scott, *1878)*

response to the publication of the Nazarene artist Schnorr von Carolsfeld's *Bible Pictures* (published in Germany 1851 and in England by Williams and Norgate in 1855 and in several editions thereafter; *Golden Threads from an Ancient Loom*, a volume featuring Schnorr's fine wood-engravings for *Das Nibelungenlied*, was published in London in 1880). The Dalziels also commissioned one of their favorite artists, Frederick Pickersgill, to do a pictorial *Life of Christ* after seeing Alfred Rethel's collection of woodcuts published by Georg Wigland in Leipzig in 1848, *Ein Todtentanz aus dem Jahre* (Holbein's "Dance of Death" updated to comment on the continental revolutions of 1848). Rethel's prints, with their expert and naturalistic drawing, their sureness of line, and their sophisticated tonal effects, update Dürer and might be perfectly at home in a book illustrated by Shields or Sandys or Paton or Poynter. Holman Hunt in his *Pre-Raphaelitism and the Pre-Raphaelite Brotherhood* denies the common nineteenth-

Albrecht Dürer: **St. Jerome in a Cave** *(woodcut, Dürer, 1512; 6 3/4 x 4 7/8)*

Alfred Rethel: **Death as a Friend** *(wood-engraving, Dalziels; 5 1/2 x 5;* Sunday Magazine, *vol. 7, 1870–71 [1871], p. 473)*

century assumption that the realistic, free-flowing illustrations of contemporary German artist Adolph Menzel were favored by the Pre-Raphaelites but acknowledges their appreciation for the woodcuts of Ludwig Richter and Rethel's famous "Death the Friend" and "Death the Enemy" prints (vol. 2, p. 104). William Morris had also written of these works in an 1856 article in his *Oxford and Cambridge Magazine*. English editions of books illustrated by Ludwig Richter—the artist in many ways closest to the precise, firm-lined woodcut style of the Pre-Raphaelites, especially Shields—appeared in the 1840s and 1850s (*The Vicar of Wakefield, Nut-Cracker and Sugar-Dolly, The Lord's Prayer,* and *The Book of German Songs*).

It is obvious from the publications and notices of the time that in the mid- and late 1850s the German approach was in the air—just as the Pre-Raphaelites (and the artists in their stylistic orbit) were inaugurating a new approach to illustration. As far back as 1833 there appeared a review of the book *Relics of Albert Dürer, Dedicated to His Admirers: A Pocket-book for the Lovers of German Art, on Account of His Third Centenary Celebration*; the article in *Foreign Quarterly Review* (vol. 11, pp. 73–89) eulogized van Eyck in a way Ruskin and the future Pre-Raphaelites would appreciate ("His chief merits were fidelity to truth and nature") and praised Dürer for his brilliant colors and as the greatest of all woodcutters and engravers.

The link between the vastly improving quality of wood-engraved works during the early 1850s and the artistry of the Germans past and present was clearly seen in the pages of the *Art Journal* during this period. In reviewing Scott's *The Lay of the Last Minstrel* in 1853 (vol. 15, p. 314), with art by Birket Foster and John Gilbert, the writer gushed:

"There is scarcely one out of the hundred engravings it contains that is not a gem of Art, and does not prove that wood-engraving has reached a very high position among us in the present day, taking the place of the prints from steel and copper, with which a few years since the illustrated literature of the period was ornamented. The designs for such a work as that before us could not have been entrusted to better hands than those of Mr. Gilbert for the figure subjects and Mr. Foster for the landscapes; who have here well sustained the reputation they have long since earned and have been most ably seconded by the engravers, Mr. Whymper and Mr. Evans."

In 1854 the *Art Journal* published six pages of engravings of biblical subjects in a Dürerish style by prominent German artists, including Ludwig Richter, G. Jager, and Julius Schnorr (vol. 16, pp. 16, 41, 140, 201, 328, 360). In the same volume (pp. 293–96) there appeared an article entitled "Wood Engraving. F. Bürkner of Dresden," which decried that English wood-engravings had lost all the characteristics that were part of their nature and were trying to imitate steel-engravings; preference was for the high standard of Bürkner, who had founded a school for wood-engravers and who had cut Rethel's *Todtentanz* and designs by Schnorr and Richter; to accompany the story, four of Rethel's designs were reproduced. The *Art Journal* for 1855 (vol. 17) printed a major article on Dürer, accompanied by many of his engravings, over four parts (pp. 1–5, 61–63, 82–84, 122–24). Finally, giving the Sixties illustrators that final nudge, there is the *Art Journal*'s 1859 (vol. 21, p. 63) review of recent London editions of *Holbein's Dance of Death* and *Holbein's Bible Cuts*.

As will be seen in the sections on the individual artists, the Dürer/Rethel–inspired wood-block drawing style was a hallmark of many of the Pre-Raphaelites, who, openly acknowledging their debts to the Germans in style as well as approach, crammed innumer-

able details, all of significance and symbolism, into their tiny illustrations. Rossetti's "St. Cecily" and Hunt's "The Lady of Shalott" for the Moxon *Tennyson*; Sandys's "Yet Once

Julius Schnorr von Carolsfeld: **The Slaughter in the Banquet Hall** *(wood-engraving, Rehle; 8 x 5 1/4;* Golden Threads from an Ancient Loom, *1880)*

More on the Organ Play," "Rosamund, Queen of the Lombards," and "The Old Chartist" in *Once a Week*; Brown's "The Prisoner of Chillon" in *The Poets of the Nineteenth Century*; Poynter's "The Broken Vow," "The Castle by the Sea," and "Ballad of the Page and the King's Daughter" in *Once a Week* (1862 and 1863); Shields's "Vanity Fair" in *Illustrations to Bunyan's Pilgrim's Progress* (1864); and many other examples combine

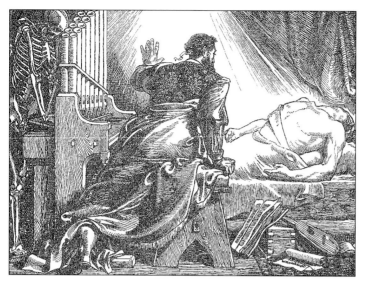

Frederick Sandys: **Yet Once More on the Organ Play** *(wood-engraving, Swain; 3 3/4 x 5 1/8;* Once a Week, *vol. 4, 1861, p. 350;* Historical and Legendary Ballads and Songs; Reproductions of Woodcuts by F. Sandys)*

the linear- and allegorical-detail qualities of their German models with the Pre-Raphaelite practice in painting of presenting an idea by realistic details built into a flattened, decorative composition. This approach resulted in a far-reaching, revolutionary style of illustration that honors drawing and lines and wood-engraving effects as an art—an attitude quite different than one (often the case before the Pre-Raphaelites and after them in certain schools of Victorian illustration) that creates a sketch or a finished scene and then expects commercial engravers to *somehow* reproduce it. Devoid of substance but heightened in style and even more reverential toward past roots, this late-century respect for line produced a true woodcut revival, with its thick lines, lack of shading, and open spaces, in the Kelmscott books of William Morris and the Vale books of Charles Ricketts.

5. *An "eccentric realism" marks both paintings and illustrations.* This may be the most intriguing aspect of Pre-Raphaelite illustration—the quirky poses of the figures. Many Pre-Raphaelite paintings, full of their own brand of realism and modeled from life, pur-

posely added the telling characteristics of individual emotions and psychological states to their characters. Following Ruskin's observations in *Modern Painters* to represent facts and make every element, no matter how small, significant, the realistic environments of Arthur Hughes's *The Long Engagement* and Madox Brown's *Work* are as Pre-Raphaelite as Rossetti's flat, medieval, decorative watercolors of the 1850s, because they all seek to depict timeless truths or poetic ideas through meaningful details.

Pre-Raphaelite pictures are invariably filled with individually delineated components, massed together (often claustrophobically) to form a poetic composition that expresses feelings and ideas rather than to merely capture a prosaic scene from literature or re-create exact visual reality. To say that Pre-Raphaelitism is realistic in character would be a mistake, and one that constructs unnecessary divisions with the direct-from-nature landscape paintings of John Brett and John Inchbold and Thomas Seddon. Ford Madox Brown may have claimed that his *Pretty Baa Lambs* (1851–59 / R.A., 1852) was simply an exercise in depicting the natural effects of sunlight, but the result is a painting as frozen in time and ideal as anything by Rossetti. Pre-Raphaelitism's attention to realistic detail is always realism in the service of poetic feeling, moral ideas, or eternal truths. In these artists' works of social and moral concern that feature contemporary figures and settings, specific ideas (usually tragic consequences of unethical behavior or untrammeled passion, and usually romantic) are conveyed about a societal issue. Both the tragic possibilities and the supreme dignity of manual labor are ideas promulgated in Henry Wallis's *The Stonebreaker*, William Bell Scott's *Iron and Coal* mural (c. 1860) in Northumberland, and Brown's *Work*. Rossetti's unfinished *Found*, Hunt's *The Awakening*

Conscience, Millais's terrific pen-and-ink drawing *The Race-Meeting* of 1853, and Hughes's *The Long Engagement* are all comments on the ethical consequences of wrong-headed love.

The specific element of *eccentric* realism, however, is one that defines style and approach, and in particular the treatment of human faces and bodies. The figures in Pre-

Dante Gabriel Rossetti: **Mary Magdalene at the House of Simon the Pharisee** *(ink drawing, 1858; 21 1/4 x 18 3/8; Fitzwilliam Museum, Cambridge; photogravure, as published in Elisabeth Luther Cary's* Poems of Dante Gabriel Rossetti, *vol. 1, 1903)*

Raphaelite art, derived initially from an effort to jettison the conventions of academic painting and scenic illustration, are not only physically based upon real people but express the various emotional states that real people, in the situations depicted, might possess. The results are often eccentrically posed figures whose facial expressions and bodily positions betray—or cause us to wonder at—their inner feelings.

It is noteworthy that all of the original Pre-Raphaelites worked with these considerations in mind, from the very beginning. Ford Madox Brown's early paintings *Wycliffe Reading His Translation of the Bible to John of Gaunt* (1848)—which so impressed Rossetti—and *Chaucer at the Court of King Edward III* contain figures that do not merely support the drama of the situations but also imply individual inner stories. In addition, Brown's moon-shaped, deep-eyed, bow-lipped, introspective faces became a Pre-Raphaelite type, appearing in the works of Rossetti, Solomon, and Burne-Jones—and of the latter's followers, Spencer-Stanhope, Thomas Rooke, John Strudwick, and Evelyn de Morgan. In pictures like Brown's *Jesus Washing Peter's Feet* and *Work*, Hunt's *A Converted British Family*, Millais's *Lorenzo and Isabella*, and Rossetti's *Mary Magdalene at the House of Simon the Pharisee* (pen and ink, 1858), each figure in a large group is given a specific character, interest, and emotion.

A number of figural poses grew to make up a Pre-Raphaelite vocabulary over the years: the clasped hands and awkwardly intertwined arms of lovers, the heads tilted back in melancholy awe or buried under hands and arms. Hands became a major focus, and are often expressionistically displayed. It sometimes seems, in Pre-Raphaelite art, that everyone is holding hands; otherwise, something else is usually found—objects, flowers, hair, drapery—to fill the clutches of the Pre-Raphaelite man or woman. Examples abound in painting: Hughes's *The Long Engagement*; Hunt's *Valentine Rescuing Sylvia from Proteus* (1851); Rossetti's *Paolo and Francesca da Rimini* (watercolor, 1855), *Beata Beatrix*, and *Astarte Syriaca* (1877); and Brown's *The Last of England*. Among wood-engravings, there are Hunt's "The Beggar Maid" and "The Lady of Shalott" (*Poems by Alfred Tennyson*); Lawless's "The Secret That Can't Be Kept" and "The Lay of the Lady and the Hound" (both *Once a Week*, 1860); Sandys's "The Waiting Time" and "Rosamund, Queen of the Lombards"

John Everett Millais: **Love** *(wood-engraving, Dalziels; 5 x 3 5/8;* The Poets of the Nineteenth Century, *1857; Millais's Illustrations)*

early-Renaissance Campo Santo frescoes in Pisa; we can see those angular, ascetic figures of early-Italian art, as well as the cold, crisp figures of Nazarene art, as contributing to a "style" of draughtsmanship that permeates especially the early drawings and published graphics of the group. Contorted, pointy (just look at those feet and noses and chins), elongated, wiry outline figures (that somehow betray solidity) are hallmarks of the fascinatingly original drawings of Millais and Rossetti and even Hunt in the late 1840s and 1850s— for example, Millais's 1849 drawing *The Disentombment of Queen Matilda*. This wonderfully original and eccentric composition is full of figures quirkily posed, each of equal yet very individual emotional intensity, each of the same pictorial importance. The effect, ultimately the effect of all Pre-Raphaelite art, is beautifully decorative, interestingly psychological, and poetically engaging. Based on superficial resemblances, Rossetti's *Dante Drawing an Angel on the First Anniversary of the Death of Beatrice* could almost be from the same hand, as could Hunt's Keatsian *He Knew Whose Gentle Hand Was at the Latch* and his first design for his *Druids* painting—all of them 1849 drawings.

(*Churchman's Family Magazine*, 1863, and *Once a Week*, 1861); and Millais's "Love" (*The Poets of the Nineteenth Century*) and "The Border Widow" (*The Home Affections*).

All of these approaches apply equally to painting and illustration. The whole Pre-Raphaelite movement is often described as appearing in a flash of explosive inspiration at the brothers' 1848 sight of Carlo Lasinio's engravings of the

Similar stylistic effects are seen in illustration: Hunt's *Germ* etching *Of My Lady in Death*; Rossetti's "The Maids of Elfen-Mere" and Hughes's "Lady Alice" and "A Boy's Burial" in *The Music Master*; Scott's "Rosamunda" in his

John Everett Millais: **The Disentombment of Queen Matilda** *(ink drawing, 1849; 9 x 16 3/4; Tate Gallery, London; photo-engraving, as published in John Guille Millais's* The Life and Letters of Sir John Everett Millais, *vol. 1, 1899)*

William Holman Hunt: **A Converted British Family Sheltering a Christian Priest from the Persecution of the Druids** *(ink drawing, 9 x 11 3/4; for the 1850 painting; Johannesburg Art Gallery; photo-engraving, as published in William Holman Hunt's* Pre-Raphaelitism and the Pre-Raphaelite Brotherhood, *vol. 1, 1905)*

Poems by a Painter (1854); Millais's "modern" designs for the Moxon *Tennyson*, such as those for "Dora" and "Locksley Hall," and his etching for *Mr. Wray's Cash-box*; much of Clayton's and Armstead's art for books and periodicals; and for wildly massed individualized figures, Frederic Shields's "Vanity Fair" wood-engraving in *Illustrations to Bunyan's Pilgrim's Progress*.

The wiry-lined, pointy-figured "early-Italian" style gradually disappeared from Pre-Raphaelite work, but the quirky poses and the individualized personalities/emotions remained: the odd faces so realistic and so personal—

ultimately even caricatures of themselves—and, especially from the paintings (almost anything from the 1860s and 1870s by Rossetti and Sandys), the female form elegant and sensual and enveloped by decoratively arranged, wild hair. In that regard, for illustration one can visit—in addition to the picture-filling single female figures that ubiquitously appear in the wood-engravings of Lawless, Watson, Millais, and Poynter—Hughes's North Wind–character drawings (*At the Back of the North Wind* in *Good Words for the Young*, 1868–69), Hunt's "The Lady of Shalott," and Sandys's "Rosamund, Queen of the Lombards," "Danae in the Brazen Chamber," and "If."

Eccentric realists, German-woodcut revivalists, literary visualizers, love-and-death obsessives, and illustration reformers—all are characterizations of the Pre-Raphaelite illustrators. The fascinating individual stories of these artists follow.

Arthur Hughes: **Out in the Storm** *[#3] for* **"At the Back of the North Wind"** *(wood-engraving, Dalziels; 3 1/8 x 2 3/8; Good Words for the Young, vol. 1, 1868–69, p. 441)*

Joseph Noel Paton

1

The Artists and
Their Works
~
Illustrations
of the Major
Pre-Raphaelites

Henry Hugh Armstead

(1828–1905)

H. H. Armstead was one of the few sculptors to work in the Pre-Raphaelite style (Thomas Woolner, Alexander Munro, and John Lucas Tupper were the most prominent). He studied at the Royal Academy Schools, and was initially involved in silverwork. For the supporting podium of the Albert Memorial, dedicated to Queen Victoria's recently deceased husband, Armstead in 1863 created reliefs of allegorical figures (*Astronomy*, *Chemistry*, *Rhetoric*, *Medicine*). In the late 1860s, he designed statues for a tower at the restored Llandaff Cathedral, working with Pre-Raphaelite–disposed architects John Pritchard and John Pollard Seddon; the project also attracted contributions by Dante Gabriel Rossetti (*The Seed of David* triptych) and stained-glass cartoons by Ford Madox Brown and Edward Burne-Jones. In the same period Armstead carved wooden relief panels with Arthurian themes for the Royal Robing Room in the Houses of Parliament.

Moses, St. Peter, St. Paul, and David, detail: *St. Peter* (wood-engraving, Dalziels; 4 7/8 x 7 3/4 [detail: 4 7/8 x 1 7/8]; after Armstead's sculptures for Westminster Abbey; Good Words, vol. 12, 1871, p. 680)

Armstead regularly exhibited busts and reliefs at the Royal Academy from 1851. In the 1870s, he produced a series of exterior sculptures for the Government Offices at Whitehall, again utilizing allegorical figures (*Valour*, *Justice*, *Truth*); for the Continents, his *Africa* is especially bold and Pre-Raphaelite—a hippopotamus and a woman, the leaves and

A Dream (wood-engraving, Dalziels; 5 1/2 x 4; English Sacred Poetry, 1862)

foliage forcefully extended, the whole full of naturalistic detail, such as the woman's hair and chains. In 1871 Armstead sculpted four niche statues for Westminster Abbey—*Moses*, *St. Peter*, *St. Paul*, and *David* (resulting in a characteristically attenuated drawing of them, engraved by the Dalziels, in *Good Words* that year).

Armstead produced a small amount of drawings for the wood-engraver, but like Frederick Sandys's mere twenty-five, they are uniformly wonderful and reputation building. Armstead's illustrations betray the Pre-Raphaelite characteristics of shallow space, massing of forms, "early-Italian" elongated shapes, and Germanic wood-engravings' treatment of drapery, highlights, and lines. Of his four drawings cut by the Dalziels for *English Sacred Poetry* (1862), the best are "The Dead Man of Bethany," a New Testament Lazarus picture linearly reminiscent of John Tenniel's work for *Lalla Rookh* (1861), and "A Dream," an odd image with a central medieval female in the best Sandys-Rossetti spirit.

In "Sea-Weeds" (*Good Words*, 1862), Rossettian multiplied-face water nymphs press together and envelop a drowning victim. "A Song" (*Good Words*, 1861) has a massed-together, shallow-spaced crowd of crusaders and children, the spiky yet delicate figures looking much like Arthur Hughes or John Everett Millais or even J. R. Clayton characters from their earliest illustrations. "Angel Teachers" (*Churchman's Family Magazine*, 1863) shows a strikingly graphic, elongated woman in black, who feels relief in watching children at play; if there ever were Pre-Raphaelite children, it's these two—certainly cousins of the even more contorted and round-faced kids of Arthur Boyd Houghton's *Home Thoughts and Home Scenes* illustrations. Armstead's four *Dalziels' Bible*

Gallery drawings (two only published in the 1894 *Art Pictures* collection that expands on the contents of the 1881 *Gallery*), done in the 1860s, reflect his experience in sculptural friezes and show an Edward Poynter–like dedication to historical/biblical decoration. "The Sun and Moon Stand Still" is an incomparable battle scene, the masses of horses and soldiers swirling from background to foreground around the cliff where Joshua looks to the sun; every player is involved in a telling incident, and the energy and excitement are palpable. "The Fall of the Walls of Jericho," with its four separate groups of figures, each angled and swaying in one direction but each different than the other, has a rhythm, composition, and firmness of technique matched in this book only by some of Leighton's and Brown's drawings.

The Sun and Moon Stand Still (*wood-engraving, Dalziels; 6 7/8 x 6 1/4;* Dalziels' Bible Gallery, *1881;* Art Pictures from the Old Testament*)*

Catalogue

PERIODICALS

Churchman's Family Magazine
Vol. 1, 1863:
¶ **The Fourth Sunday in Lent*** (p. 225, W. Thomas)
¶ **Angel Teachers*** (p. 449, W. Thomas)

Good Words
Vol. 2, 1861:
¶ **A Song (Which None but the Redeemed Can Sing)*** (p. 411, Dalziels; reprinted in *Touches of Nature*)
Vol. 3, 1862:
¶ **Sea-Weeds*** (p. 568, Dalziels; reprinted in *Touches of Nature*)
Vol. 12, 1871:
¶ **Moses, St. Peter, St. Paul, and David** (p. 680, Dalziels; after the artist's sculptures for Westminster Abbey)

Sunday Magazine
Vol. 1, 1864–65 [1865]:
¶ **Blessed Are They That Mourn*** (p. 409, Dalziels)

BOOKS

Art Pictures from the Old Testament (Aley Fox, text; Society for Promoting Christian Knowledge, 1894)
¶ **Samuel and His Mother*** (Dalziels)
¶ **Samuel and Eli*** (Dalziels)
• Plus 2 illustrations reprinted from *Dalziels' Bible Gallery*
• Reissued as *Art Pictures from the Old Testament and Our Lord's Parables* by Dalton, c. 1905, with 20 additional illustrations by Millais reprinted from *The Parables of Our Lord and Saviour Jesus Christ*

[Cook] *Poems by Eliza Cook* (Routledge, Warne, and Routledge, 1861)
¶ **The Trysting-Place*** (Dalziels)

A Song (Which None but the Redeemed Can Sing) *(wood-engraving, Dalziels; 5 1/8 x 4 1/16; Good Words, vol. 2, 1861, p. 411; Touches of Nature)*

Sea-Weeds *(wood-engraving, Dalziels; 5 1/2 x 4 1/4; Good Words, vol. 3, 1862, p. 568; Touches of Nature)*

Left: ***Samuel and His Mother*** *(wood-engraving, Dalziels; 6 1/2 x 4 3/4;* Art Pictures from the Old Testament, *1894)*

Right: ***Samuel and Eli*** *(wood-engraving, Dalziels; 6 5/8 x 4 3/4;* Art Pictures from the Old Testament, *1894)*

The Fall of the Walls of Jericho *(wood-engraving, Dalziels; 6 1/4 x 7;* Dalziels' Bible Gallery, *1881;* Art Pictures from the Old Testament*)*

Dalziels' Bible Gallery (Routledge, 1881)
 ¶ **The Fall of the Walls of Jericho*** (Dalziels)
 ¶ **The Sun and Moon Stand Still*** (Dalziels)
 • Reprinted in *Art Pictures from the Old Testament*
 • The artist's name is misspelled as "Armistead"
 • The book was issued in a limited (bound) edition and in proof presentation copies (portfolio, 1880), the engravings by the Dalziels printed from the original wood-blocks on india paper mounted on heavy paper. The book's illustrations were reprinted, with the addition of others not included in 1881, in *Art Pictures from the Old Testament* (S.P.C.K., 1894; also Virtue, 1894) and, adding a reprint of Millais's *The Parables of Our Lord and Saviour Jesus Christ*, as *Art Pictures from the Old Testament and Our Lord's Parables* (Dalton, c. 1905).
 • Most drawings for the *Bible Gallery* were created in the 1860s

English Art in 1884 (Henry Blackburn; New York: Appleton, 1885)
 ¶ **Egypt** (drawing by the artist [?] after his sculpture; photo-engraving)

English Artists of the Present Day (Seeley,

Jackson, and Halliday, 1872)
   ¶ **Dedication of a Saxon Church**
(drawing, dated 1861, for a church frieze;
Woodburytype)

English Sacred Poetry (Rev. Robert Aris
Willmott, ed.; Routledge, 1862)
   ¶ **The Dead Man of Bethany***
   ¶ **A Dream***
   ¶ **Evening Hymn***
   ¶ **In Prison***
   • Eng. Dalziels

BOOKS CONTAINING REPRINTS

Art Pictures from the Old Testament (Aley
Fox, text; Society for Promoting Christian
Knowledge, 1894)
   ¶ **The Fall of the Walls of Jericho**
   ¶ **The Sun and Moon Stand Still**
   • Reprinted from *Dalziels' Bible
Gallery*
   • Plus 2 original illustrations

Touches of Nature (Strahan, 1867)
   ¶ **A Song (Which None but the
Redeemed Can Sing)**
   ¶ **Sea-Weeds**
   • Reprinted from *Good Words*
   • *Touches of Nature* was published in
two versions: one with 98 illustrations,
and one with 47 (both 1867 and 1872
[Cassell] editions; the 1871 Strahan edition also has 47). Some artists' complete
contributions to the title are contained
only in the larger version. Both editions
contain the two Armstead illustrations.

INDIVIDUAL PRINTS

¶ **St. George and the Dragon*** (wood-
engraving proof, Dalziels, 1863; 7 x 3 1/2;
signed with initials in block)
   • British Museum, London,
Department of Prints and Drawings,
Dalziel Collection (vol. 17, 1863, no. 28);
probably unpublished

The Trysting-Place (wood-engraving, Dalziels; 4 1/8 x
5 3/8; Poems by Eliza Cook, *1861*)

*The Dead
Man of
Bethany*
(wood-engrav-
ing, Dalziels;
5 1/2 x 3 3/4;
English
Sacred
Poetry, *1862*)

Ford Madox Brown

(1821–1893)

Although the Pre-Raphaelite Brotherhood was formed principally by Dante Gabriel Rossetti, John Everett Millais, and William Holman Hunt in September 1848, it can be said that Ford Madox Brown—never a member of that group, but a stylistic supporter of Pre-Raphaelitism throughout his career—was its inspiration and elder statesman.

Born in Calais, Brown studied art in Belgium (in Ghent he was taught by a pupil of David, and he studied with Baron Wappers at the Antwerp Academy) and Rome, where he came under the influence of the German Nazarene artists. He aimed in the 1840s to establish himself in the upper tier of Academicians, the history painters; his first two paintings in England, *Wycliffe Reading His Translation of the Bible to John of Gaunt* and *Chaucer at the Court of King Edward III*, both begun in the mid-1840s, were in this tradition.

Brown joined many of the artists of this period in submitting works to the Houses of Parliament competitions, where the Nazarene fresco style was appreciated: *The Body of Harold Brought Before William the Conqueror* (1844–61) was the painting that he entered. Lucy Rabin, in her perceptive 1978 study *Ford Madox Brown and the Pre-Raphaelite History Picture*, notes its proto–Pre-

Ford Madox Brown, c. 1862 (photograph; photo-engraving, as published in Some Reminiscences of William Michael Rossetti, *vol. 1, 1906)*

Raphaelite concerns: eccentric figures; use of the living model (Brown as Harold); characters engaged in lifelike action; individualized expressions—frozen, contorted; inadequate space; and the idea that the representation of incomplete portions of human anatomy, animals, objects, and space duplicates the appearance of these things as they exist in the world and as the eye can grasp them in a glance (pp. 73, 80). When Brown revisited Italy in 1845 he met the Nazarenes and developed an appreciation for the early-Italian artists. His submission to the Free Exhibition of 1848 was *Wycliffe*, in which he used life models and a wet white undercoat for bright colors.

In spring 1848 Rossetti wrote to Brown of his admiration for his work, asking to become a pupil. At Brown's studio, Rossetti soaked up the stylistic innovations in his teacher's works-in-progress, while at the same time introducing Brown to Keats and other literary enthusiasms. The Pre-Raphaelite facial types that Rossetti passed along to his followers, like Simeon Solomon and Edward Burne-Jones, were direct adaptations of Brown's style. Rossetti's first Pre-Raphaelite painting, *The Girlhood of Mary Virgin* (1849), was begun in Brown's studio—and finished in Hunt's, to whom he trans-

GONERILL: REGAN: LEAR: FOOL: CORDELIA: FRANCE:

Cordelia (etching, Brown; 7 1/8 x 8 5/8;
frontispiece for the Germ, no. 3, March
1850)

etching, *Cordelia*, to the 1850
P.R.B. journal, the *Germ*.
Thomas Seddon, for many
years a friend of Brown, origi-
nated the idea of the North
London School of Drawing and
Modeling for Artisans and
Working Men, which opened in
1850; Brown was on the com-
mittee and taught evening
classes. He also taught at F. D.
Maurice's Working Men's
College (1857), as did Rossetti
and John Ruskin.

Brown exhibited with
Rossetti at the Free Exhibition
of 1849. For the continually
worked-on *Chaucer* painting, Dante Rossetti
sat for Chaucer, his brother William for the
troubadour. Brown was organizer of the
famous Free Exhibition of 1857 (the Russell
Place exhibit of Pre-Raphaelite works), where
he was finally associated with the movement.
In 1857 he helped found the Hogarth Club (an
expanded group of Pre-Raphaelites formed to
hold exhibitions to rival the Royal Academy).
In 1861 he was among the founding members
of the decorative-arts firm of Morris, Marshall,
Faulkner, and Co., for which he worked
(through 1874) at designing furniture and
stained-glass windows (e.g., St. Oswald's,
Durham, 1865).

Ford Madox Brown's paintings are some
of the most interesting and unusual in all
nineteenth-century art. They are Pre-
Raphaelite down to their bones—even though
his subjects are often from modern life.
Important recognition came with a masterpiece of religious art, *Jesus Washing Peter's
Feet* (1852–56), for which he received a prize
at the Liverpool Academy Exhibition in 1856.
Brown used F. G. Stephens (of the 1848

ferred his artistic allegiance and began talking
of a revolutionary movement, which would end
in the formation of the Pre-Raphaelite
Brotherhood (P.R.B.) a few months later.

Lucy Rabin comes down firmly on the side
of Brown's important role in the creation of
Pre-Raphaelitism, and quite convincingly,
when she declares: "These Brethren, having
no revolutionary style of their own, borrowed
Brown's and gave it the Pre-Raphaelite label.
Pre-Raphaelite pictures after 1849 showed
deliberate distortions of space and figure
relationships like Brown's and a similar effect
of the highly charged pictorial energy which
had become the hallmark of his style. These
paintings were amalgams of detailed elements, many of them flat, linear patterning
that taught the Pre-Raphaelites to give a stylistic and compositional coherence to their
works" (p. 143).

Although John Ruskin seems never once
to have mentioned Brown's works in his writings, by his own unstinting efforts and personal associations Brown became an integral part
of the circle. He contributed essays and an

Brotherhood), Christina, William, and Gabriel Rossetti, and Holman Hunt as models. Its eccentrically posed apostles are meant to convey what the scene actually might have been like at the time. One of the most famous Pre-Raphaelite works is the circular *The Last of England* (1855), social commentary on emigration inspired by Pre-Raphaelite brother Thomas Woolner's move to Australia in 1852. *Work* (1852–65), probably Brown's most renowned painting, depicts social activists F. D. Maurice and Thomas Carlyle in a spectacularly sunlit scene of London life and "excavators,"

Work (oil, 1852–65; 53 x 77 1/8; Manchester City Art Galleries; autotype, as published in Ford Madox Hueffer's Ford Madox Brown: A Record of His Life and Work, 1896)

contrasting symbolic (but highly realistic) figures of various classes, idle and working.

The people in Brown's 1860s-and-after

The Prisoner of Chillon (wood-engraving, Dalziels; 5 x 3 5/8; The Poets of the Nineteenth Century, 1857)

compositions take on a dynamic, slightly undulating character, and the faces are unmistakably in the Pre-Raphaelite mold that he originated. These works have appeared to some critics then and since as mannered, but their originality cannot be denied: Brown's pictures, full of round shapes and swirling drapery, and odd poses and rubbery figures, seem to reach beyond Pre-Raphaelitism toward such twentieth-century compositional concerns as those of Thomas Hart Benton and other American muralists. Both Brown's wood-engraved illustrations and his paintings (which are frequently related) fall into this category: his twelve murals at Manchester's Town Hall and the figures in his wood-engravings for *Lyra Germanica* (2d ser., 1868); "The Traveller" in *Once a Week* (1869) and its companion watercolor of 1884; and the 1866 painting *The Coat of Many Colours*, even better than its inspiration, the Dalziels' engraving of "Joseph's Coat" of the early 1860s, published in the *Bible Gallery* two decades later. The main illustration (of two) for his friend Dante Rossetti's poem "Down Stream" (*Dark Blue*, 1871) also fits into this personal scheme of swirling Pre-Raphaelitism. The genesis of this collaboration is another example of the creative reciprocity among the Pre-Raphaelites, as Rossetti described to his brother William: "I'm Dark-Blued at last, owing to Brown, who was asked to illustrate something of mine for them if I would contribute" (letter of September 10, 1871; William Michael Rossetti, ed., *Dante Gabriel Rossetti: His Family-Letters*, vol. 2, 1895, p. 246).

In addition to these engravings (he did two others for the *Bible Gallery*, "Elijah and the Widow's Son" and "The Death of Eglon"), in the field of illustration Brown created six outstanding miniatures (apparently steel-engravings) for the Moxon edition of *Byron's Poetical Works* in 1870, turning some into watercolor replicas (*The Corsair's Return*, 1870–71, *Byron's Dream*, 1889, et al.). Brown's first book illustration, "The Prisoner of Chillon," was also for Byron, and he appears to have worked over a hundred hours on it in spring 1856 and studied corpses at the hospital for days for the proper "decomposition" effects for the image (*Diary of Ford Madox Brown*, pp. 165–82). In the early 1890s he did frontispieces, all photo-engraved, for several minor books by friends and relatives: *The Brown Owl* and *The Feather* by his grandson, Ford Madox Hueffer, and Mathilde Blind's *Dramas in Miniature* —"The Perfume of the Breath of May." Pre-

Raphaelite in style and theme even at this late date, the latter drawing illustrates a poem that describes a young woman, with golden hair, dying prematurely; she had been a prostitute; a girl brings her flowers and causes her to imagine talking to her mother and the nice country life she led as a child.

Brown, whose social conscience was keen, was probably the most unselfish and generous artist in England, always concerned not only for the financial situations and success of his fellow artists, but constantly raising funds for widows and their families. In his book *Fifty Years of Work Without Wages*, Charles Rowley characterizes Brown, whose life seemed beset by as many bad times as good (his first wife had died in 1846 and his son Oliver died in 1874). Rowley knew him as a man who "would do anything for his friends, for no one was ever so self-sacrificing. . . . No man could be more altruistic. . . . [His was a] most hospitable house. . . . [He was] the best talker in London" (pp. 96–97). Indeed, Brown may also have been the best *artist* in London.

The Traveller (*wood-engraving, Swain; 7 1/4 x 4 3/4; Once a Week, new ser. [ser. 3], vol. 3, 1869, p. 145*)

Top: **Down Stream** *[#1] (wood-engraving, C. M. Jenkin; 4 1/4 x 5 7/8; Dark Blue, vol. 2, 1871, p. 211)*

Right: **Down Stream** *[#2] (wood-engraving, C. M. Jenkin; 1 3/4 x 4 1/4; Dark Blue, vol. 2, 1871, p. 212)*

Childe Harold's Pilgrimage *(steel-engraving, 4 1/4 x 2 1/2; Byron's Poetical Works, 1870)*

Catalogue

PERIODICALS

Dark Blue
Vol. 2, 1871:
¶ **"Down Stream"** by Dante Gabriel Rossetti, 2 illustrations* (pp. 211, 212; C. M. Jenkin)

Once a Week
New ser. [ser. 3], vol. 3, 1869:
¶ **The Traveller*** (p. 145, Swain)

BOOKS

A Beggar and Other Fantasies (Grace Black; Garnett, 1889)
¶ *Titlepage illustration:* **The Footpath Way** (photo-engraving)
• Also used as a bookplate by Edward Garnett

The Brown Owl (Ford Madox Hueffer; Unwin, 1892)
¶ 2 illustrations* (photo-engravings)

Byron's Poetical Works (Moxon, 1870)
¶ *Titlepage illustration:* **The Grass upon My Grave***
¶ **Childe Harold's Pilgrimage*** (a.k.a. **My Native Land—Good Night**)
¶ **The Corsair*** (a.k.a. **His Steps the Chamber Gain**)
¶ **Sardanapalus*** (a.k.a. **I Must Awake Him**)
¶ **The Two Foscari*** (a.k.a. **Marina**)
¶ **Don Juan*** (a.k.a. **His Slender**

Frame of Pallid Aspect Lay)
- Steel-engravings (most, if not all, variations and editions of this book do not contain "original" steel-engravings but probably graphotype or anastatic reproductions of the engravings)
- Plus 2 other illustrations by Oliver Madox Brown (the artist's son)
- Reissued c. 1872 without ***titlepage illustration*** and **Sardanapalus**; reissued in 1880 without **Sardanapalus**

Dalziels' Bible Gallery (Routledge, 1881)
¶ **The Death of Eglon*** (Dalziels)
¶ **Elijah and the Widow's Son*** (Dalziels)
¶ **Joseph's Coat*** (Dalziels)
- Reprinted in *Art Pictures from the Old Testament*

Dramas in Miniature (Mathilde Blind; Chatto and Windus, 1891)
¶ **The Perfume of the Breath of May** (photo-engraving)

Top: ***The Corsair*** *(steel-engraving, 2 1/2 x 4 1/4;* Byron's Poetical Works, *1870)*

Middle: ***Sardanapalus*** *(steel-engraving, 2 1/2 x 4 1/4;* Byron's Poetical Works, *1870)*

Bottom left: ***The Two Foscari*** *(steel-engraving, 4 1/4 x 2 1/2;* Byron's Poetical Works, *1870)*

Bottom right: ***Don Juan*** *(steel-engraving, 2 1/2 x 4 1/4;* Byron's Poetical Works, *1870)*

The Death of Eglon *(wood-engraving, Dalziels; 6 x 7 1/4;* Dalziels' Bible Gallery, *1881;* Art Pictures from the Old Testament*)*

Elijah and the Widow's Son *(wood-engraving, Dalziels; 9 x 5 3/4;* Dalziels' Bible Gallery, *1881;* Art Pictures from the Old Testament*)*

The Dwale Bluth: Hebditch's Legacy and Other Literary Remains of Oliver Madox Brown (Ford Madox Hueffer and William Michael Rossetti, eds.; Tinsley, 2 vols., 1876)

¶ **Oliver Madox Brown** (vol. 1; etching, Brown)

¶ **The Author at the Age of Four** (vol. 2; etching, Brown)

The Feather (Ford Madox Hueffer; Unwin, 1892)

¶ *Frontispiece:* **All but the Eagle Had the Best of It After All** (photo-engraving)

¶ 3 *titlepage illustrations* (photo-engravings)

Lyra Germanica (Catherine Winkworth, trans.; Longmans, Green, Reader, and Dyer, 2d ser., 1868)

¶ **Abraham*** (Swain; a.k.a. **Seest Thou How Faith Wrought with His Works and by Works Was Faith Made Perfect**)

¶ **O Blessed Rock*** (T. Bolton)

¶ **The Sower*** (Dalziels; a.k.a. **He That Soweth to the Spirit Shall of the Spirit Reap Life Everlasting**)

• There are two series of this book, containing varying lists of artistic contributors; the 1861 edition has illustrations by Lawless and Marks

Oliver Madox Brown (John H. Ingram; Stock, 1883)

¶ *Frontispiece:* **Portrait of Oliver Madox Brown** (photogravure)

• Plus **Oliver Madox Brown at the Age of Five** (photogravure; reproduction from an existing oil painting, *The English Boy*)

• Plus 2 other illustrations by Oliver Madox Brown

The Poets of the Nineteenth Century (Rev. Robert Aris Willmott, ed.; Routledge, 1857)

¶ **The Prisoner of Chillon*** (Dalziels)

BOOKS CONTAINING REPRINTS

Art Pictures from the Old Testament (Aley Fox, text; Society for Promoting Christian Knowledge, 1894)

¶ **The Death of Eglon**

¶ **Elijah and the Widow's Son**
¶ **Joseph's Coat**
• Reprinted from *Dalziels' Bible Gallery*

§ Paul Goldman (*Victorian Illustration*, 1996, p. 335) notes a reprint of **The Prisoner of Chillon** in a c. 1878 edition of Byron's *Poetical Works* published by Warne

§ Brown designed the cover for *Gabriel Denver* (Oliver Madox Brown; Smith, Elder, 1873)

INDIVIDUAL PRINTS

¶ **Cordelia** (etching, Brown; 7 1/8 x 8 5/8; signed with initials in plate)
• Published in the *Germ*, no. 3, March 1850
• The Pre-Raphaelite journal the *Germ* lasted four (monthly) issues, January to April 1850, and contained literary works by Brown, Dante Gabriel Rossetti, Coventry Patmore, Thomas Woolner, William Michael Rossetti, et al., and etchings (one in each issue) by Brown, James Collinson, Walter Deverell, and William Holman Hunt. The last two issues have the title changed to *Art and Poetry*. Significant reprints were published by Mosher (1898) and Stock (1901).

¶ **Invitation Card to View the Picture of Shakespeare by Ford Madox Brown** (wood-engraving, 1850; Galleries of Art, Messrs. Dickinson and Co., London)
• Birmingham Museums and Art Gallery

¶ **Windermere** (lithograph, Brown, 1854)
• Possibly two proofs only exist, one hand-colored (private collections)

Joseph's Coat (*wood-engraving, Dalziels; 7 x 6 7/8;* Dalziels' Bible Gallery, *1881;* Art Pictures from the Old Testament*)*

O Blessed Rock (*wood-engraving, T. Bolton; 4 1/4 x 3 3/4;* Lyra Germanica, *1868)*

Edward Burne-Jones

(1833-1898)

What the Pre-Raphaelite Brotherhood—with its primary aims of painting life honestly and directly from nature, expressing ideas, and rebelling against the conventions of Royal Academy artists—eventually evolved into was in no small part due to the direction taken by Edward Burne-Jones and his friend and artistic colleague, William Morris. Morris and Burne-Jones met while studying for the religious ministry at Exeter College, Oxford, but soon understood that their lives would take more of an artistic and literary direction. They were both fired up by the love of Malory, Tennyson, and the medieval legends of chivalry. Sir Galahad was Burne-Jones's favorite in Tennyson's works, and Morris gave him a copy of the 1817 edition of Malory; Morris's own poetic collection *The Defence of Guinevere* (1858) includes "Sir Galahad: A Christian Mystery." Burne-Jones even signed letters "General of the Order of Sir Galahad" (*Memorials of Edward Burne-Jones*, vol. 1, p. 77). Like the Pre-Raphaelites, the Oxford duo enthusiastically read Keats, Shelley, and Coleridge.

Georgiana Burne-Jones in her *Memorials* quotes her husband as writing, "It must have been at the end of the summer term of this year [1855] that we got permission to look at the Pre-Raphaelite pictures in the house of Mr. Combe . . . and there we saw two pictures by Holman Hunt. . . . But our greatest wonder and delight was reserved for a water-colour of Rossetti's, of Dante drawing the head of Beatrice and disturbed by people of importance. We had already fallen in with a copy of

the *Germ*, and at once he seemed to us the chief figure in the Pre-Raphaelite Brotherhood" (vol. 1, p. 110).

The founding of the *Oxford and Cambridge Magazine* was next. Burne-Jones wrote to his cousin Maria Joyce in early fall 1855: "Shall I tell you about our Magazine, as you are so good as to take an interest in it? In the enclosed envelope I have sent you a prospectus. It appeared in nearly all the magazines of the month, and will be in the *Quarterly Review* of January and in the *Times*. We have thoroughly set ourselves to the work now, banded ourselves into an exclusive Brotherhood of seven. Mr. Morris is proprietor. The expenses

Edward Burne-Jones in his studio, working on the painting **The Star of Bethlehem**, *1889 (photograph; photo-engraving, as published in Georgiana Burne-Jones's* Memorials of Edward Burne-Jones, *vol. 2, 1904)*

will fall very heavily upon him, I fear. . . ." Continuing, Burne-Jones gives a list of pieces in the first two issues, including two tales by him and his review of Thackeray's *The Newcomes*, a poem and two articles on churches by Morris, and essays on Tennyson and Carlyle by others of the group (*Memorials of Edward Burne-Jones*, vol. 1, pp. 121–22). Rossetti himself later contributed to the magazine, during the course of its twelve monthly issues that year.

This led to Burne-Jones introducing the 1856 publication to another hero, the author of *Modern Painters*, John Ruskin—who responded favorably. The same year Burne-Jones sought out Rossetti, who had been gratified by the former's praise of his *Music Master* wood-engraving "The Maids of Elfen-Mere" in the *Oxford* magazine's *Newcomes* article (which also referred to Hunt's etching in the *Germ*). That year the two students left college, Morris off to the architectural firm of G. E. Street and Burne-Jones to quarters in Chelsea, where Rossetti became his good friend and mentor.

In fall 1857, Rossetti led a group of enthusiastic artists in the famous mural-painting adventure at the Debating Society Hall of the Oxford Union. This enterprise is often seen as the point when Pre-Raphaelitism evolved into a second phase—more medieval, more decorative, more poetic. Burne-Jones, especially in his later art, symbolizes that direction, which finally turned into something else in the Aesthetic movement. The youthful muralists, knowing little of technique but a lot about their uniformly Arthurian subjects, included Arthur Hughes (whose *April Love* had recently been purchased by Morris), Valentine Prinsep, Hungerford Pollen, John Spencer-Stanhope, Morris, Rossetti, and Burne-Jones.

Burne-Jones stayed at Val Prinsep's Little Holland House in 1858, along with another famous painter, George F. Watts, who remained for decades; Tennyson also visited there awhile, as he worked on "Elaine" for his

Design for the 1887 painting **The Vision of St. Francis** *(photo-engraving, as published in Georgiana Burne-Jones's* Memorials of Edward Burne-Jones, *vol. 2, 1904)*

Idylls of the King. Burne-Jones's themes in his watercolors, drawings, and oil paintings for the remainder of his life would be primarily Arthurian and medieval, taking inspiration from Rossetti and—owing to Watts and several trips to Italy—the Italian Renaissance, particularly Botticelli. Ruskin remained a friend and patron, sponsoring Burne-Jones's Italian trips and even accompanying the artist and his wife to the continent in 1862.

Through the mid-1860s the artist concentrated on watercolors, elaborate pen-and-ink drawings, and numerous designs for stained glass and tapestries in conjunction with work for the Morris decorative-arts firm. Burne-Jones in this period produced watercolors like *Clara von Bork* (1860), *The Annunciation* (1863), and *Le Chant d'Amour* (1865) that take Rossettian themes and faces and figures and begin to transform them into otherworldly, almost decorative ideal figures, but lacking Rossetti's sensuality. Despite his being from 1877 the symbol of the Grosvenor Gallery, which was the symbol of the "new wave" of Aesthetic art, Burne-Jones nevertheless remained a true Pre-Raphaelite in many ways, assiduous in making studies from models for his paintings, his always detailed realism serving poetic and ideal ends.

Sidney Colvin, writing in the *Portfolio* in 1870 ("English Painters of the Present Day: Edward Burne-Jones," vol. 1, pp. 17–21), offers that in the years 1869–70 Burne-Jones's art was changing, attaining a greater strength and wider scope, and "the obviously powerful qualities of . . . [his art were] pronouncing themselves every day more vehemently." Of prime importance was love of beauty for beauty's sake; Burne-Jones was painting ideal nature: "A flower painted by him is like a flower described by Keats; all the fragrance and colour and purity of it are caught and concentrated in the magic pencil-strokes."

By the late 1870s, when the highly successful Grosvenor Gallery was making reputations and exposing the public to a greater variety of artists, Burne-Jones's style had matured and become so refined, so recognizable and personal, that almost overnight he became an internationally acclaimed painter. Among this period's works, still with medieval themes, are: *Merlin and Vivien* (1870–74), *The Beguiling of Merlin* (1874; exhibited at the Grosvenor's opening in 1877), and *King Cophetua and the Beggar Maid* (1884).

In the field of book illustration, Burne-Jones, of course, will ever be associated with William Morris and the Kelmscott Press. This fruitful collaboration produced numerous book-art masterpieces in the 1890s, preeminent among them the famed Kelmscott *Chaucer*, with eighty-seven woodcuts after

the artist. These works, and drawings in a similar style that Burne-Jones did for Morris's never-completed, massive "Earthly Paradise" project, belong to an "Aesthetic" school of illustration that emphasizes the decorative possibilities of the woodcut (as opposed to wood-engraving) in harmony with a printed page—a school that is well removed from the principles of Pre-Raphaelite graphics. This thick-lined, open-spaced woodcut style was followed by Morris's other Kelmscott artists, such as Walter Crane, Charles Gere, and Arthur Gaskin, and is seen in the pages of the 1880s–'90s art periodicals *Century Guild Hobby Horse*, *English Illustrated Magazine*, and the *Studio*, and in the woodcuts of Charles Ricketts for his Vale Press.

William Morris, 1857 (photograph; photo-engraving, as published in Georgiana Burne-Jones's Memorials of Edward Burne-Jones, *vol. 1, 1904)*

Burne-Jones's earlier commercial illustrations were of course greatly influenced by Rossetti's for *The Music Master* and the Moxon *Tennyson*. His elaborate 1858 pen-and-ink drawing *Going into Battle* seems to take much, in its background details, from Rossetti's "St. Cecily" for "The Palace of Art" in the *Tennyson* book. Burne-Jones reprised the design's basic elements in a wood-engraved illustration, unpublished, called "Ladies Watching Knights Depart for Battle" of the same year, the cutting of which is traditionally ascribed to his fiancée, Georgiana Macdonald. Another unpublished wood-engraving is "Christ in the Garden of Gethsemene," c. 1863, cut by the Dalziels; several proofs exist, and a note on the mount of the version in the Hartley Collection (Museum of Fine Arts, Boston) indicates that it was originally intended for an 1864 issue of *Good Words*.

But by this time Burne-Jones had dived into the field of published illustration. He had previously done nearly ninety drawings for his friend Archibald Maclaren's 1857 book *The Fairy Family*, only three of which were used; these are full of fussy details and penwork and lots of imagination, but in a totally amateurish and uncharacteristic style. Burne-Jones's first major commission, from the Dalziels, came by way of an introduction from Holman Hunt in a November 21, 1861, letter to the wood-engravers: "I write to speak of a friend of mine who I feel very strongly might be of great value to you in the illustrating of *Good Words*. He is perhaps the most remarkable of all the younger men of the profession for talent, and will, undeniably, in a few years fill the high position in general public favour which at present he holds in the professional world. He has yet, I think, made but few if any drawings on wood, but he has had much more practice in working with the point both with pencil and pen and ink on paper, and so would have no difficulty with the material. I have not seen him lately, but remember that

he has sometimes said that he should like to try his hand at drawing on wood, so without further ceremony I will enclose a letter to him which you may use at your own discretion. His name, as you will see by the enclosed, is Edward Jones" (*Brothers Dalziel*, p. 162).

Burne-Jones's "King Sigurd, the Crusader" appeared in *Good Words* in 1862, followed by "The Summer Snow" in 1863. Both have all the elements of Pre-Raphaelite style and themes, yet the drawing and linework are not quite as sure as they should be. The Dalziels nevertheless asked Burne-Jones to join the list of *Bible Gallery* contributors working in the 1860s. The artist seems to have prepared three drawings on wood-blocks for the project, two of which remain uncut ("Noah Entering the Ark" and "The Return of the Dove to the Ark," both in the Victoria and Albert Museum, London). The third finally appeared in the 1881 *Bible Gallery*—"The Parable of the Boiling Pot," with its linear denseness and Pre-Raphaelite figures, but still just missing the technical quality of most other Pre-Raphaelite illustrations. For a little-known 1888 book, Joseph Jacobs's edition of *The Fables of Bidpai*, Burne-Jones provided a frontispiece, reproduced directly from a pen-and-ink drawing; it's a rare example of a non-Kelmscott mature Burne-Jones illustration—both ideal and Pre-Raphaelite, yet clearly anticipating the style of his extraordinary drawings for Morris's press.

King Sigurd, the Crusader *(wood-engraving, Dalziels; 6 x 4 1/2;* Good Words, *vol. 3, 1862, p. 248)*

Catalogue

PERIODICALS

Daily Chronicle
Feb. 11, 1895:
¶ **Labour (When Adam Delved and Eve Span** reprinted from *A Dream of John Ball,* 1892)

Good Words
Vol. 3, 1862:
¶ **King Sigurd, the Crusader*** (p. 248, Dalziels)
Vol. 4, 1863:
¶ **The Summer Snow*** (p. 380, Dalziels)
• Erroneously credited to "Christopher Jones"

Quarto
Vol. 3, 1897:
¶ **The Parable of the Boiling Pot** (p. 60; reprinted, using the original wood-block, from *Dalziels' Bible Gallery*)

BOOKS

The Beginning of the World: Twenty-five Pictures by Edward Burne-Jones (Longmans, Green, 1902)
¶ 25 illustrations
• Prepared for engraving for this (limited) edition by R. Catterson-Smith; originally planned for the Kelmscott edition of J. W. Mackail's *Biblia Innocentum,* 1892
• Published in the U.S. as *In the Dawn of the World* (Boston: Goodspeed, 1903)

Dalziels' Bible Gallery (Routledge, 1881)
¶ **The Parable of the Boiling Pot*** (reprinted in the *Quarto* and *Art Pictures from the Old Testament*)

A Dream of John Ball (William Morris; Reeves and Turner, 1888)
¶ *Frontispiece:* **When Adam Delved and Eve Span*** (etching)

• Another version of this etching (possibly by Burne-Jones) has alternate (less refined) lettering of the title beneath the image; 5 1/2 x 4 1/4; proof: Pierpont Morgan Library, New York, Print Room

• Re-created as a woodcut for the Kelmscott edition, 1892; reprinted in the *Daily Chronicle* as **Labour**

The Earliest English Version of the Fables of Bidpai (Joseph Jacobs, ed.; Nutt, 1888)
　¶ *Frontispiece* (photogravure)

The Earthly Paradise (William Morris; Ellis, 3 vols., 1868–70)
　¶ *Titlepage illustration* (Morris)
　• Art recut (by G. Campbell) for numerous subsequent editions (number of volumes vary) published by Ellis and White and Reeves and Turner; notably reissued, 1-vol. edition, 1890 (1891 binding by Morris; Reeves and Turner)

English Art in 1884 (Henry Blackburn; New York: Appleton, 1885)
　¶ **King Cophetua and the Beggar Maid** (drawing by the artist [?] after his painting; photo-engraving)

Exhibition of Venetian Art (Catalogue; New Gallery, 1894–95)
　¶ *Titlepage illustration* (woodcut)
　• Plus cover design by the artist

The Fairy Family (Archibald Maclaren; Longmans, 1857)
　¶ *Frontispiece* (steel-engraving)
　¶ *Titlepage illustration* (steel-engraving)
　¶ *Tailpiece* (wood-engraving)
　• Reissued by Macmillan in 1874
　• A special limited edition of the book was published in 1985 (Dalrymple), reproducing the 3 original illustrations, plus 85 other unengraved and unpublished drawings designed for the book by the artist

King Poppy: A Story Without End (Edward Robert Bulwer-Lytton; Longmans, 1892)
　¶ *Frontispiece* (photo-engraving)
　¶ *Titlepage illustration* (photo-engraving)
　• Plus cover design by the artist

Parables from Nature (Mrs. Alfred Gatty;

*The **Summer Snow** (wood-engraving, Dalziels; 5 5/8 x 4 3/16; Good Words, vol. 4, 1863, p. 380)*

The Parable of the Boiling Pot *(wood-engraving, Dalziels; 7 x 5 1/4;* Dalziels' Bible Gallery, *1881;* Art Pictures from the Old Testament*)*

Bell and Daldy, 3d and 4th ser., 1865)

¶ **The Deliverer*** (H. Harral; a.k.a. **The Nativity**)

• This book was published in several series in various years (and multiple editions), often with different and overlapping artist-contributors; the entire series (1 through 5) is collected in the 1880 ("new and complete") edition, published by Bell

Pygmalion and the Image (William Morris; New York: Russell, 1903)

¶ ***Frontispiece portrait*** and 4 illustrations (from the *Earthly Paradise* series)

The Queen Who Flew: A Fairy Tale (Ford Madox Hueffer; Bliss, Sands, and Foster, 1894)

¶ ***Frontispiece*** (photo-engraving; also reproduced on cover)

Saint Eva (Amelia Pain; Osgood, McIlvaine, 1897)

¶ ***Frontispiece*** (Derbier)

Select Epigrams from the Greek Anthology (J. W. Mackail, ed.; Longmans, 1890)

¶ ***Titlepage illustration***

§ *Studies in Both Arts* (John Ruskin; Orpington, Kent: Allen, 1895) features a cover design based on an unused ***titlepage illustration***, c. 1864, for Ruskin's *Munera Pulveris*

§ A book well known for its Burne-Jones illustrations, but which contains only photo-engraved reproductions of previous works (15 illustrations), is *The Doom of King Acrisius* (William Morris; New York: Russell, 1902)

KELMSCOTT PRESS BOOKS

[Chaucer] *The Works of Geoffrey Chaucer* (F. S. Ellis, ed.; 1896; a.k.a. the Kelmscott *Chaucer*)

¶ 87 illustrations

A Dream of John Ball and A King's Lesson (William Morris; 1892)

¶ ***Frontispiece*** (redrawn from the 1888 edition; woodcut, W. H. Hooper;

reprinted in the *Daily Chronicle* as **Labour**)

The Golden Legend (Jacobus da Voragine; William Caxton, trans.; F. S. Ellis, ed.; 3 vols., 1892)
    ¶ 2 illustrations (vol. 1)

The Life and Death of Jason (William Morris; 1895)
    ¶ 2 illustrations (W. Spielmeyer)

Love Is Enough (William Morris; 1897)
    ¶ *Frontispiece* (W. H. Hooper)
    ¶ **Quia Multum Amavit** (W. H. Hooper)
    • Designed in 1872 for a proposed decorated edition of *Love Is Enough*, which was published in 1873 without illustrations. A woodcut proof of **Four Putti** (W. Morris), designed for the 1873 edition, is in the Pierpont Morgan Library, New York, Print Room.

A Note by William Morris on His Aims in Founding the Kelmscott Press (William Morris; 1898)
    ¶ 1 illustration (Morris; from the unpublished woodcuts for *The Earthly Paradise*)

The Order of Chivalry (William Caxton, trans.; F. S. Ellis, ed.; 1893)
    ¶ *Frontispiece*

Sire Degrevaunt (F. S. Ellis, ed.; 1897)
    ¶ *Frontispiece*

The Story of Sigurd the Volsung and the Fall of the Nibelungs (William Morris; 1898)
    ¶ *Frontispiece* (W. H. Hooper)
    ¶ Full-page *tailpiece* (W. H. Hooper)

Syr Perecyvelle of Gales (F. S. Ellis, ed.; 1895)
    ¶ *Frontispiece*

Syr Ysambrace (F. S. Ellis, ed.; 1897)
    ¶ *Frontispiece*

The Well at the World's End (William Morris; 1896)
    ¶ 4 illustrations

The Deliverer (wood-engraving, H. Harral; 5 1/2 x 3; Parables from Nature, 1865)

Womanly Noblesse *(woodcut, W. H. Hooper; 5 x 5 1/2;* The Works of Geoffrey Chaucer, *1896)*

Ladies Watching Knights Depart for Battle *(wood-engraving proof [only impression], Georgiana Macdonald [Burne-Jones], c. 1858; 4 3/8 x 2 3/4; courtesy William Morris Gallery, London Borough of Waltham Forest)*

The Wood Beyond the World (William Morris; 1894)
  ¶ **Frontispiece** (W. Spielmeyer)

§ In most cases, Burne-Jones's Kelmscott designs were redrawn in ink by R. Catterson-Smith, corrected by Burne-Jones, photographed onto wood-blocks, then cut by W. H. Hooper; place of publication is Hammersmith

§ For a projected edition of *Froissart's Chronycles*, two trial pages were printed at the Kelmscott Press; the half-border was engraved by W. Spielmeyer (1894), the large border engraved by C. E. Keates (Fitzwilliam Museum, Cambridge, Department of Manuscripts and Printed Books)

BOOKS CONTAINING REPRINTS

Art Pictures from the Old Testament (Aley Fox, text; Society for Promoting Christian Knowledge, 1894)
  ¶ **The Parable of the Boiling Pot** (reprinted from *Dalziels' Bible Gallery*; reprinted in the *Quarto*)

INDIVIDUAL PRINTS

  ¶ **Christ in the Garden of Gethsemene*** (wood-engraving proof, Dalziels, c. 1863; 5 1/2 x 4 3/8)
    • Unpublished; according to Harold Hartley (in a note on the mount of two trial proofs), this was originally planned for *Good Words* in 1864
    • British Museum, London, Department of Prints and Drawings, Dalziel Collection; Museum of Fine Arts, Boston, Hartley Collection

The Earthly Paradise **prints:** originally unpublished graphics, c. 1865–68, for a proposed book of this title by Morris
  ¶ **Psyche Before Pan*** (wood-engraving proof, Swain, c. 1865; 6 3/8 x 4 5/8)
    • Pierpont Morgan Library, New York, Print Room
  ¶ **Pygmalion Sculpting Galatea** (copper-engraving proof; 4 1/16 x 3 1/8)
    • Possibly engraved by Burne-Jones

• Pierpont Morgan Library, New York, Print Room

¶ **"The Ring Given to Venus"** (2 copper-engraving proofs, Burne-Jones, c. 1867)
- **No. 1: A room with figures** (4 3/8 x 6 1/4)
- **No. 2: 3 figures** (4 3/8 x 3 1/8)
• Pierpont Morgan Library, New York, Print Room

¶ **"The Story of Cupid and Psyche"**: 44 illustrations (c. 1865–68; woodcuts cut and printed by Morris and his staff; other sets printed by F. S. Ellis)
• Published in *Eros and Psyche* (Robert Bridges; Gregynog, 1935): 24 illustrations
• Published in *The Story of Cupid and Psyche* (William Morris; Rampart Lion / Clover Hill, 2 vols., 1974): 44 illustrations; also published in 3 vols., one of which is a boxed portfolio containing collotype prints of 47 drawings plus a set of proofs printed from the original 44 wood-blocks
• "Woodcuts for an Edition of *Cupid and Psyche*": an album of 44 woodcut proofs, plus 3 pages of woodcut borders, including the **Four Putti** intended for *Love Is Enough* (Pierpont Morgan Library, New York, Print Room)
• William Morris Gallery, London Borough of Waltham Forest

¶ **Ladies Watching Knights Depart for Battle*** (wood-engraving proof, Georgiana Macdonald [Burne-Jones], c. 1858; 4 3/8 x 2 3/4)
• William Morris Gallery, London Borough of Waltham Forest

§ **Noah Entering the Ark** (7 x 5 1/4) and **The Return of the Dove to the Ark** (7 x 5 1/4) are uncut drawings (pen and ink and wash) on wood-blocks, 1863, intended for *Dalziels' Bible Gallery* (Victoria and Albert Museum, London)

§ Two Burne-Jones bookplates: ***Bookplate for Cicely Horner*** (vase of leaves and berries) and ***bookplate* for Frances Horner** (c. 1892; wood-engraving of 2 cupids and a shield); Brian North Lee (*British Bookplates*, 1979, p. 96) also notes a bookplate for the Cambridge Musical Society with a Burne-Jones drawing

Christ in the Garden of Gethsemene (*wood-engraving proof, Dalziels, c. 1863; 5 1/2 x 4 3/8; corrected by Burne-Jones; courtesy Museum of Fine Arts, Boston, John H. and Ernestine A. Payne Fund [Hartley Collection]*)

Arthur Hughes

(1832–1915)

A strong case can be made that Arthur Hughes was one of the greatest Pre-Raphaelites, just after Hunt, Rossetti, Millais, and Brown. Over his long life he produced hundreds of paintings, highly personal in style and according to Pre-Raphaelite principles; and like Hunt, his late works were often as good as his earliest ones. Among his associates in the movement, Hughes shares with Millais the distinction of being equally known as a painter and an illustrator.

It would be an understatement to say that Hughes was a prolific supplier of black-and-white graphics for books and such periodicals such as *Good Words*, *London Society*, *Sunday Magazine*, and especially *Good Words for the Young*, on whose pages in the early 1870s he built his lasting reputation as the illustrator of George MacDonald's fairy tales. As a painter, he quietly continued his work in the 1880s and 1890s, to lesser and lesser notice, but his reputation as an illustrator revived in the early years of the twentieth century with a series of books written or edited by his old friend's son, Greville MacDonald, in which Hughes's mastery of line and grasp of book-page design are gloriously revealed, unhindered by wood-engraver interpretations.

William Michael Rossetti's description of Hughes and his career gives an idea of the reason for the artist's low profile during his lifetime. "If I had to pick out, from amid my once-numerous acquaintances of the male sex, the sweetest and most ingenuous nature of all, the least carking and querulous, and the freest from 'envy, hatred and malice, and all

uncharitableness,' I should probably find myself bound to select Mr. Hughes. . . . [He] married early and had a numerous family. . . . As a painter he was one of those who most sympathized with the ideas which guided the Pre-Raphaelite Brotherhood, and his style conformed pretty faithfully (not servilely) to theirs. . . . He has produced many charming pictures—of a kind which, without being didactic, appeals intimately to the feelings; yet, as they had (like himself) no 'pushing' quality whether in subject or in execution, they never brought him into a position of great prominence, and he has reached the twilight of life without receiving the full measure of his due" (*Some Reminiscences of William Michael Rossetti*, 1906, vol. 1, pp. 147–48).

The quality of Hughes's paintings is so consistently high that one cannot help but feel, as did William Rossetti, that Hughes was undeservedly neglected. After attending the Government School of Design at Somerset House, from age fourteen, Hughes enrolled in the Royal Academy Schools, in 1847. Like Burne-Jones and William Morris, he was ensnared by the spirit of Pre-Raphaelitism as soon as he read the *Germ* in 1850. His friend, the Pre-Raphaelite sculptor Alexander Munro, introduced him to Ford Madox Brown and Dante Rossetti. Next he met Millais—in 1852, when his first Pre-Raphaelite work, *Ophelia*, was exhibited at the Royal Academy. Hughes later wrote that Millais introduced himself to the younger man at the exhibition and gave him encouragement about his picture—with which his own exhibited painting shared its subject (John Guille Millais, *The Life and Letters of Sir John Everett Millais*, 1899, vol. 1, p. 146); the next year Hughes sat for the cavalier in Millais's painting *The Proscribed Royalist*.

Ophelia was followed by the masterpieces on themes he would return to throughout his life—tragic lovers and familial sentiment, in both modern and literary settings: *April Love* (1855–56; vastly admired by Ruskin and his first big success, with the press, at the Royal

April Love (oil, 1855–56; 35 x 19 1/2; Tate Gallery, London; photo-engraving, as published in William Holman Hunt's Pre-Raphaelitism and the Pre-Raphaelite Brotherhood, vol. 2, 1906)

Academy), *The Long Engagement* (1859), *The Woodman's Child* (1860), *The Rift Within the Lute* (c. 1862), and *Home from the Sea* (1863). His other thematic preference was Arthurian legend. He had joined Rossetti, Burne-Jones, Morris, and a few others in their mural painting adventure (all did Arthurian subjects) on the walls of the Oxford Union in 1857. His subsequent Arthurian paintings, often noted for their intense colors and sunsets, include *The Knight of the Sun* (c. 1860), *Geraint and Enid* (1860), and *Sir Galahad* (1865–70). From Keats, there's *The Eve of St. Agnes* (triptych, 1855–56; a second version is from 1858), with its contorted poses reminiscent of Hunt's and Millais's early paintings.

Hughes's work is perfectly Pre-Raphaelite, yet bears the stamp of a strong and original personality. His faces are "of the movement" without affecting the proportions of the typical Burne-Jones/Brown/Rossetti features. His colors are practically a style—bright and strong, yet almost playful in their emphasis on luminous greens and purples; Hughes's women frequently have golden-red hair and are dressed in velvety purple garments. His lavish depictions of ivy and other botanicals seem to go beyond Millais's need to be faithful to nature in his backgrounds and take on a poetic symbolism that makes these elements partners in the emotional play of the scene. His portrayals of loves lost or families and children (*The Home Quartette*, 1883) seldom devolved into prettiness or sentimentality or hackneyed, muted compositions, as Millais's similar subjects did.

Hughes's illustrations, spanning a period of fifty years, were in a variety of styles. The Gothic-figured manner of the early pieces (*The Music Master*, 1855) gave way to the detailed, overall-composed, and modeled-from-life typical 1860s Pre-Raphaelite images in *Good Words*. For the children's stories of George MacDonald, Hughes produced small pictures full of imagination—simple yet unforgettable images, somewhat less assured in linework and often fussy and slightly composed. The "adult" illustrations in this style, such as those for *England's Antiphon* (1868) and *Tom Brown's School Days* (1869), are less satisfactory, relying on types and exhibiting little control over lines. But for some wood-engraved works, like the drawings for Tennyson's *Enoch Arden* (1866), Hughes exhibited the perfectly composed and solid figural style and exacting linear pattern-making that would appear in his amazing late children's books for Greville MacDonald (e.g., *Phantastes*, 1905).

With such a publishing career before him, it is not surprising that Arthur Hughes was the initiator of the first significant Pre-Raphaelite (Millais, Rossetti, and himself) contributions to a book, William Allingham's *The Music Master: A Love Story, and Two Series of Day and Night Songs* (see Introduction). Allingham, also a friend of Rossetti, and a real Pre-Raphaelite in his insistence on accuracy of natural detail in these illustrations, worked arm in arm with Hughes on the book. Allingham wrote to the artist on seeing the proofs of his wood-engravings, in March 1855, recommending changes that Hughes ask the Dalziels to make: "Are not the bounding lines of the figures [in the frontispiece] somewhat hard (lines in woodcuts can be heightened or softened, can't they?), especially at the small of the young man's back & the lower edge of the girl's frock?. . . Give Dalziel nothing but praise, though I wish he had been a trifle more Pre-Raphaelite in the texture of the lines of the bank running down to the water. There *is* a diff'ce between grass & dealboards.

"As to the 'Fairies,' it is Bravo the engraver!, and Bravissimo il Maestro! . . .

"'Lady Alice': successful. Could the lady's nostril be made the least thing less dilated? And her robe, where it is rolled at the waist, be made to cut on her left arm less blackly?" (quoted in Leonard Roberts, *Arthur Hughes, His Life and Works*, 1997, p. 253).

Hughes concentrated on succeeding as a painter from the late 1850s through late

Crossing the Stile *(wood-engraving, Dalziels; 5 x 3; **frontispiece** for* The Music Master, *1855)*

1860s—only beginning his illustration career in earnest in the period after most of the other Pre-Raphaelite artists had already created their best graphic work. With the exception of a fairy picture in the *Music Master* style for *The Poets of the Nineteenth Century* (1857), Hughes's nonjuvenile illustrations are usually detailed, realistic, and quirkily posed pieces in the best Pre-Raphaelite wood-engraving manner. Exceptionally fine drawings for periodicals include: "At the Sepulchre" (1864), "The Mariner's Cave" (1870), "Go, Little Letter, Apace, Apace" and "The Dial" (1871), and

"Ev'n to the Last Dip of the Vanishing Sail" *(wood-engraving, T. Bolton; 5 1/4 x 4 1/4; Enoch Arden, 1866)*

"The Carpenter" (1872), all for *Good Words*; and for *Sunday Magazine*, "Blessing in Disguise" (1869) and "My Heart" (1871).

Some of these are typical of the religious themes and the imagery—especially angels and children—that often appear in Hughes illustrations of the 1860s and '70s, whether juvenile related or not. "Daria" (*Sunday Magazine*, 1872) is based on a poem wherein a beautiful Roman girl, later a Christian convert and martyr, declares while yet

pagan that she'll never love until she finds someone who has died to prove his love for her; a very Pre-Raphaelite Daria is at the center, an angel typically holds its head and Daria's hand, and magnificently detailed plants grow upward along the base of the crucifixion cross. Hughes continued his religious pictures for *The Shepherd Lady* (1876), which the Dalziels cut for a Boston publisher: the four drawings exhibit nicely detailed, controlled work, especially the quasi-medieval "The Dear White Lady," one of the least seen but most Pre-Raphaelite images of the era.

One book especially stands out for its illustrations of sure composition and precise linear technique: Tennyson's *Enoch Arden*, for which Hughes did twenty-five drawings. Interestingly, Thomas Bolton, known as one of the first engravers to use photography to transfer original drawings onto wood, engraved the *Enoch Arden* art—possibly freeing Hughes from the quick-sketch lines he sometimes used and revealing a technique close in style to that of his directly reproduced, precise-lined art for the MacDonald books of the early 1900s. Hughes also created steel-engraved frontispiece and titlepage art: *My Beautiful Lady* (1866), *Alec Forbes of Howglen* (1867), *Tom Brown's School Days* (1868), and *The Five Days' Entertainments at*

Left: ***Out in the Storm [#1] for "At the Back of the North Wind"*** *(wood-engraving, Dalziels; 3 1/8 x 2 3/8; Good Words for the Young, vol. 1, 1868–69, p. 440; At the Back of the North Wind)*

Right: ***Out in the Storm [#2] for "At the Back of the North Wind"*** *(wood-engraving, Dalziels; 3 1/8 x 2 3/8; Good Words for the Young, vol. 1, 1868–69, p. 440; At the Back of the North Wind)*

Left: ***Diamond Questions North Wind*** *[#1] for* ***"At the Back of the North Wind"*** *(wood-engraving, Dalziels; 3 1/8 x 2 3/8;* Good Words for the Young, *vol. 2, 1869–70, p. 664;* At the Back of the North Wind*)*

Right: ***Diamond Questions North Wind*** *[#2] for* ***"At the Back of the North Wind"*** *(wood-engraving, Dalziels; 3 1/8 x 2 3/8;* Good Words for the Young, *vol. 2, 1869–70, p. 664;* At the Back of the North Wind*)*

Wentworth Grange (1868) boast lovely, miniature masterpieces reminiscent of his paintings.

Clearly, there is a spirit of Pre-Raphaelitism in much of Hughes's wood-engraved juvenile illustration, although strictly speaking, it falls short of the style in form. Occasionally, some images are so striking and so in keeping with Pre-Raphaelite types (the wild-haired wind-woman in *At the Back of the North Wind*, for instance) that they seem to find a place among Hughes's other successes. In its review of *At the Back of the North Wind*, the *Art Journal* recognized this, as well as Hughes's growing reputation as an artist for children: "The book is lavishly illustrated; the engravings are 'peculiar,' as the story is. Both may be somewhat 'dry'; but the artist, as well as the author, may be tried by a high standard, and maintain unquestioned right to public approval" (vol. 33 [new ser., vol. 10], 1871, p. 96). Laurence Housman assessed Hughes's deserved high standing in this area of illustration, recognizing that, even in these, his scratchy yet studiously built-up lines have much of Pre-Raphaelite integrity about them: "In drawing for the young Arthur Hughes drew also for himself; from beginning to end his work is absolutely serious and sincere. . . . His slightly decorative and very orderly compositions . . . are based on an interweav-

ing of parallel lines, or where it is a matter of curves, of one curve lying in the concentric embrace of another" ("The Illustrations of Arthur Hughes," *Bibliophile*, vol. 1, 1908, pp. 234, 236).

Almost all of the children's stories that Hughes illustrated originated in *Good Words for the Young* from 1868 through 1872, soon thereafter making their way into books: *At the Back of the North Wind*, *The Boy in Grey*, *Ranald Bannerman's Boyhood*, *The Princess and the Goblin*, and *Gutta-Percha Willie*. Every one of these was written by George MacDonald, a kindred spirit of childhood fantasy and innocence. In 1904 the author's son embarked upon a series of projects with his father's old friend that are among the high points of Hughes's illustration career: *Fairy Tales* was followed by *Phantastes*, *The Magic Crook* (1911), *Jack and Jill* (1913), and *Trystie's Quest* (1913). In *The Magic Crook*, like the others done in pen and ink and reproduced photo-mechanically, there are lots of vignettes and small drawings of different shapes and sizes. The tiny, beautiful lines are very careful and delicate, yet Dürerish. The mood is bucolic, with its sheep (another Hughes favorite element) and landscapes recalling *Enoch Arden*. Herein appear all the charming and full-of-character, odd yet non-threatening fantasies Hughes understood perfectly to be in a child's story-world—fish that walk, octopuses, lots of animals (and some animal-like humans), cherub babies, ghosts, and goblins.

One other author regarded Hughes as integral to her children's books: Christina Rossetti's famed collection of nursery verse, *Sing-Song* (1871), contains 123 sympathetic small drawings by Hughes. William Michael Rossetti (diary entry, May 15, 1871) suggested to the Dalziels that Hughes would be the perfect illustrator for his sister's book, and they agreed (William Michael Rossetti, ed., *The Family Letters of Christina Georgina Rossetti*, 1908, p. 207). On August 3, 1871, Christina wrote to the Dalziels, asking them to put Hughes's name in large type on the titlepage: "We shall certainly owe so much to him" (*Rossetti-Macmillan Letters*, p. 94). Further diary entries by William Rossetti note Ford Madox Brown's reaction on seeing proofs of *Sing-Song* ("He was singularly pleased, . . . going so far as to say that the poems are about Christina's finest things, and Hughes the first of living book-illustrators") and Hughes's dedication to the project: "Hughes says that the illustrating of Christina's book took up his whole time for a while. At first he worked tolerably leisurely, but after a certain time Dalziels asked him to furnish ten designs per week; he furnished twenty the first time" (entries of October 19 and November 13, 1871; *Family Letters of Christina Georgina Rossetti*, pp. 207–08). The collaboration had been so successful that Christina wrote to Macmillan about her forthcoming book, *Speaking Likenesses*, on April 20, 1874: "About illustrations. Nothing would please me more than Mr. Arthur Hughes . . . should do them. His in my *SingSong* were reckoned charming by Gabriel, not to speak of other verdicts. This would give me pleasure, but of course the question is yours & not mine" (*Rossetti-Macmillan Letters*, p. 100).

Arthur Hughes in all that he did displayed a mildness and sincerity of emotion, a commitment to creating personal and honest art, and a childlike innocence of spirit that saw children (he had a large family himself) and their outlooks, their worlds of fantasy, as central to art and literature. In the twilight years of his long life Hughes began to see his associates from the early days passing from the

She Lay with Closed Eyes *(photo-engraving, 2 1/2 x 3 1/4; Phantastes, 1905)*

scene. William Morris had died in 1896, and some of the old gang got together at Hunt's home in April 1897. At the time Burne-Jones commented: "Last night we were at Holman Hunt's. He looked such a dear, fine old thing, so unworldly and strange. . . . Arthur Hughes was there too, and he reminded me of our first meeting which I had forgotten. It was when I took him Morris' cheque for his *April Love*." Georgiana Burne-Jones (*Memorials of Edward Burne-Jones*, vol. 2, p. 303) continues: "The result of this meeting with Arthur Hughes, whom we had not seen for a long time, was that he came to the Grange, and we spent an evening together recalling the things that belonged to our youth."

Go, Little Letter, Apace, Apace (wood-engraving, Dalziels; 7 1/8 x 5; frontispiece for Good Words, *vol. 12, 1871)*

Catalogue

PERIODICALS

Cornhill Magazine
Vol. 8, 1863:
 ¶ **At the Brook** (p. 582, Swain; a.k.a. **Margaret Denzil's History**)

Good Words
Vol. 3, 1862:
 ¶ **The Farewell Valentine** (p. 188, W. Thomas; reprinted in *London Society*)
Vol. 5, 1864:
 ¶ **At the Sepulchre*** (p. 728, Swain)
Vol. 9, Christmas Number, 1868 (*Good Cheer*):
 ¶ **A Will of Her Own*** (p. 27, Dalziels)
Vol. 10, 1869:
 ¶ **"Carmina Nuptiala"** by Gerald Massey, 2 illustrations (p. 625, reprinted as *frontispiece* for *Lilliput Legends*; p. 688; Dalziels)
Vol. 11, 1870:
 ¶ **Fancy** (p. 777; a.k.a. **The Flax That Old Fate Spun**)
 ¶ **The Mariner's Cave*** (p. 865, Dalziels)
Vol. 12, 1871:
 ¶ *Frontispiece:* **Go, Little Letter, Apace, Apace***
 ¶ **And I May Die but the Grass Will Grow*** (p. 113)
 ¶ **The Dial*** (p. 183)
 • 3 illustrations (Dalziels) originally intended for a book, Tennyson's *The Window; or, Songs of the Wrens*
 ¶ **The Mother and the Angel*** (p. 648, Dalziels)
Vol. 13, 1872:
 ¶ **Will o' the Wisp** (p. 49, Dalziels)
 ¶ **The Carpenter*** (p. 97, Dalziels)
 ¶ **"Vanity Fair"** by Robert Buchanan, 2 illustrations (**Dr. Paracelsus Agrippa**,* p. 128; **Vanity Fair**, p. 129)
 ¶ **The Man with Three Friends*** (p. 241, Dalziels)
Vol. 14, 1873:
 ¶ **Looking Back*** (p. 640, Dalziels;

reprinted, in trimmed format, from *Sunday Magazine*)

Good Words for the Young
Vol. 1, 1868–69 [1869]:
    ¶ **"At the Back of the North Wind"** by George MacDonald, 28 illustrations (2 per page: pp. 16, 17,* 113, 116, 180, 181,** 296, 297, 388, 389, 440,** 441,* 540, 541; Dalziels)
    ¶ **"The Boy in Grey"** by Henry Kingsley, 10 illustrations (pp. 240, 241, 284, 335, 337, 340, 408, 409, 520, 521; Dalziels)
Vol. 2, 1870:
    ¶ **"Ranald Bannerman's Boyhood"** by George MacDonald, 36 illustrations (pp. 1, 5, 8, 57, 61, 64, 113, 117, 120, 169, 172, 176, 225, 228, 232, 281, 284, 285, 337, 341, 344, 393, 396, 400, 449, 452, 456, 505, 508, 509, 561, 562 [2 illus.], 617, 620, 621; plus *pictorial initials*, pp. 1, 57, 113, 169, 225, 281, 337, 393, 449, 505, 561, 617; Dalziels; reprinted in *Ranald Bannerman's Boyhood*)
    ¶ **"At the Back of the North Wind"** by George MacDonald, 48 illustrations (2 per page: pp. 24, 25, 84, 85, 148, 152, 204, 205, 244 [1 illus.], 245 [1 illus.], 248 [1 illus.], 249 [1 illus.], 300, 301, 377, 380 [1 illus.], 381 [1 illus.], 424, 425, 472, 473, 528, 529, 588 [2 reprinted in *Rural England*], 589, 664,** 665; Dalziels)
    • 76 illustrations from vols. 1 and 2 reprinted in *At the Back of the North Wind*
    ¶ **"A Lilliput Revel"** by Matthew Browne [William Brighty Rands], 2 illustrations (**Touching the Moon**, p. 37; **The White Princess**, p. 268; Dalziels)
    ¶ **"The Boy in Grey"** by Henry Kingsley, 4 illustrations (pp. 440, 441, 488, 489; Dalziels)
    • 14 illustrations from vols. 1 and 2 reprinted in *The Boy in Grey*
Vol. 3, 1871:
    ¶ **"The Princess and the Goblin"** by George MacDonald, 30 illustrations (2 per page: pp. 4, 5, 68, 69, 132, 133, 188, 189, 280, 281, 300, 301, 360 [1 illus.], 361 [1 illus.], 416, 417; Dalziels; reprinted in *The Princess and the Goblin*)
    • 1 illustration reprinted in *Sunday Magazine* as **I'm in the Dark**
    ¶ **"A Lilliput Revel"** by Matthew Browne [William Brighty Rands], 7 illustra-

And I May Die but the Grass Will Grow (wood-engraving, Dalziels; 7 1/4 x 5 1/4; Good Words, *vol. 12, 1871, p. 113*)

The Dial (wood-engraving, Dalziels; 7 3/8 x 5; Good Words, vol. 12, 1871, p. 183)

tions (**The Black Showman and the White Showman**,* p. 17; **Barbara Petlamb**,* p. 161; **The Pedlar's Diamond**, p. 172; **Lock and Key**,* p. 264; **Little Keeper**,* p. 321; **Handsome Is as Handsome Does**, p. 449; **The Nephew of Charlemagne**, p. 641; Dalziels)

¶ **"A Lilliput Lecture"** by Matthew Browne [William Brighty Rands], 6 illustrations* (**Government**, p. 33; **Science and Philosophy**, p. 72; **Justice, Mercy, Charity**, p. 145; **Trade,** p. 201 [all 4 reprinted in *Lilliput Lectures*]; **Let Be, and You Will See**, p. 537; **Helpfulness**, p. 585; Dalziels)

¶ **The Whisper*** (p. 225, Dalziels)

¶ **"King Arthur's Great Boar Hunt,"** 2 illustrations* (pp. 249, 329; Dalziels)

• Plus cover design by the artist for the December 1870 issue

Vol. 4, 1872:

¶ **The Wind and the Moon** (p. 80)

¶ **"Innocents' Island"** by Matthew Browne [William Brighty Rands], 25 illustrations (pp. 120 [reprinted in several volumes of *Good Things*], 121, 123, 124, 183, 184, 185, 186, 216, 217 [2 illus.], 219, 256 [2 illus.], 257 [2 illus.], 376, 377, 416, 417, 464, 504, 505, 552, 553; Dalziels)

¶ **"The History of Gutta-Percha Willie"** by George MacDonald, 8 illustrations (pp. 153, 232, 288, 321, 361, 424, 464, 520*; Dalziels; reprinted in *Gutta-Percha Willie*)

Good Things for the Young of All Ages [*Good Words for the Young*, continued]

Vol. 1, 1873:

¶ **A Secret About a Poor Hunchback** (p. 17, Dalziels)

¶ **The Wonderful Organ** (p. 24, Dalziels)

¶ **"Henry and Amy"** by Captain Felix, 2 illustrations (pp. 72, 73; Dalziels)

¶ **"Sinbad in England"** by William Gilbert, 10 illustrations (*frontispiece*, pp. 80, 129, 193, 256, 320, 432, 481, 592, 641; Dalziels)

¶ **My Daughter*** (p. 136, Dalziels)

Vol. 2, 1874:

¶ **"Cottage Songs for Cottage Children"** by George MacDonald, 3 illustrations* (**By the Cradle**, p. 24; **Washing the Clothes**, p. 25; **Sweeping**

The Carpenter
(wood-engraving, Dalziels; 4 1/2 x 6 3/8; Good Words, *vol. 13, 1872, p. 97)*

the Floor, p. 25; Dalziels)
Vol. 6, 1877:
¶ **"The Princess and Curdie"** by George MacDonald, 3 illustrations (pp. 193, 257, 321; Dalziels)
• The vignette on page 1 introduces this volume (as well as several other *Good Things* volumes) and is reprinted from **"Innocents' Island"** in *Good Words for the Young*

Graphic
Vol. 36, Christmas Number, 1887:
¶ **Peace and Goodwill** (photo-engraved drawing with wood-engraved color; p. 26)
Vol. 38, Christmas Number, 1889:
¶ **An Old-Fashioned Christmas** (photo-engraved drawing with wood-engraved color; p. 804)

Illustrated London News
Vol. 27, 1855:
¶ **The Lovers' Walk** (p. 125, Orrinsmith; after a sculpture by Alexander Munro)

London Home Monthly
Vol. 1, 1895:
¶ **"Graih My Chree: A Manx Ballad"**

The Man with Three Friends *(wood-engraving, Dalziels; 4 3/8 x 6 3/4;* Good Words, *vol. 13, 1872, p. 241)*

My Heart (wood-engraving, Dalziels; 7 1/8 x 4 1/2; Sunday Magazine, *vol. 7, 1870–71 [1871], p. 11*)

Tares and Wheat (wood-engraving, 5 x 5 1/2; Sunday Magazine, *vol. 7, 1870–71 [1871], p. 353*)

by Hall Caine, 5 illustrations (pp. 33, 35, 37, 39, 40; photo-engravings)
   ¶ **"Good Night"** by Frederick Greenwood, 2 illustrations (pp. 90, 91; photo-engravings)

London Society
Vol. 7, 1865:
   ¶ **The Farewell Valentine*** (p. 181, W. Thomas; reprinted from *Good Words*)
Vol. 18, 1870:
   ¶ **Not Mine** (p. 480, W. Thomas)

Queen
Vol. 13, Christmas Number, 1861:
   ¶ **Hark the Herald Angels Sing** (p. 297)
   ¶ **Born on Christmas Eve and Died on Christmas Eve** (p. 297)

Sunday Magazine
Vol. 5, 1868–69 [1869]:
   ¶ **Blessing in Disguise*** (p. 156, Dalziels; reprinted as **Looking Back** in *Good Words* and as **Silversail and the Carrier-Pigeon** in *Lilliput Legends*)
Vol. 7, 1870–71 [1871]:
   ¶ **My Heart*** (p. 11, Dalziels)
   ¶ **The First Sunrise** (p. 303; reprinted [detail] as *tailpiece* in *Lilliput Legends*)
   ¶ **Tares and Wheat*** (p. 353)
New ser., vol. 1, 1872:
   ¶ **Sunday Musings** (p. 24, Dalziels)
   ¶ **Daria*** (p. 473, Dalziels)
   ¶ **Night and Day** (p. 505, Dalziels)
New ser., vol. 6, 1877:
   ¶ **I'm in the Dark** (p. 640; reprinted from **"The Princess and the Goblin"** in *Good Words for the Young*)

Vineyard
Vol. 1, 1910:
   ¶ **Angels o'er the Realms of Glory** (p. 165; photo-engraving)
   ¶ **Bethlehem** (p. 190; photo-engraving)
   ¶ **Noel** (p. 221; photo-engraving)
   ¶ **"The Shepherds' Gifts,"** decorations (pp. 260, 261; photo-engravings)
Vol. 2, 1911:
   ¶ **Good Friday** (p. 489; photo-engraving)
Vol. 3, 1911:
   ¶ **Bethlehem** (p. 190; photo-engraving; a second, different illustration)

Daria *(wood-engraving, Dalziels; 4 1/2 x 6 3/4;* Sunday Magazine, *new ser., vol. 1, 1872, p. 473)*

Welcome Guest
Vol. 1, 1858:
¶ **Girolamo at the Tentmaker's Door** (p. 393, S. M. Slader; a.k.a. **The Tent-Maker's Story**)
Vol. 1, Christmas Number, 1858:
¶ **Philip and Mildred** (p. 12, S. M. Slader; a.k.a. **The Wedding-Rings of Shrimpington-Super-Mare**)

BOOKS

Alec Forbes of Howglen (George MacDonald; Hurst and Blackett, 1867)
¶ *Frontispiece* (steel-engraving, J. Saddler)

Babies' Classics (Lilia Scott MacDonald, comp.; Winifred Troup, ed.; Longmans, Green, 1904)
¶ 67 illustrations, plus numerous *pictorial initials* and ornaments (photo-engravings)
• Plus cover design by the artist

Chamber Dramas for Children (Mrs. George [Louisa Powell] MacDonald; Strahan, 1870)
¶ *Titlepage illustration* (Dalziels)

Christmas Carols, New and Old (Rev. H. R. Bramley, words, and John Stainer, music;

Frontispiece for Alec Forbes of Howglen, *1867 (steel-engraving, J. Saddler; 5 1/4 x 3 1/4)*

David's Song (photo-engraving, 3 1/2 x 5 1/2; Babies' Classics, *1904)*

The New Danaides (wood-engraving, J. D. Cooper; 5 3/4 x 3 1/4; The Five Days' Entertainments at Wentworth Grange, *1868)*

Novello, Ewer / Routledge, [1871])
 ¶ *Frontispiece* (Dalziels)
 ¶ **Sleep! Holy Babe!** (Dalziels)
 ¶ **When Christ Was Born of Mary Free** (Dalziels)
 • Reissued in 1872

Dealings with the Fairies (George MacDonald; Strahan, 1867)
 ¶ *Frontispiece:* **The Christening**
 ¶ **Mossy and Tangle in the Wood**
 ¶ **Playing at Ball**
 ¶ **The Princess Swimming**
 ¶ **The Prince Lost in the Forest**
 ¶ **On the Water**
 ¶ **The Giant's Heart**
 ¶ **The Giant on His Knees**
 ¶ **The Shadowy Funeral**
 ¶ **The Miser and His Nurse**
 ¶ **The Odd Little Man and His Umbrellas**
 ¶ **Richard and Olive in Trouble**
 • Eng. Dalziels
 • Also published in 5 paper volumes
 • "Reprinted" in *Fairy Tales*

England's Antiphon (George MacDonald; Macmillan Sunday Library of Household Reading, 1868, published in 3 parts; book: 1874)
 ¶ **England's Antiphon** (J. D. Cooper)
 ¶ **His Volant Touch** (J. D. Cooper?)
 ¶ **He Was Dead and There He Sits** (J. D. Cooper?)
 • Book of 1874 adds *titlepage illustration*

Enoch Arden (Alfred Tennyson; Moxon, 1866)
 ¶ 25 illustrations* (T. Bolton)
 • Plus cover design by the artist

Fairy Tales (George MacDonald; Greville MacDonald, ed.; Fifield, 1904)
 ¶ *Titlepage illustration* (photo-engraving)
 ¶ **Photogen and Nycteris** (photo-engraving; a.k.a. **"Could He Believe His Eyes?"**)
 ¶ 12 illustrations from *Dealings with the Fairies* (photo-engravings from the original pen-and-ink drawings of the 1860s)
 • Reissued by Allen and Unwin in 1920 and 1924

The Five Days' Entertainments at Wentworth

Grange (Francis Turner Palgrave; Macmillan, 1868)

¶ 18 illustrations, including ***titlepage illustration*** (steel-engraving, C. H. Jeens) and 17 wood-engravings (J. D. Cooper)

Jack and Jill: A Fairy Story (Greville MacDonald; Dent, 1913)

¶ 29 illustrations (photo-engravings), including ***frontispiece:* The Second Round** (photo-engraving, color), ***titlepage illustration***, and 27 **headpieces** and full-page illustrations

• Plus cover design by the artist

The Magic Crook (Greville MacDonald; Vineyard, 1911)

¶ 62 illustrations (photo-engravings)
• Plus cover design by the artist

The Music Master: A Love Story, and Two Series of Day and Night Songs (William Allingham; Routledge, 1855)

¶ *Frontispiece:* **Crossing the Stile***
¶ *Titlepage illustration*
¶ **Lady Alice***
¶ **The Fairies**
¶ **"The Music Master,"** 2 illustrations*
¶ **A Boy's Burial***
¶ *Tailpiece*
• Plus 4 ornamental devices
• Eng. Dalziels
• Reissued as *Day and Night Songs and the Music Master* by Bell and Daldy in 1860

My Beautiful Lady (Thomas Woolner; Macmillan Golden Treasury Series, 3d ed., 1866)

¶ *Titlepage illustration** (steel-engraving, C. H. Jeens)

National Nursery Rhymes and Nursery Songs (J. W. Elliott, music; Novello, Ewer / Routledge, [1870])

¶ **My Lady Wind** (Dalziels)
¶ **Little Tommy Tucker** (Dalziels)
• Reissued as *Mother Goose* (New York: Routledge, 1872, and New York: McLoughlin, [1880])

Parables and Tales (Thomas Gordon Hake; Chapman and Hall, 1872)

¶ 9 illustrations, including ***frontispiece*** (Dalziels)

Lady Alice *(wood-engraving, Dalziels; 5 x 3;* The Music Master, *1855)*

The Music Master
[#1] (wood-engraving, Dalziels; 5 x 3;
The Music Master,
1855)

The Music Master *[#2] (wood-engraving, Dalziels; 5 x 3;* The Music Master, *1855)*

Phantastes (George MacDonald; Greville MacDonald, ed.; Fifield, 1905)
¶ 33 illustrations, including ***frontispiece*** (photo-engravings)

The Poets of the Nineteenth Century (Rev. Robert Aris Willmott, ed.; Routledge, 1857)
¶ **The Vision of Serena** (Dalziels)

Pre-Raphaelitism and the Pre-Raphaelite Brotherhood (William Holman Hunt; Macmillan, 2 vols., 1905–06)
¶ **Ewell Spring** (vol. 1; photo-engraving)
¶ **The Pre-Raphaelite Meeting, 1848** (vol.1; photo-engraving; after a sketch by Hunt)
¶ **Halt at the Well** (vol. 1; photo-engraving; after a sketch by Hunt)
¶ **The Vision City** (vol. 1; photo-engraving; after a sketch by Hunt)
¶ **Lake of Tiberias** (vol. 2; photo-engraving; after a sketch by Hunt)

[Scott] *Autobiographical Notes of the Life of William Bell Scott* (W. Minto, ed.; Osgood, 2 vols., 1892)
¶ **Penkill Castle: Staircase** (vol. 2; photogravure)
¶ **Penkill Castle: Interior of Hall** (vol. 2; photogravure)

Seekers After God (F. W. Farrar; Macmillan Standard Library of Household Reading, 1868, published in 3 parts; book: 1873)
¶ ***Frontispiece:* Aurelius and His Mother** (J. D. Cooper)

The Shepherd Lady and Other Poems (Jean Ingelow; Boston: Roberts, 1876)
¶ **"The Shepherd Lady,"** 3 illustrations* (Dalziels)
¶ **Above the Clouds** (Dalziels)

Sing-Song (Christina Rossetti; Routledge, 1872)
¶ 123 illustrations, including ***frontispiece*** and ***titlepage illustration*** (Dalziels)
• Plus cover design by the artist

Speaking Likenesses (Christina Rossetti; Macmillan, 1874)
¶ 12 illustrations, including ***frontispiece*** and ***titlepage illustration***, which are repeated, for a total of 14 (Dalziels)

• Plus cover design by the artist

[Thackeray] *The Works of Miss Thackeray* ([Anne Thackeray Ritchie]; Smith, Elder, 10 vols., 1875–90?)
 ¶ 10 illustrations* (1 **titlepage illustration** for each of 10 volumes): • *Old Kensington* • *The Village on the Cliff* • *Five Old Friends / A Young Prince* • *To Esther and Other Sketches* • *Bluebeard's Keys and Other Stories* • *The Story of Elizabeth / Two Hours / From an Island* • *Toilers and Spinsters and Other Essays* • *Miss Angel / Fulham Lawn* • *Miss Williamson's Divignations* • *Mrs. Dymond*

Tom Brown's School Days ([Thomas Hughes]; Macmillan Golden Treasury Series, 6th ed., 1868)
 ¶ **Titlepage illustration*** (steel-engraving, C. H. Jeens)

Tom Brown's School Days ([Thomas Hughes]; Macmillan, new [first illustrated] ed., 1869)
 ¶ 43 illustrations (J. D. Cooper)
 • The 16 other illustrations are not by Hughes

Trystie's Quest; or Kit, King of the Pigwidgeons (Greville MacDonald; Vineyard/Fifield, [1913])
 ¶ 29 illustrations (photo-engravings)
 • Plus cover design by the artist
 • Plus two small illustrations advertising *The Magic Crook*

BOOKS CONTAINING REPRINTS

At the Back of the North Wind (George MacDonald; Strahan, 1871)
 ¶ 76 illustrations (reprinted from *Good Words for the Young*)
 • Plus cover design by the artist

Ballads of Life, Love, and Humour (Robert Buchanan; Chatto and Windus, 1882)
 ¶ **Frontispiece (Dr. Paracelsus Agrippa** reprinted from *Good Words*)

The Boy in Grey (Henry Kingsley; Strahan, 1871)
 ¶ 14 illustrations (reprinted from *Good*

A Boy's Burial (wood-engraving, Dalziels; 5 x 3; The Music Master, 1855)

Old Morality (wood-engraving, Dalziels; 3 x 3; Parables and Tales, 1872)

Words for the Young), including **frontispiece**

Gutta-Percha Willie, the Working Genius (George MacDonald; King, 1873)
¶ 8 illustrations (reprinted from *Good Words for the Young*), including **frontispiece**
• A 9th illustration is not by Hughes

Life and Phantasy (William Allingham; Reeves and Turner, 1889)
¶ **The Fairies** (reprinted from *The Music Master*)

Lilliput Lectures ([William Brighty Rands]; Strahan, 1871)
¶ *Frontispiece:* **Trade**
¶ **Science and Philosophy**
¶ **Government**
¶ **Justice, Mercy, Charity**
• Reprinted from *Good Words for the Young*

Lilliput Legends ([William Brighty Rands]; Strahan, 1872)
¶ *Frontispiece:* **Pharronida (Carmina Nuptiale** reprinted from *Good Words*)
¶ **Silversail and the Carrier-Pigeon (Blessing in Disguise** reprinted from *Sunday Magazine*)
¶ **Twopenny Trudge (The First Sunrise**

Top: ***The Dear White Lady in Yon High Tower*** *for* ***"The Shepherd Lady"*** *(wood-engraving, Dalziels; 6 1/8 x 4 3/8;* The Shepherd Lady and Other Poems, *1876)*

Bottom left: ***Take Now This Crook*** *for* ***"The Shepherd Lady"*** *(wood-engraving, Dalziels; 6 1/4 x 4;* The Shepherd Lady and Other Poems, *1876)*

Bottom right: ***On Sunny Slopes, ah!*** *for* ***"The Shepherd Lady"*** *(wood-engraving, Dalziels; 6 3/8 x 4;* The Shepherd Lady and Other Poems, *1876)*

[detail], reprinted from *Good Words)*
  • All signatures deleted

Mother Goose (New York: Routledge, 1872;
New York: McLoughlin, [1880])
  ¶ **My Lady Wind**
  ¶ **Little Tommy Tucker**
  • Reprinted from *National Nursery
Rhymes*

The Princess and the Goblin (George
MacDonald; Strahan, 1872)
  ¶ 30 illustrations (reprinted from *Good
Words for the Young)*

Ranald Bannerman's Boyhood (George
MacDonald; Strahan, 1871)
  ¶ 36 illustrations plus 11 *pictorial ini-
tials* (reprinted from *Good Words for the
Young)*
  • Reissued by Blackie in 1885

Rural England (L. G. Seguin; Strahan, 1867)
  ¶ **The Hamlet** (introductory vignette)
  ¶ **The Hall** (introductory vignette)
  • Reprinted from **"At the Back of the
North Wind"** in *Good Words*
  • Reissued c. 1885 in a limited edition
with proof wood-engravings on mounted
india paper

§ A wood-engraving proof for an unknown
illustration of 1878, engraved by the
Dalziels, is in the British Museum,
London, Department of Prints and
Drawings, Dalziel Collection (1878 volume, no. 430; see *Arthur Hughes: His Life
and Works*, p. 282)

Titlepage illustration *for* Tom Brown's
School Days, *1868 (steel-engraving, C. H.
Jeens; 2 1/2 x 2)*

Tom's First Exploit at Football *(wood-
engraving, J. D. Cooper; 6 1/2 x 4 1/4;
Tom Brown's School Days, 1869)*

William Holman Hunt

(1827-1910)

There is no more succinct and accurate assessment of the art of William Holman Hunt than that supplied by Mary Bennett for the Hunt exhibition of 1969: "William Holman Hunt's purpose was to use realism and original imagery to express significant moral ideas. To do this he discarded conventional composition and subject matter, and developed a detailed realistic technique. In the process he discovered the importance of the effect of light on colour.

"The formation of the Pre-Raphaelite Brotherhood in 1848 was largely due to his questioning and rejection of contemporary artistic principles. It aspired to return to Nature for a renewal of vitality in painting and to early-Italian masters for inspiration" (Introduction, Walker Art Gallery/ Victoria and Albert Museum, Catalogue: *William Holman Hunt*, 1969, p. 4).

Of course, a strong case has been made by Lucy Rabin (see Brown essay) that Pre-Raphaelitism derived from Ford Madox Brown.

William Holman Hunt, c. 1870s (photograph; photo-engraving, clipping)

And Burne-Jones, Val Prinsep, and others enthralled by the unique works of Dante Gabriel Rossetti believed him to be the ultimate Pre-Raphaelite. But Hunt himself had no doubts that it was he who most purely espoused, and most consistently carried the torch of, Pre-Raphaelitism for a half-century: agreed upon by the Brotherhood founders from the outset was that, in the words of Holman Hunt, the work they "were bent on producing [was] to be more persistently derived from Nature than any having a dramatic significance yet done in the world" (*Pre-Raphaelitism*, vol. 1, p. 135).

The truth is that Hunt painted his earliest works (*Christ and the Two Marys*, *The Eve of St. Agnes*, and much of *Rienzi*, all before September 1848) according to "Pre-Raphaelite" principles and the "return to nature" edict of John Ruskin in *Modern Painters*, and convinced his friend John Everett Millais to begin to work in the same rebellious manner. Rossetti, full of ideas, having worked side by side with both Brown and Hunt, in 1848 joined Hunt and Millais in declaring unified principles in an attempt to renew art. A book of Lasinio's "early-Italian" engravings of the Campo Santo frescoes at Pisa finally inspired them all to form a guild or club or secret society—the Pre-Raphaelite Brotherhood of September 1848, expanded to seven members.

Hunt was the son of a warehouse manager and worked as a clerk for an estate agent; he studied at the Royal Academy Schools beginning in 1844—when he met Millais. At the time of the formation of the Brotherhood, he was sharing a studio with Rossetti, who was teaching Hunt how to be poetic and rebellious just as Hunt tried to impart to him the discipline of painting from nature. The first exhibited paintings of Millais, Rossetti, and Hunt (*Rienzi*) in 1849 had the initials *P.R.B.*, overlooked by the critics, who saw much to praise. By the 1850 Royal Academy Exhibition the "brotherhood" secret was revealed in the press, and the group's paintings (including Hunt's *A Converted British Family Sheltering a Christian Priest from the Persecution of the Druids*) suddenly were attacked by the critics.

Hunt, nevertheless, with the help of John Ruskin (who had written the famous Pre-Raphaelite defense letters to the London *Times* in 1851), gained patrons and buyers for some of his paintings; he won prizes for *Valentine Rescuing Sylvia from Proteus* at the Liverpool Academy in 1852 (the year he showed *The Hireling Shepherd* at the Royal Academy) and in 1853 for *Strayed Sheep* at the Birmingham exhibit. By the 1853 and 1854 Royal Academy Exhibitions (*Claudio and Isabella, Our English Coasts* [a.k.a. *Strayed Sheep*], and *The Awakening Conscience*), Hunt had gained much in reputation, especially with the crowd-pleasing, easily understood religious work, *The Light of the World*. These early paintings show that Hunt was absolutely dedicated— and he remained so throughout his life—to working directly from live models, authentic costumes and artifacts, and outdoor scenery, especially in capturing the sunlit hues of nature. The light-suffused colors of *Valentine* are so striking, even shrill, that they seem unreal, yet somehow right; the decorative designs, garment textures, and even wool

A Converted British Family Sheltering a Christian Priest from the Persecution of the Druids (*oil, 1850; 43 3/4 x 52 1/2; Ashmolean Museum, Oxford; photogravure, as published in* William Holman Hunt's Pre-Raphaelitism and the Pre-Raphaelite Brotherhood, *vol. 1, 1905*)

coats of his sheep in all of these early works are painted with breathtaking precision. As with his Pre-Raphaelite brothers' paintings, his models in these canvases were his friends—Elizabeth Siddal, the two Rossetti boys, and Millais.

Hunt's dedication to religious truths, through ideas and allegory, impelled him to undertake a true artist's adventure by spending most of 1854 and 1855 in the Middle East, sketching and painting the actual landscapes and native people that would best represent the realities of his religious faith. Out of the trip came *The Scapegoat* (1854), *The Finding of the Saviour in the Temple* (1854–60), and *Afterglow in Egypt* (1854–63; also an etched version). When he returned to London in early 1856, he was already working on the drawings for his first illustration project, the Moxon *Tennyson*. Hunt writes in his introduction to a 1901 reprinting of the Pre-Raphaelite wood-engravings for that book: "Being in Jerusalem in the year 1855, I received notice from Millais that Mr. Moxon was undertaking the publication of an illustrated edition of Tennyson's Works, that Millais had already begun to make designs, and that he had been requested to ask me to join in the undertaking. He told me also that Rossetti had been invited to contribute. . . . I rejoiced at the prospect of taking my part in the project, and began to consider whether in some of the poems of Oriental story I could not use my special opportunities, and I made experimen-

The Awakening Conscience *(oil, 1854; 30 x 22; Tate Gallery, London; photogravure, as published in William Holman Hunt's* Pre-Raphaelitism and the Pre-Raphaelite Brotherhood, *vol. 1, 1905)*

tal sketches at once" (Joseph Pennell, ed., *Some Poems by Alfred, Lord Tennyson*, 1901, p. xix).

Hunt soon developed a friendship with the Tennyson family (and with their friend, Val

Prinsep, who was also a Rossetti protégé), and maintained good relations with Charles Collins and Thomas Woolner. But the P.R.B. had virtually dissolved and Rossetti would shortly spin off his coterie of followers into a more poetic Pre-Raphaelite direction. Although he joined the expansive Hogarth Club, Hunt would from then on basically pursue his own course, exhibiting his works privately with detailed explanations of their symbolism, making more trips to the Holy Land, and becoming successful and wealthy without ever joining the Royal Academy. Hunt's reputation and fame were enhanced, as were Millais's, by the engravings for popular prints made from his paintings: *The Light of the World* (1858) was an enormous success; *Finding the Saviour in the Temple* (1863) was issued by Gambart, who paid Hunt the then-unheard-of sum of 5,500 pounds for the copyright—only to be topped by the Agnew firm's offer of 10,500 pounds for Hunt's *The Shadow of Death* (engraving published 1877).

In 1866 Hunt returned to the Holy Land; en route his new wife, Fanny Waugh, died of cholera in Florence. *Isabella and the Pot of Basil* (1867, from Keats; one of his loveliest paintings and very Rossettian in spirit) was dedicated to his deceased wife, its rights also purchased for a print by Gambart. From 1869 through 1872, Hunt traveled through Italy and the Middle East. Before his third visit to Palestine in 1876 he married Fanny's sister, Edith. That trip produced one of his most haunting works, *The Triumph of the Innocents* (1876–87). To the end Hunt remained true to his principles: *May Morning on Magdalen Tower* (1888–90) and *The Lady of Shalott* (1887–1905; based on his Moxon *Tennyson* wood-engraving) are in every sense great Pre-Raphaelite paintings.

Hunt's P.R.B. black-and-white art was in the same "quirky" early-Italian mold as Rossetti's and Millais's, owing much to the Campo Santo engravings—for example, his 1849 drawing *He Knew Whose Gentle Hand*

Was at the Latch, from Keats's "Isabella." Here Hunt portrays realistic emotions and people doing unusual things, as if the scene actually

My Beautiful Lady (etching, Hunt, 1849; 7 7/8 x 4 3/4; 2 images on one plate: *My Beautiful Lady* and *Of My Lady in Death*; *frontispiece* for the Germ, no. 1, January 1850)

happened. In the *Germ*, his etching *My Beautiful Lady/Of My Lady in Death*, based on Pre-Raphaelite brother Thomas Woolner's poems, are in this early-Italian vein—ascetic, angular, yet oddly emotive, with the standard Pre-Raphaelite hand-covered head, held hands, and oddly positioned legs. Still, in

technique they seem tentative, certainly no match for Millais's drawings of the same period. In his autobiography Hunt claims that this particular style of drawing (which Rossetti, too, adopted) was also based on a joint decision of Hunt's and Millais's in 1848, before Rossetti went to work in Hunt's studio: "Millais had now become as ardent an admirer of Keats as myself, and we soon resolved to begin a series of illustrations in slightly shaded outline; we worked these with a fine brush in line in preference to a pen for the sake of greater freedom. The drawings were to be preparations for copperplate engravings in illustration of the magnificent poem of 'Isabella'" (*Pre-Raphaelitism*, vol. 1, pp. 103–04). The early emphasis on Keats was important too, for it was Rossetti's admiration for the subject of Hunt's Keats-inspired painting *The Eve of St. Agnes* at the Royal Academy Exhibition in 1848—with its odd poses, foreshortening, and introduction of dogs as elements of realism (seen also in the following year's more famous *Lorenzo and Isabella* by Millais)—that drew him into Hunt's and Millais's little conspiracy.

The *Afterglow* etching, a result of Hunt's sketches in Egypt, was completed in 1855 and shows a firmer technique. But Hunt's career as an wood-engraving artist began with the Moxon *Tennyson*, to which he contributed seven exceptional drawings, "The Lady of Shalott" being one of the masterpieces of the school. Hunt's recollection of a conversation he had with Tennyson about this illustration points to the Pre-Raphaelite practice of creating whole new universes in their illustrations rather than merely depicting described scenes. Tennyson protested that he hadn't *described* the Lady of Shalott's hair as "wildly tossed about as if by a tornado" and he "did not say the web floated round and round her," expecting that "the illustrator should always adhere to the words of the poet!" Hunt argued that an artist has only a small space to convey an impression or idea or the whole mean-

Go and Come—The Sun Is High in Heaven, the Harvest but Begun *(wood-engraving proof, Dalziels; 5 1/2 x 4 1/4; corrected in white by Hunt; for the illustration in* Good Words, *vol. 3, 1862, p. 32;* Touches of Nature*)*

ing of a poem, and a poet has pages and pages (*Pre-Raphaelitism*, vol. 2, 1906, pp. 124–25). A comparison of Hunt's *Tennyson* engravings with some of his photographically preserved images on the blocks before cutting reveals Hunt a bit more tentative and less detailed, and less reliant on the linear-woodcut techniques of Dürer or Rethel, than artists like Sandys, Shields, and Poynter.

In general, Hunt's illustration output was modest, but of relatively high quality—although one can safely say that, unlike many of the other artists in that book, his engraved work does not attain the level of his paintings; even his most mature Pre-Raphaelite drawings are lacking the fine details in a Rossetti, Sandys, or Millais engraving. Nevertheless, there are a few real gems in this output: the fine biblical illustration "The Lent Jewels" for

English Sacred Poetry (1862; better by far than his rather tepid *Bible Gallery* drawing "Eliezer and Rebekah at the Well"); the superb steel-engraved frontispiece for *Studies from Life* (1862)—an interior so lovingly detailed that it rivals his virtuosic painting *The Awakening Conscience*; "Go and Come—The Sun Is High in Heaven, the Harvest but Begun" for *Good Words* (1862); and a very oddly composed costume piece, "Temujin," for *Once a Week* (1860). Also for *Once a Week* of 1860, there's the tender love-and-death-themed engraving "At Night."

For the frontispiece to the book *Days of Old* (1859), Hunt made a drawing that was apparently not prepared on boxwood. Another Hunt piece, "A Morning Song of Praise" for Isaac Watts's *Divine and Moral Songs for Children* of 1867, was reproduced without a middleman, through the new graphotype process. Despite wood-engraver W. J. Linton's involvement with the *Days of Old* art, Hunt's correspondence, and the lines of the illustration themselves, imply that a similar nonengraved method was used—and at the same time reveals Hunt's approach to his illustrations. In a letter to the publisher, Macmillan, of October 27, 1858, Hunt talks of reading the book and finding good things to

Frontispiece *for* Days of Old, *1859 (anastatic print?, W. J. Linton; 3 3/4 x 5 1/8)*

The Lent Jewels *(wood-engraving proof, Dalziels; 5 x 4; initialed by Hunt; for the **frontispiece** for* English Sacred Poetry, *1862)*

illustrate; he has chosen the scene "Early British Family Listening to the Reading by the Roman Soldiers of the Gospel": "I am now far enough advanced with it to be ready for the plate or block. . . . [I wrote to] Mr. Linton . . . on the subject of his process. I am always slow in my work but I think I can safely promise to let you have it a fortnight after I have got the proper tablet to work upon." On November 26, 1858, Hunt writes to the publisher that he's waiting for the "proof of the Plate" and assures him he's punctual and "any delay must arise from causes . . . in the mechanical process." Four days later, he communicates to Macmillan: "I am certainly surprised that Mr. Linton has not sent me proofs of the plate . . . having more than one or two struck off. I took the greatest possible pains to get the drawing complete throughout, but the process is so very deceptive that it is quite impossible to make it right without retouching" (New York Public Library, Berg Collection).

Hunt's most satisfying prints may be the plates he produced for the Etching Club; two

Middle East souvenirs were originally etched on one plate in 1855 and found their way (separately) into 1857's *Etchings for the Art Union of London*—*The Abundance of Egypt* (the print related to the *Afterglow* painting; a lovely female figure carrying grain on her head, and perhaps Hunt's best etching) and *The Desolation of Egypt*, a tiny, murky depiction of the Sphinx. *The Day in the Country* (in 1865's *A Selection of Etchings by the Etching Club*) is such a perfectly Pre-Raphaelite, thoroughly worked-over piece that it almost seems not to be an etching; certainly its odd perspective and landscape details make it a triumph of shallow-spaced Pre-Raphaelite decorative art. *The Father's Leave-Taking* (in *Twenty-one Etchings Published by the Etching Club*, 1879) is a carefully rendered—especially the practically in-motion clothing material—and tender image of a mother and her child.

The Abundance of Egypt *(etching, Hunt, 1855; 5 1/2 x 4 1/8; Etchings for the Art Union of London, 1857)*

Witches and Witchcraft *(wood-engraving, Dalziels; 4 x 4 7/8;* Once a Week, *vol. 2, 1860, p. 438)*

At Night *(wood-engraving, Swain; 3 x 5;* Once a Week, *vol. 3, 1860, p. 102)*

Catalogue

PERIODICALS

Good Words
Vol. 3, 1862:
 ¶ **Go and Come—The Sun Is High in Heaven, the Harvest but Begun*** (p. 32, Dalziels; reprinted as **Go, Work While It Is Called Today** in *Touches of Nature*; reprinted as **The Harvest** in *Routledge's Sunday Album for Children*)
Vol. 19, 1878:
 ¶ **Born at Jerusalem** (p. 473)

Once a Week
Vol. 2, 1860:
 ¶ **Witches and Witchcraft*** (p. 438, Dalziels)
Vol. 3, 1860:
 ¶ **At Night*** (p. 102, Swain)
 ¶ **Temujin*** (p. 630, Swain; reprinted in *The Piccadilly Annual*)

Queen
Vol. 13, Christmas Number, 1861:
 ¶ **The Eve of St. Agnes** (p. 293)

BOOKS

Dalziels' Bible Gallery (Routledge, 1881)
 ¶ **Eliezer and Rebekah at the Well*** (Dalziels; reprinted in *Art Pictures from the Old Testament*)

Days of Old: Three Stories from Old English History (Macmillan, 1859)
 ¶ *Frontispiece:* **Days of Old*** (anastatic print?, [supervised by] W. J. Linton)

Divine and Moral Songs for Children (Isaac Watts; Nisbet, 1867)
 ¶ **A Morning Song of Praise*** (graphotype, supervised by H. Fitzcook)

English Sacred Poetry (Rev. Robert Aris Willmott, ed.; Routledge, Warne, and Routledge, 1862)

Temujin (wood-engraving, Swain; 5 x 4; Once a Week, *vol. 3, 1860, p. 630)*

¶ *Frontispiece:* **The Lent Jewels*** (Dalziels; a.k.a. **The Rabbi and the Lost Treasure**; reprinted in *Routledge's Sunday Album for Children*)

The Life of Christ (Frederic W. Farrar; Cassell, Petter, and Galpin, 11th ed., 2 vols., [1874])
¶ *Frontispiece:* **Interior of a Carpenter's Shop at Nazareth** (vol. 1)
¶ *Frontispiece:* **Nablous: The Ancient Shechem** (vol. 2)

The Light of the World (Edwin Arnold; Longmans, 1893)
¶ **The Importunate Neighbour**
¶ **Jerusalem**
¶ **Christ and Mary Magdalene** (photo-engraving)
¶ **Tyre** (photo-engraving)
¶ **Glory to God in the Highest** (photogravure)
¶ **Bethlehem**
¶ **Christ Before Pilate***

The Light of Truth (wood-engraving, H. Harral; 3 3/4 x 5; *frontispiece* for Parables from Nature, *1861)*

Eliezer and Rebekah at the Well (wood-engraving, Dalziels; 7 x 5 3/8; Dalziels' Bible Gallery, *1881*; Art Pictures from the Old Testament*)

Active and Passive (*wood-engraving, H. Harral; 5 x 3 7/8;* Parables from Nature, *1861*)

Middle: *Recollections of the Arabian Nights [#1] (wood-engraving, T. Williams; 3 1/8 x 3 5/8;* Poems by Alfred Tennyson, *1857)*

Bottom: *Recollections of the Arabian Nights [#2] (wood-engraving, J. Thompson; 3 5/8 x 3 1/8;* Poems by Alfred Tennyson, *1857)*

¶ **"Did Some Man Find Hid Shekels in a Field"***

¶ **Capital of a Column**

• Plus 5 reproductions (photogravures) of existing paintings: • *Frontispiece:* **The Light of the World** • **The Triumph of the Innocents** • **The Plains of Esdraelon from the Heights Above Nazareth** • **The Finding of the Saviour in the Temple** • **The Shadow of Death**

• The preface to the book notes a Longmans edition (1863) of *The Illustrated New Testament* containing four (unidentified) illustrations reprinted in *The Light of the World*; the 1863 book has not been located

Parables from Nature (Mrs. Alfred Gatty; Bell and Daldy, 1st and 2d ser., 1861)

¶ *Frontispiece:* **The Light of Truth*** (H. Harral)

¶ **Active and Passive*** (H. Harral)

Pearl: An English Poem of the Fourteenth Century (Israel Gollancz, ed.; Nutt, 1891)

¶ *Frontispiece:* **Pearl**

Pilgrim's Progress (John Bunyan; Macmillan Golden Treasury Series, 1862)

¶ *Titlepage illustration* (steel-engraving, C. H. Jeens)

The Story of the Christians and Moors of Spain (C. M. Yonge; Macmillan, 1878)

¶ *Titlepage illustration** (steel-engraving, C. H. Jeens)

Studies from Life ([Dinah Mulock Craik]; Hurst and Blackett, [1862])

¶ *Frontispiece:* **Lost*** (steel-engraving, J. Brown)

[Tennyson] *Poems by Alfred Tennyson* (Moxon, 1857)

¶ **"Recollections of the Arabian Nights,"** 2 illustrations* (T. Williams [reprinted in *Gems from Tennyson*]; J. Thompson)

¶ **"The Ballad of Oriana,"** 2 illustrations* (Dalziels)

¶ **The Lady of Shalott*** (J. Thompson; reprinted in *Gems from Tennyson*)

¶ **Godiva*** (Dalziels; reprinted in *Gems from Tennyson*)

¶ **The Beggar Maid*** (T. Williams;

reprinted in *Gems from Tennyson*)

• Tennyson's *Poems* (a.k.a. the Moxon *Tennyson*) was reissued in 1864 (Routledge, Warne, and Routledge) and again, newly engraved, in 1866 (Moxon). A deluxe edition was published by Macmillan in 1893 that printed the illustrations from the original wood-blocks. Joseph Pennell's *Some Poems by Alfred, Lord Tennyson* (Freemantle, 1901; introduction by Holman Hunt) reduces the contents of the book to only those poems with illustrations by the Pre-Raphaelites; the 30 wood-engravings are again printed from the original wood-blocks, and there are also photogravures of 6 of the drawings before they were engraved.

BOOKS CONTAINING REPRINTS

Art Pictures from the Old Testament (Aley Fox, text; Society for Promoting Christian Knowledge, 1894)
    ¶ **Eliezer and Rebekah at the Well** (reprinted from *Dalziels' Bible Gallery*)

Gems from Tennyson (Boston: Ticknor and Fields, 1866)
    ¶ **The Beggar Maid**
    ¶ **Godiva**
    ¶ **The Lady of Shalott**
    ¶ **Recollections of the Arabian Nights** [#1]
    • Reprinted from *Poems by Alfred Tennyson*

The Piccadilly Annual of Entertaining Literature (Hotten, 1870)
    ¶ **Temujin** (reprinted from *Once a Week*)

Routledge's Sunday Album for Children ([Mrs. Charles H. Heaton, ed.]; Routledge, [1873])
    ¶ **The Lent Jewels** (reprinted from *English Sacred Poetry*)
    ¶ **The Harvest (Go and Come—The Sun Is High in Heaven, the Harvest but Begun** reprinted from *Good Words*)
    • Reprinted in *Sunday Reading for Good Children* (Routledge, [1873])

Touches of Nature (Strahan, 1867)
    ¶ **Go, Work While It Is Called Today (Go and Come—The Sun Is High in**

The Ballad of Oriana *[#1] (wood-engraving, Dalziels; 3 5/8 x 3 1/4; Poems by Alfred Tennyson, 1857)*

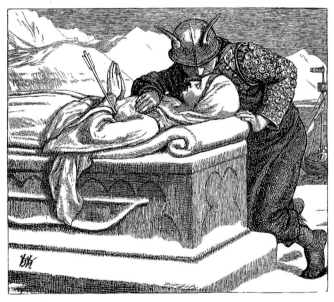

The Ballad of Oriana *[#2] (wood-engraving, Dalziels; 3 1/4 x 3 5/8; Poems by Alfred Tennyson, 1857)*

The Lady of Shalott *(wood-engraving, J. Thompson; 3 5/8 x 3 1/4;* Poems by Alfred Tennyson, *1857)*

Right: ***Godiva*** *(wood-engraving, Dalziels; 3 5/8 x 3 1/4;* Poems by Alfred Tennyson, *1857)*

Left: ***The Beggar Maid*** *(wood-engraving, T. Williams; 3 5/8 x 3 1/8;* Poems by Alfred Tennyson, *1857)*

Heaven, the Harvest but Begun reprinted from *Good Words*)

§ Holman Hunt's classic autobiography, *Pre-Raphaelitism and the Pre-Raphaelite Brotherhood* (Macmillan, 2 vols., 1905–06) contains photogravures of Hunt paintings and photo-engravings of numerous sketches, drawings, and original designs for illustrations

INDIVIDUAL PRINTS

¶ **The Abundance of Egypt*** (etching, Hunt, 1855; 5 1/2 x 4 1/8; signed in plate)
  • Published in *Etchings for the Art Union of London* (Etching Club; Cundall, 1857)
  • Another state: on the same plate with **The Desolation of Egypt** (7 3/8 x 4 1/8)

¶ **The Day in the Country*** (etching, Hunt; 5 1/2 x 8 1/4; signed with monogram in plate)
  • Published in *A Selection of Etchings by the Etching Club* (Cundall, 1865)

¶ **The Desolation of Egypt** (etching, Hunt, 1855; 1 1/2 x 4 1/8; signed in plate)
  • Published in *Etchings for the Art Union of London* (Etching Club; Cundall, 1857)

• Another state: on the same plate with **The Abundance of Egypt** (7 3/8 x 4 1/8)

¶ **The Father's Leave-Taking*** (etching, Hunt, 1879; 7 3/8 x 10; signed with monogram and dated in plate)
• Published in [*A Series of*] *Twenty-one Etchings Published by the Etching Club* (Ansdell, 1879)

¶ **My Beautiful Lady*** (etching, Hunt, 1849; 7 7/8 x 4 3/4; signed in plate)
• 2 images on one plate: **My Beautiful Lady** and **Of My Lady in Death**
• Published in the *Germ*, vol. 1, January 1850

§ Hunt may also have etched a **Portrait of W. Howes Hunt** (see Rodney Engen's *Pre-Raphaelite Prints*, 1995, p. 121)

Lost *(steel-engraving, J. Brown; 5 1/8 x 3 1/4;* **frontispiece** *for* Studies from Life, *[1862])*

The Day in the Country *(etching, Hunt; 5 1/2 x 8 1/4;* A Selection of Etchings by the Etching Club, *1865)*

Matthew J. Lawless

(1837-1864)

In his important work of 1971, *Victorian Illustrated Books*, Percy Muir makes a single mention of Matthew Lawless, in relation to Thornbury's *Historical and Legendary Ballads and Songs* (1876): "There are twenty drawings by M. J. Lawless—not to be despised—ten by J. Lawson. . . ." Lawless had fallen since his early death in 1864 into increasing obscurity, although the Dalziels' memoir has some kind things to say about him, in a single paragraph (understandably short, given that they seldom engraved his designs): "His drawings were of such a refined and accomplished character that he at once took a place amongst the distinguished men of the time" (*Brothers Dalziel*, p. 236). The *Art Journal* in

its obituary ("Mr. M. J. Lawless," vol. 26 [new ser., vol. 3], 1864, p. 290) offered that Lawless's "pictures were always well hung at the [Royal] Academy [exhibitions]." *The Sick Call* of 1863 was chief among these.

Lawless was born in Dublin, trained at Cary's and Leigh's art schools in London, and studied with the painter Henry O'Neill. It's generally recognized that his paintings and illustrations were in the Pre-Raphaelite school. In his *Illustrators of the Sixties* (1928) Forrest Reid, in keeping with his typically thorough treatment for each artist discussed, devotes a number of pages to Lawless. "Though he was faithful to the Pre-Raphaelite tradition, his drawings are stamped with a personal note that makes them as easy to identify as those of that very different artist, Charles Keene," states Reid. "Whether he would ever have developed into a great draughtsman it is impossible to say. At his death he had not yet done so; a certain laboriousness is traceable in most of his work up to the end, though the clumsiness of his first efforts is no longer there. But he is always interesting, always sincere, and the later designs do seem to show that eventually he would have abandoned the heaviness of line which is so marked a feature of his style" (p. 51).

Lawless's illustration career spanned a mere five years, but he

Sisters of Mercy (etching, Lawless, 1859; 3 1/2 x 5; Passages from Modern English Poets, *1862*)

produced nearly seventy-five illustrations, mostly for *Once a Week* (starting with the first issue of December 1859), which were engraved by Swain. His work also appeared in *Punch, Good Words, Churchman's Family Magazine,* and *London Society,* and then moved from these periodicals into *Pictures of Society* (1866) and other reprint collections. Lawless's major contributions to books were three illustrations for Catherine Winkworth's *Lyra Germanica* (1st ser., 1861) and four etchings in *Passages from Modern English Poets* by the Junior Etching Club (1862); the best, most Pre-Raphaelite of these is the intriguing *Sisters of Mercy.*

Dead Love *(wood-engraving, Swain?; 4 x 5 1/8;* Once a Week, *vol. 7, 1862, p. 434;* Historical and Legendary Ballads and Songs*)*

Lawless's interesting Pre-Raphaelite wood-engravings are very numerous, although many fall short of successfully uniting all of the elements of the style. Most seem to combine a sincere observation of reality and models with a kind of shorthand approach to Dürerish-woodcut linear effects. Lawless's designs could range from those with carefully controlled lines building up beautiful tones ("A Legend of Swaffham" and "The Secret That Can't Be Kept," both for *Once a Week,* 1860) to compositions with much white space and chunky, sometimes haphazard, lines (the second illustration for "Effie Gordon," 1861; "Faint Heart Never Won Fair Ladye," 1863; and "Heinrich Frauenlob," 1863; all for *Once a Week*). Often his figures look like miniature dolls posed in incorrect spatial environments ("The Minstrel's Curse," 1860, and "Fleurette," 1861, for *Once a Week*). Yet he could be just as fastidious as any Pre-Raphaelite, as evidenced in his directions for Swain on a touched proof of "Easter" (*Lyra Germanica,* 1861): "Don't touch the child's face again

except first to lighten the eyebrows a little where I've marked. I marked more light around the edge of the cheek and just the edge of the nostril" (Museum of Fine Arts, Boston, Hartley Collection).

Lawless's best illustrations are solid Pre-Raphaelite designs, often of strange and morbid subjects, of death and love, where the people look absolutely real. The two pictures for "The Death of Oenone" (*Once a Week,* 1860) are mystical and subtle depictions of lovers in death, wholly original and beautifully modeled; the long, flowing female hair in these works, a hallmark of much Pre-Raphaelite art, is featured also in "King Dyring" (*Once a Week,* 1861) and "The Lay of the Lady and the Hound" (*Once a Week,* 1860), both with an effective variety of linear modeling techniques. The "King Dyring" poem relates that after a king's wife—a good mother—dies, she comes back for a while, and appears to her children. "Dead Love" (*Once a Week,* 1862), a work in the spirit of Dürer and Sandys, is based on Swinburne's macabre tale of the love of woman for a corpse—a great hero, whose coffin she keeps by her bed; she's seen as evil, is killed, and then both their souls are released. "Rung into Heaven" (*Good Words*, 1862) illustrates a poem by Horace Moule with a typical innocence-and-tragedy theme: at Yuletide, three children stand beside a belfry door, counting the bells; the little girl is killed by a bell, and her soul goes to heaven.

In keeping with the Pre-Raphaelite tradition, in Lawless illustrations there is plenty of hand-clasp-

ing, lovers tightly clutching, and people burying their heads in their hands. In fact, "The Betrayed" (*Once a Week*, 1860), "Broken Toys" (*Once a Week*, 1863), and "Florinda" (*Once a Week*, 1860) are almost identical in subject and composition, featuring the same seated, head-bowed woman in a dark dress, center stage.

Twenty of Lawless's *Once a Week* illustrations can be found reprinted in *Historical and Legendary Ballads and Songs*, and all three from *Good Words* return in the pages of *Touches of Nature*.

Rung into Heaven (*wood-engraving, Dalziels; 5 1/2 x 4;* Good Words, *vol. 3, 1862, p. 153;* Touches of Nature*)*

Catalogue

PERIODICALS

Churchman's Family Magazine
Vol. 2, 1863:
¶ **One Dead*** (p. 275, W. Barker;
reprinted as **The Silent Chamber** in *Pictures of Society*)
Vol. 3, 1864:
¶ **Harold Massey's Confession**
(p. 65)

Good Words
Vol. 3, 1862:
¶ **Rung into Heaven*** (p. 153, Dalziels;
reprinted in *Touches of Nature*)
¶ **Bands of Love*** (p. 632, Dalziels;
reprinted in *Touches of Nature*)
Vol. 5, 1864:
¶ **The Player and the Listeners*** (p. 168,
Dalziels; reprinted in *Touches of Nature* [full
edition only])

London Society
Vol. 1, 1862:
¶ **Beauty's Toilette*** (p. 265, Dalziels)
Vol. 2, 1862:
¶ **The First Night at the Sea-Side***
(p. 220, W. Barker)
¶ **A Box on the Ears and Its
Consequences*** (p. 382, W. Barker)
¶ **Surreptitious Correspondence***
(p. 480, W. Barker; reprinted as **The Letter**
in *Pictures of Society*)
Vol. 4, 1863:
¶ **Honeydew** (p. 554, W. Barker)
Vol. 5, 1864:
¶ **Not for You** (p. 85, W. Barker)
Vol. 13, 1868:
¶ **Expectation*** (p. 361, W. Barker;
dated 1862 in block)
Vol. 18, 1870:
¶ **An Episode in the Italian War** (p. 97;
early 1860s)

Once a Week
Vol. 1, 1859:
¶ **"Sentiment from the Shambles"** by

One Dead *(wood-engraving, W. Barker; 4 x 5; Churchman's Family Magazine, vol. 2, 1863, p. 275; Pictures of Society)*

***The Bridal of Galtrim** [#1] (wood-engraving, Swain; 2 5/8 x 4 3/4;* Once a Week, *vol. 2, 1860, p. 88;* Historical and Legendary Ballads and Songs*)*

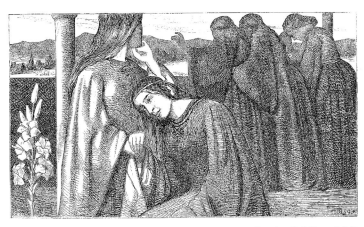

***The Bridal of Galtrim** [#2] (wood-engraving, Swain; 2 5/8 x 4 3/4;* Once a Week, *vol. 2, 1860, p. 88)*

Olive Keese, 3 illustrations (pp. 505, 507, 509*; Swain)

Vol. 2, 1860:

¶ **"The Bridal of Galtrim"** by Samuel Lover, 2 illustrations* (p. 88 [2 illus.], Swain; [#1] reprinted as **The Legend of the Prince's Plume: After the Battle** in *Historical and Legendary Ballads and Songs* [hereafter *HLBS*])

¶ **The Lay of the Lady and the Hound*** (p. 164, Swain; reprinted as **The Young Queen-Wife** in *HLBS*)

¶ **Florinda** (p. 220, Swain; reprinted as **Faces in the Fire** in *HLBS*)

¶ **Only for Something to Say*** (p. 352, Swain)

¶ **"The Headmaster's Sister"** by Herbert Vaughan, 3 illustrations (pp. 386, 389, 393; Swain)

¶ **The Secret That Can't Be Kept** (p. 430, Swain)

¶ **A Legend of Swaffham** (p. 540, Swain; reprinted as **The Apparitor of the Secret Tribunal** [#1] in *HLBS*)

¶ **The Lots upon the Raft** (p. 620, Swain)

Vol. 3, 1860:

¶ **The Betrayed** (p. 155, Swain; reprinted as **The Wreck Off Calais** in *HLBS*)

¶ **Elfie Meadows** (p. 304, Swain)

¶ **The Minstrel's Curse** (p. 351; reprinted as **The Legend of the Prince's Plume: Before the Battle** in *HLBS*)

¶ **The Two Beauties of the Camberwell Assemblies, 1778** (p. 462, Swain)

¶ **My Angel's Visit** (p. 658, Swain)

• 2 illustrations for "Pearl Wearers and Pearl Winners" on p. 79 are credited to Lawless but are not by him

Vol. 4, 1861:

¶ **"The Death of Oenone"** by H.M.M., 2 illustrations* (pp. 14, 15; Swain; reprinted as 2 illustrations for **"The Madman of Corinth"** in *HLBS*)

¶ **Confessions of St. Valentine's Day** (p. 208, Swain; a.k.a. **Valentine's Day**)

¶ **"Effie Gordon"** by B. S. Montgomery, 2 illustrations* (pp. 406, 407; Swain; reprinted as **The Night After Culloden** and **The Death of Rufus** in *HLBS*)

¶ **The Cavalier's Escape** (p. 687, Swain; reprinted [same title] in *HLBS*)

Vol. 5, 1861:

¶ **High Elms** (p. 420, Swain)

¶ **Twilight** (p. 532, Swain)

¶ **King Dyring*** (p. 575, Swain)

¶ **Fleurette** (p. 700, Swain; reprinted as **Basking** in *HLBS*)

Vol. 6, 1862:

¶ **Dr. Johnson's Penance*** (p. 14, Swain; reprinted in *The Piccadilly Annual*; reprinted [same title] in *HLBS*)

¶ **What Befell Me at the Assizes** (p. 194)

¶ **The Dead Bride*** (p. 462, Swain; reprinted as **The Dead Bride** [#1] in *HLBS*)

Vol. 7, 1862:

¶ **Dead Love*** (p. 434, Swain?; reprinted as **The Lady Witch** in *HLBS*)

Vol. 8, 1863:

¶ **The Linden Trees** (p. 644, Swain; reprinted as **German Hussar Songs** in *HLBS*)

¶ **Gifts** (p. 712, Swain; reprinted as **In Clover** in *HLBS*)

Vol. 9, 1863:

¶ **Faint Heart Never Won Fair Ladye** (p. 98, Swain?; reprinted as **The Jester's Passing Bell** in *HLBS*)

¶ **Heinrich Frauenlob*** (p. 393, Swain; reprinted as **The Dead Bride** [#2] in *HLBS*)

¶ **Broken Toys** (p. 672, Swain?)

Vol. 10, 1864:

¶ **John of Padua** (p. 71, Swain; reprinted [same title] in *HLBS*)

Punch

Vol. 39, 1860:

¶ **The Ideal** (p. 114)

¶ **The Real** (p. 120)

¶ **Cum Marte Minerva** (p. 130)

¶ **A Rise in Bread-Stuffs! Effects of Eating Aerated Bread** (p. 200)

¶ **G.W.R. Engaged** (p. 240; a.k.a. **Isn't It Melancholy . . . Hodge, Our Artist, Walking About the Station**)

Vol. 40, 1861:

¶ **Latest Importation in Sweets** (p. 12)

BOOKS

Lyra Germanica (Catherine Winkworth, trans.; Longmans, 1st ser., 1861)

¶ **Unworthy** (Dalziels)

¶ **My Jesus, Help Me to Pray** (Dalziels)

The Lay of the Lady and the Hound (wood-engraving, Swain; 5 1/8 x 2 3/4; Once a Week, vol. 2, 1860, p. 164; Historical and Legendary Ballads and Songs)

The Death of Oenone *[#1] (wood-engraving, Swain; 3 1/2 x 5;* Once a Week, *vol. 4, 1861, p. 14;* Historical and Legendary Ballads and Songs*)*

The Death of Oenone *[#2] (wood-engraving, Swain; 3 1/2 x 5;* Once a Week, *vol. 4, 1861, p. 15;* Historical and Legendary Ballads and Songs*)*

¶ **Let Who Will in Thee Rejoice** (Dalziels; a.k.a. **Watch! and Pray**)

Pictorial Bible and Church History Stories (Henry Formby; Longmans, Brown, Green, and Longmans, vol. 3, parts 6 and 7, 1862)
    ¶ **St. Bernard** (part 6)
    ¶ **Thomas à Becket** (part 6)
    ¶ **St. Francis of Assisi** (part 7)
    ¶ **St. Francis of Assisi: Homage of Dumb Creatures** (part 7)
    ¶ **St. Francis of Assisi: Before the Court of Sultan Mendi** (part 7)
    ¶ **Meeting of St. Francis and St. Dominic** (part 7)
    ¶ **St. Charles Boromeo** (part 7)
    ¶ **St. Philip Neri** (part 7)
    ¶ **Kill the Wretches** (part 7)
    ¶ **Carmelite Community** (part 7)
    ¶ **Aged Mother Prioress** (part 7)
    • Eng. Dalziels and Bale and Holman

BOOKS CONTAINING REPRINTS

Historical and Legendary Ballads and Songs (Walter Thornbury; Chatto and Windus, 1876)
    ¶ **The Death of Rufus (Effie Gordon** [#2] reprinted from *Once a Week*)
    ¶ **The Legend of the Prince's Plume: Before the Battle (The Minstrel's Curse** reprinted from *Once a Week*)
    ¶ **The Legend of the Prince's Plume: After the Battle (The Bridal of Galtrim** reprinted from *Once a Week*)
    ¶ **The Dead Bride** [#1] (reprinted [same title] from *Once a Week*)
    ¶ **The Dead Bride** [#2] (**Heinrich Frauenlob** reprinted from *Once a Week*)
    ¶ **The Apparitor of the Secret Tribunal** [#1] (**A Legend of Swatham** reprinted from *Once a Week*)
    ¶ **The Jester's Passing Bell (Faint Heart Never Won Fair Ladye** reprinted from *Once a Week*)
    ¶ **The Lady Witch (Dead Love** reprinted from *Once a Week*)
    ¶ **The Cavalier's Escape** (reprinted [same title] from *Once a Week*)
    ¶ **The Night After Culloden (Effie Gordon** [#1] reprinted from *Once a Week*)
    ¶ **Dr. Johnson's Penance** (reprinted [same title] from *Once a Week*)

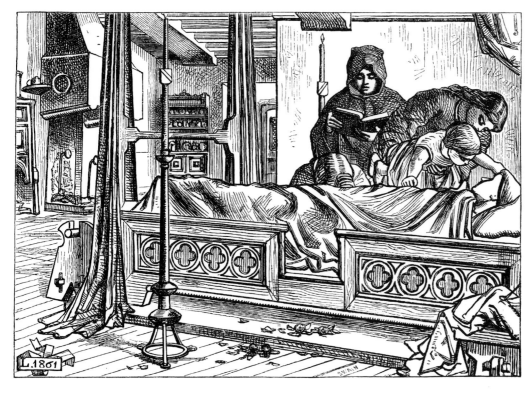

*Effie Gordon [#2]
(wood-engraving,
Swain; 3 1/2 x 5;
Once a Week, vol. 4,
1861, p. 407;
Historical and
Legendary Ballads
and Songs)*

¶ **John of Padua** (reprinted [same title] from *Once a Week*)

¶ **The Young Queen-Wife** (**The Lay of the Lady and the Hound** reprinted from *Once a Week*)

¶ **The Madman of Corinth** [#1] (**The Death of Oenone** [#1] reprinted from *Once a Week*)

¶ **The Madman of Corinth** [#2] (**The Death of Oenone** [#2] reprinted from *Once a Week*)

¶ **German Hussar Songs** (**The Linden Trees** reprinted from *Once a Week*)

¶ **The Wreck Off Calais** (**The Betrayed** reprinted from *Once a Week*)

¶ **Basking** (**Fleurette** reprinted from *Once a Week*)

¶ **In Clover** (**Gifts** reprinted from *Once a Week*)

¶ **Faces in the Fire** (**Florinda** reprinted from *Once a Week*)

The Piccadilly Annual of Entertaining Literature (Hotten, 1870)
¶ **Dr. Johnson's Penance** (reprinted from *Once a Week*)

Pictures of Society (Low, Son, and Marston, 1866)

King Dyring (wood-engraving, Swain; 6 1/2 x 3 1/2; Once a Week, vol. 5, 1861, p. 575)

Heinrich Frauenlob *(wood-engraving, Swain; 6 3/8 x 4 1/2;* Once a Week, *vol. 9, 1863, p. 393;* Historical and Legendary Ballads and Songs*)*

¶ **The Silent Chamber** (**One Dead** reprinted from *Churchman's Family Magazine*)

¶ **Harold Massey's Confession** (reprinted from *Churchman's Family Magazine*)

¶ **Special Correspondence** (**Surreptitious Correspondence** [a.k.a. **The Letter**], another state, with lines removed from face, reprinted from *London Society*)

• Reissued by Routledge in 1871

Touches of Nature (Strahan, 1867)

¶ **Rung into Heaven**

¶ **The Bands of Love**

¶ **The Player and the Listeners**

• Reprinted from *Good Words*

§ *Sunday Reading for Good Children* (Routledge, [1873]) may contain one or more reprints by Lawless

INDIVIDUAL PRINTS

¶ **The Bivouac** (etching, Lawless, 1859; 4 3/8 x 6 1/8; signed and dated in plate)

• Published in *Passages from Modern English Poets* (Junior Etching Club; Day, [1862]); reissued by Tegg in 1874 and, with the etchings transferred to stone for lithographic prints, in 1875

¶ **The Drummer** (etching, Lawless, 1859; 5 1/2 x 3 1/4; signed with monogram and dated in plate)

• Published in *Passages from Modern English Poets*

¶ **The Little Shipwrights** (etching, Lawless, 1859; 3 3/8 x 2 1/4; signed and dated in plate)

• Published in *Passages from Modern English Poets*

¶ **Sisters of Mercy*** (etching, Lawless, 1859; 3 1/2 x 5; signed and dated in plate)

• Published in *Passages from Modern English Poets*

Frederic Leighton

(1830-1896)

Frederic Leighton was the savior of a Victorian art establishment annoyed by the growing influence of the rebellious Pre-Raphaelites. He had the sophistication of a continental artist, and was a student of the classics and the revered Italian Renaissance. He had studied drawing in Rome, attended the Florence Academy, and studied with another acceptable source, a Nazarene artist (Edward von Steinle, in Frankfurt); in the 1850s he painted in Rome and Paris. Before he settled in London in 1859, he made his reputation through a flamboyant entrance to the Royal Academy: in 1855, his *Cimabue's Celebrated Madonna Is Carried in Procession Through the Streets of Florence*, a technically superb piece of historical "journalism" without the despised Pre-Raphaelite shrillness and quirkiness, took the Academy by storm and was purchased by Queen Victoria.

Leighton at first concentrated on medieval and biblical subjects, but by the 1860s and 1870s he was considered the finest representative of the new school of classical mythology-genre painters who valued beautiful forms above even narrative concerns. Leighton's mature paintings are more than theatrical scenes recreating bourgeois incidents

Frederic Leighton, c. 1890s (photograph; photo-engraving, clipping)

in the ancient world, as are Alma-Tadema's then-popular canvases, more than Albert Moore's simplified arrangements of classically draped females. Leighton's works are intensely realistic and always intriguingly composed; they flirt with sensuality, but their robust (though not necessarily Pre-Raphaelite) colors and cloudlike drapery bring to mind mouth-watering confections more than smoldering eroticism. Leighton produced memorable painting after memorable painting with that focus: *Orpheus and Eurydice* (1864), *Daedalus and Icarus* (1869), *Hercules Wrestling with Death for the Body of Alcestis* (1871), *The Music Lesson* (1877), *Cymon and Iphigenia* (1884), *The Bath of Psyche* (1890), and *Perseus and Andromeda* (1891).

William Michael Rossetti described the qualities that, combined with his virtuoso painter's skills, obtained for Leighton the presidency of the Royal Academy in 1878: "Leighton always presented the appearance of a favourite of fortune, and his great and varied abilities enabled him to sustain the position with éclat; the protagonist of the painting profession, the darling of society, the recipient of multiform flatteries" (*Some Reminiscences*, vol. 1, p. 206). Leighton received the ultimate Victorian flattery when in 1896 he became the first English artist made a peer, as Frederic, Lord Leighton.

But Leighton was more than an academic in his work, sharing much with the Pre-Raphaelites besides friendship. By the Nazarene connection with Steinle, he was influenced by early-Italian art; Peter Cornelius

The Music Lesson (oil, 1877; 36 1/2 x 37 1/2; Guildhall Art Gallery, London; photo-engraving, as published in Masters in Art: Leighton, 1908)

himself suggested changes to *Cimabue* as Leighton worked on it; and Edward Poynter (a young kindred spirit in painting and fellow Pre-Raphaelite illustrator), visiting Leighton's Paris studio, was inspired to adopt a path similar to Leighton's. After his Royal Academy success in 1855, he established himself in Paris, where he renewed his acquaintance with Poynter, who was studying at Charles Gleyre's studio with Du Maurier and other English artists. Leighton's early paintings are spiritual cousins of the Pre-Raphaelites': *Paolo and Francesca* (1861), *Jezebel and Ahab* (1863),

Dante at Verona (1864), and with its Robert Browning poetry inspiration, *Orpheus and Eurydice*. Leighton exhibited with the Pre-Raphaelites' Hogarth Club, notably a lemon-tree drawing praised for its realism by Ruskin. In all his works, Leighton was the master of the perfectly drawn figure (from life models), his classicism based on the High Renaissance but informed by the spirit of the Romantic era and an innate drama. Also like the Pre-Raphaelite approach, his figures are dynamically posed and his pictorial structure is always unusual and intriguing—a notable example being the pretzel-like (but somehow tranquil) female figure swathed in melting orange cloth who fills the entire surface of *Flaming June* (1895).

In illustration, Leighton joins the Pre-Raphaelites in their revolutionary approach of the 1850s and 1860s—daring to devote his full powers to every inch of the wood-block surface; taking a precise linear style, with sharp contrasts of light and shade, from the Nazarenes and early-Renaissance Germans; making careful studies from life; and employing remarkably inventive compositions. Leighton is especially remembered for two projects, to each of which he contributed numerous drawings: George Eliot's *Romola* and *Dalziels' Bible Gallery*.

For Eliot's Florentine romance, first serialized in the *Cornhill Magazine* in 1862 and 1863, Leighton's Italian experience seemed perfectly suited; he produced thirty-nine wood-block drawings, including pictorial initials. The realistic figures, the hooded characters, the Düreresque drapery, the dramatic lighting, and the dynamic poses all link these to the best Pre-Raphaelite work. "The Dying Message," a deathbed scene replete with supine mourner, recalls Lawless and Sandys and is W. J. Linton's best engraving here; Linton's others are all produced in his lifeless, uniformly thin-lined method. Swain engraved the remainder, whose tonal balance and richness of line make for wood-engravings vastly superior to his colleague's. Especially fine collaborations of Leighton and Swain in *Romola* are "The Peasants' Fair," "A Florentine Joke," and "Drifting Away." For the *Cornhill Magazine*, Leighton also produced a few other illustrations, notably "The Great God Pan," cut by the Dalziels, in 1860.

George Smith, of the *Cornhill* publishers Smith, Elder, described Leighton's concern for his work in doing these drawings. "Leighton, . . . when the proofs of the first wood engravings were sent to him, . . . came to me in great agitation. The engraver, he declared, had entirely spoilt his drawing, leaving out certain essential lines, and putting [in] other irrelevant ones of his own. . . . The wood engraver . . . swore . . . he had engraved every line conscientiously. . . . Lying awake one night, it suddenly occurred to me that I might manufacture evidence.

"I sent the next drawing to a photographer and instructed him to photograph it with the utmost care. When Leighton next made his appearance to complain of the injustice done to his drawing, I produced my photograph, sent for the engraver, and the two fought it out together. Leighton became more

The Dying Message for ***"Romola"*** *(wood-engraving, W. J. Linton; 4 x 6 1/4;* Cornhill Magazine, *vol. 6, 1862, p. 433;* The Cornhill Gallery; Twenty-five Illustrations by Frederic Leighton; Romola*)*

A Florentine Joke for ***"Romola"*** *(wood-engraving, Swain; 4 x 6 1/4;* Cornhill Magazine, *vol. 6, 1862, p. 450;* The Cornhill Gallery; Twenty-five Illustrations by Frederic Leighton; Romola*)*

accustomed to drawing on wood and the other engravings gave him greater satisfaction" (*House of Smith, Elder*, p. 140).

Leighton's other major set of wood-engravings was commissioned by the Dalziels for their *Bible Gallery* in the early 1860s. These were even in their time regarded as among the finest wood-block drawings ever done. "Samson Carrying the Gates," with its striking composition of the figure of Samson hunched over and almost obscured by the large pictorial element of the gates, set off by the rhythmic serration of the wall tops, has always attracted critical praise. In "Samson at the Mill," "Samson and the Lion" (an unforgettable depiction of violent motion), "Abram and the Angel," and "Moses Views the Promised Land," large, solid figures predominate, the massive shapes and background details depicted with the certainty of more elaborate Pre-Raphaelite illustrations. As in the usual German models, Leighton's lines are masterful, sure. While his drawings for *Romola* were done in pencil and the *Bible* ones in fine ink lines by brush, an examination of the original drawings preserved in photographs for both books shows how perfectly Leighton—like Sandys—understood his medium. His "Death of the First-Born" in the *Bible Gallery*, for example, is essentially no different in the drawing than it became in the Dalziels' perfect facsimile engraving (Museum of Fine Arts, Boston, Hartley Collection).

At the end of his life, when heart disease assured that he could no longer fulfill his duties as president of the Royal Academy, Leighton wrote on March 27, 1895, to John Everett Millais. Though the position was to be temporary, he was essentially passing the academic brush and

palette to the original Pre-Raphaelite: "My dear old friend, there is *only one man* whom *everybody*, without exception, will acclaim in the chair of the President on May 4th—a great artist, loved by all—yourself. You will do it admirably, that I well know; and you will have the huge advantage of doing it for once only instead of year after year. . . .

"Dear Millais, every man in the profession will rejoice to see you in that chair on that night; and let an old friend of forty years say you *may* not refuse this honour" (*Life and Letters of Sir John Everett Millais*, vol. 2, p. 315). Millais officially assumed the presidency of the Royal Academy the month after his friend passed on in January 1896.

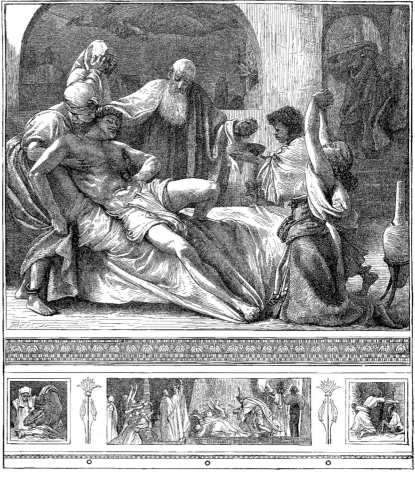

Death of the First-Born *(wood-engraving, Dalziels; 7 5/8 x 6 7/8;* Dalziels' Bible Gallery, *1881;* Art Pictures from the Old Testament*)*

Catalogue

PERIODICALS

Cornhill Magazine
Vol. 2, 1860:
¶ **The Great God Pan*** (p. 84, Dalziels; reprinted in *The Cornhill Gallery* and in *Twenty-five Illustrations by Frederic Leighton*)
¶ **Ariadne** (p. 674)
Vol. 6, 1862:
¶ **"Romola"** by George Eliot, 19 illustrations* (see information below [§])
Vol. 7, 1863:
¶ **"Romola"** by George Eliot, 16 illustrations* (see information below [§])
Vol. 8, 1863:
¶ **"Romola"** by George Eliot, 4 illustrations* (see information below [§])
• 39 illustrations from vols. 6–8 reprinted in *Romola*, 1880; 24 full-page illustrations reprinted in *The Cornhill Gallery* and *Twenty-five Illustrations by Frederic Leighton;* 3 illustrations (**"Will His Eyes Open?"**, **The Dying Message**, and **A Dangerous Colleague**) reprinted in *Romola*, 1865
Vol. 15, 1867:
¶ **"A Week in a French Country-House"** by Mrs. Sartoris, 4 illustrations (**An Evening in a French Country-House**, fac. p. 192, Swain [reprinted in *A Week in a French Country-House*]; *pictorial initial*, p. 192, Swain; **Drifting**, fac. p. 457, Swain [reprinted in *A Week in a French Country-House*]; *pictorial initial*, p. 457, Swain)

Punch
Vol. 90, 1886:
¶ **An Ideal "Rural Dene," or Cassandra Chez Elle** (p. 254; a.k.a. **Portrait of Dorothy Dene**)

§ Since Leighton's illustrations for *Romola* have often been exhibited, reprinted in various collections, and reproduced separately, here follows a listing of the individual engravings, including the ***pictorial***

The Great God Pan *(wood-engraving, Dalziels; 7 x 4;* Cornhill Magazine, *vol. 2, 1860, p. 84;* The Cornhill Gallery; Twenty-five Illustrations by Frederic Leighton*)*

Coming Home *for **"Romola"** (wood-engraving, Swain; 6 1/4 x 4;* Cornhill Magazine, *vol. 6, 1862, p. 726;* The Cornhill Gallery; Twenty-five Illustrations by Frederic Leighton; Romola*)*

Escaped for *"Romola"* (wood-engraving,
W. J. Linton; 6 1/4 x 4; Cornhill Magazine, *vol. 7,
1863, p. 29;* The Cornhill Gallery; Twenty-five
Illustrations by Frederic Leighton; Romola)

Tessa at Home for *"Romola"* (wood-engraving, Swain; 4 x 6 1/4;
Cornhill Magazine, *vol. 7, 1863, p. 569;* The Cornhill Gallery;
Twenty-five Illustrations by Frederic Leighton; Romola)

initials, as they appeared in the *Cornhill
Magazine*:

Vol. 6: • *Frontispiece:* **The Painted
Record** (W. J. Linton) • **The Blind Scholar**
(p. 1, Linton) • *Tailpiece* **for "Proem"**
(p. 7, Swain) • *Pictorial initial* (p. 8,
Swain) • **"Suppose You Let Me Look at
Myself"** (p. 27, Swain) • **A Recognition**
(fac. p. 145, Swain) • *Pictorial initial*
(p. 145) • **Under the Plane-Tree** (p. 185,
Linton) • **The First Kiss** (fac. p. 289,
Linton) • *Pictorial initial* (p. 289)
• **The Peasants' Fair** (p. 311, Swain) • **The
Dying Message** (fac. p. 433, Linton)
• *Pictorial initial* (p. 433) • **A Florentine
Joke** (p. 450, Swain) • **The Escaped
Prisoner** (fac. p. 577, Linton)
• *Pictorial initial* (p. 577) • **Niccolo at Work**
(p. 603, Swain) • *Pictorial initial* (p. 721)
• **Coming Home** (p. 726, Swain)

Vol. 7: • **"You Didn't Think It Was
So Pretty, Did You?"** (fac. p. 1, Swain)
• *Pictorial initial* (p. 1) • **Escaped** (p. 29,
Linton) • **"Father, I Will Be Guided"** (fac.
p. 145, Swain) • *Pictorial initial* (p. 145)
• **A Supper in the Rucellai Gardens**
(p. 153, Linton) • **The Visible Madonna**
(fac. p. 281, Swain) • *Pictorial initial*
(p. 281) • **A Dangerous Colleague** (p. 306,
Linton) • **Monna Brigida's Conversion**
(fac. p. 417, Swain) • *Pictorial initial*
(p. 417) • **"But You Will Help Me?"** (fac.
p. 553, Linton) • *Pictorial initial* (p. 553)
• **Tessa at Home** (p. 569, Swain) • **Drifting
Away** (fac. p. 681, Swain) • *Pictorial initial* (p. 681)

Vol. 8: • **"Will His Eyes Open?"** (fac.
p. 1, Swain) • *Pictorial initial* (p. 1) • **At
the Well** (fac. p. 129, Swain) • *Pictorial
initial* (p. 129)

§ The *Portfolio* of 1881 (vol. 12) reprints
Samson Carrying the Gates from *Dalziels'
Bible Gallery* to accompany the article
"Recent Biblical Designs" (p. 13)

BOOKS

Dalziels' Bible Gallery (Routledge, 1881)
¶ **Moses Views the Promised Land***
¶ **Cain and Abel***
¶ **Escape of the Spies***
¶ **Samson Carrying the Gates***

Left: ***Moses Views the Promised Land*** *(wood-engraving, Dalziels; 9 x 5 1/2;* Dalziels' Bible Gallery, *1881;* Art Pictures from the Old Testament)

Right: ***Cain and Abel*** *(wood-engraving, Dalziels; 7 x 6 1/8;* Dalziels' Bible Gallery, *1881;* Art Pictures from the Old Testament)

¶ **Abram and the Angel***
¶ **Eliezer and Rebekah***
¶ **Death of the First-Born***
¶ **Samson and the Lion***
¶ **Samson at the Mill***
• Eng. Dalziels
• Reprinted in *Art Pictures from the Old Testament*

English Art in 1884 (Henry Blackburn; New York: Appleton, 1885)
¶ **Cymon and Iphigenia** (drawing by the artist [?] after his painting; photo-engraving)

"My Face Is My Fortune, Sir," She Said (Mrs. John White; Simpkin, Marshall, [1886])
¶ 6 illustrations (photo-engravings?)
• Plus cover design by the artist

Romola (George Eliot; Smith, Elder, 1865)
¶ ***Titlepage illustration*** (Swain)
• Plus 3 illustrations reprinted from the *Cornhill Magazine* and *The Cornhill Gallery* (reprinted in *Twenty-five Illustrations by Frederic Leighton* and *Romola*, 1880)

Woodland Gossip (Mary Louise Boyle; McLean, 1864)

Escape of the Spies *(wood-engraving, Dalziels; 6 1/2 x 7;* Dalziels' Bible Gallery, *1881;* Art Pictures from the Old Testament)

Samson Carrying the Gates *(wood-engraving, Dalziels; 6 1/2 x 7 3/8;* Dalziels' Bible Gallery, *1881;* Art Pictures from the Old Testament*)*

Abram and the Angel *(wood-engraving, Dalziels; 8 3/8 x 6;* Dalziels' Bible Gallery, *1881;* Art Pictures from the Old Testament*)*

¶ ***Frontispiece*** (photographic print)

§ **A Contrast**, a drawing reproduced in Ernest Rhys's *Frederic Leighton* (Bell, 1900, p. 72), is said to have been used as a ***frontispiece*** for a book of fairy tales

BOOKS CONTAINING REPRINTS

Art Pictures from the Old Testament (Aley Fox, text; Society for Promoting Christian Knowledge, 1894)
   ¶ 9 illustrations (reprinted from *Dalziels' Bible Gallery*; **Escape of the Spies** reprinted as **The Spies Escape**)

The Cornhill Gallery (Smith, Elder, 1864)
   ¶ **"Romola,"** 24 full-page illustrations (reprinted from the *Cornhill Magazine*; reprinted in *Romola*, 1865 [3 illus.], and *Romola*, 1880)
   ¶ **The Great God Pan** (reprinted from the *Cornhill Magazine*; reprinted in *Twenty-five Illustrations by Frederic Leighton*)
     • Printed from the original wood-blocks
     • Reissued in 1865

Romola (George Eliot; Smith, Elder, 1865)
   ¶ ***Frontispiece: "Will His Eyes Open?"***
     ¶ **The Dying Message**
     ¶ **A Dangerous Colleague**
     • Reprinted from the *Cornhill Magazine* and *The Cornhill Gallery*
     • Reprinted in *Twenty-five Illustrations by Frederic Leighton* and *Romola*, 1880
     • Plus ***titlepage illustration*** (new)

Romola (George Eliot; Smith, Elder, 2 vols., 1880)
   ¶ 39 illustrations (reprinted from the *Cornhill Magazine*, from *The Cornhill Gallery* [24 full-page illus.], from *Romola*, 1865 [3 illus.], and from *Twenty-five Illustrations by Frederic Leighton* [24 full-page illus.])
     • Printed from the original wood-blocks, in a limited edition

Twenty-five Illustrations by Frederic Leighton Designed for the Cornhill Magazine (Smith, Elder, 1867)
   ¶ **"Romola,"** 24 full-page illustrations

(reprinted from the *Cornhill Magazine*, from *The Cornhill Gallery*, and from *Romola*, 1865 [3 illus.])

¶ **The Great God Pan** (reprinted from the *Cornhill Magazine* and *The Cornhill Gallery*)

A Week in a French Country-House (Adelaide Sartoris; Macmillan, 1902)

¶ **An Evening in a French Country House**

¶ **Drifting**

• Reprinted from the *Cornhill Magazine*

INDIVIDUAL PRINTS

¶ **Pastorale** (etching, Leighton, 1867; 6 3/8 x 3 1/4)

• Published in *Gazette de Beaux-Arts*, vol. 23 (ser. 1), 1867 (p. 90)

Eliezer and Rebekah *(wood-engraving, Dalziels; 6 7/8 x 5 7/8;* Dalziels' Bible Gallery, *1881;* Art Pictures from the Old Testament*)*

Samson and the Lion *(wood-engraving, Dalziels; 7 1/4 x 7 1/4;* Dalziels' Bible Gallery, *1881;* Art Pictures from the Old Testament*)*

Samson at the Mill *(wood-engraving, Dalziels; 7 1/2 x 6 7/8;* Dalziels' Bible Gallery, *1881;* Art Pictures from the Old Testament*)*

Henry Stacy Marks

(1829-1898)

In his early work Henry S. Marks was associated with the Pre-Raphaelites, joining them notably as a practitioner of the decorative arts, with an emphasis on the Middle Ages. He worked in the spirit of Rossetti, Burne-Jones, and the Morris firm, and was known for his stained-glass designs.

J. Beavington Atkinson's review of Marks's career in the *Portfolio* mentioned a large variety of other decorative accomplishments: an exhibited study for a Kensington Museum mural *May-day in the Olden Time*—revealing "German Gothic" influence in its "firm lines" and "flat treatment"; a frieze of Shakespearean characters painted above the proscenium of Prince's Theatre in Manchester; designs for a ceramic frieze encircling Royal Albert Hall; a cabinet, exhibited in 1862, decorated with Gothic-style "grotesques"; art for the studio of a colleague, also utilizing subjects from Shakespeare (*The Tempest* and *As You Like It*), whose general approach Atkinson compared to that of "old German prints slightly washed with color" and of paintings by the Nazarenes Cornelius and Overbeck. Atkinson added that at fellow illustrator Birket Foster's country house, Marks joined Burne-Jones and J. D. Watson in painting furniture, glass, and walls in a medieval, Pre-Raphaelite style ("English Painters of the Present Day: H. S. Marks," vol. 1, pp. 131–34). Like William Bell Scott, Marks was also a prolific designer of bookplates, many reproduced by the new photolithographic processes and featuring his trademark medieval jester.

Marks, who studied at Leigh's school and

the Royal Academy Schools, and at the École des Beaux-Arts in Paris in 1852, first exhibited at the Royal Academy in 1853. He was a prolific painter of genre, Shakespearean, and medieval subjects, and later in his career

Henry Stacy Marks, c. 1880s (wood-engraving, as published in the Magazine of Art, *vol. 6, 1883)*

seemed to be obsessed with drawing and painting birds. Many of his medieval subjects are of the "humorous genre" type, whose titles express his purpose: *Toothache in the Middle Ages* (1856), *Bottom as Pyramus* (1857), *Dogberry's Charge to the Watch* (1859), *The Franciscan Sculptor and His Model* (1861), *The Jester's Text* (1862), *How Shakespeare Studied* (1863), *The Jolly Post-boys* (1875), and *A Merry Jest* (1875). Marks's pictures, noted W. W. Fenn in 1879, reflected his personality's "sedately humorous expression, the quiet twinkle in his bright eye, and the sly fun playing about the corners of his mouth. . . . Socially he is one of the most amusing and delightful companions that it is possible to meet. With Shakespeare at his fingers' ends, with an inexhaustible fund of anecdote at his command, an able versifier, a singer of a good song, a teller of a good story, he is indeed hard to match . . ." ("Our Living Artists: Henry Stacy Marks," *Magazine of Art*, vol. 2, p. 99–100).

As an illustrator, Marks was uneven and often lapsed into a thick-lined, minimum-detail, cartoony style that seemed suited to his bird pictures and mock-medieval illustrations for children, sometimes in color (*The Good Old Days*, 1876). His best historical illustrations, in the transitional period when he was simplifying his lines and still valued Pre-Raphaelite detail and composition, are "Fetching the Doctor" (*Once a Week*, 1867) and "Paying Labourers" (Walter Thornbury's *Two Centuries of Song*, 1867). Many of his drawings and graphic designs and bookplates are reproduced in his own book *Pen and Pencil Sketches* (1894)—and in some of these in particular one can see that Dürer and Holbein are behind much of Marks's style.

Marks illustrated for *Once a Week*, *Churchman's Family Magazine*, the *Illustrated London News*, *London Society*, and the *Quiver*. His finest work by far, however, is for two books, Willmott's *English Sacred Poetry* (1862) and Winkworth's *Lyra Germanica* (1st ser., 1861). These show Marks brimming with realistic detail, clearly indebted to Dürer and working in the gorgeous tonal-woodcut style, with beautiful highlights, of Sandys, Paton, Shields, and early Millais. At least four of his drawings for *English Sacred Poetry*, eloquently cut by the Dalziels, are exceptional Pre-Raphaelite works: "A Quiet Mind," "Inscription in a Hermitage," "The Two Weavers," and "A Father Reading the Bible." His two etchings for the Junior Etching Club, *The Last Man* (in *Passages from the Poems of Thomas Hood*, 1858) and *To an Egyptian Mummy in the British Museum* (*Passages from Modern English Poets*, 1862) are in this detailed style, but not as serious, and considerably overworked.

The Waits in the Olden Time (*wood-engraving, W. I. Mosses; 11 3/4 x 8 1/2;* Illustrated London News, *vol. 75, Christmas Number, 1879, p. 8)*

Fetching the Doctor (wood-engraving, Swain; 6 7/8 x 4 7/8; *Once a Week,* new ser. [ser. 2], vol. 4, 1867, p. 494)

A Father Reading the Bible (wood-engraving, Dalziels; 5 x 4; *English Sacred Poetry, 1862*)

Catalogue

PERIODICALS

Churchman's Family Magazine
Vol. 1, 1863:
¶ **Home Longing** (p. 113, W. Thomas)
¶ **Age and Youth** (p. 337)

Illustrated London News
Vol. 69, Christmas Number, 1876:
¶ **A Christmas Present** (p. 20, M. Klinkicht)
Vol. 75, Christmas Number, 1879:
¶ **The Waits in the Olden Time** (p. 8, W. I. Mosses)

London Society
Vol. 18, Christmas Number, 1870:
¶ **"Masquers and Mummers,"** 3 illustrations (fac. p. 1, color wood-engraving, H. Harral; pp. 1, 7)

Once a Week
New ser. [ser. 2], vol. 1, 1866:
¶ **The Servants' Hall*** (p. 560, Swain)
New ser. [ser. 2], vol. 4, 1867:
¶ **Fetching the Doctor*** (p. 494, Swain)

Quiver
Ser. 3, vol. 8, 1873 [1872–73]:
¶ **Truth Will Out** (p. 84)

§ **Mansion House Marbles** in *Punch*, vol. 40, 1861 (p. 145), may also be by Marks. Simon Houfe (*Dictionary of British Book Illustrators and Caricaturists*, 1981, p. 383) reports an illustration in *Punch* for 1882 and notes there are perhaps a few illustrations by Marks in the *Home Circle* for 1855 and the *Graphic* in the 1870s (although these may be wood-engravings after his paintings **St. Francis Preaches to the Birds** and **The Convent Drudge**, which are reprinted in *The Graphic Portfolio* [Chatto and Windus, 1877]).

BOOKS

English Art in 1884 (Henry Blackburn; New York: Appleton, 1885)
¶ **The Angler's Rest** (drawing by the artist after his painting; photo-engraving)

English Sacred Poetry (Rev. Robert Aris Willmott, ed.; Routledge, 1862)
¶ **A Father Reading the Bible*** (reprinted in *A Thousand and One Gems of English Poetry*)
¶ **The Atheist and the Acorn**
¶ **A Quiet Mind*** (reprinted in *Aunt Mary's Sunday Picture Book*)
¶ **The Dirge of the Famous**
¶ **The Ring***
¶ **Inscription in a Hermitage***
¶ **The Two Weavers***
• Eng. Dalziels

The Good Old Days (Esmé Stuart; Ward, 1876)
¶ *Frontispiece:* **"The Queen Is Coming!"** (double-page foldout)
¶ **Ye Silent Joe Getteth into Hot Water**
¶ **Ye Butcher Roche—Good Turkeys and Bad News**
¶ **Ye Birds of Evil Omen**
¶ **"All's Well That Ends Well"** (also used, in trimmed format, mounted on the cover)
• Color wood-engravings

Half-Hours with Our Sacred Poets (Alexander H. Grant; Hogg, [1863])
¶ Illustrations
• Reissued by Blackwood in 1869

Lyra Elegantiarum (Frederick Locker, ed.; London: n.p., 1867 / New York: White, Stokes, and Allen, 1884)
¶ *Titlepage illustration:* **Frederick Locker, Fear God, Fear Nought** (etching, Marks?; printed in sepia)
• Also used as a bookplate, in redrawn format

Lyra Germanica (Catherine Winkworth, trans.; Longmans, Green, Reader, and Dyer, 1st ser., 1861)
¶ **Except the Lord Keep the City*** (H. Harral)

A Quiet Mind (wood-engraving, Dalziels; 5 x 4; English Sacred Poetry, *1862*)

Inscription in a Hermitage (wood-engraving, Dalziels; 5 x 4; English Sacred Poetry, *1862*)

The Two Weavers *(wood-engraving, Dalziels; 5 x 4;*
English Sacred Poetry, *1862)*

The Ring *(wood-engraving, Dalziels; 4 x 4 1/2;* English Sacred
Poetry, *1862)*

¶ **St. Stephen's Day*** (H. Leighton)
¶ **Quinquagesima Sunday*** (Pearson)
¶ **First Sunday After Easter***
(H. Leighton)

National Nursery Rhymes (Novello, Ewer /
Routledge, [1870])
  ¶ **Humpty Dumpty** (Dalziels)
  ¶ **Taffy Was a Welshman** (Dalziels)
  ¶ **The Old Man Clothed in Leather**
(Dalziels)

Pen and Pencil Sketches (Henry Stacy
Marks; Chatto and Windus, 2 vols., 1894)
  ¶ 13 illustrations (vol. 1)
  ¶ 11 illustrations (vol. 2)
  • Plus numerous reproductions of
existing drawings and graphic designs
  • Photo-engravings

Ridiculous Rhymes (Henry Stacy Marks;
Routledge, c. 1870)
  ¶ Color wood-engravings

Sketching from Nature (T. J. Ellis; Macmillan,
1883)
  ¶ *Frontispiece*
  • Plus 10 illustrations reproduced
from existing drawings
  • Photo-engravings

*Songs of the Cavaliers and Roundheads,
Jacobite Ballads, Etc.* (Walter Thornbury;
Hurst and Blackett, 1857)
  ¶ *Frontispiece:* **The Jacobite Plate**
  ¶ **Melting the Earl's Plate**
  ¶ **The Dance Round the Plague Pit**
  ¶ **The Jacobite on Tower Hill**
  ¶ **The Jester's Sermon**
  ¶ **The Masked Ball**
  • Eng. W. Thomas

Two Centuries of Song (Walter Thornbury,
ed.; Low, 1867)
  ¶ *Frontispiece:* **Paying Labourers**
(Orrinsmith)

§ Marks is said to have made illustrations
for *A Child's History of England* but the
1873 Chapman and Hall edition of the
Dickens work does not have Marks illustrations; the reference may be to a 4-part
series of Routledge shilling toy books in
color, *The History of England*

BOOKS CONTAINING REPRINTS

Aunt Mary's Sunday Picture Book
(Routledge, n.d.)
¶ **A Quiet Mind** (reprinted from
English Sacred Poetry)

Mother Goose (New York: Routledge, 1872;
New York: McLoughlin, [1880])
¶ **Humpty Dumpty**
¶ **Taffy Was a Welshman**
¶ **The Old Man Clothed in Leather**
• Reprinted from *National Nursery
Rhymes*

Sunday Reading for Good Children
(Routledge, [1873])
¶ Reprinted illustration[s]

*A Thousand and One Gems of English
Poetry* (Charles Mackay, ed.; Routledge,
1867)
¶ **A Father Reading the Bible** (reprinted from *English Sacred Poetry*)

Paying Labourers
*(wood-engraving,
Orrinsmith; 5 5/8 x
4 1/4;* **frontispiece**
for Two Centuries of
Song, *1867)*

INDIVIDUAL PRINTS

¶ **The Last Man*** (etching, Marks, 1858; 5 1/2
x 4; signed with monogram in plate)
• Published in *Passages from the
Poems of Thomas Hood* (Junior Etching
Club; Gambart, 1858)

¶ **To an Egyptian Mummy in the British
Museum*** (etching, Marks, 1859; 5 3/8 x
3 5/8; signed with monogram and dated in
plate; a.k.a. **A Study in the Egyptian
Antiquity Department in the British
Museum** and **Rustic Wonder**)
• Published in *Passages from Modern
English Poets* (Junior Etching Club; Day,
[1862]); reissued by Tegg in 1874 and,
with the etchings transferred to stone for
lithographic prints, in 1875

§ Graphics reproduced in *Pen and Pencil
Sketches*
¶ **1880 General Exhibition of Water
Colours** (advertising card, 1879; vol. 1,
p. 175)
¶ **Henry Stacy Marks invitation card,
1880** (vol. 2, p. 28)
¶ **New Year's Card, 1886** (vol. 2, p. 30)

The Last Man *(etching, Marks; 5 1/2 x 4;* Passages from
the Poems of Thomas Hood, *1858)*

To an Egyptian Mummy in the British Museum (etch-ing, Marks, 1859; 5 3/8 x 3 5/8; Passages from Modern English Poets, [1862])

¶ **Henry Stacy Marks invitation card, 1890s** (vol. 2, p. 91)

¶ **The Seven Ages** (poster for Calvert Memorial Performance, Theatre Royal, Manchester, 1879; vol. 2, p. 112)

¶ **New Year's card, 1885** (vol. 2, p. 139)

¶ **Fine Art Society Second Bond Street Bird Exhibition, 1890** (private view card; vol. 2, p. 159)

¶ **Marks Exhibition, Bond St.** [#1] (poster; vol. 2, p. 161)

¶ **Marks Exhibition, Bond St.** [#2] (poster; vol. 2, p. 161)

¶ **Henry Stacy Marks "At Home" card, 1880s** (vol. 2, p. 235)

¶ *Bookplate* **for R. T. Pritchett** (vol. 2, p. 252)

¶ *Bookplate* **for Robinson Duckworth** (vol. 2, p. 253)

¶ *Bookplate* **for H. S. Marks** (vol. 2, p. 254)

§ 45 bookplates by Marks (52 if size varia-tions are included) are listed in H. W. Fincham's *The Artists and Engravers of British and American Book Plates*, 1897 (p. 62). Among these (mostly reproduced by photolithography) are ***bookplates* for Frederick Locker** (version of etching for *Lyra Elegantiarum*); **James Roberts Brown** (1892); **Robert Jackson**; and **Walter D. Marks** (1892).

John Everett Millais

(1829-1896)

Destined for a brilliant career in art from an early age, John Everett Millais, the rebellious wonder boy of the Pre-Raphaelite Brotherhood, ultimately became one of the stars of the Royal Academy: elected A.R.A. in 1853, he was made a full member in 1863—an "honor" his Pre-Raphaelite colleagues Rossetti, Holman Hunt, and Burne-Jones (after a brief membership) proudly eschewed. For a short while before his death in 1896, he served as president of the Royal Academy; by then he had received one of the utmost Victorian accolades, adding *Sir* to his name in 1885. From about 1860 onward, through his popular genre paintings and portraits and the more than one hundred successful commercial prints based upon them, and most of all through his ubiquitous illustrations (he may not have been a *Punch* artist, but "Illustrated by Millais" was among the better selling points for any book or magazine serial), Millais achieved fame and wealth.

The mystery of Millais is how in the 1840s and 1850s he swerved from the fast track to success and fell in with some dubious artistic company—William Holman Hunt and Dante Gabriel Rossetti. Millais was a child prodigy, attending the Royal Academy Schools from 1840, the amazingly gifted darling of his well-to-do parents, and as a student first in honors and renowned for his draughtsmanship. He met Hunt at the Academy in 1844, but it was about 1847 when they mutually began to consider following John Ruskin's *Modern Painters* advice and painting directly from nature. In this Hunt seemed to lead in determination and evolving reformist dogma; Millais, with the cockiness of self-perceived genius and youthful enthusiasm and loads of talent, just wanted to paint better and produce uniquely original works. Hunt's painting for the Royal

John Everett Millais, 1854 (photograph; photo-engraving, as published in John Guille Millais's The Life and Letters of John Everett Millais, *vol. 2, 1899)*

Academy of 1848, *The Eve of St. Agnes* (after Keats, a growing enthusiasm of the duo), inspired Millais to discard his old style in creating his *Cymon and Iphigenia*, upon which

Hunt commented to his friend at the time, "You see what a dangerous rebel I am, but you are every bit as bad as myself! Here are you painting a poetic subject in which you know all authorities would insist upon conventional treatment, and you cannot pretend that this work of yours is academic. . . . You've made beings of varied form as you see them in Nature. You've made living persons, not tinted effigies. Oh, that'll never do! it is too revolutionary" (*Pre-Raphaelitism*, vol. 1, pp. 85–86). The die was cast; and after Rossetti, enamored of Hunt's Keats painting of 1848, joined the conspiracy, the Pre-Raphaelite Brotherhood came into being. Of the seven members after the September 1848 founding, Collinson, Hunt, Millais, and Rossetti attached the *P.R.B.* initials to their 1849 exhibited works.

Millais's paintings from 1848 through the mid-1850s are works of genius. He seemed able to combine the poetry of Rossetti with the technical virtuosity of Hunt—without thinking too much about it. Before his natural facility (and ambition) took over and poetry left his soul in the Academy- and crowd-pleasing works of his last four decades, Millais was the embodiment of Pre-Raphaelite art in all its forms. Hunt, too, tried to explain the mysterious Millais contradiction: "Not an hour of his life had been lost to his purpose of being a painter. The need of groping after systems by philosophic research and deductions was superseded in him by a quick instinct which enabled him to pounce as an eagle upon the prize he searched for. . . . It was strange how from behind his practical quali-ties an inspiration to convey a poetic meaning would take possession of him, which was not less mystic genius because he could give no logical reason for it, or because no type of it could be found in earlier art. He felt the fire of his message. . . . He possessed, as was already proved in his black and white designs, a true novice's devotion to poetic mysticism and beauty, and a power of invention the exercise of which is meat and drink to the real artist" (*Pre-Raphaelitism*, vol. 1, p. 139).

One of the masterworks that defines this

Christ in the House of His Parents *(oil, 1850; 34 x 55; Tate Gallery, London; photo-engraving, as published in John Guille Millais's* The Life and Letters of Sir John Everett Millais, *vol. 1, 1899)*

side of Millais is his first exhibited Pre-Raphaelite painting, *Lorenzo and Isabella* (1849), based of course on Keats. The realism and colors were and are startling, from the clothing textures to the brocaded wall pattern; the space is compressed so the scene itself is a pattern, a composition, rather than a stage setting; the figures were modeled after many of the artist's family and friends, including Dante Rossetti; the characters are individualized personalities that make the scene come alive, as it might have been; there are stylistic parallels with early-Italian and

Nazarene art; and the often-used early Pre-Raphaelite device of lounging dogs is so central that the bizarre pose, in the foreground, of Lorenzo's brother, who extends his leg to kick a dog, becomes the most memorable thing about the picture.

A succession of incredible Pre-Raphaelite works followed: *Christ in the House of His Parents* (a.k.a. *The Carpenter's Shop*) and *Ferdinand Lured by Ariel* (both exhibited in 1850); *Mariana* and *The Woodman's Daughter* (both 1851); *Ophelia* (1852); and *Autumn Leaves* and *The Blind Girl* (both 1856). In 1859 Millais produced one of the most disturbingly poetic of all Pre-Raphaelite paintings, *The Vale of Rest*, which was to be the last work in which this side of his inspiration emerged. The influential John Ruskin had championed everything Millais did—even after the artist in 1855 married Effie Gray, who had obtained an annulment from Ruskin on grounds that their marriage had not been "consummated." Ruskin did turn against him in 1857, however, disliking his approach in his painting *A Dream of the Past: Sir Isumbras at the Ford.*

Millais, feeling destined for greater success, also grew tired of the critical bashing the artists associated with Pre-Raphaelitism had been taking in the press since 1850. Throughout the following decade his output of "inspired" paintings was interspersed with canvases holding little mystery or poetry—canvases of large figures in fairly conventional compositions, of romantic and sentimental themes, the technical treatment becoming more and more broad: *The Huguenot* (1852), *The Order of Release* (1853), *The Proscribed Royalist* (1853),

*Design for the 1853 painting **The Order of Release** (photo-engraving, as published in John Guille Millais's* The Life and Letters of Sir John Everett Millais, *vol. 1, 1899)*

The Rescue (1855), *Peace Concluded* (1856), and *The Black Brunswicker* (1860). For all their lessened motivations, these paintings are all relatively fine works. But for the rest of his career, Millais seemed satisfied with his reputation for society portraits and sentimental historical and modern genre paintings. In composition, technique, and emotional impact, these prettified popular works—*The Bride of Lammermoor* (1878), *The Princes in the Tower* (1878), *Cherry Ripe* (1879), *Bubbles* (1886), and many others—are ciphers.

Despite Holman Hunt's lead in forming the P.R.B., Millais's enthusiasm for the revolt should not be taken for granted. Indeed, it was his copy of a collection of engravings of the Campo Santo frescoes at Pisa that got the group fired up for their rebellion, in an 1848 meeting at his house. These early-Italian engravings are in the linear style that Rossetti, Hunt, and Millais all adopted in their early drawings, which feature huddled masses of pointy, slightly modeled, angular, and quirkily posed figures. Millais's drawings are by far the most finished and finest of the group: he seems to have regarded these black-and-white works as important compositions, fully equal to his paintings in inspiration and technique—perhaps pointing to his coming role as one of the masters of English Victorian illustration.

The Disentombment of Queen Matilda of 1849 (pen and ink) is a picture teeming with these eccentrically posed, Gothically angular figures, better than anything Rossetti could have drawn at the time but striking for the morbidly weird and mystical spirit, and stylistic parallels, it has in common with his

Pre-Raphaelite brother's works. For the group's magazine the *Germ*, Millais intended a rather simplified drawing in this style, *St. Agnes of Intercession* (1850), but since the fifth issue of the journal never came out, Millais's etching of the subject exists only in a few proofs.

The personally trying summer of 1853, during which Millais and his brother William accompanied John Ruskin and his wife on a painting tour of Scotland, resulted in Millais's love affair and eventual marriage to Effie Gray Ruskin, an incredible Pre-Raphaelite portrait painting of John Ruskin, and Millais's most symbolic, emotionally felt, and stylistically superb drawings, in a slightly more realistic and modeled approach than in *Queen Matilda*. Most are of lovers in bad relationships, based on the situation with Effie: *Rejected, The Ghost, Virtue and Vice, The Race-Meeting* (all 1853); and *The Man with Two Wives* of 1854, in which a bigamist is confronted by both families. Similar in style and emotional power is "When I First Met Thee," engraved for Moore's *Irish Melodies* of 1856. This is a drawing of a

Titlepage illustration for Robinson Crusoe, *1866 (steel-engraving, 3 1/8 x 2 5/8)*

woman in church watching her former lover getting married, done earlier under the spell of the difficult 1853–54 period. Millais had made a rather feeble etching of a man and a woman for Wilkie Collins's *Mr. Wray's Cash-box* (1852) and drew a fine group of figures for "The Fireside Story" wood-engraving in *The Music Master* (1855); but the appearance of this first really substantial Pre-Raphaelite illustration, in *Irish Melodies*, immediately marked Millais as an extraordinary illustrator, with a unique Pre-Raphaelite perspective.

Millais drew more "tonally" (i.e., wash/watercolors) for many other steel-engraved illustrations during his career, and these are usually equally fine and detailed works, notably the frontispieces for *John Halifax, Gentleman* (1861), *The Valley of a Hundred Fires* (1861), *Mistress and Maid* (1863), and *No Name* (1864) and a titlepage vignette for *Robinson Crusoe* (1866). In a similar medium, the naturally dense and sketchy style of Millais's mature illustrations lent itself nicely to his published etchings. He was a member of both the Etching Club and Junior Etching Club; for their publications he produced, among others, *The Young Mother* (1856), *Happy Springtime* (1860), *Summer Indolence* (1861), *Going to the Park* (1872), and *The Baby-House* (1872). All of these feature mothers (or nannies) and children; the earliest three display a Pre-Raphaelite spirit in the poses and figure drawing, although none show a line treatment as highly detailed as in the etchings of Hunt. In *The Bridge of Sighs* (published in *Passages from the Poems of Thomas Hood*, 1858), a destitute woman is about to throw herself (and her bundled child) into the river; it is a study in rich blacks, expertly contrasted with the frightened figure's illuminated face. Certainly, of all the Pre-Raphaelites, Millais had the best understanding of the etching medium.

It was in periodical and book illustration, drawn for the wood-block, that Millais gained his reputation as perhaps the greatest mid-Victorian illustrator. He began with many Pre-

vignettes are uniquely Pre-Raphaelite, but hardly inspired or elaborate. Even for these relatively uncomplicated compositions Millais was characteristically finicky in his instructions to the Dalziels on the proofs. For "The Talking Oak"—the image of a bride dressing with three other women—his comments are extensive: "Simplify the lines of the eyelids, they look gummy. . . . This head is too blotchy about the mouth. . . . You have cut one line into two with the little girl's shoe and face. . . . Compare this with another proof—wherever you see white paint, make the lines more delicate. . . . Make the lines in the middle of the waist of the bride more delicate" (Museum of Fine Arts, Boston, Hartley Collection).

The alternate-style Tennyson works, which include "Mariana," "The Death of the Old Year," "The Lord of Burleigh," and two illustrations each for "The Day-Dream" and "A Dream of Fair Women," are clearly superior—more complete compositions filled with decorative and realistic detail. With "The Dream" and "Love," published the same year, Millais made—temporarily—his decision in regard to style direction, choosing the more fully designed method for these two evocative Pre-Raphaelite cuts in *The Poets of the Nineteenth Century*. This approach reaches perfection in a great drawing for *Lays of the Holy Land* (1858), "The Finding of Moses," and two pieces for *The Home Affections by the Poets* (1858). In the latter volume's "The Border Widow" with its unbelievably convoluted

Raphaelite–style works but, as in his paintings, he soon adjusted his approach to be more facile and less challenging. Certainly, without those voluminous women's dresses of the era, Millais would have lost much of his composition and would have had to invest a greater effort in covering his block. However, in the case of his illustrations, with their subjects predetermined, the quality always remained high, their sentimentality was in check, and their psychological statements were appropriate to the material. Whether Pre-Raphaelite or not, these fine black-and-white works are regarded as uniformly quite successful.

With the Moxon *Tennyson* of 1857, Millais joined his Pre-Raphaelite brothers in affirming a new style of illustration. Actually, he affirmed two new styles, for as quirky as the poses are in all eighteen of his drawings, some are done as bare-bones vignettes in his slightly modeled, even outline, method of the earlier pen drawings, and others in the highly detailed, tonally sophisticated manner that honors the German woodcut artists in stark contrasts of light and shade and linear control. The

body positions, a woman mourns her dead lover—a knight, slain by enemies—and must bury him (and "love no other"); "There's Nae Luck About the House," a simple poem about a wife's love for her husband, inspired Millais to create a personal and poetic Pre-Raphaelite visual drama.

Although much of Millais's late illustrations were to be cut brilliantly by Swain, these earliest works were by the Dalziels, who valued Millais's art so much that they commissioned, just before the appearance of the above books, a series of drawings on the Parables of Jesus. The book finally stopped at twenty drawings, published as *The Parables of Our Lord and Saviour Jesus Christ* in 1864. As the work progressed, the Dalziels obviously realized they had a rare treasure: they showed proofs of some of the engravings at the Royal Academy (1862) and sold the rights to print twelve of them to *Good Words* (1863). (Millais also employed the designs for many watercolor paintings during this time.) Millais did not join his fellow illustrators in contributing to *Dalziels' Bible Gallery*, though his biblical works were the only ones that were published at the time they were created. Both Dalziel books were finally combined in *Art Pictures from the Old Testament and Our Lord's Parables* in 1905.

In their memoir, the Dalziels recall the genesis and progress of Millais's *Parables*. After the firm suggested the project, Millais wrote back on August 13, 1857: "I would set about them immediately if you will send me some blocks. . . . There is so much labour in these drawings that I trust you will give me my own time, otherwise I could not undertake the commission. I should make it a labour of love

like yourselves." Millais's time in finishing each drawing grew longer as the work went on; he had promised thirty but managed only twenty. (For the *Bible Gallery*, he offered an

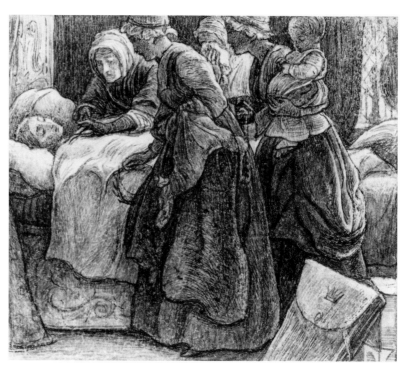

The Lord of Burleigh *(ink and wash drawing, 3 1/8 x 3 3/8; for the illustration in* Poems by Alfred Tennyson, *1857; courtesy Ashmolean Museum, Oxford, Department of Western Art)*

"Adam and Eve in the Garden of Eden" but never did it.) In the course of the work, Millais clearly understood that these were no ordinary illustrations, writing to the engravers on January 14, 1859, "Nothing can be more exquisitely rendered than the 'Importunate Widow'"—that is, "The Unjust Judge"—and in a later (undated) letter, "I can do ordinary illustrations as quickly as most men, but these designs can scarcely be regarded in the same light—each Parable I illustrate perhaps a dozen times before I fix and the 'Hidden Treasures' I have altered on the wood at least six times" (*Brothers Dalziel*, pp. 94, 97, 98, 100, 102, 104).

At the Hartley Collection in Boston (Museum of Fine Arts), there is significant material relating to the *Parables*. The studies for "The Pharisee and the Publican" show Millais's working method: four poses on one sheet in sepia-ink sketches—as if he's trying out bends of legs and shading; he does the same with "The Foolish Virgins," with a nice pencil sketch on paper, very quick, working with poses. There is also an original drawing on an uncut wood-block (as photography came to be used to transfer drawings to blocks, the Dalziels made use of the process to preserve the valuable original artworks, even ones already drawn on wood). For "The Unmerciful Servant" Millais worked in pencil, ink, and wash; the background is indicated in light pencil lines; the figures have been heightened with more definite ink lines, all very exact and well planned; it appears that "Chinese" white was used to paint out white areas afterward, and paint out pencil marks. At the bottom of the proof for this engraving, Millais, showing his dedication to the project, writes: "I am working at *Parables* at this moment. Could you not find a day to touch this one & others under my superintendence?" And on the burnished proof of "The Importunate Friend" he has drawn pictures of an eye and hand and even a thumbnail—"take out thumbnail"—and whitened many edge areas, like those of the dog, hat, scarf, and cloak.

Millais's *Parables* was such an event, such a tour de force, that the *Art Journal* not only devoted a lengthy and gushing review to the

The Crown of Love *(wood-engraving, Swain; 5 x 3;* Once a Week, *vol. 2, 1860, p. 10)*

book in 1864, but followed it a few issues later with another essay accompanied by two *Parables* cuts. Millais, commented the review's writer, "brings to his work an earnest, thoughtful, and reverential mind, a truly poetical imagination, and a thorough knowledge of the technicalities of Art. . . . There is not one of these subjects which does not stand out in striking and noble contrast with the prettiness and sentimentalism that too frequently characterises the works purporting to express sacred Art, and which are so often mistaken for it. . . . The engravers seem to have fully entered into the spirit and feelings of the artist, and to have worked with him" (vol. 26 [new ser., vol. 3], 1864, p. 59).

After these masterpieces, the remainder of Millais's work for periodicals was devoted to novels of contemporary society, in which the artist excelled, albeit in an altered style. He had spent many years turning out fine work for *Once a Week* (nearly seventy illustrations from 1859 through 1868), the early ones like "Magenta," "On the Water," and "The Crown of Love" (which inspired a painting of 1875) adhering somewhat to Pre-Raphaelitism. He was Anthony Trollope's illustrator for the serialized novels (and subsequently their book versions) in the *Cornhill Magazine* (*Framley Parsonage* and *The Small House at Allington*) and in *St. Paul's Magazine* (*Phineas Finn*), and for

The Young Mother *(etching, Millais, 1856; 6 x 5 3/4;* Etchings for the Art Union of London, *1857)*

Chapman and Hall's *Orley Farm* (2 vols., 1862) and *Rachel Ray* (1864). Millais might not have been a Pre-Raphaelite in these later illustrations, but the figures, supported often by very sketchy backgrounds, remain full of character and true to life; and he still dogged his engravers at every turn, noting to the Dalziels on the corrected proof for "Peregrine's Eloquence," the frontispiece to volume two of *Orley Farm*: "Chimney piece slab all wrong—

cut away. . . . Light on boot at top. . . . Cut away the two other coils of hair [on the woman]" (Museum of Fine Arts, Boston, Hartley Collection). In his autobiography, Trollope writes of his appreciation for his collaborator's work: "I do not think that more conscientious work was ever done by man. . . . In every figure that he drew it was his object to promote the views of the writer whose work he had undertaken to illustrate, and he never spared himself any pains in studying the work so as to enable him to do so" (quoted in *Life and Letters of Sir John Everett Millais*, vol. 1, pp. 282–83).

Strahan, the publisher of *Good Words*, felt Millais was such a star that he deserved a book devoted solely to his wood-engraved art. *Millais's Illustrations* of 1866 includes eighty splendid pieces, each surrounded by the white of a generous page; the book contains most of his important engravings (regardless of original publisher) up to that time. The *Art Journal* review of this book (vol. 28 [new ser., vol. 5], 1866, p. 64) once again gave tribute to this quintessential Victorian illustrator:

"There is a wonderful truth and power of expression in all he does, united with a purpose and a meaning such as are conveyed by language once vigorous and eloquent."

Bookplate for Christopher Sykes, M.P. *(wood-engraving proof, Dalziels, 1863; 2 7/8 x 1 7/8)*

Catalogue

PERIODICALS
Many of Millais's periodical illustrations
were reprinted in three major book collec-
tions, indicated in this section as follows:
Δ *Millais's [Collected] Illustrations*
Ω *The Cornhill Gallery*
∞ *Twenty-nine Illustrations by John
Everett Millais Designed for the Cornhill
Magazine*

Argosy
Vol. 2, 1866:
¶ **The Sighing of the Shell** (p. 64,
Dalziels)

Churchman's Family Magazine
Vol. 1, 1863:
¶ **"The New Curate,"** 2 illustrations
(pp. 15, 221; Swain; 1 reprinted in *Pictures
of Society*)

Cornhill Magazine
Vol. 1, 1860:
¶ **Unspoken Dialogue** (p. 194,
Dalziels) Ω ∞
¶ **"Framley Parsonage"** by Anthony
Trollope, 2 illustrations (pp. 449, 691;
Dalziels) Ω ∞
Vol. 2, 1860:
¶ **"Framley Parsonage"** by Anthony
Trollope, 2 illustrations (pp. 129, 462;
Dalziels) Ω ∞
¶ **Last Words** (p. 513, Dalziels) ∞
Vol. 3, 1861:
¶ **"Framley Parsonage"** by Anthony
Trollope, 2 illustrations (pp. 48, 342;
Dalziels) Ω ∞
• 6 **"Framley Parsonage"** illustrations
in vols. 1–3 reprinted in *Framley Parsonage*
¶ **Horace Saltoun** (p. 229, Dalziels;
a.k.a. **Temptation**) Ω ∞
Vol. 5, 1862:
¶ **Irene** (p. 478, Swain) Ω ∞
Vol. 6, 1862:
¶ **The Bishop and the Knight** (p. 100,
Dalziels) Ω ∞
¶ **"The Small House at Allington"** by

In the Churchyard for **"Mistress and Maid"** *(wood-
engraving, Dalziels; 6 x 4 3/8;* **frontispiece** *for* Good
Words, *vol. 3, 1862;* Touches of Nature; Millais's
Illustrations*)*

Magenta *(wood-engraving, Dalziels; 3 1/8 x 3;*
Once a Week, *vol. 1, 1859, p. 10)*

The Grandmother's Apology *(wood-engraving, Dalziels; 4 x 4 7/8;*
Once a Week, *vol. 1, 1859, p. 41;* Millais's Illustrations*)*

On the Water *(wood-engraving, Dalziels; 3 x 5;* Once a Week,
vol. 1, 1859, p. 70; Millais's Illustrations*)*

Anthony Trollope, 4 illustrations (fac. pp.
364,* 552, 663,* 758; Dalziels) Ω
• Plus 4 *pictorial initials* (pp. 364,
552, 663, 789; Dalziels)
Vol. 7, 1863:
¶ **"The Small House at Allington"** by
Anthony Trollope, 6 illustrations (fac. pp.
56,* 214, 349, 469, 657, 756; Dalziels) Ω
• Plus 6 *pictorial initials* (pp. 56, 214,
349, 469, 657, 756; Dalziels)
Vol. 8, 1863:
¶ **"The Small House at Allington"** by
Anthony Trollope, 6 illustrations (fac. pp.
59, 208, 257, 385, 513, 641; Dalziels) Ω
• Plus 6 *pictorial initials* (pp. 59, 208,
257, 385, 513, 641; Dalziels)
Vol. 9, 1864:
¶ **"The Small House at Allington"** by
Anthony Trollope, 2 illustrations (fac. pp.
1, 232; Dalziels) Ω
• Plus 3 *pictorial initials* (pp. 1, 232,
442; Dalziels)
• 18 full-page illustrations in vols. 6–9
reprinted in *The Small House at Allington*
Vol. 10, 1864:
¶ **An Old Song** (p. 434; a.k.a. **Madame
de Monferrato**)
• The full-page illustration faces p. 434;
a *pictorial initial* appears on p. 434

Good Words
Vol. 3, 1862:
¶ **Olaf** (p. 25, Dalziels)
¶ **"Mistress and Maid"** by [Dinah
Mulock Craik], 12 illustrations (*frontispiece:* **In the Churchyard,*** pp. 33, 97,
161 [reprinted as **The Parting** in *Touches
of Nature* and *Routledge's Sunday Album
for Children*], 225, 289, 353, 417 [reprinted
as **Arrested** in *Touches of Nature*], 481,
545, 609, 673; Dalziels) Δ
• Cropped versions of some of the
illustrations from **"Mistress and Maid"**
appear in *Good Cheer* (the Christmas
Number of *Good Words*) for 1867
¶ **Highland Flora** (p. 393, Dalziels)
Vol. 4, 1863:
¶ **"The Parables Read in the Light of
the Present Day"** by Thomas Guthrie,
12 illustrations* (Dalziels): • *Frontispiece:*
The Labourers in the Vineyard • **The
Parable of the Leaven** (p. 1) • **The
Parable of the [Ten] Virgins** (p. 81) Δ • **The
Prodigal Son** (p. 161) • **The Good**

Samaritan (p. 241) • **The Unjust Judge** (p. 313) Δ • **The Pharisee and the Publican** (p. 385; reprinted as **A Contrast** in *Touches of Nature* [full edition only]) • **The Hid Treasure** (p. 461) • **The Pearl of Great Price** (p. 533) • **The Lost Piece of Silver** (p. 605; reprinted in *Touches of Nature* [full edition only]) • **The Sower** (p. 677) • **The Unmerciful Servant** (p. 749)ⁱ
     • Reprinted in *The Parables of Our Lord and Saviour Jesus Christ*, together with 8 additional illustrations; the 20 are reprinted in *Art Pictures from the Old Testament and Our Lord's Parables*
Vol. 5, 1864:
     ¶ **Oh, The Lark Is Singing in the Sky** (p. 65, Swain; reprinted in *Rural England*) Δ
     ¶ **Scene for a Study** (p. 161, Swain)
     ¶ **Polly** (p. 248, Swain; reprinted in *Lilliput Levée*) Δ
     ¶ **The Bridal of Dandelot** (p. 304, Swain) Δ
     ¶ **Prince Philibert** (p. 481, Swain; reprinted in *Lilliput Levée*; revised as an etching for *Voices of the Summer*) Δ
Vol. 19, 1878:
     ¶ **MacLeod of Dare** (p. 651, Swain; reprinted in *MacLeod of Dare*)
Vol. 23, 1882:
     ¶ **Kept in the Dark** (p. 364, Swain; reprinted in *The First Hunt*)

Illustrated London News
Vol. 41, Christmas Number, 1862:
     ¶ **Christmas Story-Telling** (p. 672, Dalziels)

Leisure Hour
Vol. 25, 1876:
     ¶ *Frontispiece:* **The Grandmother** (color wood-engraving, E. Evans; from Millais's original watercolor, based on his illustration **The Grandmother's Apology** in *Once a Week*)

London Society
Vol. 2, 1862:
     ¶ **The Border Witch** (p. 181, Dalziels; a.k.a. **Ah, Me, She Was a Winsome Maid**; reprinted as **I Remember** in *Pictures of Society*)
Vol. 2, Christmas Number, 1862:
     ¶ **The Christmas Wreaths of Rockton** (p. 65, Swain; a.k.a. **"Yes, Lewis," She**

There's Nae Luck About the House (*wood-engraving, Dalziels; 4 7/8 x 3 5/8;* The Home Affections, *1858;* Millais's Illustrations*)*

The Border Widow (*wood-engraving, Dalziels; 3 5/8 x 4 7/8;* The Home Affections, *1858)*

The Finding of Moses (wood-engraving, Dalziels; 5 3/8 x 4 7/8; Lays of the Holy Land, *1858;* Millais's Illustrations)

The Labourers in the Vineyard for "The Parables Read in the Light of the Present Day" *(wood-engraving, Dalziels; 5 1/2 x 4 1/4;* **frontispiece** for Good Words, *vol. 4, 1863;* The Parables of Our Lord and Saviour Jesus Christ*)*

Said, "Quite Satisfied"; reprinted as **A Moment of Suspense** in *Pictures of Society*)
Vol. 6, 1864:
 ¶ *Frontispiece:* **Knightly Worth**
(p. 193, Dalziels)
 ¶ **The Tale of a Chivalrous Life** (p. 247)

Magazine of Art
Vol. 1, 1878:
 ¶ **Two Fair Maidens** (p. 50, Swain; reprinted as **These Twin Girls** in *Sunday Magazine*; reprinted in vol. 20 of the *Magazine of Art*)
Vol. 16, 1892:
 ¶ **Thomas Bewick** (p. 233, R. Taylor; wood-engraved version of autotype illustration from *Game Birds and Shooting Sketches*)
Vol. 20, 1896:
 ¶ **A Reverie** (p. xiv; steel-engraving, C. H. Jeens; reprinted from *Leslie's Musical Annual*)
 ¶ **Two Fair Maidens** (p. viii; reprinted from the *Magazine of Art*)
 • Both illustrations contained in a special section on Millais, pp. i–xvi

Once a Week
Vol. 1, 1859:
 ¶ **Magenta*** (p. 10, Dalziels)
 ¶ **The Grandmother's Apology***
(p. 41, Dalziels; published as **The Grandmother**, a wood-engraved color version, in the *Leisure Hour*) ∆
 ¶ **On the Water*** (p. 70, Dalziels) ∆
 ¶ **La Fille Bien Gardée*** (p. 306, Swain) ∆
 ¶ **The Plague of Elliant** (p. 316, Swain; reprinted in *Ballads and Songs of Brittany*) ∆
 ¶ **Maude Clare** (p. 382, Swain) ∆
 ¶ **A Lost Love** (p. 482, Dalziels)
 ¶ **St. Bartholemew*** (p. 514, Dalziels) ∆
Vol. 2, 1860:
 ¶ **The Crown of Love*** (p. 10, Swain)
 ¶ **A Wife*** (p. 32, Swain)
 ¶ **The Head of Bran** (p. 132, Swain) ∆
 ¶ **Practising** (p. 242, Dalziels)
 ¶ **Musa** (p. 598, Dalziels)
Vol. 3, 1860:
 ¶ **Master Olaf** (p. 63, Swain)
 ¶ **Violet** (p. 140, Swain)
 ¶ **Dark Gordon's Bride** (p. 238, Swain) ∆
 ¶ **The Meeting** (p. 276, Swain) ∆
 ¶ **"The Iceberg"** by A. Stuart Harrison,

2 illustrations (p. 407, reprinted in *The Queen of the Arena and Other Stories*; p. 435; Swain)

¶ **A Head of Hair for Sale** (p. 519, Swain)
Vol. 4, 1861:

¶ **Iphis and Anaxarete** (p. 98, Swain)

¶ **Thorr's Hunt for His Hammer** (p. 126)
Vol. 5, 1861:

¶ **Tannhäuser** (p. 211, Swain)

¶ **Swing Song** (p. 434, Swain; reprinted as **Tommy's Swing** in *Our Little Sunbeam's Picture Book*; reprinted as **Swinging** in *Little Valentine and Other Tales*)
Vol. 6, 1862:

¶ **Schwerting of Saxony** (p. 43, Swain)

¶ **The Ballad of the Thirty** (p. 155, Swain; reprinted as **The Prayer of the Thirty to St. Kado** in *Ballads and Songs of Brittany*) ∆

¶ **The Fair Jacobite** (p. 239, Swain) ∆

¶ **"Sister Anna's Probation"** by Miss [Harriet] Martineau, 5 illustrations (pp. 309∆, 337, 365∆, 393∆, 421; Swain)

¶ **Sir Tristem** (p. 350, Swain)

¶ **The Crusader's Wife** (p. 546, Swain; reprinted in *Ballads and Songs of Brittany*)

¶ **The Chase of the Siren** (p. 630, Swain)

¶ **The Drowning of Kaer-Is** (p. 687, Swain; reprinted in *Ballads and Songs of Brittany*) ∆
Vol. 7, 1862:

¶ **Margaret Wilson** (p. 42, Swain) ∆

¶ **"Anglers of the Dove"** by Miss [Harriet] Martineau, 5 illustrations (pp. 85∆, 113∆, 141∆, 169, 197; Swain)

¶ **Maid Avoraine*** (p. 98, Swain)

¶ **The Mite of Dorcas** (p. 224, Swain) ∆

¶ **The Spirit of the Vanished Island** (p. 546, Swain)

¶ **The Parting of Ulysses** (p. 658, Swain)

¶ **Limerick Bells** (p. 710, Swain) ∆
Vol. 8, 1863:

¶ **Endymion on Latmos** (p. 42, Swain)

¶ **"The Hamdens"** by Miss [Harriet] Martineau, 10 illustrations (pp. 211, 239∆, 267∆, 281, 309, 337, 365, 393∆, 421, 449; Swain; reprinted in *The Hamdens*)
Vol. 9, 1863:

¶ **"Son Christopher"** by Miss [Harriet] Martineau, 8 illustrations (pp. 491, 519, 547, 575∆, 603, 631, 659, 687; Swain)

¶ **Hacho the Dane** (p. 504, Swain)
New ser. [ser. 3], vol. 1, 1868:

¶ **Death Dealing Arrows** (p. 79, Swain?)

The Parable of the Leaven for *"The Parables Read in the Light of the Present Day"* (wood-engraving, Dalziels; 5 1/2 x 4 1/4; Good Words, *vol. 4, 1863, p. 1;* The Parables of Our Lord and Saviour Jesus Christ)

The Parable of the [Ten] Virgins for *"The Parables Read in the Light of the Present Day"* (wood-engraving, Dalziels; 5 1/2 x 4 1/4; Good Words, *vol. 4, 1863, p. 81;* The Parables of Our Lord and Saviour Jesus Christ; Millais's Illustrations)

The Prodigal Son for *"The Parables Read in the Light of the Present Day"* (wood-engraving, Dalziels; 5 1/2 x 4 1/4; Good Words, *vol. 4, 1863, p. 161;* The Parables of Our Lord and Saviour Jesus Christ)

The Good Samaritan for *"The Parables Read in the Light of the Present Day"* (wood-engraving, Dalziels; 5 1/2 x 4 1/4; Good Words, *vol. 4, 1863, p. 241;* The Parables of Our Lord and Saviour Jesus Christ)

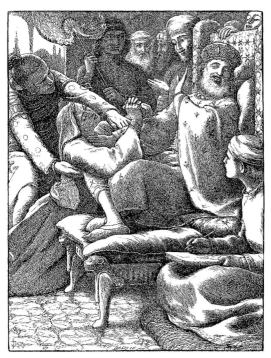

The Unjust Judge for *"The Parables Read in the Light of the Present Day"* (wood-engraving, Dalziels; 5 1/2 x 4 1/4; Good Words, *vol. 4, 1863, p. 313;* The Parables of Our Lord and Saviour Jesus Christ; Millais's Illustrations)

New ser. [ser. 3], vol. 2, Christmas Number, 1868:
¶ **Taking His Ease** (p. 64, Swain)

Punch
Vol. 44, 1863:
¶ **"It Is the Chapeau Blanc, the White Witness"** (p. 115, Swain; a.k.a. **Mokeanna**; reprinted in *Mokeanna!*)

Quarto
Vol. 2, 1896:
¶ **The Foolish Virgins** (p. 8; reprinted from *The Parables of Our Lord*)

St. Paul's Magazine
Vol. 1, 1867–68:
¶ **"Phineas Finn"** by Anthony Trollope, 6 illustrations (***frontispiece***, pp. 247, 375, 486, 637, 750; Swain)
Vol. 2, 1868:
¶ **"Phineas Finn,"** 6 illustrations (pp. 113, 253, 376, 510, 638, 747; Swain)
Vol. 3, 1868–69:
¶ **"Phineas Finn,"** 6 illustrations

The Pharisee and the Publican for *"The Parables Read in the Light of the Present Day"* (wood-engraving, Dalziels; 5 1/2 x 4 1/4; Good Words, *vol. 4, 1863, p. 385;* The Parables of Our Lord and Saviour Jesus Christ; Touches of Nature)

(pp. 128, 233, 381, 503, 636, 737; Swain)
Vol. 4, 1869:
 ¶ **"Phineas Finn,"** 2 illustrations (**frontispiece**, p. 256; Swain)
 • 20 illustrations in vols. 1–4 reprinted in *Phineas Finn, the Irish Member*; 3 illustrations reprinted for **"The Hall"** in *Rural England*

Sunday Magazine
New ser., vol. 12, 1883:
 ¶ **These Twin Girls** (p. 756; **Two Fair Maidens** reprinted, without signatures of Millais or Swain, from the *Magazine of Art*)

§ *Day of Rest* (c. 1874) is said to contain an enlarged version of **The Lost Piece of Silver** (originally designed for **"The Parables"** in *Good Words*); see Forrest Reid's *Illustrators of the Sixties*, 1928, p. 75

BOOKS

A Breath from the Veldt (John Guille Millais; Sotheran, 1895)
 ¶ *Frontispiece:* **The Last Trek**
 • Photogravure reproduction of black-and-white watercolor; John Everett Millais did the three foreground figures; the author (his son) created the frieze of zebras in the background

Dalziels' Illustrated Arabian Nights' Entertainments (H. W. Dulcken, ed.; Ward and Lock, 2 vols., 1865)
 ¶ **Zobeide Discovers the Young Man Reciting the Koran** (Dalziels)
 ¶ **Armire and the Lady** (Dalziels)
 • Originally issued in parts, 1864–65; also published in 1 vol., 1865 (Ward, Lock, and Tyler)

Egmont (Johann Wolfgang von Goethe; A. D. Coleridge, ed.; Chapman and Hall, 1868)
 ¶ *Frontispiece:* **Egmont Asleep in Prison** (Swain)

English Art in 1884 (Henry Blackburn; New York: Appleton, 1885)
 ¶ **An Idyll, 1745** (drawing by the artist [?] based on his painting; photo-engraving)
 ¶ **Portrait of the Marquis of Lorne**

The Hid Treasure for **"The Parables Read in the Light of the Present Day"** (*wood-engraving, Dalziels; 5 1/2 x 4 1/4; Good Words, vol. 4, 1863, p. 461; The Parables of Our Lord and Saviour Jesus Christ*)

The Pearl of Great Price for **"The Parables Read in the Light of the Present Day"** (*wood-engraving, Dalziels; 5 1/2 x 4 1/4; Good Words, vol. 4, 1863, p. 533; The Parables of Our Lord and Saviour Jesus Christ*)

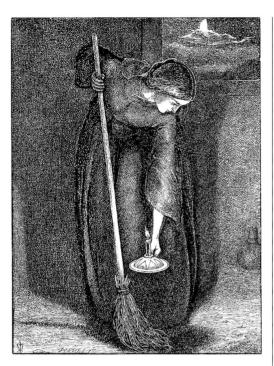

The Lost Piece of Silver *for* ***"The Parables Read in the Light of the Present Day"*** *(wood-engraving, Dalziels; 5 1/2 x 4 1/4; Good Words, vol. 4, 1863, p. 605; The Parables of Our Lord and Saviour Jesus Christ; Touches of Nature)*

Right: ***The Sower*** *for* ***"The Parables Read in the Light of the Present Day"*** *(wood-engraving, Dalziels; 5 1/2 x 4 1/4; Good Words, vol. 4, 1863, p. 677; The Parables of Our Lord and Saviour Jesus Christ)*

Left: ***The Unmerciful Servant*** *for* ***"The Parables Read in the Light of the Present Day"*** *(wood-engraving, Dalziels; 5 1/2 x 4 1/4; Good Words, vol. 4, 1863, p. 749)*

(drawing by the artist based on his painting; photo-engraving)

Game Birds and Shooting Sketches (John Guille Millais; Sotheran, 1892)
¶ ***Frontispiece:*** **Thomas Bewick** (autotype)
• Image wood-engraved by R. Taylor for the *Magazine of Art*, 1892

The Home Affections [Pourtrayed] by the Poets (Charles Mackay, ed.; Routledge, 1858)
¶ **There's Nae Luck About the House*** (Dalziels; reprinted as **The Father's Departure** in *Routledge's Album for Children* and in *Little Lily's Picture Book*) ∆
¶ **The Border Widow*** (Dalziels)
• Reissued by Routledge in 1866

Irish Melodies (Thomas Moore; Longmans, Brown, Green, and Longmans, 1856)
¶ **When I First Met Thee*** (steel-engraving, T. O. Barlow)

John Halifax, Gentleman ([Dinah Mulock Craik]; Hurst and Blackett, [1861])
¶ ***Frontispiece:*** **Ursula March** (steel-engraving)

Lays of the Holy Land (Nisbet, 1858)
¶ **The Finding of Moses*** (Dalziels) Δ
• Reissued in 1871

Leslie's Musical Annual (Henry Leslie; Cassell, 1870)
¶ **A Reverie** (steel-engraving, C. H. Jeens; reprinted in the *Magazine of Art*)
¶ **A Line Drawing**

The Tares *(wood-engraving, Dalziels; 5 1/2 x 4 1/4; The Parables of Our Lord and Saviour Jesus Christ, 1864)*

Left: **The Wicked Husbandman** *(wood-engraving, Dalziels; 5 1/2 x 4 1/4; The Parables of Our Lord and Saviour Jesus Christ, 1864)*

Bottom: **The Foolish Virgins** *(wood-engraving, Dalziels; 5 1/2 x 4 1/4; The Parables of Our Lord and Saviour Jesus Christ, 1864)*

Leslie's Songs for Little Folks (Henry Leslie; Cassell, [1883])
¶ *Frontispiece:* **St. Agnes' Eve***
• Plus 7 illustrations reprinted from *Little Songs for Me to Sing*

Les Misèrables (Victor Hugo; Hurst and Blackett, [1864])
¶ *Frontispiece:* **Cosette** (steel-engraving)

Little Songs for Me to Sing (Henry Leslie; Cassell, Petter, and Galpin, [1865])
¶ *Frontispiece*
¶ **Morning and Evening Hymns**
¶ **God's Work**
¶ **Mary's Little Lamb**
¶ **The Sweet Story of Old**

The Importunate Friend (wood-engraving, Dalziels; 5 1/2 x 4 1/4; The Parables of Our Lord and Saviour Jesus Christ, 1864)

The Marriage Feast (wood-engraving, Dalziels; 5 1/2 x 4 1/4; The Parables of Our Lord and Saviour Jesus Christ, 1864)

¶ **Twinkle, Twinkle Little Star**
¶ **Little Brother Charlie**
• Eng. Swain
• Reprinted in *Leslie's Songs for Little Folks*

[Locker] *Selections from the Works of Frederick Locker* (Moxon, 1865)
    ¶ *Frontispiece:* **Portrait of Frederick Locker** (etching, Millais)

Lost and Saved (Mrs. Norton; Hurst and Blackett, [1863])
    ¶ *Frontispiece* (steel-engraving, J. Saddler)

The Memoirs of Barry Lyndon, Esq. (William Makepeace Thackeray; Smith, Elder, 1879; vol. 19 [of 24] of *The Works of William Makepeace Thackeray*)
    ¶ 4 illustrations (Swain)

Millais's [Collected] Illustrations (Strahan, 1866)
    ¶ *Titlepage illustration* (Swain)
    ¶ **Pick-a-pack** (Swain; also published in 1866 in *Studies for Stories from Girls' Lives*)
    ¶ **Watching** (Swain)
    • Plus 77 others reprinted from *Once a Week* Δ and *Good Words* Δ

Mr. Wray's Cash-box (Wilkie Collins; Bentley, 1852)
    ¶ *Frontispiece:* **Annie Wray Ties Martin Blunt's New Cravat** (etching, Millais)

Mistress and Maid ([Dinah Mulock Craik]; Hurst and Blackett, 1863)
    ¶ *Frontispiece** (steel-engraving, J. Saddler)

The Music Master: A Love Story, and Two Series of Day and Night Songs (William Allingham; Routledge, 1855)
    ¶ **The Fireside Story** (Dalziels)

No Name (Wilkie Collins; Low, 1864)
    ¶ *Frontispiece:* **One Half-Hour*** (steel-engraving, J. Saddler)

Nothing New ([Dinah Mulock Craik]; Hurst and Blackett, 1861)
    ¶ *Frontispiece:* **Jean Douglas** (steel-engraving, J. Saddler)

An Old Story (Virtue, Spalding, [1875])
    ¶ *Frontispiece:* **Watching and Waiting** (J. D. Cooper)

Orley Farm (Anthony Trollope; Chapman and Hall, 2 vols., 1862)
    ¶ 39 illustrations (19 in vol. 1; 20 in vol. 2; Dalziels)
    • Also issued in 20 monthly parts, March 1861–October 1862
    • The following titles are reprinted in *Millais's Illustrations* ∆:
    Vol. 1: • *Frontispiece:* **Orley Farm • There Was Sorrow in Her Heart • Van Brauhr's Dream • Christmas at Noningsby—Morning • Christmas at Noningsby—Evening • Footsteps in the Corridor • Lady Staveley**
    Vol. 2: • **John Kenneby • Guilty • Lady Mason After Her Confession • Never Is a Very Long Word • Lady Mason Before the Magistrates • No Surrender • And How Are They All at Noningsby? • Farewell! • Farewell / Sir Peregrine Orme**

Papers for Thoughtful Girls (Sarah Tytler [Henrietta Keddie]; Strahan, 3d ed., 1862)
    ¶ *Frontispiece:* **Ciss Berry's Arrival** ∆
    ¶ **Our Sister Grizel** ∆
    ¶ **Herr Willy Koenig** ∆
    ¶ **Dame Dorothy** ∆
    • Eng. Dalziels

The Parables of Our Lord and Saviour Jesus Christ (Routledge, Warne, and Routledge, 1864)
    ¶ **The Tares**
    ¶ **The Wicked Husbandman**
    ¶ **The Foolish Virgins** (reprinted in the *Quarto*)
    ¶ **The Importunate Friend**
    ¶ **The Marriage Feast**
    ¶ **The Lost Sheep**
    ¶ **The Rich Man and Lazarus**
    ¶ **The Good Shepherd**
    • Eng. Dalziels
    • Plus 12 others reprinted from *Good Words*; of these, **The Pharisee and the Publican** is reprinted as **A Contrast** and **The Lost Piece of Silver** as **The Lost Piece of Money** in *Touches of Nature* [full edition only]
    • Reissued by the S.P.C.K. in 1882
    • 20 illustrations reprinted, as mounted

The Lost Sheep (*wood-engraving, Dalziels; 5 1/2 x 4 1/4;* The Parables of Our Lord and Saviour Jesus Christ, *1864*)

The Rich Man and Lazarus (*wood-engraving, Dalziels; 5 1/2 x 4 1/4;* The Parables of Our Lord and Saviour Jesus Christ, *1864*)

The Good Shepherd *(wood-engraving, Dalziels; 5 1/2 x 4 1/4; The Parables of Our Lord and Saviour Jesus Christ, 1864)*

The Dream *(wood-engraving, Dalziels; 5 x 3 5/8; The Poets of the Nineteenth Century, 1857; Millais's Illustrations)*

india-paper proofs from original wood-blocks printed by the Dalziels in 1864, in *Twenty India Paper Proofs of the Drawings of Sir John Everett Millais, Bart., P.R.A., to the Parables of Our Lord* (Camden / Charles Dalziel, 1902; large-paper limited edition, with facsimile drawings and letters relating to the original project)

• 20 illustrations reprinted in *Art Pictures from the Old Testament and Our Lord's Parables* (Dalton, c. 1905)

Paul Faber, Surgeon (George MacDonald; Chatto and Windus, new ed., 1883)
¶ ***Frontispiece*** (Swain)

The Pleasures of Hope (Rev. John Anderson; Hall, Virtue, [1856])
¶ ***Frontispiece*** (T. Williams)

The Poets of the Nineteenth Century (Rev. Robert Aris Willmott, ed.; Routledge, 1857)
¶ **The Dream*** (Dalziels) Δ: as **Both Were Young and One Was Beautiful**
¶ **Love*** (Dalziels) Δ

Puck on Pegasus (H. Cholmondeley-Pennell; Hotten, 6th ed., rev. and enl., 1869)
¶ **The Fire Brigade** (Swain; a.k.a. **Fire!**)

Punch's Almanack for 1865 (Bradbury and Evans, 1865)
¶ **Mr. Vandyke Brown** (Swain; a.k.a. **Children in the Studio**)

Rachel Ray (Anthony Trollope; Chapman and Hall, 7th ed., 1864)
¶ ***Frontispiece*** (steel-engraving)

Robinson Crusoe (Daniel Defoe; Macmillan Golden Treasury Series, 1866)
¶ ***Titlepage illustration*** (steel-engraving)

St. Olaves (Eliza Tabor; Hurst and Blackett, [1865])
¶ ***Frontispiece:*** **Alice** (steel-engraving, J. Saddler)

Studies for Stories from Girls' Lives ([Jean Ingelow]; Strahan, 1866)
¶ **The Cumberers** (Swain)
¶ **The Stolen Treasure** (Swain; a.k.a. **The Merry Little Face Peeped Out**) Δ: as **Pick-a-pack**

[Tennyson] *Poems by Alfred Tennyson* (Moxon, 1857)

¶ **Mariana*** (Dalziels; reprinted in *Gems from Tennyson*) ∆: as **"I Am Aweary, Aweary!"**

¶ **"The Miller's Daughter,"** 2 illustrations* (T. Williams; J. Thompson) ∆: [#1] as **"Yet Fill My Glass; Give Me One Kiss";** [#2] as **The Miller's Daughter**

¶ **The Sisters*** (Dalziels) ∆: as **"The Wind Is Blowing in Turret and Tree"**

¶ **"A Dream of Fair Women,"** 2 illustrations* (W. J. Linton; Dalziels) ∆: [#1] as **Cleopatra**; [#2] as **"Drew Forth the Poison with Her Balmy Breath"**

¶ **The Death of the Old Year*** (Dalziels) ∆: as **"Toll Ye the Church Bell"**

¶ **"Dora,"** 2 illustrations* (T. Williams; J. Thompson [reprinted in *Gems from Tennyson*])

¶ **"The Talking Oak,"** 2 illustrations* (J. Thompson; Dalziels)

¶ **"Locksley Hall,"** 2 illustrations* (J. Thompson; Dalziels) ∆: [#1] as **Many an Evening by the Waters**; [#2] as **"Preaching Down a Daughter's Heart"**

¶ **St. Agnes' Eve*** (Dalziels; reprinted in *Gems from Tennyson*) ∆

¶ **"The Day-Dream,"** 2 illustrations* (W. J. Linton; C. T. Thompson [reprinted in *Gems from Tennyson*]) ∆: [#1] as **The Sleeping Palace**; [#2] as **The Revival**

¶ **Edward Gray*** (J. Thompson) ∆: as **"Bitterly Weeping I Turned Away"**

¶ **The Lord of Burleigh*** (Dalziels) ∆: as **"Bring the Dress and Put It on Her"**

The Valley of a Hundred Fires (Julia [De Winton] Stretton; Hurst and Blackett, 1861)

¶ ***Frontispiece: Mrs. Leslie** (steel-engraving, J. Saddler)

Wordsworth's Poems for the Young (Strahan, 1863)

¶ ***Titlepage illustration** (Dalziels; reprinted in *Lilliput Levée*)

• Reproduced in color on the front cover for the 1866 reissue

• Also reprinted (as **The Picture-Book**) in the *Infant's Magazine*, no. 23, 1867 (p. 175)

§ *The Industrial Arts of the Nineteenth Century* (Matthew Digby Wyatt; Day, 2 vols., 1851 and 1853; also issued in 40 parts) in

Top: ***Mariana*** *(wood-engraving, Dalziels; 3 5/8 x 3 1/8;* Poems by Alfred Tennyson, *1857;* Millais's Illustrations*)*

Middle left: ***The Miller's Daughter** [#1] (wood-engraving, T. Williams; 3 3/4 x 3 1/4;* Poems by Alfred Tennyson, *1857;* Millais's Illustrations*)*

Middle right: ***The Miller's Daughter** [#2] (wood-engraving, J. Thompson; 3 3/4 x 3 1/4;* Poems by Alfred Tennyson, *1857;* Millais's Illustrations*)*

Bottom: ***The Sisters** (wood-engraving, Dalziels; 3 5/8 x 2 7/8;* Poems by Alfred Tennyson, *1857;* Millais's Illustrations*)*

A Dream of Fair Women *[#1] (wood-engraving, W. J. Linton; 3 3/4 x 3 1/4;* Poems by Alfred Tennyson, *1857;* Millais's Illustrations*)*

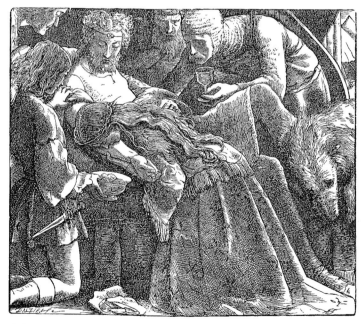

A Dream of Fair Women *[#2] (wood-engraving, Dalziels; 3 1/4 x 3 3/4;* Poems by Alfred Tennyson, *1857;* Millais's Illustrations*)*

vol. 1, 1851, lists Millais as a contributor (chromolithographs, F. Bedford)

§ Millais produced a ***frontispiece illustration*** (Swain) for *Wace, Ses Oeuvres, Sa Partie* (by John Sullivan; after 1865; see William Fredeman's *Pre-Raphaelitism: A Bibliocritical Study*, 1965, p. 293); proof: British Museum, London, Robin de Beaumont Collection

§ For *Maggie Band* (Low, 1862) Millais supposedly did two drawings (see *Life and Letters of Sir John Everett Millais*, vol. 2, p. 493)

BOOKS CONTAINING REPRINTS

Ballads and Songs of Brittany (Hersart de la Villemarqué; Tom Taylor, trans.; Macmillan, 1865)
    ¶ **The Plague of Elliant**
    ¶ **The Drowning of Kaer-Is**
    ¶ **The Prayer of the Thirty to St. Kado**
(**The Ballad of the Thirty** in *Once a Week*)
    ¶ **The Crusader's Wife**
    • Reprinted from *Once a Week*

The Cornhill Gallery (Smith, Elder, 1864)
    ¶ 28 illustrations (reprinted from the *Cornhill Magazine*, as indicated Ω)

The First Hunt (W. J. Woodbury; Boston: Lothrap, n.d.)
    ¶ 1 illustration (**Kept in the Dark** reprinted from *Good Words*)

Framley Parsonage (Anthony Trollope; Smith, Elder, 3 vols., 1861)
    ¶ 6 illustrations (reprinted from the *Cornhill Magazine*) Ω

Gems from Tennyson (Boston: Ticknor and Fields, 1866)
    ¶ **The Day-Dream** [#2]
    ¶ **Mariana**
    ¶ **Dora**
    ¶ **St. Agnes** (a.k.a. **St. Agnes' Eve**)
    • Reprinted from *Poems by Alfred Tennyson*

The Hamdens (Miss [Harriet] Martineau; Routledge, 1880)

¶ 10 illustrations (reprinted from *Once a Week*)

Holiday Album for Children (Henry Frith; Routledge, 1877)
    ¶ Reprinted illustration[s]
    • Also published in 2 parts as *Routledge's Holiday Album for Boys* and *Routledge's Holiday Album for Girls*

Leslie's Songs for Little Folks (Henry Leslie; Cassell, [1883])
    ¶ *Frontispiece* (of *Little Songs for Me to Sing*)
        ¶ **Morning and Evening Hymns**
        ¶ **God's Work**
        ¶ **Mary's Little Lamb**
        ¶ **The Sweet Story of Old**
        ¶ **Twinkle, Twinkle Little Star**
        ¶ **Little Brother Charlie**
    • Reprinted from *Little Songs for Me to Sing*
        ¶ Plus 1 original illustration

Life and Phantasy (William Allingham; Reeves and Turner, 1889)
    ¶ *Frontispiece* (**The Fireside Story** reprinted from *The Music Master*)

Lilliput Legends ([William Brighty Rands]; Strahan, 1872)
    ¶ *Halftitle vignette* (reprinted from *Wordsworth's Poems for the Young* and *Lilliput Levée*)

Lilliput Levée ([William Brighty Rands]; Strahan, [1864])
    ¶ *Halftitle vignette* (reprinted from *Wordsworth's Poems for the Young*)
    ¶ **Prince Philibert** (revised as an etching for *Voices of the Summer*)
        ¶ **Polly**
        • Reprinted from *Good Words*
        • Reissued by Strahan in 1867

Little Lily's Picture Book (Routledge, [1872])
    ¶ **The Father's Departure** (reprinted from *Routledge's Album for Children* and **There's Nae Luck About the House** reprinted from *The Home Affections*)

Little Valentine and Other Tales (Henry Frith; Routledge, 1878)
    ¶ **Swinging** (**Swing Song** reprinted

The Death of the Old Year *(wood-engraving, Dalziels; 3 3/4 x 3 1/4; Poems by Alfred Tennyson, 1857; Millais's Illustrations)*

Dora *[#1] (wood-engraving, T. Williams; 3 3/4 x 3 1/4; Poems by Alfred Tennyson, 1857)*

Dora *[#2] (wood-engraving, J. Thompson; 3 3/4 x 3 1/4; Poems by Alfred Tennyson, 1857)*

Top: ***The Talking Oak** [#1] (wood-engraving, J. Thompson; 3 1/4 x 3 3/4;* Poems by Alfred Tennyson, *1857)*

Left: ***The Talking Oak** [#2] (wood-engraving, Dalziels; 3 3/4 x 3 1/4;* Poems by Alfred Tennyson, *1857)*

***Locksley Hall** [#1] (wood-engraving, J. Thompson; 3 3/4 x 3 1/4;* Poems by Alfred Tennyson, *1857;* Millais's Illustrations*)*

***Locksley Hall** [#2] (wood-engraving, Dalziels; 3 3/4 x 3 1/4;* Poems by Alfred Tennyson, *1857;* Millais's Illustrations*)*

from *Once a Week* and **Tommy's Swing** reprinted from *Our Little Sunbeam's Picture Book*)

MacLeod of Dare (William Black; Macmillan, 1879)
 ¶ **MacLeod of Dare** (reprinted from *Good Words*)

Millais's [Collected] Illustrations (Strahan, 1866)
 ¶ 77 illustrations (reprinted from sources indicated △)
 • Plus 3 original illustrations
 • Reissued by Cassell, Petter, and Galpin in 1870, with a new titlepage

Mokeanna! (F. C. Burnand; Bradbury, Agnew, 1873)
 ¶ **Mokeanna** (reprinted from *Punch*; a.k.a. **"It Is the Chapeau Blanc, the White Witness"**)

Our Little Sunbeam's Picture Book (Mrs. Semple Garrett; Routledge, 1877)
 ¶ **Tommy's Swing** (**Swing Song** reprinted from *Once a Week* and reprinted in *Little Valentine and Other Tales*)
 ¶ **In the Fields** (reprint?)

The Parables of Our Lord and Saviour Jesus Christ (Routledge, Warne, and Routledge, 1864)
 ¶ **Labourers in the Vineyard**
 ¶ **The Leaven**
 ¶ **The Ten Virgins**
 ¶ **The Prodigal Son**
 ¶ **The Good Samaritan**
 ¶ **The Unjust Judge**
 ¶ **The Pharisee and the Publican** (reprinted as **A Contrast** in *Touches of Nature* [full edition only])
 ¶ **The Hidden Treasure**
 ¶ **The Pearl of Great Price**
 ¶ **The Lost Piece of Silver** (reprinted as **The Lost Piece of Money** in *Touches of Nature* [full edition only])
 ¶ **The Sower**
 ¶ **The Unmerciful Servant**
 • Reprinted from *Good Words*
 • Plus 8 original illustrations

Phineas Finn, the Irish Member (Anthony Trollope; Virtue, 2 vols., 1869)

¶ 20 illustrations (reprinted from
St. Paul's Magazine)

Pictures of Society (Low, Son, and Marston,
1866)
   ¶ **I Remember (The Border Witch**
reprinted from *London Society*)
   ¶ **Moment of Suspense (The Christmas
Wreaths of Rockton** reprinted from *London
Society*)
   ¶ **A Matter of Moment** (illustration for
"The New Curate" reprinted from
Churchman's Family Magazine)

The Queen of the Arena and Other Stories
(A. Stewart Harrison; Unwin, 1886)
   ¶ **The Iceberg** (reprinted from *Once a
Week*)

Routledge's Album for Children (Mrs.
Charles Heaton, ed.; Routledge, 1871)
   ¶ **The Father's Departure (There's Nae
Luck About the House** reprinted from *The
Home Affections* and reprinted in *Little Lily's
Picture Book*)

Routledge's Sunday Album for Children
([Mrs. Charles Heaton, ed.]; Routledge,
1873)
   ¶ **The Parting** (reprinted from
"Mistress and Maid" in *Good Words* [p. 161]
and *Touches of Nature*; reprinted in *Sunday
Reading for Good Children*, [1873])

Rural England (L. G. Seguin; Strahan, 1867)
   ¶ **"The Hall,"** 3 illustrations (reprinted
from **"Phineas Finn"** in *St. Paul's
Magazine*; reprinted in *Phineas Finn, the
Irish Member*)
   ¶ **Theodora (Oh, the Lark Is Singing in
the Sky** reprinted from *Good Words*)

The Small House at Allington (Anthony
Trollope; Smith, Elder, 2 vols., 1864)
   ¶ 18 illustrations (reprinted from the
Cornhill Magazine) Ω

Sunday Reading for Good Children
(Routledge, [1873])
   ¶ **The Parting** (reprinted from
Routledge's Sunday Album for Children)

A Thousand and One Gems of English Poetry
(Charles Mackay, ed.; Routledge, 1867)

St. Agnes' Eve *(wood-engraving, Dalziels; 3 3/4
x 2 7/8;* Poems by Alfred Tennyson, *1857;*
Millais's Illustrations*)*

The Day-Dream *[#1] (wood-engraving, W. J. Linton; 3 1/4 x 3 3/4;*
Poems by Alfred Tennyson, *1857)*

The Day-Dream *[#2] (wood-engraving, C. T. Thompson; 3 1/4 x 3 3/4; Poems by Alfred Tennyson, 1857; Millais's Illustrations)*

Edward Gray *(wood-engraving, J. Thompson; 3 1/2 x 3 1/4; Poems by Alfred Tennyson, 1857; Millais's Illustrations)*

¶ **Edward Gray** (reprinted from *Poems by Alfred Tennyson*)

Touches of Nature (Strahan, 1867)
¶ **The Parting** (reprinted from **"Mistress and Maid"** [p. 161] in *Good Words*)
¶ **Arrested** (reprinted from **"Mistress and Maid"** [p. 417] in *Good Words*)
¶ **A Contrast** (**The Pharisee and the Publican** reprinted from *Good Words* and *The Parables of Our Lord*)
¶ **The Lost Piece of Money** (**The Lost Piece of Silver** reprinted from *Good Words* and *The Parables of Our Lord*)
• The abbreviated edition with 47 illustrations omits the **Contrast** and **Money** wood-engravings

Twenty-nine Illustrations by John Everett Millais Designed for the Cornhill Magazine (Smith, Elder, 1867)
¶ 29 illustrations (reprinted from the *Cornhill Magazine*, as indicated ∞)

Voices of the Summer (Edinburgh: Grant, 1899)
¶ **Once More Who Would Not Be a Boy?** (etching, C. Smart; reworking of **Prince Philibert** image from *Good Words* and *Lilliput Levée*, with additional background)

§ Paul Goldman (*Victorian Illustration*, pp. 296, 324, 335) notes reprinted designs by Millais in the *Infant's Magazine* (no. 23, 1867), *Dawn to Daylight* (Warne, [1874]), and Byron's *Poetical Works* (Warne, c. 1878; **A Dream** from *The Poets of the Nineteenth Century*). Acknowledgment is also made to *Victorian Illustration* (pp. 321, 343, 353, 359, 363) for the catalogue listings of several scarce Millais titles with original illustrations: *The Pleasures of Home*, *An Old Story*, *Lost and Saved*, and *St. Olaves*, and for *Kept in the Dark* (Anthony Trollope; Chapman and Hall, 1882), whose ***frontispiece*** may reprint the **Kept in the Dark** illustration from *Good Words*, 1882 (see also Fredeman's *Pre-Raphaelitism*, p. 295).

INDIVIDUAL PRINTS

¶ **The Baby-House** (etching, Millais; 5 1/8 x 7; signed with monogram in plate)

• Published in *Etchings for the Art Union of London by the Etching Club* (1872)

¶ *Bookplate* for **Christopher Sykes, M.P.*** (wood-engraving proof, Dalziels, 1863; oval, 2 7/8 x 1 7/8; signed with monogram in block)
  • British Museum, London, Department of Prints and Drawings, Dalziel Collection (vol. 17, 1863, no. 36); et al.

¶ *Bookplate* for the **Millais Family** (etching, Millais; circular, 2 5/8 in. diam.)
  • Published in *The Lineage and Pedigree of the Family of Millais* (J. Bertrand Payne; privately printed, 1865)

¶ **The Bridge of Sighs*** (etching, Millais, 1857; 4 5/8 x 3 5/8; signed with monogram in plate)
  • Published in *Passages from the Poems of Thomas Hood* (Junior Etching Club; Gambart, 1858)

¶ **Design for a Gothic Window*** (wood-engraving proof, Dalziels, 1853; 5 7/8 x 7 3/4)
  • British Museum, London, Department of Prints and Drawings, Dalziel Collection (vol. 5, 1853, no. 1154)

¶ **Going to the Park** (etching, Millais; 6 1/2 x 5; signed with monogram in plate)
  • Published in *Etchings for the Art Union of London by the Etching Club* (1872)

¶ **Happy Springtime*** (etching, Millais, 1860; 5 1/4 x 4; signed with monogram and dated in plate)
  • Published in *A Selection of Etchings by the Etching Club* (Cundall, 1865)

¶ **A Penny for Her Thoughts** (etching, Millais, 1878; 9 15/16 x 7 7/16 [plate]; signed with monogram and dated in plate)
  • Published in [*A Series of*] *Twenty-one Etchings Published by the Etching Club* (Ansdell, 1879)

¶ **Ruth** (etching, Millais; 5 x 3 7/16; signed with monogram and dated in plate)
  • Published in *Passages from the Poems of Thomas Hood* (Junior Etching Club; Gambart, 1858)

The Lord of Burleigh (*wood-engraving, Dalziels; 3 1/4 x 3 3/4;* Poems by Alfred Tennyson, *1857;* Millais's Illustrations)

The Bridge of Sighs (*etching, Millais, 1857; 4 5/8 x 3 5/8;* Passages from the Poems of Thomas Hood, *1858*)

Happy Springtime *(etching, Millais, 1860; 5 1/4 x 4;*
A Selection of Etchings by the Etching Club, *1865)*

¶ **St. Agnes of Intercession*** (etching,
Millais, 1850; 4 1/2 x 7 3/8)

• Originally intended for the fifth
(unpublished) issue of the *Germ*

• Proofs: Birmingham Museums and
Art Gallery; Victoria and Albert Museum,
London; Ashmolean Museum, Oxford (a.k.a.
The Reluctant Sitter)

¶ **Summer Indolence*** (etching, Millais,
1861; 3 1/2 x 6; signed with monogram and
dated in plate)

• Published in *Passages from Modern
English Poets* (Junior Etching Club; Day,
[1862]); reissued by Tegg in 1874 and, with
the etchings transferred to stone for lithographic prints, in 1875

¶ [**Woman on the Shore**] (etching, Millais,
1867; 4 5/16 x 3 1/8; signed with monogram
and dated in plate)

• Proof (only impression?): British
Museum, London, Department of Prints
and Drawings

¶ **The Young Mother*** (etching, Millais,
1856; 6 x 5 3/4; signed with monogram and
dated in plate)

• Published in *Etchings for the Art Union
of London* (Etching Club; Cundall, 1857)

Summer Indolence *(etching,
Millais, 1861; 3 1/2 x 6;* Passages
from Modern English Poets,
[1862])

Joseph Noel Paton

(1821–1901)

A Scottish painter who became known for his religious and fairy paintings, Joseph Noel Paton began his career in a more auspicious and Pre-Raphaelite manner. He was associated early on with illustrations and paintings from Shakespeare and Scottish history, and he entered the 1845 competition for the Houses of Parliament cartoons, winning a prize for *The Spirit of Religion* (an allegory of Christianity—the World, Flesh, and Devil). He became a member of the Royal Scottish Academy in 1850, and also exhibited prominently at London's Royal Academy, from 1856 to 1883. Paton was so well regarded that he was knighted in 1867—years before such honors were given to Millais and Leighton.

Paton was linked with, and influenced by, the Pre-Raphaelites, and like many of them wrote books of poetry (*Poems by a Painter*, 1861, and *Spindrift*, 1867). Because he resided far from London, Paton spent little time associating with the usual Pre-Raphaelites. William Rossetti claimed that neither he nor Brown had met Paton before 1875, when in a visit to Scotland they learned that he was a great admirer of Gabriel (*Some Reminiscences*, vol. 2, p. 495). In 1898 (June 16) Paton wrote to the director of the Berlin Photographic Company, Arthur Levi, about a print after one of Rossetti's paintings: "I hasten to acknowledge, with many thanks,

receipt of the admirable reproduction of the great *Dante's Dream* which you have been so good as to send me; and which, I need scarcely say, I am exceedingly glad to possess. No work of art ever affected me so profoundly as did that most noble and pathetic picture, when I saw it—still unfinished—in Rossetti's studio" (manuscript letter, collection of the author). Rossetti's oil, *Dante's Dream at the Time of the Death of Beatrice*, was completed in 1871, possessed by two patrons, and eventually found its way back to Rossetti, who kept retouching it. Paton's letter apparently refers to this later state of the work, for on August 6, 1881, Rossetti wrote to his sister Christina: "Sir Noel Paton (always a generous friend to my work) was here lately and most enthusiastic about the large picture [*Dante's*

Plate 10 for Compositions from Shakespeare's Tempest, *1845 (steel-engraving, Paton; 8 1/4 x 12 1/4)*

Dream]" (*Rossetti: His Family-Letters*, vol. 2, p. 385).

After 1880 Paton corresponded regularly with Frederic Shields. He was a lifelong friend of Millais (from their student days), whose painting *The Order of Release* (1853) seems a basis for Paton's similar canvas, *Home* (1856)—the meeting of a guardsman and his wife and mother on his return from the Crimean War. *Home* won praise from Ruskin, who for decades maintained a friendship, and corresponded, with Paton.

Paton had first exhibited "fairy pictures" at the Royal Scottish Academy (1847's *The Reconciliation of Oberon and Titania* and *The Quarrel of Oberon and Titania* of 1850) but soon began painting a series of Pre-Raphaelite–inspired works, in keeping with Millais's approach of "truth to nature": *Dante Meditating the Episode of Francesca da Rimini and Paolo Malatesta* (1852), *The Eve of St. Agnes* (1852), *The Dead Lady* (1854), *The Pursuit of Pleasure* (1855), and his two best

Titlepage illustration for The Fairy Book, *1863 (steel-engraving, C. H. Jeens; 3 in. diam.)*

works in the style, *The Bluidie Tryst* (1855)—a tour-de-force of Millais-like botanical detail enveloping tragic lovers—and *Hesperus*, an Arthurian subject of 1857.

Illustration and metal-engraving were part of Paton's artistic output from the very beginning. Obviously indebted to John Flaxman's art, his early graphics were in outline; he designed and engraved thirteen drawings for *Compositions from Shelley's Prometheus Unbound* (1844), sixteen for *Compositions from Shakespeare's Tempest* (1845), and twelve for *Silent Love* (1845). In the 1840s his illustrations, both wood-engraved and etched, graced numerous books by Scottish publishers, and he was one of the artists involved in the seminal illustrated volume of the period, *The Book of British Ballads* (1842, 1844). Paton often contributed single drawings such as frontispieces and titlepage art for books through the 1880s, two of these being among the most interesting titlepage illustrations, engraved on steel by Jeens, in Macmillan's Golden Treasury Series: for Dinah Mulock Craik's *The Fairy Book* (1863) and William Allingham's *The Ballad Book* (1864). The most magnificent of his steel-engraved prints can be found in *The Dowie Dens o' Yarrow* of 1860.

Paton's wood-engraved illustrations are among the finest of the time, crisply Pre-Raphaelite in detail and even closer to Rethel and Dürer in the feeling of Germanic woodcuts than Sandys's. For the *Cornhill Magazine* (1864), he drew "Ulysses," apparently his only commissioned magazine illustration after the 1850s. He is remembered as the illustrator

O Fare Ye Weel, My Ladye Gay! *(steel-engraving, L. Stocks; 6 1/2 x 8; The Dowie Dens o' Yarrow, 1860)*

for Charles Kingsley's *The Water-Babies* (1863), although he contributed only two illustrations, which are charming but not terribly distinguished. In *The Rime of the Ancient Mariner*, issued by the Art Union of London (1863), with its sure, clean lines and well-conceived compositions and figures massed together in a neo-Romantic Pre-Raphaelite whirl, Paton provides a much-enlivened version of the illustration style of the Nazarene Schnorr von Carolsfeld's *Bible Pictures* (several English editions, from 1855). Yet despite appearances, the plates are not cut on wood at all but are reproduced lithographically.

Definitely wood-engraved (by the Dalziels, Linton, and several others) are the pictures in Aytoun's *Lays of the Scottish Cavaliers* (1863). The book brims with Paton's half-page illustrations, headpieces, and tailpieces (augmented by a few landscapes by his brother, Waller Paton)—the armor and historical costumes (Paton was a noted collector of these) perfectly realized to the last detail, the compositions unusual and forceful, the squeezed-together figures wild, Romantic, and brimming with personality, the effects of light and shade Germanic but dazzlingly tonal in the spirit of Sandys and Poynter.

The book was deemed impressive at the time as well, for the *Art Journal* in 1864 gave it a full-page review, reproducing two of the illustrations and calling the drawings "powerful in expression," "spirited," and well

engraved. The reviewer continued: "The majority of them seem based upon that [method] usually employed by the best artists of Germany, but with greater richness in design, and with more freedom of pencilling. They combine, in fact, the truth of drawing and the deep feeling of the former school with the fertile invention, and picturesque manner,

At Length Did Cross an Albatross *(ink drawing, 11 5/8 x 15; for the illustration in* The Rime of the Ancient Mariner, *1863; courtesy Glasgow Museums: Art Gallery and Museum)*

of our own" (vol. 26 [n.s, vol. 3], p. 19). The *Journal*, however, missed some of the best work in the book by mentioning Linton and Thompson but not the Dalziel Brothers. Paton himself had approached the Dalziels, writing to them on October 8, 1858: "Judging from your work in the [Moxon] *Tennyson*, and from proofs now before me, I can with perfect security and confidence recommend the Messrs. Blackwood [publishers of *Lays*] to entrust you with as many of my drawings as you care to undertake" (*Brothers Dalziel*, p. 108).

Ulysses *(wood-engraving, Swain; 6 x 4 3/8; Cornhill Magazine, vol. 9, 1864, p. 66; The Cornhill Gallery)*

Capture of the Slave-Ship *(wood-engraving, 4 7/8 x 6 5/8; Sunday Magazine, vol. 1, 1864–65 [1865], p. 289)*

Catalogue

PERIODICALS

Art Union
Vol. 9, 1847:
    ¶ **"Midsummer Eve"** by Mrs. S. C. [Anna Maria] Hall, 39 illustrations (pp. 13 [2 illus.], 14 [3 illus.], 15 [2 illus.], 17 [2 illus.], 53, 55, 56 [3 illus.], 58, 103, 104, 132, 133, 136, 165, 166, 167, 217, 221 [2 illus.], 248, 250, 289, 315, 317, et al.; reprinted in *Midsummer Eve: A Fairy Tale of Love*)

Cornhill Magazine
Vol. 9, 1864:
    ¶ **Ulysses*** (p. 66, Swain; reprinted in *The Cornhill Gallery*)

Illustrated London News
Vol. 5, 1844:
    ¶ **"The Burns Festival at Ayr,"** 27 illustrations (pp. 80, 81, 88, 89 [8 illus.], 92 [5 illus.], 93, 94, 104 [2 illus.], 105 [3 illus.], 108 [4 illus.], 389)

Quiver
Ser. 3, vol. 20, 1885:
    ¶ **Queen Margaret and King Malcolm*** (p. 57, W. Ballingall; **Queen Margaret and Malcolm Canmore** reprinted from *Classic Scenes in Scotland*)

Sunday Magazine
Vol. 1, 1864–65 [1865]:
    ¶ **Capture of the Slave-Ship*** (p. 289)
    ¶ **"The Song of the Freed Woman"** by Isa Craig, 2 illustrations* (**Slavery**, p. 672; **Freedom**, p. 673)
    • Engraved for *Sunday Magazine* from pictures by Paton "by permission of the Glasgow Art Union"; newly engraved as illustrations here, but originally drawings reproduced photographically in *Bond and Free*

BOOKS

The Ballad Book (William Allingham, ed.; Macmillan Golden Treasury Series, 1864)
   ¶ ***Titlepage illustration**** (steel-engraving, C. H. Jeens)

Bond and Free: Five Sketches Illustrative of Slavery (Joseph Noel Paton; Art Union of Glasgow, 1863)
   ¶ **Verbum Dei***
   ¶ **The Sale*** (wood-engraved and published in *Sunday Magazine* as **Slavery**)
   ¶ **The Capture***
   ¶ **The Rescue*** (wood-engraved and published in *Sunday Magazine* as **Capture of the Slave-Ship**)
   ¶ **Freedom*** (wood-engraved and published in *Sunday Magazine*)
   • Photographic prints of drawings, some of which are dated 1858

The Book of British Ballads (Samuel Carter Hall, ed.; How, ser. 2, 1844)
   ¶ **"Elfinland Wud,"** 6 illustrations (T. Armstrong)
   ¶ **"The Eve of St. John,"** 8 illustrations (F. Branston)
   • The series 1 edition was published in 1842, in a trade edition and in a large-paper edition with india-paper proofs of the wood-engravings
   • Both series were reissued in a 1-vol. edition by Bohn in 1853

Classic Scenes in Scotland by Modern Artists (William Ballingall, eng. and ed.; Edinburgh: Ballingall, 1875)
   ¶ **Queen Margaret and Malcolm Canmore** (W. Ballingall; reprinted as **Queen Margaret and King Malcolm** in the *Quiver*)

Compositions from Shakespeare's Tempest (Joseph Noel Paton; Chapman and Hall, 1845)
   ¶ 16 illustrations, including ***titlepage illustration*** (steel-engravings, Paton; see information below [§])
   • Reissued by Nimmo in 1877
   • Reprinted in *Compositions from Shakespeare's Tempest / Compositions from Shelley's Prometheus Unbound*

Compositions from Shelley's Prometheus Unbound (Joseph Noel Paton; Holloway, 1844)

Slavery *for **"The Song of the Freed Woman"*** *(wood-engraving, 4 7/8 x 5 3/4; Sunday Magazine, vol. 1, 1864–65 [1865], p. 672)*

Freedom *for **"The Song of the Freed Woman"*** *(wood-engraving, 4 7/8 x 5 5/8; Sunday Magazine, vol. 1, 1864–65 [1865], p. 673)*

Top: ***Finis*** *(steel-engraving, L. Stocks; 6 5/8 x 8 1/8;* The Dowie Dens o' Yarrow, *1860)*

Bottom: ***For, with a Father's Pride*** *(wood-engraving, Dalziels; 5 1/2 x 4 3/8;* Lays of the Scottish Cavaliers, *1863)*

¶ 13 illustrations, including ***titlepage illustration*** (steel-engravings, Paton; see information below [§])
• Reissued by Nimmo in 1877
• Reprinted in *Compositions from Shakespeare's Tempest / Compositions from Shelley's Prometheus Unbound*

The Dowie Dens o' Yarrow (Glasgow: Royal Association for the Promotion of the Fine Arts in Scotland, 1860)
¶ **Late at E'en, Drinking the Wine*** (steel-engraving, R. C. Bell)
¶ **O Fare Ye Weel, My Ladye Gay!*** (steel-engraving, L. Stocks)
¶ **Four Has He Hurt, and Five Has Slain*** (steel-engraving, C. W. Sharpe)
¶ **Oh Gentle Wind That Bloweth South*** (steel-engraving, L. Stocks)
¶ **She's Taen Him in Her Armis Twa*** (steel-engraving, C. W. Sharpe)
¶ **Finis*** (steel-engraving, L. Stocks)

The Fairy Book ([Dinah Mulock Craik]; Macmillan Golden Treasury Series, 1863)
¶ ***Titlepage illustration**** (steel-engraving, C. H. Jeens)

Come Hither, Evan Cameron! *(wood-engraving, Dalziels; 5 x 4 3/8;* Lays of the Scottish Cavaliers, *1863)*

Five Gateways of Knowledge (George Wilson; Macmillan, c. 1858)
¶ *Frontispiece*

Gems of Literature (Edinburgh: Nimmo, 1866)
¶ **"Una and the Lion"** by Edmund Spenser, 2 illustrations* (R. Paterson)
• Reprinted in *Gems of Literature / Pen and Pencil Pictures from the Poets*

Gudrun: A Story of the North Sea (E. Letherbrow, ed.; Edinburgh: Edmonston and Douglas, 1863)
¶ *Frontispiece*

The Impeachment of Mary Stuart, Sometime Queen of Scots . . . "In Defence!" (John Skelton; Edinburgh/London: Blackwood, 1876)
¶ *Frontispiece:* **Portrait of Mary Queen of Scots** (collotype)

Lays of the Scottish Cavaliers (W. E. Aytoun; Edinburgh/London: Blackwood, 1863)
¶ 37 illustrations* (J. Thompson, Dalziels, W. L. Thomas, J. Whymper, W. J. Linton)
• Plus numerous spot vignettes and cover design by the artist
• The landscape illustrations are by the artist's brother, Waller Paton

They Brought Him to the Watergate *(wood-engraving, W. J. Linton; 5 1/2 x 4 1/2;* Lays of the Scottish Cavaliers, *1863)*

But Alone He Bent the Knee *(wood-engraving, Dalziels; 5 3/4 x 4 1/2;* Lays of the Scottish Cavaliers, *1863)*

The Motherless Boy (Margaret Maria Brewster [Gordon]; Edinburgh: Edmonston and Douglas, 1856 [or 1860])
¶ ***Frontispiece***

My Indian Journal (Walter Campbell; Edinburgh: Edmonston and Douglas, 1864)
¶ **Bianca**

The National Shakespeare (MacKenzie, 3 vols., 1889)
¶ 20 illustrations* (photogravures)

An Old Story (Virtue, Spalding, [1875])
¶ 1 illustration

Passages from the Poets (John Allen Giles; 1849)
¶ **The Cyclops in Love**

The Past in the Present: What Is Civilisation? (Arthur Mitchell; Edinburgh: Edmonston and Douglas, 1880)
¶ ***Titlepage illustration****

The Prince of the Fair Family (Mrs. S. C. [Anna Maria] Hall; Chapman and Hall, [1867])
¶ **The Seedling Head of a Dandelion*** (J. D. Cooper)

The Princess of Silverland and Other Tales (Elsie Strivelyne; Macmillan, 1874)
¶ ***Frontispiece***

Top: ***Lo! We Bring with Us the Hero*** *(wood-engraving, Dalziels; 4 x 4 3/4;* Lays of the Scottish Cavaliers, *1863)*

Middle: ***Tailpiece*** for ***"The Widow of Glencoe"*** *(wood-engraving, Dalziels; 2 x 3 1/2;* Lays of the Scottish Cavaliers, *1863)*

Bottom: ***And the Hanoverian Horsemen*** *(wood-engraving, Dalziels; 4 x 4 3/4;* Lays of the Scottish Cavaliers, *1863)*

Puck on Pegasus (H. Cholmondeley-Pennell; Hotten, 6th ed., rev. and enl., 1869)
  ¶ **The Night Mail North*** (H. Harral)

Rab and His Friends (Dr. John Brown; Edinburgh: Douglas, 1878)
  ¶ **Dead Ailie*** (steel-engraving, R. C. Bell)
  ¶ **James and His Burden*** (steel-engraving, R. C. Bell)
  • Originally published by Edmonston and Douglas in 1864?

Religio Chemici (George Wilson; Macmillan, 1862)
  ¶ ***Titlepage illustration***

Renfrewshire Annual (Mrs. Maxwell, ed.; Paisley: Murray and Stewart/Neilson; London: Tilt and Bogue, 1842)
  ¶ ***Frontispiece*: The Duke of Lennox** (steel-engraving, R. C. Bell)
  ¶ ***Titlepage illustration*** (steel-engraving, J. Smith)
  ¶ **Io! Evoke!** (steel-engraving, J. Smith)
  ¶ **The Poor Scholar** (etching, Paton)
  ¶ **Anglers in a Highland Cottage** (etching, Paton)
  ¶ **"Spare Me, Good Sirs, I'm a Robber Myself"** (etching, Paton)
  ¶ **Don Ferdinand** (etching, Paton)
  ¶ **Francesco** (steel-engraving, J. Gallatly)

The Rime of the Ancient Mariner (Samuel Taylor Coleridge; Art Union of London, 1863)
  ¶ **20 illustrations*** (lithographs, W. H. McFarlane/F.H.; see information below [§])
  • Reprinted in *The Rime of the Ancient Mariner* (New York: Pollard and Moss, 1887), with additional illustrations by Gustave Doré

St. Giles', Edinburgh (James Cameron Lees; Edinburgh/London: Chambers, 1889)
  ¶ **In St. Giles After Flodden**

Silent Love: A Poem by the Late James Wilson of Paisley (Andrew Park; Paisley: Murray and Stewart, 4th ed., 1845)
  ¶ **12 illustrations** (steel-engravings, Paton)

Spindrift (Joseph Noel Paton; Edinburgh/London: Blackwood, 1867)

Ailie Dead *(steel-engraving, R. C. Bell; 4 x 5;* Rab and His Friends, *1878)*

The Bride Hath Paced into the Hall *(lithograph, W. H. McFarlane/F.H.; 9 1/2 x 12 3/8;* The Rime of the Ancient Mariner, *1863)*

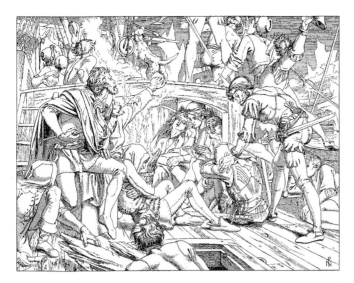

¶ *Titlepage illustration* (R. Paterson)
¶ *Contents-page illustration*
(R. Paterson)

The Story of Wandering Willie (Lady
Augusta Noel; Macmillan, 1870)
¶ *Frontispiece*

Tales of Women's Trials (Mrs. S. C. [Anna
Maria] Hall; Chapman and Hall, 1847)
¶ 4 illustrations (G. Dalziel, J. G.
Nicholls)

The Trial of Sir Jasper (Samuel Carter Hall;
Virtue, Spalding, 1873)
¶ **"Is It Too Late to Save Him?"**
(W. Ballingall)
• Reissued in 1874 by Virtue, Spalding,
and Daldy

The Union of Christians (Rev. J. T. Brown;
1846)
¶ *Frontispiece*

The Water-Babies (Rev. Charles Kingsley;
Macmillan, 3d ed., 1863)
¶ 2 illustrations, including *frontispiece* (J. D. Cooper)

Waverley Novels (Walter Scott; Edinburgh:
Cadell, Abbotsford ed.; 12 vols., 1842–48,
and 5 vols., 1846)
¶ Illustrations

Top: ***At Length Did Cross an Albatross***
*(lithograph, W. H. McFarlane/F.H.; 9 3/4 x
12 1/2;* The Rime of the Ancient Mariner,
1863)

Middle: ***And a Good South Wind Sprung
Up Behind*** *(lithograph, W. H. McFarlane/F.H.;
9 1/2 x 12 1/8;* The Rime of the Ancient
Mariner, *1863)*

Bottom: ***Then All Averred I Had Killed the
Bird*** *(lithograph, W. H. McFarlane/F.H.; 9 3/4
x 12 5/8;* The Rime of the Ancient Mariner,
1863)

§ Paton's own book, *Poems by a Painter* (Edinburgh/London: Blackwood, 1861), has no illustrations but has a cover design by the artist

§ J. P. Campbell in her and M. H. Noel-Paton's *Noel Paton, 1821–1901* (1990, p. 97) lists Alex Maclagan's *Balmoral: Lays of the Highlands* (1871) as having a **frontispiece** by the artist

§ Acknowledgment is given to Paul Goldman's *Victorian Illustration* (p. 343) for the catalogue listing of *An Old Story*

Ah! Well a-Day! What Evil Looks *(lithograph, W. H. McFarlane/F.H.; 9 3/4 x 12 5/8;* The Rime of the Ancient Mariner, *1863)*

The Naked Hulk Alongside Came *(lithograph, W. H. McFarlane/F.H.; 9 3/4 x 12 5/8;* The Rime of the Ancient Mariner, *1863)*

The Souls Did from Their Bodies Fly *(lithograph, W. H. McFarlane/F.H.; 9 3/4 x 12 5/8;* The Rime of the Ancient Mariner, *1863)*

BOOKS CONTAINING REPRINTS

Compositions from Shakespeare's Tempest / Compositions from Shelley's Prometheus Unbound (Edinburgh: Nimmo, 1845)
   ¶ 16 illustrations reprinted from *Compositions from Shakespeare's Tempest*
   ¶ 13 illustrations reprinted from *Compositions from Shelley's Prometheus Unbound*
   • Reissued by Nimmo in 1877

The Cornhill Gallery (Smith, Elder, 1864)
   ¶ **Ulysses** (reprinted from the *Cornhill Magazine*)

Gems of Literature / Pen and Pencil Pictures from the Poets (Edinburgh: Nimmo, 1883)
¶ **"Una and the Lion"** by Edmund Spenser, 2 illustrations (reprinted from *Gems of Literature*)

Midsummer Eve: A Fairy Tale of Love (Mrs. S. C. [Anna Maria] Hall; Longman, Brown, Green, and Longmans, 1848)
¶ 39 illustrations (reprinted from the *Art Union*)
• Reissued by Hotten in 1870

INDIVIDUAL PRINTS

§ **Members of the Peace Society, City of Edinburgh Branch, 1861** (lithograph, Paton?, 1861; 9 1/8 x 11 3/4)
• Scottish National Portrait Gallery, Edinburgh

¶ **Memorial of the War of Independence Under William Wallace and Robert the Bruce** (lithograph, Paton?, 1859; 15 1/2 x 9 1/2)

§ Paton also designed at least two ephemeral pieces related to the Royal Scottish Academy: an **1852 Season Ticket** and the cover of the Academy's **Twenty-sixth Exhibition Catalogue** (1852); these

Top: *The Selfsame Moment I Could Pray (lithograph, W. H. McFarlane/F.H.; 9 3/4 x 12 1/2; The Rime of the Ancient Mariner, 1863)*

Middle: *This Seraph-Band, Each Waved His Hand (lithograph, W. H. McFarlane/F.H.; 9 1/2 x 12 1/8; The Rime of the Ancient Mariner, 1863)*

Bottom: *"Dear Lord! It Hath a Fiendish Look" (lithograph, W. H. McFarlane/F.H.; 9 3/4 x 12 1/2; The Rime of the Ancient Mariner, 1863)*

Top: ***Upon the Whirl, Where Sank the Ship*** *(lithograph, W. H. McFarlane/F.H.; 9 1/2 x 12 1/8;* The Rime of the Ancient Mariner, *1863)*

Middle: ***But in the Garden Bower the Bride*** *(lithograph, W. H. McFarlane/F.H.; 9 1/2 x 12 1/4;* The Rime of the Ancient Mariner, *1863)*

Bottom: ***While Each to His Great Father Bends*** *(lithograph, W. H. McFarlane/F.H.; 9 5/8 x 12 5/8;* The Rime of the Ancient Mariner, *1863)*

images are reprinted (lithographs) in the lithography firm Schenck and McFarlane's specimen book *Ornamental, Architectural, and Monumental Designs, Rare Alphabets, Etc.* (c. 1857). Acknowledgment is given to English author David Schenck for providing this and the **Peace Society** print information, as well as other material on Paton and the lithographic practices in Scotland during the period.

§ See also: • *Compositions from Shelley's Prometheus Unbound* (13 illustrations; steel-engravings, Paton; each 8 1/4 x 12 1/4) • *Compositions from Shakespeare's Tempest* (16 illustrations; steel-engravings, Paton; each 8 1/4 x 12 1/4) • *Rime of the Ancient Mariner* (20 illustrations; lithographs, W. H. McFarlane/F.H.; each 9 3/4 x 12 1/2, avg. [see captions])

Edward J. Poynter

(1836–1919)

Born in Paris, the son of an architect, Edward Poynter first attended the Royal Academy Schools and then studied at Charles Gleyre's Paris atelier in the late 1850s, along with George Du Maurier, James McNeill Whistler, and Val Prinsep. Like Frederic Leighton—also an influence in Paris—he became very much a part of England's establishment art community and divided his time between painting and teaching/administration (Slade Professor of University College, 1871–75; principal of the South Kensington Schools, 1875–81; director of the National Gallery, 1894–1904). After Leighton died in 1896, John Everett Millais served a short tenure as president of the Royal Academy (he died later the same year), to be succeeded by Poynter, who watched over English art in that capacity until 1918. And like his predecessors, he was knighted. It was recognized even in 1878 ("Contemporary Portraits, New Series, No. 7: E. J. Poynter, R.A.," *Dublin University Magazine*, vol. 92, p. 29) that Poynter was a forward-looking teacher: he encouraged the participation of women in his classes, allowed nude models in mixed classes, and stressed the importance of good drawing and working from life models.

Despite such official success, Poynter's art was initially Pre-Raphaelite in spirit, following William Holman Hunt's and Ford Madox Brown's prescription to re-create history (and interpret literature) as if their subjects' real lives were being viewed. (Poynter was a friend of William Morris and Edward Burne-Jones, and in fact married a sister of Burne-Jones's wife, Georgiana.) Poynter became known for his marvelously finished studies from nature and life models for every picture, including his illustrations. He exhibited at the Royal Academy from 1861, as well as at the British Institution, the Old Water Colour Society, the Royal Society of Painter-Etchers and Engravers, and the Grosvenor Gallery. Like the above gentlemen, and many other Pre-Raphaelites, Poynter throughout his career dedicated his full talents to the decorative and "minor" arts, designing stained-glass windows and tilework and painting furniture (e.g., Murrietta sideboard series, "Three Summer Days," 1871).

Edward Poynter, c. 1876 (etching by Alphonse Legros)

If Leighton took the Academy by storm with his sensational *Cimabue* of 1855, Poynter's *Israel in Egypt* in 1867 created a similar furor, with its huge crowd scene of individually delineated figures, high finish, and Hunt-like depiction of biblical architecture and decorative elements. Of all the painters of ancient-historical scenes, such as Alma-Tadema and even Leighton, Poynter is the most Pre-Raphaelite and hard-edged, the least stagy and sentimental. His subjects run the gamut from ancient Greece, Rome, and Egypt to the Bible and Dante. Despite his appreciation for Italian art, his crisp, unmuddied realism is unlike Leighton's and Alma-Tadema's diffused-light, atmospheric, Renaissance-inspired works and more like the Nazarenes' and Pre-Raphaelites'— as seen in *An Egyptian Sentinel* (1864), *The Catapult* (1868), *Atalanta's Race* (1876), and *The Fortune-Teller* (1877), among others.

Poynter's 1871 painting *Feeding the Sacred Ibis in the Halls of Karnac* is a masterpiece of historical realism—and, like many Pre-Raphaelite paintings, linked thematically with his contemporaneous illustration work. The Dalziels, in fact, may be given credit for Poynter's Egyptian obsession (although there is certainly the influence from Gleyre's Paris studio in the 1850s), since the story is that after Poynter's return to London in 1860, the Dalziels saw (and purchased) at an exhibition his watercolor of two Egyptian girls carrying waterpots near the Nile; they soon commissioned him to draw for their *Bible Gallery* project (*Brothers Dalziel*, p. 250), Poynter selecting the lives of Joseph and Moses. These subjects inspired his paintings, culminating in *Israel in Egypt* (which he worked on for four years).

As he labored over his magnum opus, Poynter also concentrated on book and periodical illustration. He did ten wood-engraved drawings for *Once a Week*—nine in 1862 and 1863; the tenth, "Feeding the Sacred Ibis in the Halls of Karnac" (1867), was not only the inspiration for his painting but is basically the same composition—and no less detailed, realistic,

and gorgeous than the painting. Poynter contributed scenes of modern life to *Churchman's Family Magazine* and *London Society*; he etched thirty-one works, mostly after past artists, for Anna Jameson's and Lady Eastlake's *The History of Our Lord as Exemplified in Works of Art* (1864); he drew a superb "Persephone" for *Poems by Jean Ingelow* (1867); and he created twelve drawings for the *Bible Gallery* (1881)—the most by any artist other than Simeon Solomon (whose complete set of twenty designs only appeared years later in *Art Pictures from the Old Testament*).

With the exception of the five slightly comical illustrations for the "Lord Dundreary" series in *London Society*, all of Poynter's illustrations are of the highest Pre-Raphaelite

Feeding the Sacred Ibis in the Halls of Karnac (*wood-engraving, Swain; 6 7/8 x 4 3/4; Once a Week, new ser. [ser. 2], vol. 3, 1867, p. 238)*

The Castle by the Sea *(wood-engraving, Swain; 5 5/8 x 4 1/2;* Once a Week, *vol. 6, 1862, p. 84)*

order—not as odd or mystical or poetic as some, but certainly in the finest tradition of German wood-engravings, and equal to Frederick Sandys's in technique and realism, with an effusive decorative power and every inch crammed with detail. Poynter's two illustrations for "A Dream of Love" show what Millais's similar modern-life illustrations might have become if he had remained steadfastly Pre-Raphaelite. "The Castle by the Sea" (*Once a Week*, 1862), with its medieval setting, is pure Alfred Rethel and illustrates a poem "from the German of Uhland" just as does Sandys's Rethelian "Yet Once More on the Organ Play." "Ballad of the Page and the King's Daughter" (*Once a Week*, 1863) is ravishing in its minutely depicted costume details.

"Miriam," in the *Bible Gallery*, focuses on a central female figure, with virtuosic treatment of swirling and draped cloth—also seen

in "Persephone" and "Feeding the Sacred Ibis." "Moses and Aaron Before Pharaoh," "Moses Strikes the Rock," "Joseph Distributes Corn," and just about all of Poynter's drawings in that book are almost insanely Pre-Raphaelite in their accumulation of figures and decorative/architectural details, in filling every millimeter of the picture; it is what Holman Hunt did in most of his paintings (look at *The Finding of the Saviour in the Temple*, 1854–60, and *The Miracle of Sacred Fire*, 1895) but rarely attempted in his illustrations. Poynter, true to the spirit of Pre-Raphaelite art, saw little difference between the effort exerted for a monumental painting and for a small wood-block drawing.

A letter from Poynter to the Dalziels dated November 28, 1871, shows that despite most of the book's drawings having been done in the early 1860s, the project and engraving continued for many years after—and that Poynter was as fastidious in getting an engraving right (in this case probably "Joseph Distributes Corn") as any of the Pre-Raphaelites were in their proof comments: "I have touched a little on the proof with a view to getting a little more breadth of light. The reduction so concentrates the effect that it looks rather spotty; I was a little afraid it might. The light on the floor especially seems to want shading more gradually into the background; cutting out the cross lines in the hatching on the left hand side would, I should think, do this, and thinning the lines generally as they get nearer the light. I have made a slight alteration in the head of the young lady standing up by taking out some of the shading, and one or two other points are touched with a view to simplicity. I hope I am not giving you too much trouble! The engraving is most beautiful, especially the two near figures, which are wonderful; indeed, whatever is wrong is my own fault" (*Brothers Dalziel*, p. 250).

Some of the more interesting of Poynter's prints are the large steel-engravings for Keats's *Endymion* (1873)—six were done but,

Joseph Distributes Corn *(wood-engraving, Dalziels; 6 1/4 x 7 1/4;* Dalziels' Bible Gallery, *1881;* Art Pictures from the Old Testament*)*

according to P. G. Hamerton, the whole series was not finished due to the failure of the Moxon publishing house; "they were issued, however, in their incomplete state, and make what the artist calls 'a very lame-looking volume'" ("Edward J. Poynter, R.A.," *Portfolio*, vol. 8, 1877, p. 13). One would assume

Poynter referred to the fact that his illustrations abruptly stop a quarter of the way through the book's text (although his name is gold-stamped on the cover, as large as Keats's); in quality, however, they form a wondrous set of oversize prints (just as do Paton's six steel-engravings in the *Dowie Dens o' Yarrow*), with an inky richness that can only be attained through engraving on metal.

Whence That Completed Form of All Completeness? *(steel-engraving, F. Joubert; 9 1/2 x 7 1/4;* Endymion, *1873)*

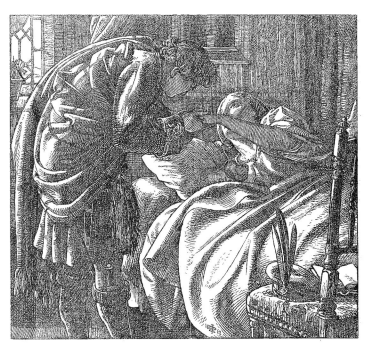

The Broken Vow (wood-engraving, Swain; 4 5/8 x 5 1/8; Once a Week, *vol. 7, 1862, p. 322)*

A Dream of Love [#2] (wood-engraving, Swain; 4 x 5; Once a Week, *vol. 7, 1862, p. 393)*

Catalogue

PERIODICALS

Churchman's Family Magazine
Vol. 1, 1863:
¶ **"The Painter's Glory,"** 3 illustrations (**Crude Efforts**,* p. 124, Swain?; **Painter's Inspiration**,* p. 131, Swain; **The Home Circle**, p. 136, Swain?)

Graphic
Vol. 1, 1869–70:
¶ **Poetry** (p. 662)

Illustrated London News
Vol. 57, Christmas Number, 1870:
¶ **A Vision of the Departing Year** (pp. 652–53)

London Society
Vol. 2, 1862:
¶ **"Lord Dundreary"** series, 5 illustrations (**A Letter from the Lord Dundreary**, p. 215, W. Corway; **Lord Dundreary in the Country,** p. 308, J.S.; **"I Can't Thmoke a Pipe,"** p. 328, R.S.M.; **Tip-Cat,** p. 331, W. Thomas; **Lord Dundreary at Brighton,** p. 472, W. Thomas)
Vol. 2, Christmas Number, 1862:
¶ **The Kissing Bush*** (p. 41, Swain)
Vol. 6, Christmas Number, 1864:
¶ **A Sprig of Holly*** (p. 29, Swain; reprinted in *Pictures of Society*)

Once a Week
Vol. 6, 1862:
¶ **The Castle by the Sea*** (p. 84, Swain)
¶ **The Wife and I*** (p. 724, Swain)
Vol. 7, 1862:
¶ **The Broken Vow*** (p. 322, Swain)
¶ **"A Dream of Love"** by D. Richmond, 2 illustrations* (pp. 365, 393; Swain)
¶ **"A Fellow-Traveller's Story,"** 2 illustrations* (pp. 699, 722; Swain)
Vol. 8, 1863:
¶ **Of a Haunted House in Mexico*** (p. 141, Swain)
¶ **My Friend's Wedding Day**

A Fellow-Traveller's Story *[#2] (wood-engraving, Swain; 6 3/8 x 4 3/4; Once a Week, vol. 7, 1862, p. 722)*

(p. 313, Swain)
¶ **Ducie of the Dale*** (p. 476, Swain)
¶ **Ballad of the Page and the King's Daughter*** (p. 658, Swain)
New ser. [ser. 2], vol. 3, 1867:
¶ **Feeding the Sacred Ibis in the Halls of Karnac*** (p. 238, Swain)

Quarto
Vol. 3, 1897:
¶ **Daniel's Prayer** (p. 8; reprinted from *Dalziels' Bible Gallery*)

BOOKS

Dalziels' Bible Gallery (Routledge, 1881)
¶ **Joseph Distributes Corn***
¶ **Joseph Before Pharaoh***
¶ **Pharaoh Honours Joseph***
¶ **Joseph Presents His Father to Pharaoh***
¶ **Moses Slaying the Egyptian***
¶ **Moses Keeping Jethro's Sheep***
¶ **Moses and Aaron Before Pharaoh***
¶ **The Israelites in Egypt: Water-Carriers***
¶ **Miriam***

Of a Haunted House in Mexico *(wood-engraving, Swain; 4 5/8 x 5 1/8; Once a Week, vol. 8, 1863, p. 141)*

Ballad of the Page and the King's Daughter *(wood-engraving, Swain; 6 5/8 x 5; Once a Week, vol. 8, 1863, p. 658)*

Right: **Persephone** (wood-engraving, Dalziels; 5 1/8 x 4; Poems by Jean Ingelow, 1867)

Left: **Joseph Before Pharaoh** (wood-engraving, Dalziels; 6 7/8 x 7 1/2; Dalziels' Bible Gallery, 1881; Art Pictures from the Old Testament)

Pharaoh Honours Joseph (wood-engraving, Dalziels; 7 3/4 x 6 7/8; Dalziels' Bible Gallery, 1881; Art Pictures from the Old Testament)

¶ **Moses Strikes the Rock***
¶ **By the Rivers of Babylon***
¶ **Daniel's Prayer*** (reprinted in the Quarto)
  • Eng. Dalziels
  • Reprinted in Art Pictures from the Old Testament

Echoes (E.M.H. [Emily Marion Harris]; Bell and Daldy, 1872)
  ¶ **Frontispiece*** (Dalziels)

Endymion (John Keats; Moxon, 1873)
  ¶ **Frontispiece: A Little Shallop***
  ¶ **Leading the Way**
  ¶ **O Thou***
  ¶ **Whence That Completed Form of All Completeness?***
  ¶ **Before the Crystal Heavens Darken**
  ¶ **Strive to Find a Half-Forgetfulness in Mountain Wind**
  • Steel-engravings, F. Joubert

The History of Our Lord as Exemplified in Works of Art (Mrs. Jameson [Anna Brownell] and Lady Eastlake; Longman, 2 vols., 1864)
  ¶ 31 illustrations (etchings [9 in vol. 1; 22 in vol. 2] by Poynter after other artists, of sculptures, paintings, and other existing works of art)
  • Reissued in 1880

Top: ***Joseph Presents His Father to Pharaoh*** (*wood-engraving, Dalziels; 5 1/4 x 7 3/8;* Dalziels' Bible Gallery, *1881;* Art Pictures from the Old Testament*)*

Middle: ***Moses Slaying the Egyptian*** (*wood-engraving, Dalziels; 7 x 6 1/4;* Dalziels' Bible Gallery, *1881;* Art Pictures from the Old Testament*)*

Bottom: ***Moses Keeping Jethro's Sheep*** (*wood-engraving, Dalziels; 7 1/8 x 6 1/4;* Dalziels' Bible Gallery, *1881;* Art Pictures from the Old Testament*)*

[Ingelow] *Poems by Jean Ingelow* (Longmans, Green, Reader, and Dyer, 1867)
　¶ **Persephone*** (Dalziels)

The Nobility of Life (L. Valentine, ed.; Warne, 1869)
　¶ **Mercy**
　¶ **Cheerfulness**
　¶ **Obedience**
　¶ **Youth**
　• Mounted color wood-engravings, J. M. Kronheim

Moses and Aaron Before Pharaoh *(wood-engraving, Dalziels; 7 7/8 x 6 7/8;* Dalziels' Bible Gallery, *1881;* Art Pictures from the Old Testament*)*

Miriam *(wood-engraving, Dalziels; 8 7/8 x 6 5/8;* Dalziels' Bible Gallery, *1881;* Art Pictures from the Old Testament*)*

§ Original drawings by Poynter may also illustrate *Poynter's Drawing Cards for the Standards* (Glasgow: Blackie, 1886–88)

BOOKS CONTAINING REPRINTS

Art Pictures from the Old Testament (Aley Fox, text; Society for Promoting Christian Knowledge, 1894)
¶ 12 illustrations (reprinted from *Dalziels' Bible Gallery*)

Pictures of Society (Low, Son, and Marston, 1866)
¶ **A Sprig of Holly** (reprinted from *London Society*)

The Israelites in Egypt: Water-Carriers *(wood-engraving, Dalziels; 7 5/8 x 5 1/2;* Dalziels' Bible Gallery, *1881;* Art Pictures from the Old Testament*)*

INDIVIDUAL PRINTS

¶ **Labour and Science** (wood-engraving, Dalziels, 1868; 10 x 15; signed with monogram and dated)

• British Museum, London, Department of Prints and Drawings, Dalziel Collection (vol. 24, 1868, no. 36); this is probably a design for a science diploma for the South Kensington Schools (see F. Hamilton Jackson, "The Work of Sir E. J. Poynter, P.R.A.: Billiard Room Decoration for Watley Hall," *Architectural Review*, vol. 2, 1897, p. 225)

§ The *Architectural Review* of 1897 (see above) notes two other graphics by Poynter: **Poster for the Guardian Insurance Office** (1886) and a chromolithograph **Border Design for Queen Victoria's Announcement of the Death of the Duke of Clarence** (1893), later published by R. Tuck

§ See also: *The History of Our Lord as Exemplified in Works of Art*, 2 vols., 1864; 9 etchings in vol. 1; 22 in vol. 2 by Poynter after other artists; page size: 8 1/4 x 6; signed with monograms and dated from 1862 through 1864 in plates

§ Poynter's ***bookplate*** (a decorative rather than illustrative design) was reproduced in the *Bibliophile* of 1909 (vol. 2, p. 17) to accompany the article "Book-plates of Celebrities" by Harold F. B. Wheeler

Top: **Moses Strikes the Rock** (*wood-engraving, Dalziels; 8 7/8 x 6 3/8;* Dalziels' Bible Gallery, *1881;* Art Pictures from the Old Testament)

Left: **By the Rivers of Babylon** (*wood-engraving, Dalziels; 8 3/4 x 7;* Dalziels' Bible Gallery, *1881;* Art Pictures from the Old Testament)

Daniel's Prayer (*wood-engraving, Dalziels; 7 1/2 x 6 7/8;* Dalziels' Bible Gallery, *1881;* Art Pictures from the Old Testament)

Dante Gabriel Rossetti

(1828~1882)

The story of Dante Gabriel Rossetti's role in the founding of the Pre-Raphaelite Brotherhood runs like a theme through most of the other essays in this book. He was the movement's most dynamic personality, a

Dante Gabriel Rossetti, 1863 (photographic print, as published in T. Hall Caine's Recollections of Dante Gabriel Rossetti, *1882)*

force—albeit a behind-the-scenes one—for artistic reform, a setter of goals and establisher of themes, and an artistic and poetic inspiration to all who knew him.

His father, Gabriele, was a political refugee from Italy and professor of Italian at King's College, London. There were four Rossetti children, all talented and literary: Maria, a very religious woman, wrote the book *A Shadow of Dante* and was a member of an Anglican sisterhood during the last two years of her life; William Michael became a significant writer on art and literature; Christina is considered one of the great women poets of the nineteenth century; and Dante Gabriel throughout his life pursued the dual goals of creating significant poetry and significant art.

Dante (he was known as Gabriel to his friends and family) intended to make his living by art and entered the Royal Academy Schools in 1844. Having been impressed with Ford Madox Brown's paintings *The Body of Harold Brought Before William the Conqueror* and *Wycliffe Reading His Translation of the Bible to John of Gaunt*, Rossetti wrote the older artist to become his pupil in spring 1848. Feeling Brown's exercises were tedious, by summer Rossetti thought he could learn more from a fellow student, whose painting *The Eve of St. Agnes* (a.k.a. *The Flight of Madeline and Porphyro*), from the work of a mutually admired poet, John Keats, had caught his attention at the Royal Academy that year; he soon was sharing a studio with William Holman Hunt, who emphasized his (and John Everett Millais's) already determined methods of painting everything honestly, from models and nature. At that studio Rossetti and Hunt produced their first Pre-Raphaelite paintings, *The Girlhood of Mary*

Virgin and *Rienzi*, respectively. Rossetti modeled for the main figure of Hunt's picture (Millais posed for the knight on the left), and Rossetti's mother and sister Christina modeled for St. Anne and Mary in his picture. (Both Brown and Hunt acknowledged that as much as Rossetti needed to learn from them the techniques of painting, they benefited from his vast knowledge of literature.)

These paintings, exhibited in 1849, were the first with the *P.R.B.* initials attached. The Brotherhood had been organized by Rossetti, Hunt, and Millais in September 1848 as a revolutionary band against the stagnancy of the Royal Academy. The new group was to follow nature exactly, paint directly from life in bright colors, reject conventional compositional techniques, and express real ideas—literary, religious, or moral. Rossetti enlisted three others—Thomas Woolner, James Collinson, and William Michael Rossetti; Hunt enlisted F. G. Stephens, to make seven original brethren. In their acknowledged influence, and that noted approvingly by the critics in 1849, all the Pre-Raphaelite paintings (including Millais's *Lorenzo and Isabella* and Collinson's *Italian Image-Makers*) seemed to reflect an early-Italian, early-German, and Nazarene style. From the Northern painters of the early Renaissance like van Eyck and Dürer the brothers adopted jewel-like colors and the portrayal of reality unhindered by centuries of distorting compositional rules. Certainly, the "unsophisticated" Cimabue's and Giotto's and Fra Angelico's flattened decorative space, with multiplied figures and heads overlapping, and emotions honestly portrayed, ended up in many Pre-Raphaelite works, especially the early drawings by Hunt, Rossetti, and Millais, and the latter's *Lorenzo and Isabella*. Rossetti's drawings throughout his life in fact show this multiplied, overlapped-figure technique, seen notably in such illustrations as "Mythic Uther's Deeply Wounded Son" for "The Palace of Art" in the Moxon *Tennyson*. But the same early-Italian spirit most noticeably informs Pre-Raphaelite drawings in the form of spiky, Gothic, angular, elongated, pointy-toed figures with crisply folded garments, clearly derived from the P.R.B.-inspiring book of Carlo Lasinio's engravings of the Campo Santo frescoes at Pisa.

Frontispiece for The Early Italian Poets, *1861; unused (wood-engraving, J. D. Cooper; 5 7/8 x 3 3/4; English Illustrated Magazine, vol. 1, 1883–84, p. 30)*

Rossetti's early pen-and-ink drawings, like Hunt's and Millais's, are all in this slightly open, medievalist style, particularly beautiful examples being his *Dante Drawing an Angel on the First Anniversary of the Death of Beatrice* (1849) and *The Salutation of Beatrice* (1849–50). Very soon, with the use of models (especially his lover, Elizabeth Siddal, resulting in relentlessly churned out drawings of her) and heightened decorative concerns, and a more realistically shaded style, Rossetti's drawings took on the well-worked form, with its designy effusion and linear perfection—and facial types and gestures—that seems to be a source for many of the great Pre-Raphaelite illustrators of the 1860s. His highly elaborate pen-and-ink drawings show him to be a creator of unique picture structures (and Pre-Raphaelite convoluted poses), an artist of original ideas, and a master of intense linework. *Hesterna Rosa* (1853), *Sir Launcelot in the Queen's Chamber* (1857), *Mary Magdalene at the House of Simon the Pharisee* (1858), *How They Met Themselves* (1860), and *Cassandra* (1861) are all among Western art's most unforgettable drawings.

At the same time, Rossetti was producing even more ambitious watercolors, sought after by patrons (sometimes procured by John Ruskin) and highly admired by a large circle of artists. These are ravishing in their colors; their themes, as in many of Rossetti's drawings, are medieval/Arthurian, from Malory, Dante, and Tennyson—and usually mystical, symbolic, and very sensual. Like Holman Hunt, but in a less obviously realistic manner, Rossetti used symbolic elements to comment on the picture and its meaning and emotions, cramming in crowd scenes or towns in a tiny corner of a work (*St. George and Princess Sabra*, watercolor, 1862; "St. Cecily," wood-engraving, Moxon *Tennyson*, 1857) or plastering backgrounds with repeated decoration.

The influence of William Blake's figural style and mystical/symbolic approach is certainly evident in much of this work. Rossetti in 1847 had acquired a notebook of autograph writings and drawings by that visionary artist, and he helped complete the first major book on Blake (published in 1863) after Alexander Gilchrist, the author, died in 1861. The work (especially in black and white) of Edward Burne-Jones, Simeon Solomon, and Frederick Sandys all replicate in some way the Rossetti style (which itself echoes the physical types

of Ford Madox Brown, his teacher).

Rossetti's Arthurianism reached a culmination in his project to decorate the walls of the Oxford Union Debating Hall. He enlisted six other artists (a new Brotherhood of seven?), among them Burne-Jones, William Morris, Arthur Hughes, and Val Prinsep. Technically the adventure was a fiasco, since the group's grasp of fresco technique was minimal. But the effort established Rossetti as the leading figure of Pre-Raphaelitism, just as Millais was turning into the darling of the Academy and Hunt was pursuing his own career as a religious painter. This gathering marked the beginning of a new phase of Pre-Raphaelitism, buoyed by Morris's and Burne-Jones's enthusiasm for medieval fantasy and decorative art and themes of legend.

As Rossetti in the early 1860s returned to painting in oils—with a new emphasis on the sumptuous handling and color of Venetian Renaissance masters, possibly influenced by Burne-Jones's Italian trips and Ruskin's writ-

***St. Cecily** for **"The Palace of Art"** (photograph of the drawing on the wood-block for the illustration in* Poems by Alfred Tennyson, *1857; photogravure, 3 3/4 x 3 1/8; as published in Joseph Pennell's* Some Poems by Alfred, Lord Tennyson, *1901)*

Beata Beatrix *(oil, 1864–70; 34 x 26; Tate Gallery, London; photogravure, as published in Elisabeth Luther Cary's* Poems of Dante Gabriel Rossetti, *vol. 2, 1903)*

By the force of his personality and the originality of his work, Rossetti mesmerized the art and literary communities of Victorian England. He maintained throughout his life a reputation as a passionate, eccentric genius; his early enthusiasm for the tragic love story of Dante and Beatrice he seemed to purposely replicate in his own life, notably in his love affair with Elizabeth Siddal, a beautiful but sickly woman who was his perpetual model. They finally married in 1860, a child was still-born, and Lizzie apparently took her own life with an overdose of the drug laudanum in 1862. Living his dream's tragedy, Rossetti buried the only manuscript of his poems in her coffin. In memory of his love for her, he painted, over the next few years, one of his masterpieces, *Beata Beatrix*, portraying Dante's Beatrice mystically transported from earth to heaven. The story only ends with Rossetti having his papers exhumed from the coffin in 1869. This first published collection of his poems (1870) established his reputation as an important poet (which overshadowed his artistic reputation, at least publicly, during his lifetime). At the same time, he was developing a dependence on chloral, a drug first taken for insomnia and then gradually leading to addiction and contributing to his death. The craving for chloral would eventually cool down his passionate relationship with William Morris's wife, Jane—another ubiquitous model for his work—in the late 1860s and early 1870s.

Despite his personal problems, and the obsessively controlling degree with which he regarded any dissemination of his art to the public and buyers, Rossetti was among the most loyal and giving of friends. Even in a circle of artists known for their generosity and kindness toward each other, Rossetti stood out as one who always had an encouraging word to say about others' works, ready to help with money or time, whose home was always open to anyone who wished to stay there, and who also made himself welcome for

ings extolling the Italians' virtues—and began concentrating on lone or multiplied female figures beautifully arranged and symbolically presented, Sandys followed. Burne-Jones soon made a career of producing dreamlike arrangements of females, existing in a world timeless and Botticellian and medieval at the same time. In this form, Burne-Jones's art proved even more clone-worthy than Rossetti's, and the works of the Burne-Jones followers Thomas M. Rooke, John M. Strudwick, and John Spencer-Stanhope seem only distinguishable from their master's by their slightly less poetic natures. Also producing female-centric compositions, artists such as Albert Moore and Frederic Leighton emphasized classical/Renaissance subjects, turning Rossettian poetic realism into the often prosaic formal arrangements of the Aesthetic movement.

long stays in his friends' homes. When their mutual friend James Smetham became mentally ill and there seemed little hope of his recovery, Rossetti and Frederic Shields tried to help his family by seeking buyers for Smetham's works, with Rossetti even finishing a few of them. On February 13, 1878, Rossetti wrote to Shields: "I wish I could report any progress with the Smetham business yet. I wrote to Mrs. Cowper-Temple, but have not her answer yet. To-day I have written to Valpy who is in Italy. Graham I have seen no more. I am very anxious about the matter and have no doubt of *some* results. Meanwhile do you know whether the Smethams are in want of funds to go on with? If so, I could consider the practicability of making some advance and reckoning on sales, which, though delayed, must I think occur to some extent. The delay in my movements has depended partly on a wish to get something done to the works (as you suggested) to give them a little better chance. . . . The truth is that to do any real good to them will cut into time, and I am most harassed to think what position our poor friend may be in. Have you any further news?" (*Life and Letters of Frederic Shields*, p. 228). Rossetti maintained lifelong friendships with both Shields and Smetham despite the latter two's obsessively and often dark religious personalities. Even amid the quarrels, estrangements, and paranoia of his last decade, Rossetti continued to possess a generous spirit.

After his wife's death, Rossetti's housemates were a varied lot: he shared his Cheyne Walk, Chelsea, quarters for a short time after 1862 with his brother, the poet Algernon Charles Swinburne, and the writer George Meredith. Rossetti's painting assistants Walter Knewstub and Henry Treffry Dunn both lived, in succession, on the premises; so did painter-illustrator Frederick Sandys, "for about a year and a quarter, terminating in the summer of 1867," according to William Michael Rossetti (*Rossetti: His Family-Letters*, vol. 1, p. 256).

Another unwavering confidant and correspondent, William Bell Scott, was a frequent visitor to Rossetti's. So was Shields, who seemed always in need of a new home or a place to stay, and partook of Rossetti's open-ended invitations many times since their friendship began in 1864, Rossetti offering him studio space and availing himself of Shields's service as photographer of his paintings. Shields, always a better draughtsman than colorist, vastly improved his painting after he started to spend a large amount of time in Rossetti's studio from about 1877; the two became very close, Shields often assisting the older, and failing, artist in his work. When Rossetti died in 1882, William Michael Rossetti requested that Shields make a drawing of the dead man's face.

With his models, Rossetti was generous in his encouragement of any artistic abilities they had. He tried to have Tennyson include Elizabeth Siddal, who did stiff but interesting Rossettian drawings, among the illustrators for the Moxon book. Better results of his support were evinced with Maria Spartali Stillman, who became the best known of the female Pre-Raphaelite painters.

One of Rossetti's most characteristic traits was his fear of, and sensitivity to, criticism. Soon after the poet Robert Buchanan's attack on his 1870 book (an infamous 1871 article called "The Fleshly School of Poetry" in the *Contemporary Review*), Rossetti suffered a nervous breakdown. This aversion to negative criticism also led to a general reluctance to exhibit after being excoriated by reviewers over the *P.R.B.* initials in his painting *Ecce Ancilla Domini*, shown in 1850. Rossetti, however, never had any hesitation in joining in the efforts sponsored or championed by his old mentor Ford Madox Brown: teaching at the Working Men's College, showing at the Free Exhibition of Pre-Raphaelite art in 1857 and over the years (1858–61) with the Hogarth Club, and designing for Morris's decorative-arts firm from 1861.

*Study [**Lancelot**] for the illustration **The Lady of Shalott** in* Poems by Alfred Tennyson, *1857 (ink drawing, 4 1/16 x 3 1/2; courtesy Delaware Art Museum, Samuel and Mary R. Bancroft Collection)*

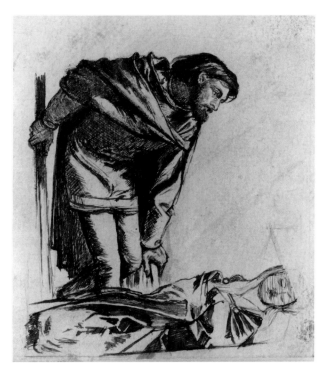

Nevertheless, Rossetti occasionally showed his works at other non–Royal Academy venues, such as the Liverpool Exhibition of 1858, and certainly was not wanting for patrons and buyers. Among many efforts on Rossetti's behalf, Ruskin procured for him a major commission, the altarpiece for Llandaff Cathedral—then being restored by John P. Seddon, the brother of Thomas Seddon (the sculptor Henry H. Armstead also was involved). This triptych, *The Seed of David* (1864), is one of Rossetti's finest works in oil, showing the artist at his most personal (with its repeated female angel heads) and symbolic, meticulously painted in the best Pre-Raphaelite realistic tradition (Jane and William Morris were models). During the following two decades, Rossetti's oil-painting technique steadily improved, the delectable sensuousness of his brushwork matching the otherworldly sensuality of his subjects—idealized "literary" females (*Monna Vanna*, 1866; *Proserpine*, 1877; *The Blue Bower*, 1865, and *The Blessed Damozel*, 1875–78, based on his own poetry; and including possibly the best oil of this later period, *Dante's Dream at the Time of the Death of Beatrice*, 1871).

Rossetti's reluctance to open himself up to negative criticism (the art critic F. G. Stephens, an original Pre-Raphaelite, was able to see the reclusive Rossetti's artworks and comment on them, with the artist's blessing, in the pages of the *Athenaeum*) also resulted in Rossetti's need to control the dissemination of his original works—and his limited use of reproductive means of showing his art. He was so fastidious about his drawings for the Moxon *Tennyson* that he delayed the book beyond its Christmas 1856 publication date and to some degree contributed to its failure. For the few illustrations for wood-engraving that he did, Rossetti

remained unapologetically curmudgeonly, constantly asking for revisions from the engravers and criticizing their efforts as not worthy of his original designs. It has been noted elsewhere how he favored W. J. Linton's engraving of his pieces, for the Moxon and his sister's two books; this was one of the few blind spots in Rossetti's taste, for Linton's lifeless technique generally lessened the impact of an artist's drawing.

For the Dalziels Rossetti reserved unrelenting scorn. On that firm's cutting of his blocks for the Moxon *Tennyson* he wrote disdainfully—and colorfully—to William Allingham in December 1856: "I have done, as yet, four [illustrations]—'Mariana in the South,' 'Sir Galahad,' and two to the 'Palace of Art.' I hope to do a second to 'Sir Galahad,' but am very uncertain as to any more. But these engravers! What ministers of wrath! Your drawing comes to them . . . and is hewn in pieces. . . . I took more pains with one block lately than I had with anything for a long while. It came back to me on paper, the other day, with Dalziel performing his cannibal jig [signature] in the corner, and I have really felt like an invalid ever since" (*Letters of Dante Gabriel Rossetti to William Allingham*, p. 191).

Rossetti's treatment of the publisher Edward Moxon is notorious; he continually delayed submission of his drawings after complaining that Hunt and Millais had received the best subjects to illustrate. According to Holman Hunt, "So often did the poor expectant publisher get disappointed in the delivery of each block, that it was said when soon after Moxon quitted this world of worry and vexation, that the book had been the death of him!" (*Pre-Raphaelitism*, vol. 2, p. 102). Rossetti wished to preserve his original images (which would be cut away on the block), and so had them photographed, writing to William Bell Scott in March 1857: "I shall not forget to keep photographs of my blocks for you—would send *one* now, did I not feel hopeful of having 2 more to send with it. I only had 3 blocks photographed. . . . Besides these 3, I have done 2 more blocks, which Linton has cut well, & of which therefore I need not regret having no photograph" (Princeton University Library, Troxell Collection).

Rossetti's most famous Moxon engraving was, however, cut by the Dalziels—"St. Cecily" (a.k.a. "St. Cecilia") for "The Palace of Art"; and despite his protestations, their clean and detailed cutting seems to clarify Rossetti's original drawing rather than harm it. Neither Tennyson nor the Dalziels quite understood what this picture had to do with its source poem (although the "gilded organ-pipes" and the "clear-wall'd city on the sea" are present); but the union of earthly sensuality with a heavenly spirit is pure Rossetti, anticipating the use of that theme in many of his paintings and drawings in the coming decades, notably *Beata Beatrix*. The Moxon's two other preeminent wood-engravings—"The Lady of Shalott" (a.k.a. "Lancelot") and "Mythic Uther's Deeply Wounded Son" for "The Palace of Art"—are also by Rossetti and the Dalziels, and as in the "St. Cecily," every medieval millimeter is preg-

nant with symbolic and decorative detail. These three unforgettable compositions surpass even the best illustrations by Hunt and Millais in the book.

The engraving of Rossetti's first book illustration, "The Maids of Elfen-Mere" for William Allingham's *The Music Master* (1855), which so affected the young Burne-Jones, was also a bone of contention for Rossetti. Indeed, Rossetti's letters to Allingham are obsessive in their anguish over the perceived mauling of the drawing by the Dalziels. At the beginning of

*Engraved wood-block for the illustration **The Maids of Elfen-Mere** in* The Music Master, *1855 (Dalziels; 4 7/8 x 3 x 7/8; courtesy Museum of Fine Arts, Boston, John H. and Ernestine A. Payne Fund [Hartley Collection])*

the process the artist was already making excuses and expecting the worst. "One thing I must not forget is to say how very busy and bothered I have been, and to beg that may plead my excuse for delay, not only with the letter, but with the more important wood-block, which is not yet sent in," Rossetti wrote in November 1854. "I hope, above all, they mean to have the drawing well cut. For my part I should like to tell them that they had better in my own case give the price of the *drawing* as an extra bonus to the *engraver*, and that then they must let me see a proof as soon as cut—the thing to be cancelled altogether if not approved of by me."

Apparently, Rossetti's worst fears came true, for in a March 1855 letter he was wailing to Allingham: "That wood-block! Dalziel has made such an incredible mull of it in the cutting that it cannot possibly appear. . . . Before I sent in my drawing, however, to the engraver, I consulted a friend—Clayton, who has drawn much on wood—as to whether it were done in the right way for cutting, and he assured me it was not only adaptable but remarkably so. . . . If you like, I will send you the proof of it, . . . though at the cost of considerable humiliation to myself, as you cannot imagine by looking at it, even after this letter, *how far* different it is from my drawing" (*Letters of Dante Gabriel Rossetti to William Allingham*, pp. 81–82, 108–09). Yet Allingham wrote to William Michael

Buy from Us with a Golden Curl (*wood-engraving, Morris, Marshall, Faulkner, and Co. [C. Faulkner]; 4 1/4 x 3 1/2;* **frontispiece** *for* Goblin Market and Other Poems, *1862*)

Rossetti on May 28, 1855: "The book is very soon to appear. What think you of the woodcuts, if you have seen them? I am on the whole delighted with them, and I unaffectedly think a great deal of Gabriel's, and see no evidence, at all events none of the *prima facie* sort, that could in the least justify the hanging of the engraver, a step which the painter seems to think desirable." William Rossetti sided "with Allingham in holding this [his brother's] was an extreme opinion" (*Ruskin: Rossetti: PreRaphaelitism*, p. 87).

For Rossetti's final illustration projects, it was obvious that the aggravation of getting his designs correctly interpreted by engravers, printers, and publishers was becoming much too taxing. His correspondence with Macmillan on his four drawings for Christina Rossetti's *Goblin Market* (1862) and *The Prince's Progress* (1866) continue his pattern of "micro-managing" every detail of the process, bristling at criticism, and still deferring to Linton. In a letter to Macmillan in December 1861, for example, Rossetti complains of a delay in cutting his blocks and asks the publisher, "Would [you] like me to take the 2 blocks at once to Linton instead? They are both good drawings & will require good cutting, though not by any means [very] elaborate. . . . I have made both drawings now from *Goblin Market*—not in the least, mind, because you told me the one you saw was mannered. That simply showed you did not understand it. My work never resembles any work but my own. So much for plain speaking!" Then Rossetti asked Macmillan, in early 1862, about the first finished block: "Shall I take it to Linton or Swain, 2 engravers in whom I have confidence?" Even after publication of the book Rossetti was still dissatisfied in his work's treatment; as he wrote to Macmillan on April 4, 1862: "They [the printed engravings] are as blurred & faint as possible & more like a penny newspaper than a careful book. I really think you should ask how this has happened . . . as the illustrations are completely ruined by it." Christina, however, wrote to Macmillan (in October 1862): "Have you seen my brother's designs? Charming, I think" (New York Public Library, Berg Collection).

Rossetti's obsession with fair treatment of his designs even extended to bindings and a minor addition of lettering to a titlepage. For the reissue of *Goblin Market* in 1865 he demanded to control the insertion of the words *Second Edition* by personally seeing to it that the sister of the Morris firm's Charles Faulkner (he had engraved the frontispiece to the first edition) cut it. Rossetti wrote to Macmillan on March 31, 1865: "Will you send me a copy of Goblin Market 2nd Ed? I am anx-

ious to see how the blocks are printed. . . . I hope to find that there is a mistake in a report I hear that my design for the binding has been somehow clipped or altered. This should no more occur without my sanction than an alteration should be made in engraving my drawings" (*Rossetti-Macmillan Letters*, p. 48).

Rossetti's final two illustrations were for *The Prince's Progress*. As fussy as ever, Rossetti himself chose Linton to engrave both designs, but it was the Moxon *Tennyson* all over in respect to deadlines. His sister intervened, corresponding with Macmillan on December 16, 1865, and apologizing that her brother could not finish the woodcuts before Christmas, even though *Prince's Progress* was scheduled—and advertised—to come out soon. She said she hoped the publisher would agree with her "in thinking Gabriel's designs too desirable to forego . . ." (*Rossetti-Macmillan Letters*, p. 56).

These four illustrations for Christina show Rossetti in his prime as an illustrator. Gone are the overworked surfaces of the Moxon drawings—replaced by a confident simplicity of style reflecting that of the designs he was making at the time for stained-glass windows. In "Buy from Us with a Golden Curl" and "Golden Head by Golden Head" (the latter framed by a fully designed titlepage border) for *Goblin Market*, and "The Long Hours Go and Come and Go" and "You Should Have Wept Her Yesterday" for *The Prince's Progress*, Rossetti is in perfect control of his thick, brushlike lines, not a wasted stoke in sight—the full-bodied figures expertly rendered, flowing garments and ample white areas taking the place of overall decorative coverage. The Moxon *Tennyson* drawings may be original and extraordinary works of art, but these four drawings are great *illustrations*.

An interesting article appeared in *Tinsley's Magazine* in 1869 about Rossetti's then-grow-

Golden Head by Golden Head (*wood-engraving, W. J. Linton; 2 3/8 x 2 5/8;* **titlepage illustration** *for* Goblin Market and Other Poems, *1862*)

ing reputation, in spite of his public low profile, as the Pre-Raphaelite leader. The quality of his art, it maintained, could only be judged on hearsay—on the opinions of others who themselves had evaluated the "mysteriously enshrined talents of that gentleman": for example, William Rossetti claiming his brother as the greatest Pre-Raphaelite painter; Swinburne in a pamphlet on a Royal Academy

A Sonnet (wood-engraving, 3 3/4 x 6 1/4; *frontispiece for* Dante Gabriel Rossetti: A Record and a Study, *1882*)

Exhibition devoting much discussion to work he had seen in Rossetti's studio or elsewhere (but not at the Academy) and describing sonnets appended to the pictures; and Swinburne and Morris both dedicating their first books of poems to Rossetti.

In one area, however, Rossetti's art could be seen and judged by all, continued the article; his public reputation at the time was largely based on his *illustrations*. "These designs show the priceless attainments of delicate fancifulness and original creation. There is not in one of them any element of commonplace or conventionality." The four illustrations for his sister's books in particular brought praise. "The picture [the frontispiece to *Goblin Market*] is noteworthy for its fullness and variety of action, and for the firm and unstrained gathering of the whole

into a composition which fills the small allotted space without crowding, and fills that space with various motion—even a few scratches of blown tree and windy sky seeming to render the sense of movement." As for the Moxon *Tennyson*, the article's author felt that Rossetti's contributions were "the chief attraction to connoisseurs" and were "all very beautiful" and important in "composition and imagination . . ." ("Criticisms on Contemporaries, No. 7. The Rossettis, Part 2: Dante Gabriel Rossetti," vol. 5, 1869–70, pp. 143–45).

After his ten illustrations, from *The Music Master* to *The Prince's Progress*, Rossetti drew nothing more for the wood-engravers, renewing instead his career as a poet and gaining a remarkable sureness in his painting, in technique and simplified symbolic-female subjects. His health—mental and physical—deteriorated, with the help of the stupefying chloral, throughout the 1870s. When he finally expired in April 1882, it was as if the flame had gone out that had illuminated English art and poetry for decades, as if everyone's friend and teacher and mentor and entertainer and correspondent had left them all alone. Ford Madox Brown wrote to Frederic Shields most poignantly when he heard of their friend's death: "I don't know how you feel [about] this sad event; to me it is the greatest blow I have received since the loss of our dear Nolly [Brown's son, in 1874]. I cannot at all get over the idea that I am never to speak to him again. . . . A great man is gone! And the effects of it on art in this country none can tell, but one may fear. . . . You have seen so much of poor dear Gabriel of late; you must be terribly cut up. To me it seems like a dream; I cannot make out how things are to go on; in so many directions things must be changed" (*Life and Letters of Frederic Shields*, p. 275).

The Maids of Elfen-Mere *(wood-engraving, Dalziels; 4 7/8 x 3; The Music Master, 1855)*

The long hours go and come and go

The Long Hours Go and Come and Go *(wood-engraving, W. J. Linton; 3 x 3 1/4; frontispiece for* The Prince's Progress and Other Poems, *1866)*

Catalogue

PERIODICALS

English Illustrated Magazine
Vol. 1, 1883–84:
¶ ***Frontispiece*** **for *The Early Italian Poets*** (p. 30; unpublished 1861 illustration; engraved for the *English Illustrated Magazine* by J. D. Cooper; see information below [§])

§ Clearly in the tradition of the wood-engraved illustrations of the period is **The Virgin at the Foot of the Cross,*** a typical facsimile wood-engraving by Swain, which accompanies Sidney Colvin's article "Rossetti as a Painter" in the *Magazine of Art*, vol. 6, 1883 (p. 180)

BOOKS

Goblin Market and Other Poems (Christina Rossetti; Macmillan, 1862)
¶ ***Frontispiece:*** **Buy from Us with a Golden Curl*** (Morris, Marshall, Faulkner, and Co. [C. Faulkner])
¶ ***Titlepage illustration:*** **Golden Head by Golden Head*** (W. J. Linton)
• Plus cover design by the artist

The Music Master: A Love Story, and Two Series of Day and Night Songs (William Allingham; Routledge, 1855)
¶ **The Maids of Elfen-Mere*** (Dalziels; reprinted in *Flower Pieces*)

The Prince's Progress and Other Poems (Christina Rossetti; Macmillan, 1866)
¶ ***Frontispiece:*** **The Long Hours Go and Come and Go*** (W. J. Linton)
¶ **You Should Have Wept Her Yesterday*** (W. J. Linton)
• Plus cover design by the artist

[Tennyson] *Poems by Alfred Tennyson* (Moxon, 1857)
¶ **The Lady of Shalott*** (Dalziels; a.k.a. **Lancelot**)

¶ **Mariana in the South*** (W. J. Linton)

¶ **"The Palace of Art,"** 2 illustrations* (Dalziels; **Mythic Uther's Deeply Wounded Son** [a.k.a. **King Arthur and the Weeping Queens**]; **St. Cecily** [a.k.a. **St. Cecilia**])

¶ **Sir Galahad*** (W. J. Linton; reprinted in *Gems from Tennyson*)

§ See also: **A Sonnet**, the wood-engraved *frontispiece* (of a previously unpublished drawing) for William Sharp's *Dante Gabriel Rossetti: A Record and a Study* (Macmillan, 1882)

BOOKS CONTAINING REPRINTS

Flower Pieces and Other Poems (William Allingham; Reeves and Turner, 1888)

¶ **The Maids of Elfen-Mere** (reprinted from *The Music Master*)

• Plus a photo-engraved reproduction of the artist's watercolor **The Queen's Page**

Gems from Tennyson (Boston: Ticknor and Fields, 1866)

¶ **Sir Galahad** (reprinted from *Poems by Alfred Tennyson*)

Goblin Market, The Prince's Progress, and Other Poems (Christina Rossetti; Macmillan, new ed., 1875)

¶ **Buy from Us with a Golden Curl**

¶ **Golden Head by Golden Curl**

• Reprinted from *Goblin Market and Other Poems*

¶ **The Long Hours Go and Come and Go**

¶ **You Should Have Wept Her Yesterday**

• Reprinted from *The Prince's Progress and Other Poems*

• Plus cover design by the artist adapted from *Goblin Market*

• Published in a new, enlarged edition in 1890 as *Christina Rossetti's Poems*

§ Rossetti designed covers for the following books (in addition to those already cited):

• *Atalanta in Calydon: A Tragedy* (Algernon Charles Swinburne; Moxon, 1865)

You Should Have Wept Her Yesterday (wood-engraving, W. J. Linton; 5 7/8 x 3 3/4; The Prince's Progress and Other Poems, *1866)*

Mariana in the South (wood-engraving, W. J. Linton; 3 3/4 x 3 1/4; Poems by Alfred Tennyson, 1857)

The Lady of Shalott *(wood-engraving, Dalziels; 3 5/8 x 3 1/8;* Poems by Alfred Tennyson, *1857)*

Mythic Uther's Deeply Wounded Son *for "The Palace of Art"* *(wood-engraving, Dalziels; 3 1/8 x 3 5/8;* Poems by Alfred Tennyson, *1857)*

• *Ballads and Sonnets* (Dante Gabriel Rossetti; Ellis and White, 1881)
• *The Comedy of Dante Alighieri. Part 1: The Hell* (William Michael Rossetti; Macmillan, 1865)
• *Dante and His Circle with the Italian Poets Preceding Him* (Dante Gabriel Rossetti, ed. and trans.; Ellis and White, 1874)
• *The Early Italian Poets from Ciullo d'Alcamo to Dante Alighieri* (Dante Gabriel Rossetti, ed. and trans.; Smith, Elder, 1861)
• *A Pageant and Other Poems* (Christina Rossetti; Macmillan, 1881)
• *Parables and Tales* (Thomas Gordon Hake; Chapman and Hall, 1872)
• [Rossetti] *Dante Gabriel Rossetti: Poems* (Ellis, 1870)
• *A Shadow of Dante* (Maria Francesca Rossetti; Rivingtons, 1871)
• [Shelley] *Percy Bysshe Shelley: Poetical Works* (Reeves and Turner, 4 vols., 1880; 2 vols., 1882)
• [Shelley] *Percy Bysshe Shelley: Prose Works* (Harry Buxton Forman, ed.; Reeves and Turner, 4 vols., 1880)
• *Songs Before Sunrise* (Algernon Charles Swinburne; Ellis, 1871)

INDIVIDUAL PRINTS

¶ **Juliette** (lithograph, Rossetti, c. 1846; 8 15/16 x 6 3/16)
• Victoria and Albert Museum, London, Department of Prints, Drawings, and Paintings

¶ **Playing Cards**, set of 5 (lithographs, Rossetti, c. 1847; each 3 1/4 x 2 1/2)
• The 5 subjects are: **The King of Spades**, **The King of Hearts**, **The Queen of Hearts**, **The King of Diamonds**, and **The King of Clubs**
• Victoria and Albert Museum, London, Department of Prints, Drawings, and Paintings

¶ **Trade Card for Murray Marks** (color wood-engraving, C. Eade, c. 1876; 3 1/4 x 4 5/8)
• Reprinted (probably using the original boxwood blocks) in G. C. Williamson's

Murray Marks and His Friends (Lane, 1919); Williamson reports that Rossetti created the gold and maroon Japanese jar with peacock feathers, James McNeill Whistler contributed the interior border designs, and William Morris did the lettering; the card advertised Murray Marks's decorative-wares shop. Possibly created by H. Treffry Dunn, Rossetti's studio assistant (see Linda Merrill's *The Peacock Room: A Cultural Biography*, 1998, pp. 176–77).

§ *The Risen Life* (3d ed., Elkins, 1889) by Richard C. Jackson has one Rossetti illustration (also used for the cover), which is a previous design for a sculptural panel, *Pelican with Young*, reproduced in *Building World*, January 2, 1888 (see Fredeman's *Pre-Raphaelitism*, p. 297)

§ Illustration for *The Early Italian Poets* in the *English Illustrated Magazine*: There are also proof prints (photogravures?) of the same drawing. Printed beneath the image is "From a drawing on a zinc plate by D. G. Rossetti intended for the title page of *The Early Italian Poets*, 1861." These appear to be impressions from the plate owned by the Kelmscott Press secretary, Sidney Cockerell (4 3/4 x 3 5/8; Beinecke Rare Book and Manuscript Library, Yale University Library, New Haven, Purdy-Hardy Collection; Birmingham Museums and Art Gallery).

St. Cecily** for **"The Palace of Art" (wood-engraving, Dalziels; 3 5/8 x 3 1/8; Poems by Alfred Tennyson, *1857*)

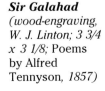

Sir Galahad (wood-engraving, W. J. Linton; 3 3/4 x 3 1/8; Poems by Alfred Tennyson, *1857*)

Frederick Sandys

(1829–1904)

It often seems that Frederick Sandys was, and is, everyone's favorite illustrator of the Sixties—a powerful, fastidious draughtsman whose Pre-Raphaelite wood-engravings represented the goal to which his fellow artists aspired. His work, particularly his twenty-five wood-block drawings, drew the praise of the "Arts-and-Crafts" enthusiasts of the 1890s; Walter Crane, Gleeson White, Joseph Pennell, and Esther Wood (in an 1896 monograph) all wrote enthusiastically about the artist. Well known is Rossetti's remark that Sandys was

Frederick Sandys, c. 1900 (photographic print; as published in Reproductions of Woodcuts by F. Sandys, *deluxe edition, [1910])*

"the greatest of living draughtsmen."

Sandys was associated, personally and stylistically, with Dante Gabriel Rossetti and other Pre-Raphaelite artists beginning in the late 1850s. Sandys was originally from Norwich, an area with its own distinctive school of art, among whose leaders were John Crome and John Sell Cotman. Cotman, an important influence on Sandys, was one of the leading etchers of his day, and he produced a number of etching collections of architectural antiquities before 1840. Sandys's early patron, the Reverend James Bulwer, was also a patron of Cotman, who together with Crome and Sandys provided original illustrations for the rector's manuscript book *The Antiquities of Norfolk*. For *Extracts from My Journal* (privately printed, 1853) by the Reverend's son J. R. Bulwer, Sandys produced four etchings; *Norfolk Portraits* (c. 1850) also contains four early etchings by Sandys (who at the time was known as Fred Sands).

Sandys's exposure to Cotman as well as his interest in "antiquities" and early-German and Gothic art was intensified through his relationship with Bulwer—important for his development as a Pre-Raphaelite practitioner of highly detailed depictions of nature and precise draughtsmanship. Those qualities in Cotman's etchings and in the graphic work of Albrecht Dürer were to inspire Sandys's drawing style both before and after he arrived in London. Early on, he signed his brilliant studies of natural details in medieval-type script (e.g., *Smoker's Hole*, 1852) and developed a monogram based on Dürer's.

Sandys first came to the attention of Rossetti and his friends in 1857, when he produced *The Nightmare*, a lithographic print caricaturing John Everett Millais's painting *Sir Isumbras at the Ford* of the same year. Both Sandys's London career in publishing and his substantial contact with the Pre-Raphaelites began about 1860. His elaborately detailed contemporary subject *Autumn*, a pen-and-ink drawing of that year, became a painting in 1862: an

The Nightmare (lithograph, Sandys, 1857; 13 x 19; also published [photo-engraving] in Reproductions of Woodcuts by F. Sandys, *deluxe edition,* [1910])

old soldier talks of his youth to a mother and child, all reclining along a riverbank. In the distance is a view of Bishop's Bridge and the town of Norwich, with its castle and cathedral (Arthur B. Chamberlain, "Works by Frederick Sandys in the Birmingham Art Gallery," *Apollo*, vol. 2, 1925, p. 263); the foreground items and botanical elements are an indication of Sandys's concern for and mastery of even the tiniest blade of grass in his works. In his oil paintings of the 1860s, Sandys concentrates on themes similar to Rossetti's—full and half figures of females surrounded by flowers, and attached to medieval/legendary/classical themes: *Oriana* (1861), *King Pelleas's*

Daughter (1862), *La Belle Ysonde* (1862), and *Mary Magdalene* (1862, and looking quite medieval). For a superb draughtsman, Sandys was unusually skilled as a colorist, his subjects often shimmering in rich harmonies of golds, greens, and reds, certainly reflective of an appreciation for the paintings of Dürer, Holbein, van Eyck, and Memling. A wonderful example is *Morgan-le-Fay* (exhibited 1864), perhaps Sandys's most famous painting; here he brings his full powers of careful observation into play to depict King Arthur's evil half-sister, and weaves the work with two- and three-dimensional symbols and perfectly rendered individual strands of hay and thread.

Female beauty in its tragic passion and terrible wrath, heroic in its proportions, was Sandys's slightly different take on the Rossetti model, also seen in his painting *Medea* of 1868 (a photograph of this work was used as the frontispiece to a book, A. B. Richards's *Medea: A Poem*, 1869). By the mid-1860s, Sandys in his exhibited works (*Gentle Spring*, 1865) was taking Rossetti's lead into the realm of the Aesthetic movement, where the beautiful arrangement of natural forms—usually with a woman as the center—became an end in itself, unrelated to any narrative or symbolic meaning. Throughout the 1870s and '80s Sandys continued to make exquisite chalk drawings and paintings of Aesthetic-spirited female figures/heads and some of the century's finest English portraits, often compared to those of Holbein.

William Michael Rossetti relates the story of his brother's relationship with Sandys, who became "a frequent visitor [after 1862], and at one period stayed continuously in the house

Until Her Death *(wood-engraving, Dalziels; 4 1/8 x 5 1/8;* Good Words, *vol. 3, 1862, p. 312;* Touches of Nature; Reproductions of Woodcuts by F. Sandys)

for many months. . . . In 1869 an unfortunate split occurred between Sandys and Dante Rossetti. The latter considered that the former imbued his mind overmuch with pictorial motives and treatment of which Rossetti was the originator, and that he reproduced them in works not indeed outwardly very conformable to Rossetti's methods, but still so far germane to them as to forestall his own hold upon his projects of work. In a very unaggressive spirit he represented this state of the facts in a letter which he addressed to Mr. Sandys; but Sandys was not at all inclined to accept such a view, and, as the upshot of a few letters interchanged, he renounced all further friendship with my brother. My own firm belief is that the latter was correct in his estimate of the facts, and was free from any blame in the tone in which he set them forth. Towards 1875 Rossetti took the first step, by writing a friendly letter, for effecting a reconciliation, and Sandys responded warmly" (*Some Reminiscences*, vol. 2, pp. 321–22).

Narrative interest and painstakingly depicted physical details, together with the pronounced influence of Dürer's prints, were the informing principles of Sandys's undeniable masterpieces, his twenty-five illustrative wood-engravings of the 1860s. After a tentative, though realistic and powerful, start with "The Legend of the Portent" in the *Cornhill Magazine* (1860), Sandys's second illustration, "Yet Once More on the Organ Play" (*Once a Week*, 1861) unveils an illustrative technique clearly based on Dürer's woodcuts and engravings. William Morris owned a collection of photographs of Dürer's work and was also interested in the efforts of the German artist Alfred Rethel to revive the art of woodcuts along the lines of Dürer; Morris in 1856 wrote an article describing two of Rethel's "Dance of Death" prints of the late 1840s in his *Oxford and Cambridge Magazine*. Rethel is held by such contemporary writers on English illustration as Joseph Pennell, Walter Crane, and Gleeson White to have influenced Sandys's style; and Rethel's figures of Death are surely models for Sandys's similar figures in "Yet Once More on the Organ Play" and "Until Her Death" (*Good Words*, 1862). Certainly another series of wood-engravings based on Dürer's methods that had recently been published in England, the Nazarene artist Schnorr von Carolsfeld's *Bible Pictures*, was essential in confirming Sandys's stylistic leanings in his own black-and-white art.

Sandys's illustrations are among the most obviously indebted to Dürer and early-German models of any others of the 1860s. Sandys's lines, regardless of the subject he's depicting—a Holbein- or Dürer-inspired theme like "Yet Once More" and "Until Her Death" or a contemporary scene like "From My Window" (*Once a Week*, 1861) or "The Old Chartist" (*Once a Week*, 1862)—are for the most part of a uniform thickness akin to Dürer's. This aspect was apparently quite important to the artist; for example, in a letter to the Dalziels (undated) about his "Jacob Hears the Voice of the Lord" engraving in their *Bible Gallery*, Sandys writes: "Do not forget to keep my lines in the cutting *very thick*" (manuscript letter, author's collection). The angular, twisting folds of the clothing in Sandys's drawings—especially seen in "Rosamund, Queen of the Lombards" (*Once a Week*, 1861), "The Three Statues of Aegina" (*Once a Week*, 1861), "Harald Harfagr" (*Once a Week*, 1862), and "Until Her Death"—recall the linear play and solidity of garments by Dürer and van Eyck. The pensive seated woman in voluminous clothing that appears in many of Sandys's wood-engravings—"Until Her Death," "If" (*Argosy*, 1866), "The Waiting Time" (*Churchman's Family Magazine*, 1863)—may derive from Dürer's famous figure in his *Melancolia* engraving of 1514. Even Sandys's monogram, based early on Dürer's, often finds itself in his engravings nestled into the sides of blocks of wood ("Manoli" for the *Cornhill Magazine*, 1862) or even inscribed on a little plaque ("The King at the Gate" and "Jacques de Caumont," both for *Once a Week*, 1862), just as Dürer treated his.

Thematically, the same females—and males—involved in tragic and often morbid circumstances as in his paintings, and as so often appealed to the Pre-Raphaelites in their illustrations, became the subjects for most of Sandys's illustrations. In the poem "The Sailor's Bride" (drawn for *Once a Week*, 1861), a sailor

Rosamund, Queen of the Lombards (*wood-engraving, Swain; 5 1/8 x 4 1/2;* Once a Week, *vol. 5, 1861, p. 631; Reproductions of Woodcuts by F. Sandys*)

returns, too late; his fiancée has died. "Yet Once More," with its Rethelian figure of Death providing the musical accompaniment, illustrates the poetic lines: " 'Tis some unearthly blessed strain / Bursts forth as he doth play— / He stops with awe—the list'ner's soul / Hath gently passed away." In Walter Thornbury's poem "The Three Statues of Aegina," a sculptor in Greece labors to make a great masterpiece—the third attempt is finally a success, but he dies just as the judge acclaims him. "Manoli" depicts a workman, laboring for nine years, whose walls kept vanishing—until he took an oath to wall up in the building the first woman he sees—which is his wife.

In discussing "Rosamund, Queen of the Lombards," Joseph Pennell provides a description of Sandys's talent as well as of the grisly scene of Rosamund, who caresses her father's skull, made into a wine cup, just after she has slain the bloodthirsty king: "She kneels before the desk, richly carved, covered with books, by which her scissors and pens hang; behind her, on his bed, is the dead king, whose blood streams down across the floor, the lamps flare and flicker in the darkness, and the morning light comes in at the back, showing the horror and disorder of the place. Save the Sandys of the next years, I know of no other English illustration in its way to approach this" ("*Once a Week*: A Great Art Magazine," *Bibliographica*, vol. 3, 1897, p. 71).

Landscape with Bridge over Stream *(etching proof, Sandys, early 1850s; 3 3/8 x 6 1/4; inscribed "Comp. The Old Chartist, 1862"; image used as background for the wood-block illustration* **The Old Chartist** *in* Once a Week, *1862; courtesy Fitzwilliam Museum, Cambridge)*

Sandys's training as a draughtsman allowed him to immediately grasp the importance of the linear qualities of the wood-engraving. "The Legend of the Portent," his first, already displays an incredible understanding of wood-engraving technique in reducing every part of the picture to highly controlled parallel lines, with a minimum of crosshatching and fussiness. In addition to innumerable studies from life for the individual elements of a piece, Sandys prepared a finished drawing for each of his twenty-five wood-engraved illustrations, and these drawings are—more than those of any other artist working in the medium—exact facsimiles of the prints themselves: stroke by stroke, he transferred his original with brush and ink to the block's surface, where it was engraved by the Dalziels or Swain.

In a Sandys cut like "Rosamund, Queen of the Lombards" there is no line that is not thoroughly thought out and related to another. Photographs of the original drawings on the blocks before cutting for "The Death of King Warwulf" (*Once a Week*, 1862), "Harald Harfagr," and "If," when compared with the engraved versions by Joseph Swain, show an absolutely exact line-for-line correspondence—which says much for Sandys's understanding of woodcut art and Swain's exceptional skill at interpretation (Museum of Fine Arts, Boston, Hartley Collection).

One of the most important aspects of Sandys's work is the equal pictorial treatment of all elements in nature, down to the smallest details. This is, of course, a characteristic of Pre-Raphaelite "realism"—based in part on the precisely rendered natural forms in every part of a Dürer wood- or copper-engraving—from the foreground plants to the patterns of the trees and buildings in the distant hills—elements that reappear in Sandys illustrations like "Until Her Death," "The Old Chartist," and "Harald Harfagr." This emphasis relates also to the symbolism the artist imbues in the detail, a particularly Pre-Raphaelite characteristic and shared with the great Flemish and German masters: like them, Rossetti, Hunt, Sandys, and their brethren carried the emphasis on symbolic detail into their graphic work. In Sandys's engravings, this is evident in "Rosamund," in "The Old Chartist"—whose figure is joined in bucolic reverie by every living element of even minor stature in his surroundings—and in "Amor Mundi" (*Shilling Magazine*, 1865), an aggressively realistic depiction of the Pre-Raphaelite theme of love and death. Here, the overgrown, entwined vegetation, almost diabolical in its confusion, reflects the dead body twisting and rotting below the two lovers. The scrupulousness of portrayal of each little root and blade of grass also adds that Pre-Raphaelite sense of eternal reality to the scene, while confusing all sense of space below the top figures—especially appropriate since it is the philosophical present/future concept of Christina Rossetti's poem—pleasure leading to death—that is portrayed.

Sandys's devotion to creating a perfect work of art for all these illustrations can be seen in his notes to engravers. One of his masterpieces, for *English Sacred Poetry* (1862), is "The Little Mourner." On the Hartley Collection (Museum of Fine Arts, Boston) proofs, touched in white for the Dalziels' corrections, Sandys writes: "Lighten very delicately the soles where I have touched. . . . Lighten and widen the heel. Of course *very, very* slightly are they to be lighten[ed]—it is only that they may more readily attract the eye. . . . Show more distinctly *the profile* of the upper and lower jaws and teeth and lighten a black patch by the nose, as marked." The Hartley Collection also has the original woodblock engraved by W. H. Hooper for "The Sailor's Bride," which Sandys, in an unusual move, actually demanded not be used; he requested that the entire work be recut by Joseph Swain. He was justified, for the extremely subtle depiction in darkened tones of the head and face of the man, in fact the whole central area, would have printed extremely muddy.

Sandys drew for the leading periodicals of the 1860s: the *Argosy*, *Churchman's Family Magazine*, the *Cornhill Magazine*, *Good Words*, *Once a Week*, the *Quiver*, and the *Shilling Magazine*, normally using Swain as his engraver. For the Dalziels he drew two unsurpassable works for Willmott's

English Sacred Poetry and one for the *Bible Gallery* (1881). John Saddler engraved two characteristic watercolors on steel for the frontispieces of George Meredith's *The Shaving of Shagpat* (1865) and Dinah Mulock Craik's *Christian's Mistake* (1866). Sandys's periodical drawings were reprinted in the books *The Cornhill Gallery* (1864), *Pictures of Society* (1866), *Idyllic Pictures* (1867), and most extensively (with some alternate titles) in Thornbury's *Historical and Legendary Ballads and Songs* of 1876. In 1910 his widow, Mary Sandys, issued a portfolio of his twenty-five illustrations, *Reproductions of Woodcuts by F. Sandys, 1860–1866*, and a deluxe limited edition with the art printed on mounted india paper and with the addition of three other works, including *The Nightmare* print of 1857—which had started it all.

*Engraved wood-block for the illustration **The Sailor's Bride** (W. H. Hooper; 3 3/8 x 5 x 7/8; unused; drawing recut by Swain and published in* Once a Week, *1861; courtesy Museum of Fine Arts, Boston, John H. and Ernestine A. Payne Fund [Hartley Collection])*

If (wood-engraving, Swain; 6 1/4 x 4 1/2; Argosy, vol. 1, 1866, p. 336; Touches of Nature; Reproductions of Woodcuts by F. Sandys)

Danae in the Brazen Chamber *(wood-engraving, Swain, [1867]; 7 x 4 1/2;* Century Guild Hobby Horse, *vol. 3, 1888, p. 47;* Reproductions of Woodcuts by F. Sandys)

Catalogue

PERIODICALS
Illustrations reprinted in *Reproductions of Woodcuts by F. Sandys, 1860–1866* are indicated thus: Δ

Argosy
Vol. 1, 1866:
    ¶ **If*** (p. 336, Swain; reprinted as **Hoping Against Hope** in *Touches of Nature*) Δ
    • The illustration also appears in a cropped circular format on the titlepage

Century Guild Hobby Horse
Vol. 3, no. 10, 1888:
    ¶ **Danae in the Brazen Chamber*** (p. 47, Swain; originally engraved for, but not published with, Swinburne's poem in *Once a Week*, 1867) Δ
    ¶ **Miranda** (photogravure in red)

Churchman's Family Magazine
Vol. 2, 1863:
    ¶ **The Waiting Time*** (p. 91, W. Thomas; reprinted as **Lancashire's Lesson** in *Pictures of Society*) Δ

Cornhill Magazine
Vol. 1, 1860:
    ¶ **The Legend of the Portent*** (p. 617, W. J. Linton; reprinted in *The Cornhill Gallery*) Δ
Vol. 6, 1862:
    ¶ **Manoli*** (p. 346, Swain; reprinted in *The Cornhill Gallery*) Δ
Vol. 14, 1866:
    ¶ **Cleopatra (Dissolving the Pearl)*** (p. 331, Dalziels; to accompany a poem by Swinburne written for Sandys's original drawing of 1862; the drawing is reproduced in the *Pall Mall Magazine*, vol. 16, 1898, p. 336) Δ

English Illustrated Magazine
Vol. 1, 1883–84:
    ¶ **Matthew Arnold** (p. 202, O. Lacour; based on one of the artist's chalk portraits of famous authors for Macmillan)

Vol. 8, 1890–91:
¶ **Proud Maisie** (p. 560, W. Spielmeyer; reprinted in the deluxe edition of *Reproductions of Woodcuts by F. Sandys*)

Good Words
Vol. 3, 1862:
¶ **Until Her Death*** (p. 312, Dalziels; reprinted in *Touches of Nature*) Δ
Vol. 4, 1863:
¶ **Sleep*** (p. 589, Dalziels; reprinted in *Touches of Nature* and *Aunt Mary's Sunday Picture Book*) Δ
• "The Sheep and the Goat" (p. 671) by J. D. Watson is erroneously credited to Sandys in the index

Once a Week
Vol. 4, 1861:
¶ **Yet Once More on the Organ Play*** (p. 350, Swain; a.k.a. **From the German of Uhland**; reprinted as **Tintoretto** in *Historical and Legendary Ballads and Songs* [hereafter *HLBS*]) Δ
¶ **The Sailor's Bride*** (p. 434, Swain) Δ
Vol. 5, 1861:
¶ **From My Window*** (p. 238, Swain) Δ
¶ **The Three Statues of Aegina*** (p. 491, Swain; reprinted [same title] in *HLBS*) Δ
¶ **Rosamund, Queen of the Lombards*** (p. 631, Swain) Δ
Vol. 6, 1862:
¶ **The Old Chartist*** (p. 184, Swain; reprinted as **The Miller's Meadow** in *HLBS*) Δ
¶ **The King at the Gate*** (p. 322, Swain; reprinted as **The Avatar of Zeus** in *HLBS*) Δ
¶ **Jacques de Caumont*** (p. 614, Swain; reprinted as **The Apparitor of the Secret Tribunal** [#2] in *HLBS*) Δ
Vol. 7, 1862:
¶ **Harald Harfagr*** (p. 154, Swain; reprinted as **The Labours of Thor** in *HLBS*) Δ
¶ **The Death of King Warwulf*** (p. 266, Swain; reprinted [same title] in *HLBS*)
¶ **The Boy Martyr*** (p. 602, Swain; reprinted [same title] in *HLBS*) Δ
New ser. [ser. 2], vol. 1, 1866:
¶ **Helen and Cassandra*** (p. 454, Swain; reprinted as **The Search of Ceres for Proserpine** in *HLBS*) Δ

The Waiting Time
(wood-engraving, W. Thomas; 7 1/8 x 4 1/2; Churchman's Family Magazine, *vol. 2, 1863, p. 91;* Pictures of Society; Reproductions of Woodcuts by F. Sandys*)*

The Legend of the Portent
(wood-engraving, W. J. Linton; 5 3/4 x 3 7/8; Cornhill Magazine, *vol. 1, 1860, p. 617;* The Cornhill Gallery; Reproductions of Woodcuts by F. Sandys*)*

Cleopatra (Dissolving the Pearl) (wood-engraving, Dalziels; 7 x 4 1/4; Cornhill Magazine, vol. 14, 1866, p. 331; Reproductions of Woodcuts by F. Sandys)

Right: **Sleep** *(wood-engraving, Dalziels; 5 3/4 x 4 1/2; Good Words, vol. 4, 1863, p. 589; Touches of Nature; Reproductions of Woodcuts by F. Sandys)*

Bottom: **The Sailor's Bride** *(wood-engraving, Swain; 3 1/4 x 4 7/8; Once a Week, vol. 4, 1861, p. 434; Reproductions of Woodcuts by F. Sandys)*

Quarto
Vol. 1, 1896:
    ¶ **The Spirit of the Storm** (p. 38; photo-engraving of an unfinished ink drawing on a wood-block)
    • Wood-block: Art Gallery of South Australia, Adelaide
    • While the *Quarto* is the traditional source for this illustration, it was also published in *A London Garland* (W. E. Henley, ed.; Macmillan, 1895) as **A Storm Fiend**

Quiver
Ser. 3, vol. 1, 1866 [1865–66]:
    ¶ **The Advent of Winter*** (p. 201, Dalziels; reprinted as **October** in *Idyllic Pictures*) Δ

Shilling Magazine
Vol. 1, 1865:
    ¶ **Amor Mundi*** (p. 193, Swain) Δ

§ A photogravure reproduction of the ink drawing **Morgan-le-Fay** appears in the *British Architect* for October 1879, and is reprinted in the deluxe edition of *Reproductions of Woodcuts by F. Sandys*

§ The *Art Journal* of 1884 (vol. 46 [new ser., vol. 23]) reproduces the wood-engravings **If**, **The Old Chartist**, **The Death of King Warwulf**, and **Harald Harfagr**, in addition to the original drawing for **The Advent of Winter** wood-engraving and **Tears**, a drawing (photogravure), and several sketches for illustrations (photo-engravings) to accompany the article "Frederick Sandys" (pp. 73–78)

BOOKS

Christian's Mistake ([Dinah Mulock Craik]; Hurst and Blackett, 1866)
 ¶ *Frontispiece:* **Christian*** (steel-engraving, J. Saddler)

The Conquest of England (John Richard Green; Macmillan, 1883)

From My Window *(wood-engraving, Swain; 5 x 3 3/8; Once a Week, vol. 5, 1861, p. 238; Reproductions of Woodcuts by F. Sandys)*

The Three Statues of Aegina *(wood-engraving, Swain; 5 x 3 1/4; Once a Week, vol. 5, 1861, p. 491; Historical and Legendary Ballads and Songs; Reproductions of Woodcuts by F. Sandys)*

The Old Chartist *(wood-engraving, Swain; 4 7/8 x 4 1/8; Once a Week, vol. 6, 1862, p. 184; Historical and Legendary Ballads and Songs; Reproductions of Woodcuts by F. Sandys)*

The King at the Gate (*wood-engraving, Swain;
5 x 4 1/4; Once a Week, vol. 6, 1862, p. 322;* Historical
and Legendary Ballads and Songs; Reproductions of
Woodcuts by F. Sandys)

Jacques de Caumont (*wood-engraving, Swain; 4 3/4
x 4 3/8;* Once a Week, *vol. 6, 1862, p. 614;* Historical
and Legendary Ballads and Songs; Reproductions of
Woodcuts by F. Sandys)

¶ *Frontispiece:* **Portrait of Prof. J. R.
Green** (steel-engraving, G. J. Stodart;
based on one of the artist's chalk portraits
of famous authors for Macmillan)

Dalziels' Bible Gallery (Routledge, 1881)
¶ **Jacob Hears the Voice of the Lord***
(Dalziels; reprinted in *Art Pictures from the
Old Testament*) Δ

English Sacred Poetry (Rev. Robert Aris
Willmott, ed.; Routledge, 1862)
¶ **Life's Journey*** (Dalziels) Δ
¶ **The Little Mourner*** (Dalziels) Δ

The Shaving of Shagpat (George Meredith;
Chapman and Hall, 2d ed., 1865)
¶ *Frontispiece:* **Bhanavar Among the
Serpents of Lake Karatis*** (steel-engrav-
ing, J. Saddler; a.k.a. **Bhanavar the
Beautiful**)

§ *Medea: A Poem* (Alfred Bate Richards;
Chapman and Hall, 1869) includes a photographic print of Sandys's painting *Medea*
as the *frontispiece*

BOOKS CONTAINING REPRINTS

Art Pictures from the Old Testament (Aley
Fox, text; Society for Promoting Christian
Knowledge, 1894)
¶ **Jacob Hears the Voice of the Lord**
(reprinted from *Dalziels' Bible Gallery*)

Aunt Mary's Sunday Picture Book
(Routledge, n.d.)
¶ **Sleep** (reprinted from *Good Words*)

The Cornhill Gallery (Smith, Elder, 1864)
¶ **The Legend of the Portent**
¶ **Manoli**
• Reprinted from the *Cornhill Magazine*

Historical and Legendary Ballads and Songs
(Walter Thornbury; Chatto and Windus,
1876)
¶ **The Apparitor of the Secret
Tribunal** [#2] (**Jacques de Caumont**
reprinted from *Once a Week*)
¶ **The Avatar of Zeus** (**The King at the
Gate** reprinted from *Once a Week*)
¶ **The Boy Martyr** (reprinted [same

title] from *Once a Week*)

¶ **The Death of King Warwolf** [#1] (reprinted [same title, alt. spelling] from *Once a Week*)

¶ **The Labours of Thor** (**Harald Harfagr** reprinted from *Once a Week*)

¶ **The Miller's Meadow** (**The Old Chartist** reprinted from *Once a Week*)

¶ **The Search of Ceres for Proserpine** (**Helen and Cassandra** reprinted from *Once a Week*)

¶ **The Three Statues of Aegina** (reprinted [same title] from *Once a Week*)

¶ **Tintoretto** (**Yet Once More on the Organ Play** reprinted from *Once a Week*)

Idyllic Pictures (Cassell, Petter, and Galpin, 1867)

¶ **October** (**The Advent of Winter** reprinted from the *Quiver*)

• All reprints in *Idyllic Pictures* are from the *Quiver* and are printed from the original wood-blocks

Laus Venertis (Algernon Charles Swinburne; Portland, Maine: Mosher, 1899)

¶ **Cleopatra** (reprinted from the *Cornhill Magazine*)

Pictures of Society (Low, Son, and Marston, 1866)

¶ **Lancashire's Lesson** (**The Waiting Time** reprinted from *Churchman's Family Magazine*)

Reproductions of Woodcuts by F. Sandys, 1860–1866 (Mary Sandys, ed.; Borough Johnson, intro.; Hentschel, [1910])

¶ 25 illustrations (photo-engraved reproductions; reprinted from sources indicated Δ)

• The book is bound in a 3-fold paper cover tied by a cord

• A deluxe, large-paper limited edition was also published, with the wood-engravings printed on mounted india paper, the pages loose in a folder; this edition contains three extra illustrations:

¶ **Proud Maisie** (photo-engraving of the wood-engraving; reprinted from the *English Illustrated Magazine*)

¶ **Morgan-le-Fay*** (photo-engraving of the ink drawing; reprinted from the *British Architect*)

Harald Harfagr (*wood-engraving, Swain; 7 1/4 x 4 1/4; Once a Week, vol. 7, 1862, p. 154; Historical and Legendary Ballads and Songs; Reproductions of Woodcuts by F. Sandys*)

The Death of King Warwulf (*wood-engraving, Swain; 5 1/2 x 4 1/2; Once a Week, vol. 7, 1862, p. 266; Historical and Legendary Ballads and Songs; Reproductions of Woodcuts by F. Sandys*)

The Boy Martyr (wood-engraving, Swain; 3 1/8 x 4 7/8; Once a Week, vol. 7, 1862, p. 602; Historical and Legendary Ballads and Songs; Reproductions of Woodcuts by F. Sandys*)*

Helen and Cassandra (wood-engraving, Swain; 6 7/8 x 4 7/8; Once a Week, new ser. [ser. 2], vol. 1, 1866, p. 454; Historical and Legendary Ballads and Songs; Reproductions of Woodcuts by F. Sandys*)*

The Advent of Winter (wood-engraving, Dalziels; 6 1/2 x 4 3/4; Quiver, ser. 3, vol. 1, 1866 [1865–66], p. 201; Idyllic Pictures; Reproductions of Woodcuts by F. Sandys*)*

¶ **The Nightmare*** (photo-engraving of the original zincotype print)

¶ Some deluxe editions have a **Portrait Photograph of Frederick Sandys** (original photographic print, mounted); others have a photogravure reproduction of the photo

Touches of Nature (Strahan, 1867)
   ¶ **Hoping Against Hope** (**If** reprinted from the *Argosy)*
   ¶ **Sleep** (reprinted from *Good Words*)
   ¶ **Until Her Death** (reprinted from *Good Words*)

§ *A Consideration of the Art of Frederick Sandys* (Esther Wood; Constable; Winter Number, 1896, of *The Artist*; limited edition) has a binding design by the artist and contains 31 photo-engravings and photogravures of Sandys's work in various media

INDIVIDUAL PRINTS
Including the etchings by the artist for several minor volumes published in Norwich

The Antiquities of Norfolk (Rev. James Bulwer; pre-1851)
   ¶ Illustrations by "Fred. Sands" (etchings, Sandys)

The Birds of Norfolk (Rev. James Bulwer; pre-1851)
   ¶ Illustrations by "Fred. Sands" (etchings, Sandys)

Extracts from My Journal, MDCCCLII (J. R. Bulwer; Norwich: Muskett, 1853)
   ¶ **Cascade des Pelerins** (3 1/8 x 5 1/4)
   ¶ **Dressed for the Glacier** (3 1/2 x 5 1/2)
   ¶ **The Grands Mulets** (4 7/8 x 3 1/2)
   ¶ **Our Bedchamber** (2 3/4 x 3 1/8)
   • Etchings (Sandys) after Bulwer's sketches (signed "Fred. Sands")

¶ **Head of a Man with a High Hat** (etching, Sandys, 1849; 5 1/4 x 3 3/4; signed "Fred. Sands")
   • Victoria and Albert Museum, London, Department of Prints, Drawings, and Paintings

¶ **Interpreter to Ibrahim Pasha** (etching, Sandys, 1849; 8 1/4 x 5 3/8; signed "Fred. Sands")
  • Victoria and Albert Museum, London, Department of Prints, Drawings, and Paintings

¶ **Landscape with Bridge over Stream** (etching, Sandys, early 1850s; 3 7/16 x 6 1/4)
  • Fitzwilliam Museum, Cambridge
  • Basis for the background of **The Old Chartist** illustration

¶ **Landscape with Deer** (etching, Sandys, early 1850s; 3 1/16 x 4 5/8)
  • Fitzwilliam Museum, Cambridge

¶ **Landscape with Gate, Field, and Trees** (etching, Sandys, early 1850s; 2 x 3 7/8)
  • Fitzwilliam Museum, Cambridge

¶ **The Nightmare*** (lithograph [zincotype], Sandys, 1857; 13 x 19; scroll-verses beneath main image increase dimensions to 18 x 19)
  • Fitzwilliam Museum, Cambridge; New York Public Library (Humanities and Social Sciences Library), Print Room; et al.
  • Included in *Reproductions of Woodcuts by F. Sandys*, deluxe edition (photo-engraving)

Norfolk Portraits: Portraits of Distinguished Characters Connected with the County of Norfolk (Norwich: Muskett, c. 1850)
  ¶ **Portrait of John Marsham, Mayor of Norwich, 1518** (etching, Sandys; 7 x 5 3/4)
  ¶ **Portrait of Philip Yonge, D.D., Bishop of Norwich, 1761** (etching, Sandys; 7 1/8 x 5 1/2; signed with initials)
  ¶ **Portrait of Thomas Green, D.D., Bishop of Norwich, 1721** (etching, Sandys; 7 1/4 x 5 1/2)
  ¶ **Portrait of William Barnham, Mayor of Norwich, 1652** (etching, Sandys; 6 7/8 x 5 3/4)
  • City of Norwich Museums; Fitzwilliam Museum, Cambridge

Notices and Illustrations of the Costume, Professions, Pageantry, Etc., Formerly Displayed by the Corporation of Norwich (Norwich: Muskett, 1850)
  ¶ **Portrait of Augustus Stewart** (etch-

Amor Mundi (*wood-engraving, Swain; 6 3/4 x 4; Shilling Magazine, vol. 1, 1865, p. 193; Reproductions of Woodcuts by F. Sandys*)

Jacob Hears the Voice of the Lord (*wood-engraving, Dalziels; 7 3/8 x 5 3/4; Dalziels' Bible Gallery, 1881; Art Pictures from the Old Testament; Reproductions of Woodcuts by F. Sandys*)

Life's Journey *(wood-engraving, Dalziels; 5 x 4;* English Sacred Poetry, *1862;* Reproductions of Woodcuts by F. Sandys*)*

The Little Mourner *(wood-engraving, Dalziels; 5 1/2 x 4 1/4;* English Sacred Poetry, *1862;* Reproductions of Woodcuts by F. Sandys*)*

ing, Sandys; 7 x 5 5/8)
  • City of Norwich Museums; Fitzwilliam Museum, Cambridge
    ¶ **Portrait of Erasmus Earl** (etching, Sandys; 11 x 5 1/2)
  • Probably intended for *Norfolk Portraits*, but unused; a version by W. C. Edwards appears in *Norfolk Portraits*
    • Fitzwilliam Museum, Cambridge
    ¶ **Portrait of Sir Edward Atkyns, Lord Chief Baron of the Exchequer** (etching, Sandys; oval, 6 1/2 x 5 3/8)
  • Intended for *Norfolk Portraits*, but unused; a version by W. C. Edwards appears in *Norfolk Portraits*

¶ **Portrait of Frederick Sand[y]s** (etching, Sandys, c. 1849; 4 1/4 x 3 1/4; after a drawing of the artist by his father)
  • Fitzwilliam Museum, Cambridge

¶ **Portrait of William Freeman** (lithograph, Sandys, 1848; 11 x 9; signed ["Fred. Sands"] and dated)
  • City of Norwich Museums

¶ **Rocky Landscape with Figures** (etching, Sandys, early 1850s; 3 x 4 7/8)
  • Fitzwilliam Museum, Cambridge

¶ **Two Male Heads, a Dog, and a Pear** (etching, Sandys, 1848; 4 11/16 x 3 9/16; signed with initials and dated)
  • Fitzwilliam Museum, Cambridge

William Bell Scott

(1811–1890)

William Bell Scott certainly deserves a place among the Pre-Raphaelite illustrators, but mostly because he was a friend of Rossetti and so involved with their circle, and because his poetry and art appeared in so many books. But he was, more than any of his "brethren," a child of the 1840s in the field of illustration, fitting in with the previous generation of Kenny Meadows and John Gilbert, and turning out overworked but ultimately sketchy drawings, showing some Pre-Raphaelite influence, but seldom enough to raise his art to the others' level. Cataloguing Scott's published works is a trying and tedious experience, because he was, in all honesty, a really boring artist. The only interesting thing about Scott's graphic work is how often he used etching as his medium (a predilection left over, no doubt, from the heyday of such illustrator-etchers as Cruikshank and Leech).

Still, there are few works in Scott's canon that are more lifeless and insipid than his etchings after his brother, David Scott, who was even less talented than William. David, a minor history/literary painter, died in 1849. This apparently affected William greatly; lamenting such a "talent" cut down in his prime, he preserved David's works by etching them for various projects (*Memoir of David Scott*, 1849; *Pilgrim's Progress*, 1851; and *Selections from the Works of the Late David Scott Etched by His Brother, W. B. Scott*, 1866–67). The less said about these fuzzied-up outline drawings, badly drawn and poorly composed, the better.

Unfortunately, this style occasionally sur-faced in William Bell Scott's own etchings—and if not that, then the Kenny Meadows–scribble/doll-figure style for wood-engravings. These tendencies are seen in most of Scott's illustrations of the 1840s and 1850s, such as for *The Book of British Ballads* (1842, 1844), *The Nursery Rhymes of England* (1853), *The Year of the World* (1846), and *Chorea Sancti Viti* (1851). The last two books are among the many that Scott wrote himself, and his poetry (which is slightly better than his art) is what initially drew Dante Gabriel Rossetti to make his acquaintance—a long-lasting relationship that forever linked him to the Pre-Raphaelites

William Bell Scott, 1879 (etching [detail] by Scott, as published in Autobiographical Notes of the Life of William Bell Scott, *vol. 1, 1892)*

and occasionally inspired works approaching their spirit.

Rossetti introduced himself to Scott by way of a letter dated November 25, 1847, praising two of the latter's published poems, "Rosabell" and "Dream of Love," as well as his book *The Year of the World*. Scott commented on this auspicious start in his autobiography: "[Gabriel] Rossetti, who very soon after began to sign himself Dante Gabriel Rossetti, Christina and Maria his sisters, and William his brother, from that day to this have been all very dear and near to me; the two men have often been to me like brothers, and every autumn one or more of the four came to us for a few weeks" (*Autobiographical Notes of the Life of William Bell Scott*, 1892, vol. 1, pp. 243, 245). Later, Scott contributed verse to the Brotherhood's journal, the *Germ*. Ford Madox Brown wrote to Scott in 1854, praising his poetry (*Poems by a Painter*, 1854), mentioning that he was also stirred by Tennyson —"great though affected"—and "the strange and exquisite poems of our friend Rossetti" (Princeton University Library, Troxell Collection). Scott also figures in Brown's diary entry of July 15, 1855: "Gabriel and Scott dined here. Emma enchanted with Scott, as all women are; a truly nice fellow and an honour to know" (*Ruskin: Rossetti: PreRaphaelitism*, pp. 40–41). Scott joined Brown and the others in their exhibiting, under the auspices of the Hogarth Club in the early 1860s. He was friendly with Thomas Woolner and Algernon Swinburne (who visited him often at Newcastle), and maintained a lively correspondence over the years with William Holman Hunt and the Pre-Raphaelite poet Coventry Patmore.

Besides the Pre-Raphaelite connection, Scott had all the proper credentials and associations to be a leading painter and illustrator. Born in Edinburgh, he was the son (and apprentice) of an engraver, tried his hand unsuccessfully at illustration in London, then returned to Scotland to concentrate on painting. He entered the Houses of Parliament competition, and beginning in 1843, he served as a master of the School of Design at Newcastle-upon-Tyne, a post he held for twenty years. When he returned to London in 1864 he taught art at the South Kensington Schools—and became Rossetti's neighbor in Chelsea; the two remained good friends (and considerate correspondents) until the latter's death in 1882. Scott was also a friend of W. J. Linton, the wood-engraver whom Rossetti preferred above all others.

Scott exhibited his paintings at the Royal Scottish Academy and British Institution from the 1830s, and at London's Royal Academy from 1842 to 1869. He also painted murals—at Wallington Hall, Northumberland (for the Trevelyan family), and at Penkill Castle, Ayrshire (for the Boyd family). One of the eight Wallington Hall murals is Scott's famous *Iron and Coal* (c. 1860), in which he assiduously attempted to incorporate Pre-Raphaelite principles of realism, a variety of telling details, and claustrophobic full-focus figural composition. This paean to the Industrial Revolution is perhaps Scott's best painting; although the placement of the various elements seems more random than composed, it somehow holds together successfully.

Like Paton and Sandys, Scott was a student of antiquities (he wrote *Antiquarian Gleanings in the North of England*, published in 1851, with twenty of his own etchings). He was also in the vanguard of those artist-illustrators who appreciated the engravings of Blake, Dürer, and Rethel. An auction of his art collection in 1885 shows a major emphasis on prints and drawings by such graphic-art masters as Aldegrever, Altdorfer, Mantegna, Schöngauer, Dürer, van Leyden, Beham, Cranach, Hollar, Goltzius, Bewick, Blake, Cruikshank, Whistler, Gilbert, and Rethel (Sotheby, Wilkinson, and Hodge, *Catalogue of the Choice Collection of Engravings and Etchings Formed by W. B. Scott, Esq.*). Not only did Scott write a book on Dürer (1869) but in 1878 he published a compilation of his etchings after drawings by Blake.

Despite his opinionated and aggressive insinuation into the world of Victorian art and literature, Scott rarely succeeded in his paintings and illustrations. His two most commercial wood-block drawings, for Mrs. Gatty's *Parables from Nature*, are clumsy and spongy in line and form, barely escaping by 1865 his early efforts influenced by his brother. Hardly more successful are his fussy and nearly tonal etchings for the 1875 collection of his own writings (*Poems, Ballads, Studies from Nature, Sonnets, Etc.*), although the best piece is a lovely and simple turret with crows, "Penkill, Ayrshire," which also appears as titlepage art for *Illustrations to The King's Quair*.

Some of Scott's most fastidiously conceived and drawn pieces are his etchings for the *Quair* book; six large prints were published in 1887, based on his Penkill Castle murals of 1865–68. The etchings are medieval and antiquarian, full of details and symbolism, and well worked over to create a variety of dense tonal effects—surely very Pre-Raphaelite in spirit, although again the drawing is somewhat amateurish and satisfies no known Pre-Raphaelite criterion for realism.

A surer hand is seen in another large etching, based on an 1876 painting: *The Norns Watering Yggdrasill* was published in the *Etcher* (1879), accompanied by Scott's poem on the Norse myth. This is a lovely Pre-Raphaelite figure-and-foliage composition with a rhythmic flow, showing more realistic treatment than almost any other of his graphics; fortunately, *Norns*'s origins as a painting inspired Scott to begin with numerous figural and botanical studies (in the collection of the National Gallery of Scotland).

A smaller illustrative etching with the same elements and very effective in composition and drawing is "Rosamunda," in *Poems by a Painter* (1854). In the spirit of Hughes's *Music Master* designs, it is perhaps Scott's most Pre-Raphaelite graphic, and one of the earliest, since it predates that book by William Allingham—who, in a letter to Scott on February 23, 1855, called the etching "charming, the face & figure living, & quietly expressive in a degree not often met with" (Princeton University Library, Troxell Collection).

This tone-producing etching style served Scott's needs for his many bookplates (the lamp-book-palette design for the *Poems by a Painter* frontispiece was used for his personal bookplates), which are packed with nice details in small spaces and work well because they are less grandly conceived.

Scott's most pleasing and best drawn illustrations may be the oval spot art that he did for his poetry collection *A Poet's Harvest Home* of 1882—three simple woodcutty designs, perfectly composed miniatures, looking very much like Bewick's vignettes.

Titlepage illustration for A Poet's Harvest Home, *1882 (wood-engraving, H.L.; 2 1/4 x 1 3/4)*

Penkill, Ayrshire *(etching, Scott; 3 1/8 x 2 1/2;* Poems, Ballads, Studies from Nature, Sonnets, Etc.*, 1875;* Illustrations to The King's Quair*)*

Catalogue

BOOKS

Ballads and Metrical Tales (James and Burns, 1845)
¶ **Gray Palfrey**
¶ **The Chattsworth Outlaw**
¶ **The Friar of Order Gray**
¶ **Glenfinlas**
¶ **Lord William**

Bob Thin (W. J. Linton; privately printed, 1845)
¶ 15 illustrations (approx.)

The Book of British Ballads (Samuel Carter Hall, ed.; How, ser. 1, 1842)
¶ **"Kempion,"** 4 illustrations (O. Smith, W. J. Linton)
¶ **"The Birth of St. George,"** 8 illustrations (W. Folkard, T. Armstrong, H. Vizetelly)
¶ **"The Nut-Brown Mayd,"** 4 illustrations (H. Vizetelly, E. Landells)

The Book of British Ballads (Samuel Carter Hall, ed.; How, ser. 2, 1844)
¶ **"Ruth,"** 4 illustrations (W. J. Linton)

[Coleridge] *Poetical Works of Samuel Taylor Coleridge* (William Bell Scott, ed.; Routledge, [1874])
¶ 5 illustrations

Half-Hour Lectures on the History and Practice of the Fine and Ornamental Arts (William Bell Scott; Longmans, Green, Longmans, Roberts, 1861)
¶ 50 illustrations (W. J. Linton)

Juvenile Verse and Picture Book (Warne, 1866)
¶ 4 illustrations

[Keats] *Poetical Works of John Keats* (William Bell Scott, ed.; Routledge, [1874])
¶ 6 illustrations

[Landon] *Poetical Works of Letitia Elizabeth*

Landon (William Bell Scott, ed.; Routledge, [1874])
¶ 6 illustrations

Lays and Legends Illustrative of English Life (Camilla Toulmin; How, 1845)
¶ **The Forest**
¶ **Winter Scene**

Love in Idleness (H. C. Beeching; Paul, Trench, 1883)
¶ *Titlepage illustration* (steel-engraving)

The Nursery Rhymes of England (James Orchard Halliwell, ed.; Smith, 5th ed., 1853)
¶ *Frontispiece* (etching, Scott)
¶ *Titlepage illustration* (etching, Scott)
¶ 38 illustrations
• Reissued in a large-paper edition, printed by the Dalziels, by Warne in 1886

The Ornamentalist, or Artisan's Manual (William Bell Scott; London / Edinburgh / Dublin: Fullarton, 1845)
¶ Includes "An Essay on Ornamental Art" by Scott, illustrated with 21 small wood-engravings probably by Scott
• Second Part, "The Ornamentalist or Artisan's Manual," includes 60 lithographic plates, not by Scott

Parables from Nature (Mrs. Alfred Gatty; Bell and Daldy, 3d and 4th ser., 1865)
¶ **Red Snow** (H. Harral)
¶ **Master of the Harvest** (H. Harral)

A Poet's Harvest Home (William Bell Scott; Stock, 1882)
¶ 3 illustrations,* including *titlepage illustration* and *tailpiece* (H.L.)
• Reissued in an enlarged and limited edition by Matthews and Lane in 1893

Routledge's Sunday Album for Children (Routledge, 1873)
¶ Illustrations

[Shelley] *Poetical Works of Percy Bysshe Shelley* (William Bell Scott, ed.; Routledge, [1874])
¶ 6 illustrations (Dalziels)

§ Several other works are reported to con-

Love Originating Art (etching, Scott; 2 7/8 x 1 3/4; titlepage illustration for Poems, Ballads, Studies from Nature, Sonnets, Etc., *1875)*

A Study from Nature (etching, Scott; 2 3/4 x 3 3/8; Poems, Ballads, Studies from Nature, Sonnets, Etc., *1875)*

Hervor (etching, Scott; 3 3/8 x 2 7/8; after Alice Boyd; Poems, Ballads, Studies from Nature, Sonnets, Etc., *1875)*

tain wood-engraved illustrations by Scott: *Landscape Lyrics* (c. 1837); the *Observer* (1842); and *The Pictorial Edition of the Works of Shakespeare* (Charles Knight, ed.; Knight, 8 vols., 1839–43); *The [Family?] Bible* (Edinburgh: Fullarton, c. 1867–74) includes **The Resurrection**, **Moses Brings Down the Tablets of the Law**, **The Rending of the Veil in the Temple**, and possibly other illustrations

§ *Sunday Reading for Good Children* (Routledge, [1873]) may include one or more reprints by Scott

§ *The British School of Sculpture* (William Bell Scott; Virtue, 1872) contains 20 steel-engravings and 50 wood-engravings; it is unlikely any of the illustrations are by Scott

BOOKS ILLUSTRATED WITH ETCHINGS BY SCOTT

Antiquarian Gleanings in the North of England (William Bell Scott; Bell, [1851])
　¶ *Titlepage illustration* (wood-engraving, G. Measom)
　¶ 20 illustrations (including aquatints)

[Blake] *William Blake: Etchings from His Works by William Bell Scott* (William Bell Scott; Chatto and Windus, 1878)
　¶ 11 illustrations* (after Blake; see information below [§])

Chorea Sancti Viti; or, Steps in the Journey of Prince Legion (William Bell Scott; Bell, 1851)
　¶ *Titlepage illustration*
　¶ **Prince Legion Is Born**
　¶ **Price Legion Is Nursed**
　¶ **The Influx of Thought**
　¶ **He Is Directed in Life**
　¶ **Love**
　¶ **He Enters into Masquerade**
　¶ **He Retains the Mask Even to His Friend and His Mistress**
　¶ **Scenery of 25 Years of Prince Legion's Life**
　¶ **Prince Legion Has Attained**
　¶ **The Soul of Prince Legion**
　¶ **He Arrives at the End of His Journey**

[Dürer] *Albert Dürer: His Life and Works* (William Bell Scott; Longmans, Green, 1869)
¶ *Frontispiece:* **Dürer at 13, 1484** (after Dürer)
¶ *Titlepage illustration* (wood-engraving)
¶ **Village of Eytas** (after Dürer)
¶ **Dürer at 28** (after Forster)
¶ **Dürer's House at Thiergartner-Thor**
¶ **Dürer's Portrait at 50** (after T. Vincidore, engraving by A. Stock, 1629)
¶ **View from the Window at Dürer's House**
¶ **Dürer's Drawing Pen** (wood-engraving)
¶ **The Dürer Shield** (wood-engraving)
¶ **Dürer's Grave, St. John's** (wood-engraving)

Hades; or, The Transit; and The Progress of the Mind (William Bell Scott; Renshaw, 1838)
¶ *Frontispiece*
¶ **Celestial Beings Playing Lyre**

Illustrations to The King's Quair (William Bell Scott; Edinburgh: Constable at University Press, 1887)
¶ 7 illustrations* (see information below [§])
• Limited edition, india-paper proofs

[Keats] *Poetical Works and Other Writings of John Keats* (Harry Buxton Forman, ed.; Reeves and Turner, 4 vols., 1883)
¶ *Frontispiece:* **Portrait of Keats** (vol. 4; reprinted from *Letters of John Keats to Fanny Brawne*)

Letters of John Keats to Fanny Brawne (Harry Buxton Forman, ed.; Reeves and Turner, 1878)
¶ *Frontispiece:* **Portrait of Keats** (after Joseph Severn)

Martyr Scenes of the Sixteenth and Seventeenth Centuries (C. Tylor; Hamilton, Adams, 1888)
¶ 12 illustrations (probably three after Edward Backhouse)

Memoir of David Scott, R.S.A. (William Bell Scott; Edinburgh: Black, 1850)
¶ *Frontispiece:* **Self-Portrait of David Scott**

Love, the Weaver of Fictions (etching, Scott; 5 1/4 in. diam.; Illustrations to The King's Quair, *1887*)

Old Windsor, Early Morning *(etching, Scott; 9 1/4 x 8;*
Illustrations to The King's Quair, *1887)*

¶ **Procession of Unknown Powers**
¶ **Discord; or, Household Gods Destroyed**
¶ **Vasco De Gama**
• All after David Scott

Pilgrim's Progress (John Bunyan; London/ Edinburgh/Dublin: Fullarton, [1851])
¶ ***Titlepage illustration***
¶ 40 illustrations (after David Scott)
• Fullarton's reissue of 1859 includes "Part Second," containing 25 additional etched illustrations by William Bell Scott (with a second ***titlepage illustration***)
• Fullarton's reissue of c. 1870 includes 74 illustrations; the titlepage still reads *65*

Poems, Ballads, Studies from Nature, Sonnets, Etc. (William Bell Scott; Longmans, Green, 1875)
¶ 13 illustrations (see information below [§])

Poems by a Painter (William Bell Scott; Smith, Elder, 1854)
¶ ***Frontispiece**** (lamp-and-palette image used in several versions for Scott's bookplates)
¶ **Rosamunda***
¶ **St. Francis***

[Scott] *Autobiographical Notes of the Life of William Bell Scott* (W. Minto, ed.; Osgood, 2 vols., 1892)
¶ ***Frontispiece:* Self-Portrait** (vol. 1)
¶ **Leigh Hunt, G. H. Lewes, Vincent Hunt, and W.B.S.** (vol. 1)
¶ **Christina Rossetti When a Child** (vol. 1)
¶ **David Scott, Two Days Before His Death** (vol. 1)
¶ **Dante Gabriel Rossetti, Age 25** (vol. 1)
• Vol. 1: Plus **View from Workshop in Old Parliament Square** (photogravure of a drawing)
¶ ***Frontispiece:* Self-Portrait** (vol. 2)
¶ **Algernon Charles Swinburne, Age 22*** (vol. 2)
¶ **Miss Boyd of Penkill*** (vol. 2; after Rossetti)
• Vol. 2: Plus **Design for Lecture Theater Door, South Kensington** (pho-

togravure of a drawing); **Strobhall: Window and Fireplace** (photogravure of a drawing); eight reproductions of drawings (photo-engravings)

Selections from the Works of the Late David Scott Etched by His Brother, W. B. Scott (Art Union of Glasgow, 1866–67)
¶ 12 illustrations (after David Scott), plus *titlepage illustration*

A Series of Seventeen Proof Etchings, Before Lettering, for the Poetical Works of Robert Burns Drawn and Etched by W. B. Scott; Never Before Published (Edinburgh: Jack, 1885)
¶ 17 illustrations* (see information below [§])

[Shelley] *The Poetical Works of Percy Bysshe Shelley* (Harry Buxton Forman, ed.; Reeves and Turner, 4 vols., 1882)
¶ *Frontispiece:* **Portrait of Beatrice Cenci** (vol. 2; after Guido; reprinted in *The Works of Percy Bysshe Shelley in Verse and Prose*)
¶ *Frontispiece:* **Shelley's Grave** (vol. 3; etching by A. Evershed after W. B. Scott; reprinted in *The Works of Percy Bysshe Shelley in Verse and Prose*)
• Also issued in 2 vols., 1882, with Scott *frontispieces*

[Shelley] *The Prose Works of Percy Bysshe Shelley* (Harry Buxton Forman, ed.; Reeves and Turner, 4 vols., 1880)
¶ *Frontispiece:* **Portrait of Shelley** (vol. 1; after Miss Curran; reprinted from *The Works of Percy Bysshe Shelley in Verse and Prose*)

[Shelley] *The Works of Percy Bysshe Shelley in Verse and Prose* (Harry Buxton Forman, ed.; privately printed, 8 vols., 1880)
¶ *Frontispiece:* **Portrait of Beatrice Cenci** (vol. 2; after Guido; reprinted in *The Poetical Works of Percy Bysshe Shelley*)
¶ *Frontispiece:* **Shelley's Grave** (vol. 3; etching by A. Evershed after W. B. Scott; reprinted in *The Poetical Works of Percy Bysshe Shelley*)
¶ *Frontispiece:* **Portrait of Shelley** (vol. 5; after Miss Curran; reprinted in *The Prose Works of Percy Bysshe Shelley*)

Lady Jane Listening to the Nightingale *(etching, Scott; 9 1/4 x 8;* Illustrations to The King's Quair, *1887)*

Titlepage illustration for Pilgrim's Progress, Part Second, *c. 1859 (etching, Scott; 4 1/4 in. diam.)*

A Simple Story; and, Nature and Art (Mrs. [Elizabeth] Inchbald; William Bell Scott, intro.; De la Rue, 1880)
¶ *Frontispiece* (etching?)

The Year of the World (William Bell Scott; Edinburgh: Tait / London: Simpkin, Marshall, 1846)
¶ **The Golden Age**
¶ **The Journey**
¶ **The Journey Continues**
¶ **The Journey Renewed**
¶ **The Future**

INDIVIDUAL PRINTS

¶ **The Brazen Serpent** (etching, Scott; circular, 10 x 11 [plate]; signed with monogram in plate)
 • Museum of Fine Arts, Boston, Hartley Collection

¶ **Fuseli's Witches** (wood-engraving, W. J. Linton; 1857)
 • Exhibited by Linton at the Royal Academy, 1857

¶ **John Blackett, M.P.: Portrait** (wood-engraving, Scott)
 • British Museum, London, Department of Prints and Drawings

¶ **Loch Leven on the Night of the Escape of Mary, Queen of Scots** (steel-engraving, Scott; 7 x 10 3/8; after D. O. Hill)
 • Published by Moon Boys and Graves
 • Museum of Fine Arts, Boston, Hartley Collection

¶ **The Norns Watering Yggdrasill** (etching, Scott, 1876; 9 3/4 x 6 1/2; signed and dated in plate)
 • Published in the *Etcher*, vol. 1, 1879

§ Scott produced many bookplates, most of them etchings; among these are: *Bookplates* **for H. Buxton Forman; Joseph Knight; Thomas Pigg; R. de Tabley; Sir Charles Edward Trevelyan and His Wife Lady Eleanora; Sir Walter Caverley Trevelyan** (at least 3)**; J. B. Leicester Warren; Henry Aylorde; George Burnett; and William Bell Scott,**

including at least 2 versions based on the
titlepage illustration for *Poems by a
Painter*

§ Books containing Scott's etched illustrations that often are treated as individual
prints:
    *William Blake: Etchings from His Works
by William Bell Scott:* • **Titlepage illustration** (wood-engraving; after Blake; also
printed on cover) • **There Shall Be No
More Death** (7 7/8 x 5 1/4; after Blake)
• **And the Waters Prevailed upon the
Earth an Hundred and Fifty Days** (6 1/4 x
4 1/2; after Blake) • **Comic Sketch, Perhaps
of John Varley** (lithograph, 7 1/2 x 5 3/4;
after Blake) • **The Nativity** (5 1/4 x 7 3/4;
after Blake) • **St. Matthew and the Angel**
(7 1/2 x 5; after Blake) • **The Queen of
Evil** (6 3/4 x 5 1/2; after Blake) • **The
Creation of Eve** (7 1/4 x 5 3/4; after Blake)
• **Adam and Eve in Paradise** (7 1/4 x 5 1/2;
after Blake) • **Eve Eating the Forbidden
Fruit** (7 1/4 x 5 1/4; after Blake) • **The
Dream of Eve** (lithograph, 7 3/8 x 5 3/4;
after Blake; a.k.a. **Paradise Lost**) (all have
signatures beneath images in plates)
    Illustrations to The King's Quair:
• **Titlepage illustration: Penkill, Ayrshire**
(3 1/8 x 2 1/2; reprinted from *Poems,
Ballads, Studies from Nature, Sonnets, Etc.*)
• **Love, the Weaver of Fictions** • **Old
Windsor, Early Morning** • **Lady Jane
Listening to the Nightingale** • **The Garden
of the Court of Venus** • **Lady Jane
Sending the Dove** • **King James Receives
the Dove** (all 9 1/4 x 8 except **titlepage
illustration** and **Love** [circular, 5 1/4 in.
diam.]; all signed with monogram except
Old Windsor ["WB Scott 1866"])
    *Poems, Ballads, Studies from Nature,
Sonnets, Etc.:* • **Titlepage illustration:
Love Originating Art** (2 7/8 x 1 3/4; signed
in plate) • **An Old Chest** (3 x 3 3/4; signed
in plate; a.k.a. **The Toy Chest**) • **Pax
Vobiscum** (3 1/2 x 2 1/2; after David Scott)
• **The Way of Life: Whither?** (3 1/4 x 2 3/8;
signed with initials in plate) • **Penkill,
Ayrshire** (3 1/8 x 2 1/2; signed with initials
in plate; reprinted in *Illustrations to The
King's Quair*) • **The Garden, Penkill**
(3 x 3; signed with monogram in plate)
• **A Study from Nature** (2 3/4 x 3 3/8;
signed with monogram in plate) • **Design**

Rosamunda *(etching, Scott; 4 7/8 x 2 7/8;* Poems by a
Painter, *1854)*

Remembered from a Dream (2 3/4 x 3 1/4; signed with initials in plate) • **Keats' Grave, Rome** (3 x 3 1/8; signed with monogram and dated in plate) • **Pygmalion** (3 x 2; signed with monogram in plate) • **Recreating Genii** (3 1/8 x 2 5/8; reworked from version in *Hades*; a.k.a. **Music of the Spheres**) • **Portrait of William Bell Scott at Age 20** (oval, 2 1/4 x 2 7/8; after David Scott) • **Hervor** (3 3/8 x 2 7/8; after Alice Boyd)

A Series of Seventeen Proof Etchings, Before Lettering, for the Poetical Works of Robert Burns Drawn and Etched by W. B. Scott; Never Before Published: • 17 illustrations (each approx. 4 x 6 1/2 oblong on sheets 12 1/8 x 10 3/4; in portfolio)

The Norns Watering Yggdrasill *(etching, Scott, 1876; 9 3/4 x 6 1/2; Etcher, vol. 1, 1879; courtesy Boston Public Library, Fine Arts Department)*

Frederic J. Shields

(1833–1911)

Given the mental flagellation over his own sins and those of the world that the very religious Frederic Shields put himself through, it is a wonder that he ever succeeded at any worldly enterprise, let alone being able to devote his life to art. Shields seems to have spent most of his time in London and Manchester seeking new houses, working hard and depriving himself of pleasure (poverty was certainly a factor in the early years), searching for temporary quarters, and staying with friends—settling anywhere that did not impinge on his overly sensitive disposition. In 1866 he suffered a nervous breakdown, partly due to overwork and undernourishment, but ostensibly because of his noise phobia. "I have counted as many as seven organs in a morning at Chelsea, with German bands," he later recalled. "It was this infliction that has brought me so low—nothing else." Shields continually rejected potential lodgings because of barking dogs, noisy birds, or organ-grinders (*Life and Letters of Frederic Shields*, pp. 109–10).

Shields was one of the most extreme of the overly religious artists that touched the Pre-Raphaelite circle, among them Charles Collins, James Collinson, Christina Rossetti, William Holman Hunt, and James Smetham. Certainly his anguish was exacerbated by his own early years in extreme poverty and the deaths of his two young brothers. Even as he tortured himself over any time-wasting hour of personal pleasure, he continued to devote efforts to teaching Sunday School, visiting the sick, and distributing religious tracts; his

diary entries for several years from 1859 inevitably begin with the initials W.P.B.B. for "Wash, Prayer, Bible, Breakfast" (*Life and Letters of Frederic Shields*, p. 59). Yet, despite his obsessive religious proselytizing and self-denial, he managed to maintain lifelong friendships with two very different yet equally generous souls, Ford Madox Brown and Dante Gabriel Rossetti.

Frederic Shields, c. 1870s? (photograph; photogravure, as published in Ernestine Mills's The Life and Letters of Frederic Shields, *1912)*

After discovering Pre-Raphaelite work at the Manchester Art Treasures Exhibition in 1857, and marveling at a copy of the Moxon *Tennyson* he came across in 1860, Shields was converted to the Pre-Raphaelite cause. Through John Ruskin, he met both Brown and Rossetti in 1864, and then Edward Poynter, Edward Burne-Jones, and Frederick Sandys; eventually he also developed an extensive correspondence with a more kindred spirit, Holman Hunt. Shields's close friendship with Brown and Rossetti ended only with their deaths; even with their differing personalities and religious views, all felt equally drawn to supporting each other's artistic efforts and helping those in need. In autumn 1872, for example, Shields wrote to Madox Brown for help in setting up an exhibition for the benefit of the widow of a young Manchester artist; immediately Brown effected his usual efforts to secure art donations from all his friends. Soon thereafter the two went about trying to similarly help the widow of a Liverpool artist, whose death left ten children unprovided for. And back in Manchester, Shields was aiding a bed-ridden man whose wife had died, leaving four children (*Life and Letters of Frederic Shields*, pp. 157–59).

Shields seemed to be very reluctant to undertake any enterprise he felt uncomfortable with, even though he was frequently in pecuniary straits. Having gained a reputation as an extraordinary draughtsman for wood-engravings, he, like Rossetti, felt so disappointed by the results that after the 1860s he usually rejected this kind of work. When Rossetti in 1865 asked him if he'd like to design stained-glass windows for his firm, Morris, Marshall, Faulkner, and Co., Shields declined. And in one of his major commissions of the late 1870s, the twelve murals for

Manchester Town Hall, he generously involved his friend Brown—who eventually painted all the scenes, rather than his original six, after Shields finally dropped out of the project.

Shields's early paintings were genre watercolors, particularly of children; he was elected Royal Water Colour Society Associate in 1865.

Paintings, Chapel of the Ascension, London (photograph, c. 1912; photo-engraving, as published in Ernestine Mills's The Life and Letters of Frederic Shields, *1912)*

Ironically, much of his success in art was due to his eventual acclimation to designing for stained glass, whose religious subjects suited his purposes. Among these are his first window series, for Sir James Houldsworth, called "The Triumph of Faith," which he worked on from 1876 through 1880. In 1878 Shields began a more important stained-glass commission, for the Duke of Westminster's Eaton Chapel. Shields's later comments about these religious-themed undertakings also point to the fact that his efforts in large-scale color work (as opposed to drawings) were continually evolving and with Rossetti's assistance becoming more Pre-Raphaelite. "My soul kindled and flamed with the subject accepted, the glorious hymn of St. Ambrose, the *Te Deum*. Nearly ninety subjects, all told, not isolated, but such as could be linked in blessed continuity—to keep the heart hot, and the mind quick, with its grand purpose—the praise of God and of His Son Jesus Christ, from the lives of apostles, prophets, martyrs, and the Holy Church of all ages. . . .

"It revolutionized all my views of design, imposing bounds upon me that purified and ennobled my style, while the practice in drawing upon a large scale gave me great increase of knowledge and power, and the necessity of grappling with the fine disposition of drapery gradually taught me how much the dignity, grace, and action of a figure depended on this feature, and made me seek after excellence in this respect eagerly" (*Life and Letters of*

The Good Shepherd (*wood-engraving, 5 7/8 x 4;* Illustrations to Bunyan's Pilgrim's Progress, 1864)

Frederic Shields, pp. 225–26). This passage goes far to explain how despite his religious seriousness, Shields also had it in him to be energized by the same aesthetic challenges that propelled his Pre-Raphaelite friends.

Rossetti and Shields shared still another unlikely passion: the art of Blake. Rossetti had helped to complete the important *Life of William Blake* by Alexander Gilchrist after the latter's death in 1861; the first edition came out in 1863, and the author's widow brought out a revised one in 1880—which Shields helped to produce and drew designs for. About this time Rossetti wrote to Brown: "The new Blake volumes are truly splendid. Shields has made the most wonderful cover from a design of Blake's, and has written a long paper on Young's *Night Thoughts* series, which reads as if he had been writing all his life. He has also drawn a most interesting plate of Blake and his wife from Blake's Sketches, and a separate one of Mrs. Blake from another sketch of Blake's. In fact he has half-made the book" (*Life and Letters of Frederic Shields*, p. 255).

From the mid-1870s until his death in 1882, Rossetti, in continuing ill-health, depended on Shields to photograph his paintings and acquire such items as fresh flowers to be used as models for his works. In return, Shields spent days at a time working in Rossetti's studio, where his friend basically gave him the technical and aesthetic tools necessary to finally achieve distinction in oil and mural painting. This legacy enabled Shields to undertake his greatest achievement in 1890, the complete wall decoration of a new chapel, designed by Herbert Horne, on London's Bayswater Road, and sponsored by Mrs. Russell-Gurney as a place of meditation and prayer. Shields covered the Chapel of the Ascension from top to bottom with dozens of self-contained paintings, many of an allegorical nature as well as biblical; these are a triumph of their kind, the dramatic religious idealism tempered by a superb drawing technique and clear influences of Hunt's and

Rossetti's styles. Within six months of his completion of this monumental work in September 1910, Shields died.

Shields may not have undertaken this extraordinary artistic journey, however, if he hadn't gained attention in the 1860s for two projects that were among his finest achievements, the wood-engraved illustrations for the books *The History of the Plague of London* (1863) and *Illustrations to Bunyan's Pilgrim's Progress* (1864). Shields had apprenticed for the commercial lithographers Maclure and Macdonald in London, and at age sixteen, back in Manchester, worked for another lithography firm, Bradshaw and Blacklock, who first dismissed him and then rehired him to design for Baxter's "oil-painting–process" color prints. "The year 1860 formed a turning-point in my career, for then, having before heard much of Rossetti, alone among the Pre-Raphaelites

unrepresented at the 'Art Treasures' [exhibition], I fell in with the edition of Tennyson's poems which contains some designs from his hand," he later recalled. "Those burning with imaginative fervour of invention appealed to forces hitherto held in subjection within me, and at this juncture a door was opened to put to trial their capacity in a proposition from the late Mr. Henry Rawson, of the *Manchester Examiner*, to illustrate the *Pilgrim's Progress*. . . . The designs elicited unstinted praise from John Ruskin, and brought me eventually the friendship, warm, helpful, and steadfast until his death, of Dante Rossetti, and also of Ford Madox Brown" (Frederic Shields, "An Autobiography," *Good Words*, vol. 30, 1889, pp. 822–24, 827). The book of *Pilgrim's Progress*, to Shields's disappointment, was published in 1864 without a text. The most ambitious drawing for the project was a large "Vanity Fair," a scene so crowded with masses of well-realized and distinctive figures that it approaches obsession in its undeniable virtuosity. Shields contacted John Ruskin in 1861 about procur-

Vanity Fair (*wood-engraving, A. Gaber; 4 x 7 1/8;* Illustrations to Bunyan's Pilgrim's Progress, *1864*)

ing a very skilled engraver for this exceptional work (Swain had engraved many of the others), and a lively correspondence ensued (Gaber, engraver for some of the great German illustrators, was used). But every single one of the drawings for *Pilgrim's Progress* is a minor masterpiece, a skillful combination of Pre-Raphaelite spirit and poses and the linear technique of the contemporary German illustrators Schnorr, Rethel, and Richter.

Shields next produced another series of illustrations in the same brilliant style.

Imprisoned Family Escaping (ink and wash drawing, 4 1/2 x 3 1/4; for the illustration in The History of the Plague of London, *[1863]; courtesy Manchester City Art Galleries)*

Predating the appearance of *Illustrations to Bunyan's Pilgrim's Progress, The History of the Plague of London* was his first important book; Ruskin and Rossetti both immensely admired its six engravings. Shields preserved the drawings on the wood-blocks through photographs, and his disappointment over their cutting prevented him from doing much more illustration work for the rest of his life. Like Brown for "The Prisoner of Chillon," Shields spent time drawing directly from dead bodies to achieve the realism of these pictures (*Life and Letters of Frederic Shields*, pp. 77–78). It seems quite amazing that a person with Shields's sensitive nature and religion-based fear of the world and its temptations could produce such powerful, emotional, and original illustrations.

One of the greatest Pre-Raphaelite draughtsmen, Shields in these same years created three more distinctive wood-block drawings (at least two admirably engraved by Swain): "The Robber Saint" and "Turberville and the Heiress of Coity" (*Once a Week*, 1861 and 1864) and "Even as Thou Wilt" (*Sunday Magazine*, 1866). A late illustration on a favorite subject (Knott Mill Fair in Manchester), "Old Clothes Market" (*Graphic*, 1870), recalls "Vanity Fair" in its masterful assemblage of people in a huge crowd. This swirling composition is packed full of figures in typically Pre-Raphaelite poses and engaged in typically Pre-Raphaelite telling incidents that define personalities and relate individual stories.

The Robber Saint (*wood-engraving, Swain; 5 1/8 x 4;*
Once a Week, *vol. 5, 1861, p. 378*)

Turberville and the Heiress of Coity (*wood-engraving,*
5 1/4 x 4 5/8; Once a Week, *vol. 10, 1864, p. 378*)

Catalogue

PERIODICALS

Good Words
Vol. 9, 1868:
  ¶ **Among the Corn** (p. 441)
Vol. 30, 1889:
  ¶ **The Nativity*** (p. 825, Swain; the
bottom portion of the original drawing is
reproduced in *A Christmas Faggot*)

Graphic
Vol. 2, 1870:
  ¶ **Old Clothes Market: Camp Field,
Manchester*** (p. 584, Swain)

Illustrated London News
Vol. 35, 1859:
  ¶ **Christmas Eve** (p. 626, Orrinsmith;
a.k.a. **The Holly Gatherers**)

London Home Monthly
Vol. 1, 1895:
  ¶ **The Old Frenchman of the Strand**
(photo-engraving)

Once a Week
Vol. 4, 1861:
  ¶ **An Hour with the Dead*** (p. 491)
Vol. 5, 1861:
  ¶ **The Robber Saint*** (p. 378, Swain)
Vol. 10, 1864:
  ¶ **Turberville and the Heiress of
Coity*** (p. 378)
New ser. [ser. 2], vol. 3, 1867:
  ¶ **Hide a Stick in a Little Hole*** (p. 569,
Swain)

Punch
Vol. 69, 1875:
  ¶ **" 'Tis an Ill Wind Blows Nobody
Good"** (p. 239)

Sunday Magazine
Vol. 2, 1865–66 [1866]:
  ¶ **Even as Thou Wilt*** (p. 33, Swain;
reprinted in *Touches of Nature*)

Even as Thou Wilt
(wood-engraving, Swain;
5 x 6 5/8; Sunday Magazine, *vol. 2,*
1865–66 [1866], p. 33; Touches of
Nature*)*

§ Shields may have done a few additional illustrations for *Punch* c. 1867–75

BOOKS

Brotherhood with Nature (Charles Rowley, ed.; spring issue to the Ancoats Brotherhood; Manchester: Sherratt and Hughes, 1904)

Bottom left: **The Decision of Faith** (*wood-engraving, Swain?; 4 1/8 x 3 1/8;* **frontispiece** *for* The History of the Plague of London, *[1863])*

Bottom middle: **The Plague-Stricken House** (*wood-engraving, W. Morton; 4 3/4 x 3 1/4;* The History of the Plague of London, *[1863])*

Bottom right: **Solomon Eagle** (*wood-engraving, W. Morton?; 4 3/4 x 2 7/8;* The History of the Plague of London, *[1863])*

Top left: ***Imprisoned Family Escaping*** *(wood-engraving, Swain; 4 1/2 x 3 3/8; The History of the Plague of London, [1863])*

Top middle: ***The Dead-Pit*** *(wood-engraving, Swain; 5 x 3 1/4; The History of the Plague of London, [1863])*

Top right: ***Fugitive Found Dead by Rustics*** *(wood-engraving, Swain; 4 1/4 x 3 1/4; The History of the Plague of London, [1863])*

Christian Reading (wood-engraving, Swain; 5 1/2 x 4; Illustrations to Bunyan's Pilgrim's Progress, 1864)

¶ 3 illustrations (**The Good Shepherd**, ***titlepage illustration***, and ***tailpiece***; photo-engravings)

A Christmas Faggot (Alfred Gurney; Paul, Trench, 1884)
    ¶ ***Frontispiece:*** **The Nativity*** (photogravure; bottom portion of a larger image, engraved in full for *Good Words*; a.k.a. **Every Knee Should Bow**)
    • Plus cover design by the artist

Dante's Pilgrim's Progress (Emelia R. Gurney; Stock, 1893)
    ¶ 1 illustration (chromolithograph graphic design)
    • Plus cover design by the artist

The History of the Plague of London (Daniel Defoe; Laurie's Entertaining Library, [1863])
    ¶ ***Frontispiece:*** **The Decision of Faith*** (Swain?)
    ¶ **The Plague-Stricken House*** (W. Morton)
    ¶ **Solomon Eagle*** (W. Morton?)
    ¶ **Imprisoned Family Escaping*** (Swain)
    ¶ **The Dead-Pit*** (Swain)
    ¶ **Fugitive Found Dead by Rustics*** (Swain)
    • Also issued with better reproduction of the art by Longman, Green, Longman, Roberts, and Green (Shilling Entertaining Library, 1863)

Illustrations to Bunyan's Pilgrim's Progress
(Frederic Shields; Manchester: Ireland /
London: Simpkin, Marshall, 1864)
¶ ***Frontispiece:* Portrait of John
Bunyan*** (Orrinsmith)
¶ ***Pictorial initial: Part 1****
¶ ***Pictorial initial: Part 2****
¶ **Christian Reading*** (Swain)
¶ **The Vision of Judgment***
(W. Thomas)
¶ **Christian at the Cross***
¶ **Christian, Sloth, Simple***
¶ **Hill Difficulty*** (Swain)
¶ **Apollyon***
¶ **Giant Pope*** (Swain)
¶ **Faithful and Wanton*** (Green)
¶ **Moses and Faithful*** (Swain)
¶ **Vanity Fair*** (A. Gaber)
¶ **Hill of Caution*** (Swain)

Christian, Sloth, Simple *(wood-engraving, 5 1/2 x 4;* Illustrations to Bunyan's Pilgrim's Progress, *1864)*

REJOICE NOT AGAINST ME ,O MINE ENEMY
WHEN I FALL . I SHALL ARISE

Apollyon *(wood-engraving, 5 x 3 5/8;* Illustrations to Bunyan's Pilgrim's Progress, *1864)*

¶ **The River of Death***
¶ **Mercy Fainting***
¶ **The Muck-rake***
¶ **Mercy Making Garments*** (Swain)
¶ **The Good Shepherd***

Moses and Faithful *(wood-engraving, Swain; 3 7/8 x 3;* Illustrations to Bunyan's Pilgrim's Progress, *1864)*

¶ **Turn-away at the Cross***
• Reissued in 1875

The Life of William Blake (Alexander Gilchrist; Macmillan, 2d, rev. ed., 2 vols., 1880)
  ¶ **Plan of Blake's Room in Fountain Court** (photogravure)
  ¶ **Catherine Blake** (photogravure; after a sketch by Blake)
  ¶ **Catherine and William Blake** (photogravure; after a sketch by Blake)
  • Plus cover design by the artist (after Blake designs)

A Rachde Felley's Visit to th' Greyt Eggshibishun ([Oliver Ormewood]; London: Hamilton, Adams and Routledge / Manchester: Heywood and Kelley and Slater / Liverpool: Philip, 3d ed., [1856])
  ¶ 19 illustrations (Langton)

BOOKS CONTAINING REPRINTS

Touches of Nature (Strahan, 1867)
  ¶ **Even as Thou Wilt** (reprinted from *Sunday Magazine*)

§ Ernestine Mills (*Life and Letters of Frederick Shields*, p. 47) notes several drawings by Shields for wood-blocks (after old master paintings) for the *Manchester Art Treasures Examiner* (1857)

Top: ***Mercy Fainting*** (*wood-engraving, 5 7/8 x 4;* Illustrations to Bunyan's Pilgrim's Progress, *1864*)

Bottom: ***Mercy Making Garments*** (*wood-engraving, Swain; 3 7/8 x 4;* Illustrations to Bunyan's Pilgrim's Progress, *1864*)

BLESSED IS (S)HE THAT CONSIDERETH YE POOR

Simeon Solomon

(1840-1905)

Simeon Solomon's paintings and drawings closely follow in the style of Dante Gabriel Rossetti and Edward Burne-Jones. With their multiplied heads and large figures, these decorative arrangements of human forms seem to have pseudo–mystical/allegorical meanings attached to them after the fact rather than serving as inspirational sources. Solomon did many watercolors and drawings, some of them extremely beautiful, and some of them crossing the line over into decadence and a sensuality of confused genders and of male-female angels. This predilection in his personal life got him into trouble; he was arrested in 1873 and soon became a social outcast, barely involved in art ("pavement artist" has been used to describe his later activities). He died penniless (despite friends' repeated attempts to help), of alcoholism, in 1905.

Two others in the Solomon family were also painters, Simeon's siblings Rebecca and Abraham. Simeon attended (with Edward Poynter and Henry Holiday) the schools of the Royal Academy, where he exhibited from 1858. He traveled in Italy in the late 1860s, soaking up influences similar to those favored by Burne-Jones and Frederic Leighton—whose artfully arranged, Renaissance-inspired figures reflect the art-for-art's-sake philosophy of one of Solomon's close friends, the art historian Walter Pater. Solomon's fine *Dante's First Meeting with Beatrice* (pen and ink, 1863) looks like a Rossetti image of the period when he worked in the style of the Lasinio engravings and the angular drawings of Millais; the social *I Am Starving* (pen and ink, 1857) and the biblical *David Dancing Before the Ark* (pen and ink, 1860) are similar drawings of real character.

Bacchus (oil, 1867) was well received at the Royal Academy; it is simply the bust of a grape-garlanded male, who is carrying a stick with grapes over his shoulder. *Amoris Sacramentum* (watercolor, 1868) depicts a standing male figure draped in an animal skin and carrying a scepter and a lamp, in a

The End of a Month *(wood-engraving, H. Harral; 4 1/4 x 6; Dark Blue, vol. 1, 1871, p. 217)*

Rossettian landscape, with flowers at his feet. *A Prelude by Bach* (watercolor, 1868) poses languid standing, reclining, and sitting people: one woman plays the harpsichord; all look exactly the same, although there are supposedly four men and five women—disturbingly decadent, the figures in this friezelike bunch of poseurs are totally unrelated, uncomposed. *The Sleepers and the One That Watcheth*, a watercolor of 1870, consists of three busts—one woman awake; one man (?) sleeping; and one "person," in the center, sleeping; they all hold onto each other for dear life. The picture seems lazy and pointless, and the effect is one of symbolism without an idea or spirit behind it. Despite their obvious stylistic debt to Rossetti, the irony of the situation was that in the 1860s Solomon's inferior works were better known than his source's.

An approach similar to that of *Sleepers*, this time consisting of merely two busts, is taken in Solomon's wood-engraved illustration to the poem "The End of a Month" by Algernon Charles Swinburne in *Dark Blue* (1871). The poem itself is extremely purple and full of allusions and symbols of the sea and lovers. Reversing the relationship, Swinburne's poem "Erotion" is based on a Solomon drawing, and Pre-Raphaelite poet John Payne composed three sonnets related to *Sleepers*. Swinburne, a friend and supporter, in an 1871 article wrote of Solomon: "Grecian form and beauty divide the allegiance of his spirit with Hebraic shadow and majesty. . . . For no painter has more love of loveliness; but the fair forms of godhead and manhood which in ancient art are purely and merely beautiful rise again under his hand with the likeness on them of a new thing, the shadow of a new sense, the hint of a new meaning. . . . Instances of . . . [a] ceremonial bias towards religious forms of splendour or solemnity are frequent in the list of the painter's works; gorgeous studies of eastern priests in church or synagogue, of young saint and rabbi and Greek bishop doing their divine service in 'full-blown dignity' of official magic. . . . Whether suffering or enjoyment be the master expression of a face, and whether that enjoy-

Top: ***The Marriage Ceremony*** for **"Jews in England"** *(wood-engraving, 3 7/8 x 5; Once a Week, vol. 7, 1862, p. 192)*

Bottom: ***Lighting the Lamps*** for **"Jews in England"** *(wood-engraving, 3 7/8 x 5; Once a Week, vol. 7, 1862, p. 193)*

ment or that suffering be merely or mainly spiritual or sensual, it is often hard to say—hard often to make sure whether the look of loveliest features be the look of a cruel or a pitiful show. . . . The subtleties and harmonies of suggestion in such studies of complex or it may be perverse nature would have drawn forth praise and sympathy from Baudelaire, most loving of all students of strange beauty and abnormal refinement, of painful pleasures

Abraham's Sacrifice *(wood-engraving, Dalziels; 7 x 5 1/4;* Art Pictures from the Old Testament, *1894)*

Abraham and the Three Angels *(wood-engraving, Dalziels; 6 7/8 x 5 3/8;* Art Pictures from the Old Testament, *1894)*

of soul and inverted raptures of sense" ("Simeon Solomon: Notes on His 'Vision of Love' and Other Studies," *Dark Blue*, vol. 1, pp. 569, 571–72, 575).

If such a sympathetic writer as Swinburne felt the need to comment on Solomon's decadence, it is not surprising that other critics of

the time equivocated even less. Sidney Colvin wrote in 1870 ("English Painters of the Present Day: Simeon Solomon," *Portfolio*, vol. 1, p. 35) that some considered the artist's work full of "affectation" and "ambiguous and indiscriminate sentimentalism." While Robert Ross in 1911 ("Simeon Solomon: A Biography," *Bibelot*, vol. 17, p. 148) stated that although Solomon's "slightest drawing is informed by an idea, nearly always a beautiful one, however exotic," his work could nevertheless be described as "unwholesome . . . morbid . . . [and] informed by odd sentiment."

Most critics, however, were enthusiastic about Solomon's paintings, drawings, and illustrations for ceremonial Jewish life, and this element of his background certainly provided the inspiration for the best works he ever did. Almost all of Solomon's wood-

engraved drawings are in fact Jewish-themed. Two illustrations for "Jews in England" (*Once a Week*, 1862) are realistic, well-designed depictions of contemporary Jewish life—"The Marriage Ceremony" and "Lighting the Lamps"—with sophisticated tonal effects that have the true spirit of Pre-Raphaelitism in them rather than superficial parallels. In his ten pictures for "Illustrations of Jewish Customs" (*Leisure Hour*, 1866) Solomon goes beyond Pre-Raphaelitism (but retains its sense of composition and structure and the occasional typical face) to create elaborately tonal, relentlessly crosshatched, mysteriously lit miniature masterpieces that are almost impressionistic in style.

In "The Veiled Bride" (*Good Words*, 1862) Solomon produced one of his many illustrations on Old Testament themes, the rest being for the *Dalziels' Bible Gallery* project. The periodical piece (also engraved by the Dalziels) and the *Bible Gallery* images are all beautifully rendered in the best strong-figured, controlled-line, and realistic fashion that is certainly Pre-Raphaelite. Of Solomon's twenty *Bible Gallery* wood-engraved drawings (fourteen did not appear until the 1881 book's republication in expanded form by the Society for Promoting Christian Knowledge in 1894), there's not a clinker in the group. His figures' long robes sway and curve in decorative counterpoints, the contrasts of tone and light are lovely, and Pre-Raphaelite realism (not to mention the occasional Rossettian face or mane of hair) clearly infuses these subjects with an inner life.

For the Junior Etching Club, Solomon created one print, *The Haunted House* (*Passages from the Poems of Thomas Hood*, 1858), a mysterious but atmospheric piece that is strange-

The Haunted House (etching, Solomon; 5 1/2 x 3 3/8; Passages from the Poems of Thomas Hood, *1858*)

ly ill-drawn while maintaining the naive Pre-Raphaelite charm of a Smetham work. A woman and young girl stand at a doorway, expressing the sentiments of the poem: "O very gloomy is the House of Woe, / Where tears are falling while the bell is knelling. / With all the dark solemnities which show / That Death is in the dwelling."

Catalogue

PERIODICALS

Dark Blue
Vol. 1, 1871:
¶ **The End of a Month*** (p. 217, H. Harral)
• Erroneously credited "S. Salaman"

Good Words
Vol. 3, 1862:
¶ **The Veiled Bride*** (p. 592, Dalziels)

Leisure Hour
Vol. 15, 1866:
¶ **"Illustrations of Jewish Customs,"** 10 illustrations* (pp. 73, 168, 217, 329, 377, 476, 540, 604, 653, 823; Butterworth and Heath)

Once a Week
Vol. 7, 1862:
¶ **"Jews in England"** by G.L., 2 illustrations* (**The Marriage Ceremony**, p. 192; **Lighting the Lamps**, p. 193)

The Veiled Bride (wood-engraving, Dalziels; 5 3/4 x 3 13/16; Good Words, vol. 3, 1862, p. 592)

Bottom left: *The Passover* (wood-engraving, Dalziels; 7 x 5 3/8; Art Pictures from the Old Testament, *1894*)

Bottom right: *The First Offering of Aaron* (wood-engraving, Dalziels; 5 1/2 x 7 1/4; Art Pictures from the Old Testament, *1894*)

The Burnt Offering *(wood-engraving, Dalziels; 6 1/4 x 4 3/4; Art Pictures from the Old Testament, 1894)*

Offering Incense *(wood-engraving, Dalziels; 7 x 5 1/4; Art Pictures from the Old Testament, 1894)*

Offering the First-Fruits of the Harvest *(wood-engraving, Dalziels; 7 x 5 3/8; Art Pictures from the Old Testament, 1894)*

Left: ***"He Shall Order the Lamps"*** *(wood-engraving, Dalziels; 6 7/8 x 5 3/8; Art Pictures from the Old Testament, 1894)*

Right: ***"Righteousness and Peace Have Kissed Each Other"*** *(wood-engraving, Dalziels; 6 1/2 x 4 3/4; Art Pictures from the Old Testament, 1894)*

BOOKS

Art Pictures from the Old Testament (Aley Fox, text; Society for the Promotion of Christian Knowledge, 1894)
¶ **Abraham and the Three Angels***

Top left: ***The Feast of Tabernacles*** (wood-engraving, Dalziels; 5 3/8 x 7; Art Pictures from the Old Testament, *1894)*

Top right: ***Ruth and Naomi*** (wood-engraving, Dalziels; 6 1/2 x 4 3/4; Art Pictures from the Old Testament, *1894)*

Middle left: ***Shadrach, Meshach, and Abednego*** (wood-engraving, Dalziels; 6 1/2 x 4 3/4; Art Pictures from the Old Testament, *1894)*

Middle right: ***"And David Took an Harp"*** (wood-engraving, Dalziels; 6 3/8 x 5; Art Pictures from the Old Testament, *1894)*

Bottom: ***Jewish Women Burning Incense: Jeremiah*** (wood-engraving, Dalziels; 6 3/8 x 4 3/4; Art Pictures from the Old Testament, *1894)*

¶ **Abraham's Sacrifice***
¶ **The Passover***
¶ **The First Offering of Aaron***
¶ **The Burnt Offering***
¶ **Offering Incense***
¶ **Offering the First-Fruits of the Harvest***
¶ **"He Shall Order the Lamps"***
¶ **"Righteousness and Peace Have Kissed Each Other"***

Abraham and Isaac
(wood-engraving,
Dalziels; 6 7/8 x 5 1/4;
Dalziels' Bible Gallery,
1881; Art Pictures from
the Old Testament*)*

Hagar and Ishmael
(wood-engraving, Dalziels;
6 1/2 x 4 3/4; Dalziels'
Bible Gallery, *1881;* Art
Pictures from the Old
Testament*)*

The Infant
Moses *(wood-*
engraving,
Dalziels; 5 1/2
x 4 1/2;
Dalziels' Bible
Gallery, *1881;*
Art Pictures
from the Old
Testament*)*

¶ **The Feast of Tabernacles***
¶ **Ruth and Naomi***
¶ **"And David Took an Harp"***
¶ **Jewish Women Burning Incense:**
Jeremiah*
¶ **Shadrach, Meshach, and**
Abednego*
• Eng. Dalziels
• Plus 6 illustrations reprinted from
Dalziels' Bible Gallery

Hosannah! *(wood-engraving, Dalziels; 6 3/8 x*
4 3/4; Dalziels' Bible Gallery, *1881;* Art Pictures
from the Old Testament*)*

Dalziels' Bible Gallery (Routledge, 1881)
¶ **Abraham and Isaac***
¶ **Hagar and Ishmael***
¶ **Hosannah!***
¶ **The Infant Moses***
¶ **Melchizedek Blesses Abram***
¶ **Naomi and the Child Obed***
• Eng. Dalziels
• Reprinted in *Art Pictures from the Old*
Testament

A Vision of Love Revealed in Sleep
(Simeon Solomon; Ellis, 1871)
¶ ***Frontispiece:*** **Then I Knew My Soul**

Left: *Melchizedek Blesses Abram* (*wood-engraving, Dalziels; 6 7/8 x 5 1/4;* Dalziels' Bible Gallery, *1881;* Art Pictures from the Old Testament)

Right: *Naomi and the Child Obed* (*wood-engraving, Dalziels; 6 1/4 x 7 7/8;* Dalziels' Bible Gallery, *1881;* Art Pictures from the Old Testament)

Stood By Me (photographic print)
  • Limited edition "printed for the author"
  • Plus cover design by the artist

§ *King Solomon and the Fair Shulamite* (Julia Ellsworth Ford, ed.; New York: Sherman, 1908) reproduces 7 drawings on the title subject done previously by the artist, and published here for the first time (photogravures)

INDIVIDUAL PRINTS

¶ *Bookplate* **for Oscar Browning*** (wood-engraving, Swain, 1870; 3 3/8 x 2 1/4; signed with monogram and dated in block)

¶ **The Haunted House*** (etching, Solomon; 5 1/2 x 3 3/8; signed with initials in plate; a.k.a. **The Schoolroom Door**)
  • Published in *Passages from the Poems of Thomas Hood* (Junior Etching Club; Gambart, 1858)

Bookplate for Oscar Browning (*wood-engraving, Swain, 1870; 3 3/8 x 2 1/4; photo-engraving, as published in Egerton Castle's* English Book-plates, *1893*)

Simeon Solomon

2

The Artists and Their Works
~
Illustrations of the
Pre-Raphaelite
Associates

William Shakespeare Burton
(1824–1916)

W. S. Burton was a minor Pre-Raphaelite painter whose works, though exhibited at the Royal Academy, seemed not to have achieved much success. His best regarded Pre-Raphaelite painting (and only one of note) is *The Wounded Cavalier*, exhibited at the Academy in 1856. This is a tour de force of naturalistic-detail and crisp-realism painting: even though the right half of the picture is almost entirely landscape, with the figures all on the left, its startling, imaginative composition works beautifully—with its inscrutable Puritan man stoically standing parallel to a tree that only barely seems not a part of him.

Burton was a member of the Hogarth Club in the period 1858–61. Lack of recognition and poor health caused a pause in his artistic output for the last decades of the century, but William Michael Rossetti in 1906 noted a recent painting by him based on Dante Gabriel Rossetti's poem "The Blessed Damozel" and called Burton "a painter of high aims, and of attainment insufficiently recognized" (*Some Reminiscences*, vol. 1, p. 226).

As far as can be determined, Burton's four wood-engravings for *Once a Week* mark the extent of his illustrative work. Their approach recalls the stylized, thick, even-lined drawings of the Dürer emulators (Sandys, Poynter), albeit with looser linework in the manner of Charles Keene. His large, sculptural, simplified figures are similar to those of John D. Watson and John Lawson at their least detailed. Of Burton's four 1864 compositions, the most Pre-Raphaelite is "The Romaunt of the Rose."

The Romaunt of the Rose (wood-engraving, Swain; 6 1/2 x 4 5/8; Once a Week, vol. 10, 1864, p. 602)

Catalogue

Once a Week
Vol. 10, 1864:
¶ **The Romaunt of the Rose*** (p. 602, Swain)
Vol. 11, 1864:
¶ **Who Was the Executioner of King Charles the First?*** (p. 14, Swain)
¶ **Dame Eleanor's Return** (p. 210, Swain)
¶ **The Whaler Fleet** (p. 638, Swain?)

Charles Allston Collins

(1828–1873)

Brought into the Pre-Raphaelite circle early on by John Everett Millais, Charles Collins submitted a painting based on the group's principles to the Royal Academy Exhibition of 1850, *Berengaria Seeing the Girdle of Richard Offered for Sale in Rome*. Millais and Collins retired to a secluded cottage for a short time in 1850 to paint from nature, Millais working on *The Woodman's Daughter* (Royal Academy, 1851). In summer 1851 the two were joined by Millais's brother William (an occasional painter and illustrator) and William Holman Hunt at a country farmhouse to once again paint directly their "backgrounds." As Millais was painting *Ophelia* and Hunt *The Hireling Shepherd*, Collins was fastidiously re-creating an old shed and tree leaves, even though he had no subject in mind. The picture was never finished, and eventually Collins gave up painting in favor of literary pursuits, as a contributor to Dickens's *Household Words* periodical and author of several books. But during that 1851 artistic excursion, Collins's extreme religious views were causing his health to deteriorate: he refused to enjoy meals in the spirit of camaraderie the others desired and was criticized for becoming "so much of an ascetic" (*Life and Letters of Sir John Everett Millais*, vol. 1, pp. 133, 137).

Interestingly, Collins shared this religious preoccupation with James Collinson, and like Collinson he became linked for a while to a Rossetti sister; but Collins's preference was for Maria rather than Christina. William Rossetti characterized him as "one of those artists who, along with very sufficient execu-

tive powers, seem to have little of the artistic nature: so at least it struck me, and so perhaps, as he relinquished the career [he stopped painting in the mid-1850s], it struck himself" (*Some Reminiscences*, vol. 1, p. 152).

Convent Thoughts *(oil, 1851; 33 1/8 x 23 1/4; Ashmolean Museum, Oxford; photogravure, as published in William Holman Hunt's* Pre-Raphaelitism and the Pre-Raphaelite Brotherhood, *vol. 2, 1906)*

Collins's best-known Pre-Raphaelite work, *Convent Thoughts* (1851), depicts compulsively detailed plant forms and a central female figure sharing space equally with the other elements, all in sharp focus, including the very legible illuminated-missal pages of the book the sister holds. The painting is a near blueprint for second-phase Pre-Raphaelitism, led by Rossetti and Sandys, with its picture-consuming females enveloped by flora and with sensuality replacing early-Italian–inspired religious subjects.

Charles Allston Collins was the younger brother of Wilkie Collins—the author of the novels *The Moonstone* and *The Woman in White* and the father of the English detective story. Not surprisingly, Charles drifted into literature, notably writing a series of travel books. It appears his only illustrations were for his own books; *A Cruise upon Wheels*, the most famous, is a fictional travelogue subtitled "The Chronicle of Some Autumn Wanderings Among the Deserted Post-roads of France." Collins married Charles Dickens's daughter in 1860, and was to illustrate Dickens's *The Mystery of Edwin Drood*, but due to illness only completed the paper cover.

Catalogue

A Cruise upon Wheels (Charles Allston Collins; Routledge, Warne, and Routledge, 1863)
> ¶ *Frontispiece:* **Monsieur Morve of Malaise***
> ¶ *Titlepage illustration*
> • Originally published in 2 vols., 1862

The Eye-witness (Charles Allston Collins; Low, 1860)
> ¶ *Titlepage illustration*

A New Sentimental Journey (Charles Allston Collins; Chapman and Hall, 1859)
> ¶ *Frontispiece* (steel-engraving)

§ Collins's *At the Bar* (Chapman and Hall, 1866) may also contain an illustration by the artist

Monsieur Morve of Malaise *(wood-engraving, Dalziels; 6 x 3 1/2;* **frontispiece** *for* A Cruise upon Wheels *[2 vols., 1862], 1863)*

James Collinson

(c. 1825–1881)

One of the more interesting figures involved with the Pre-Raphaelites in their earliest stage was James Collinson. "Interesting" is perhaps not the most appropriate word, since Collinson by all accounts seemed an unusually placid character. William Holman Hunt shared lodgings with him awhile, when he was working on his *Converted British Family* painting; Collinson's own canvas he described as "designed and painted with little promise of ultimate success." His most reproduced "Pre-Raphaelite" painting, *The Renunciation of Queen Elizabeth of Hungary* (exhibited 1851), Hunt called "a neat and at the same time timid effort, a would-be Pre-Raphaelitism" and denigrated Collinson's use of a newly built Gothic-revival church ("with Minton tiles for the Pavement") as the model for the work's thirteenth-century interior (*Pre-Raphaelitism*, vol. 1, p. 194). *The Renunciation* is a carefully painted effort in the spirit of the Campo Santo frescoes, somewhat archaic, and a composition that sprawls over a mixture of disjointed set-ups; it holds together better than fellow Pre-Raphaelite Walter Deverell's *Twelfth Night* (1850), but just barely.

Hunt also gives what appears to be the prevailing assessment of Collinson's personality: "In his personal life [about 1849] the painter seemed less awake than ever; he repined daily as he sat at breakfast on the terribly bad night he had had, yawning as he sipped his tea. If I went into his studio at noon he was asleep over the fire, while a hulking model was idly earning his shilling an hour all the same" (*Pre-Raphaelitism*, vol. 1, p. 194).

William Michael Rossetti's account is similar, though more polite, suggesting that Collinson's choice by his brother Gabriel as one of the original seven "brethren" was not appropriate. More importantly, William provides an account of Collinson's famous relationship with their sister Christina. An early friend and fellow student of Gabriel, Collinson fell in love with the then seventeen-year-old Christina, who declined his offer of marriage due to their religious differences (Collinson had earlier converted to Roman Catholicism). Collinson reconsidered, reverted to Anglicanism, and then became engaged, about fall 1848. But Collinson once more had a change of spiritual heart: by spring 1850 he was renewed in his Catholic faith, and Christina again broke off the relationship, an event that deeply affected her (*Some Reminiscences*, vol. 1, p. 73).

Shortly after showing his painting *Answering the Emigrant's Letter* at the Royal Academy Exhibition that same year, he quit the Brotherhood—owing much to the negative critical reception for the P.R.B. paintings, especially along religious grounds. In a letter of resignation to Dante Rossetti, Collinson offered that "as a sincere Catholic" he could no longer associate with the Brotherhood or its *Germ* magazine and thus help to "dishonour . . . God's faith and saints . . . if not absolutely to bring their sanctity into ridicule" (Thomas Bodkin, "James Collinson," *Apollo*, vol. 31, 1940, p. 129). William Rossetti continues the tale: "At the beginning of 1853 he entered a Jesuit College as a 'working brother,'

The Child Jesus (etching, Collinson; 4 1/2 x 6 7/8; **frontispiece** for the Germ, no. 2, February 1850)

but he soon left again, resumed his profession as a painter—he never rose to any real eminence in the art—and married a sister-in-law of the painter John Rogers Herbert, himself a Catholic convert" (*Some Reminiscences*, vol. 1, p. 74). Collinson's painting *The Empty Purse* (several versions in the 1850s) shows him retaining something of the old spirit, in the sharp and distinct forms and bright colors.

Collinson produced an etching for the *Germ* in 1850. *The Child Jesus*, in the second issue, is a nicely composed and fairly satisfying religious composition in the style of his major painting and the Rossetti/Hunt/Millais drawings of the period—that is, rather unmodeled pointy figures massed together, resembling the early-Italian style of the Nazarenes and Lasinio's engravings.

Catalogue

¶ **The Child Jesus*** (etching, Collinson; 4 1/2 x 6 7/8; signed and dated in plate)
   • Published in the *Germ*, no. 2, February 1850

Walter Deverell

(1827–1854)

Walter Deverell, though not part of the Pre-Raphaelite Brotherhood, was so close to its members that he is often thought of as having replaced James Collinson, who left the group in 1850. Deverell had been a fellow student of John Everett Millais, William Holman Hunt, and Dante Gabriel Rossetti at the Royal Academy, and he had quickly (in 1848) gained a position as assistant master at the Government School of Design. According to Hunt, Deverell was interested in social issues and was such an effervescent personality that he often took part in theatrical productions (*Pre-Raphaelitism*, vol. 1, p. 197).

After his father passed away in 1853, Deverell was obliged to support his family, even though he himself was suffering from a fatal illness. When he died in 1854, he had completed only a handful of paintings, including *The Grey Parrot* (1852–53), *Scene from As You Like It* (1852–53), and his best-known Pre-Raphaelite work, *Twelfth Night* (1850). Compositionally, this is a fairly unsatisfying and unfocused work, but the colors are bright, the treatment is early Italian, and he followed the movement's standard

Viola and Olivia (etching, Deverell; 6 7/8 x 4 5/8; **frontispiece** for the Germ, no. 4, April 1850)

procedure of using his friends as models. Rossetti posed for the Jester and Deverell based the central figure on himself. Viola was Elizabeth Siddal, Deverell's model-discovery, announced to the group in this way (according to Holman Hunt in *Pre-Raphaelitism*, vol. 1, p. 198): "You fellows can't tell what a stupendously beautiful creature I have found." Siddal thus became part of the circle: she immediately modeled for Hunt's *A Converted British Family* (1850) and also impressed Rossetti, who would make her a Pre-Raphaelite icon and eventually his wife.

Seemingly, Deverell's sole contribution to Pre-Raphaelite graphics is his etching for the fourth issue of the *Germ*, a fairly pedestrian two-figure composition again based on Shakespeare's *Twelfth Night*.

Catalogue

¶ **Viola and Olivia*** (etching, Deverell; 6 7/8 x 4 5/8; signed with initials in plate)
  • Published in the *Germ*, no. 4, April 1850

Henry Holiday

(1839–1927)

Henry Holiday attended the Royal Academy Schools in the mid-1850s, where he formed a sketching club that included Albert Moore and Simeon Solomon. Like many of the Pre-Raphaelites, he was a fine designer of stained glass (for Powell and Sons from 1861), devoting much of his career to that discipline; he even formed his own glassworks factory in 1890. He created murals and mosaics and

But the Queen Held Her Brows and Gazed *(etching, C. Waltner; 5 x 7;* **frontispiece** *for* The Illustrated British Ballads, *vol. 2, 1881)*

invented new methods of enameling on metal.

A friend of Hunt and Burne-Jones, Holiday was also a painter, who exhibited regularly at the Royal Academy from 1858. The Grosvenor

Gallery in 1883 showed his most famous (and often-reproduced) canvas, *Dante and Beatrice*, which reveals various influences, from the Rossetti-ish theme to the Poynter-Leighton historical re-creation and the Burne-Jones sensibility in the figures.

Holiday did not do many drawings for the wood-block, but those he did have elevated him to the ranks of great Victorian illustrators—owing mainly to his illustrations for Lewis Carroll's *The Hunting of the Snark* of 1876, engraved by Swain. These are rather spectacular technical achievements, showing a perfect understanding of the linear elements of the medium—despite the fact that Holiday was inexperienced as an illustrator. In his essay "The Designs for the Snark" in *Lewis Carroll's The Hunting of the Snark, Illustrated by Henry Holiday* (1981, p. 108), Charles Mitchell describes Holiday's process, which is a good indication of the way many of the Pre-Raphaelites worked: "Having decided on his pictorial formulation, he invariably made a compositional design, normally in pencil on paper and about the same size as the intended cut. . . . His next step was to make, in pencil on larger paper

"Uncover Ye His Face," She Said *for **"The Staff and Scrip"** (wood-engraving, 4 x 4 3/8;* The Illustrated British Ballads*, vol. 2, 1881)*

and usually with the aid of living models posed in the positions established by the compositional design, precisely detailed working studies of whole figures or parts of them. . . . Then, finally, he made the finished design, in pencil or ink on board and sometimes larger than the intended cut, . . . whose outlines he transferred in reverse [via tracing paper] to the wood-block, sharpening them up, with the finished design before him, in very hard pencil in the finest detail so that the engraver knew exactly what to reproduce." Holiday's wood-engraved illustrations for *Snark* are very English, very Tenniel (Carroll's illustrator for the *Alice* books) in their fantasy, with a little of the big-head caricature of *Punch*'s Linley Sambourne thrown in, but with the polished and detailed woodcuttish technique of a more fastidious Walter Crane.

Also of interest are six excellent illustrations Holiday made for *The Illustrated British Ballads* (2 vols., 1881), which are extremely

The Crew on Board *for **"The Landing"** (wood-engraving, Swain; 5 1/4 x 3 3/4;* The Hunting of the Snark, *1876;* Rhyme? and Reason?*)*

well engraved (probably all, except for the etched frontispiece, by E. Babbage) and combine several influences: in addition to the hyper-realistic depictions of knights and their horses and the decorative use of detailed foliage, there are echoes of Burne-Jones and Rossetti (the multiplied female figures) and the Aesthetic figural arrangements of Leighton and Moore.

Catalogue

The Hunting of the Snark (Lewis Carroll [Charles Lutwidge Dodgson]; Macmillan, 1876)
¶ **"The Landing,"** 3 illustrations*
(*frontispiece*; **The Crew on Board**; **The Butcher and the Beaver**)
¶ **The Baker's Tale**
¶ **The Hunting***
¶ **The Beaver's Lesson***

The Hunting (*wood-engraving, Swain; 5 1/4 x 3 1/2;* The Hunting of the Snark, *1876;* Rhyme? and Reason?*)*

¶ **The Barrister's Dream**
¶ **The Banker's Fate**
¶ **The Vanishing**
• Eng. Swain
• Plus cover design by the artist
• Reprinted in *Rhyme? and Reason?* (Lewis Carroll [Charles Lutwidge Dodgson]; Macmillan, 1883)

The Illustrated British Ballads, Old and New (George Barnett Smith, ed.; Cassell, Petter, Galpin, 2 vols., 1881)

¶ **The Bonnie Bairns** (vol. 1)
¶ *Frontispiece:* **But the Queen Held Her Brows and Gazed*** (vol. 2; etching, C. Waltner)
¶ **Riding Together** (vol. 2)
¶ **Sir Guido** (vol. 2; E. Babbage)
¶ **"The Staff and Scrip,"** 2 illustrations* (vol. 2)

§ **The Annunciation** (wood-engraving proof, Swain) is a broadside ad announcing Holiday's mural painting *Ave Maria* at the Chapel of All Saints Church, Notting Hill (Museum of Fine Arts, Boston, Hartley Collection)

The Beaver's Lesson (*wood-engraving, Swain; 5 1/8 x 3 1/2;* The Hunting of the Snark, *1876;* Rhyme? and Reason?*)*

John W. Inchbold

(1830–1888)

John Inchbold, one of the premier Pre-Raphaelite landscapists, was a favorite of John Ruskin. Having been impressed by his microscopically realistic technique and bright colors, as well as by his attached quotes from Wordsworth (a poet admired by Ruskin) in such paintings as *A Study in March* (a.k.a. *In Early Spring*, 1855) and *The White Doe of Rylstone* (1855), Ruskin frequently praised Inchbold in the critic's annual *Academy Notes*. In the late 1850s, the two men traveled to Switzerland on a painting expedition.

Inchbold was a friend of Dante Gabriel Rossetti, as well as of other literary figures like Coventry Patmore, Algernon Charles Swinburne, Alfred Tennyson, and Robert Browning, and he wrote his own volume of sonnets (*Annus Amoris*). Given this literary bent, and the fact that he was an apprentice to lithographers Day and Haghe in the late 1840s, it is surprising that he did not follow his colleagues' example and draw for the wood-engravers. He did, however, contribute an etching to the *Portfolio* in 1879, and he published his own collection of twenty-one landscape etchings in 1885, *Mountain and Vale*.

Inchbold enjoyed a long career as a landscape painter (exhibiting at the Royal Academy from 1851 to 1885), although William Michael Rossetti called him "unsuccessful . . . [and] harassed by ill-success into losing or frittering away his finer powers in the art" (*Some Reminiscences*, vol. 1, p. 229). His later paintings, as well as his etchings of natural settings, are not especially Pre-Raphaelite in style or inspiration.

Catalogue

¶ **In Westminster Abbey** (etching, Inchbold; 9 5/8 x 6 7/8 [plate])
   • Published in the *Portfolio*, vol. 10, 1879

Mountain and Vale (John W. Inchbold, 1885)
   ¶ *Titlepage illustration* (7 9/16 x 10)
   ¶ **Dent du Midi** (7 1/2 x 10 1/16)
   ¶ **Clarens** (7 7/16 x 10 3/8)
   ¶ **Petit Bouverant, Chesiese** (10 3/16 x 7 1/4)
   ¶ **Studies of Flowers and Leaves** (10 3/16 x 7 5/16)
   ¶ **Tomb of Sophia, Daughter of James I: Westminster Abbey** (10 1/8 x 7 7/16)
   ¶ **Westminster Abbey** (10 1/16 x 7 3/16)
   ¶ **At Bruges** (10 x 7 1/8)
   ¶ **Les Avants** (7 3/8 x 10 3/8)
   ¶ **Thames** (7 5/16 x 10)
   ¶ **The Thames** (7 5/16 x 10)
   ¶ **Montreux, 1881** (7 7/16 x 10 3/8)
   ¶ **Montreux** (7 3/8 x 10)
   ¶ **Kensington Gardens** (7 3/16 x 10)
   ¶ **Mountain Mist and Cloud from Chesiese** (10 1/16 x 7 3/8)
   ¶ **Aigle** (10 3/16 x 7 3/8)
   ¶ **Richmond, 1879** (6 7/8 x 10 7/16)
   ¶ **View on the Thames** (7 1/4 x 10 1/16)
   ¶ **Bouverie, 1884** (7 3/8 x 10 1/4)
   ¶ **Puteaux** (10 1/4 x 7 1/4)
   ¶ **Castle of Chillon, Lake Geneva** (11 1/8 x 14 3/8)
   • A collection of 21 landscapes etched by the artist; plate sizes given

Val Prinsep

(1838–1904)

Born in Calcutta, Valentine Prinsep studied at the Royal Academy Schools and at Gleyre's Paris studio in the late 1850s, where he met the English artists Edward Poynter and George Du Maurier (who would model a character in his novel *Trilby* on Prinsep). At his family's Little Holland House estate, Prinsep came under the influence of their permanent house guest, the Renaissance-inclined George F. Watts. In 1859 he traveled to Italy with Edward Burne-Jones. Prinsep exhibited at the Royal Academy from 1862 through 1904, and taught in its schools as professor of painting in the first few years of the twentieth century.

Percy Bate (*The English Pre-Raphaelite Painters*, 1899, p. 90) states that Prinsep pictures such as *Bianca Capello* and *Whispering Tongues Can Poison Truth* were "painted under the direct personal inspiration of Rossetti." (In general, Prinsep's paintings seem part Rossetti and part Poynter, displaying a sure technique that well serves his depictions of historical female figures against decorative backgrounds.) That the older Pre-Raphaelite would have such an effect on Prinsep is understandable, given that Prinsep got his start, so to speak, in the famous project, led by Rossetti and joined by Burne-Jones, Arthur Hughes, William Morris, and two others, to paint the Oxford Union's walls.

The extent of Rossetti's powerful personality and influence at the time can be seen in Prinsep's recollections of the event. "We all worked hard . . . and did our best. We were all wanting in experience. We had no method and but little knowledge. What we did had a cer-

tain 'cachet' which came from our being all full of the same feeling and labouring under the same enthusiasms. . . . I was told, when I returned to London, that I had caught

Val Prinsep, c. 1880s (wood-engraving, as published in the Magazine of Art, *vol. 6, 1883)*

Rossetti's intonation of voice, and I know myself I used all his slang and talked of 'stunners' with truly Rossettesque enthusiasm" ("A Chapter from a Painter's Reminiscence," *Magazine of Art*, new ser., vol. 2, 1904, p. 169).

While Prinsep wrote a number of novels (*Virginie*; *The Story of Abibal the Tsourian*), the one book illustrated by him is his own

Imperial India: An Artist's Journal (1879). The latter contains numerous wood-engraved drawings recording the artist's experiences while traveling in India; several illustrations are beautifully executed portraits with a realistic/Aesthetic attention to garment and background decoration, reminiscent of the portrait-style paintings of Rossetti and Sandys. Prinsep's only other significant illustration, "Strolling Along," appeared in *Once a Week* in 1869.

Catalogue

English Art in 1884 (Henry Blackburn; New York: Appleton, 1885)
    ¶ **The Little Bookworm** (drawing by the artist after his painting; photo-engraving)

Imperial India: An Artist's Journal (Val Prinsep; Chapman and Hall, [1879])
    ¶ 24 illustrations* (Dalziels)

Once a Week
New ser. [ser. 3], vol. 3, 1869:
    ¶ **Strolling Along** (p. 299)

H.H. Jeswant Sing, Maharajah of Jodhpore (*wood-engraving, Dalziels; 5 1/2 x 4 1/4; Imperial India: An Artist's Journal, [1879]*)

Begoo, a Kashmiree Nautch Girl (*wood-engraving, Dalziels; 5 1/4 x 3 3/4; Imperial India: An Artist's Journal, [1879]*)

John Ruskin

(1819-1900)

John Ruskin was like an annoying bumble-bee buzzing undeterred through the artistic community of Victorian England. His writings on art were relentless, his criticism (especially in the annual *Academy Notes*) making and breaking artistic reputations. He was involved in many of the socially conscious enterprises of the day—teaching drawing, for example, at the Working Men's College along with painters like Ford Madox Brown and Dante Gabriel Rossetti, and founding the Guild of St. George in 1871 for the "workmen and labourers of Great Britain." He was generous with his considerable wealth and his support of any artists he felt were worthy.

Yet he was stern and self-important, ready to challenge Whistler in court over his criticism of the artist's less-than–Pre-Raphaelite method of painting. Most damningly, one cannot read his meandering prose without feeling that pompous argument after pompous argument merely serves to prop up some personal like or dislike of the moment, in the midst of an inconsistent philosophy. William Michael Rossetti characterized him thus: "I did not find him dictatorial or pragmatic; but one element in our relative position was the tacit assumption on both sides that he knew a great deal about matters in which I also was interested, and that my cue was to profit by what he could and would impart to me. . . . He always presented the aspect of a man of very sensitive mind and feelings and a little liable to take a contrary or perverse bias. . . . [This] appeared to hint of a certain deviousness of temperament . . ."

(*Some Reminiscences*, vol. 1, pp. 179–80, 184).

Ruskin was educated at King's College, London, and Christ Church, Oxford, in the 1830s. His travels in Europe in 1840–41 included a career-shaping visit to Venice. He met the embodiment of his initial artistic passion, the great landscapist J.M.W. Turner, in 1840. The first volumes of his seminal work, *Modern Painters*, appeared in 1843 and 1846 (there were five, through 1860) and helped to inspire the young William Holman Hunt and John Everett Millais and others in the love of early-Italian painters and the need to go to nature directly in creating modern art. Ruskin was the prestigious Slade Professor of Art at Oxford from 1869 through 1884, after which time he became increasingly reclusive, until his death in 1900. In addition to *Modern Painters*, his enormous body of writings on art includes *The Seven Lamps of Architecture* (1849), *The Stones of Venice* (1851–53), and *The Elements of Drawing* (1857).

It was Ruskin's two letters to the London *Times* in 1851 that salvaged the reputations of the Pre-Raphaelites, after the critics began to excoriate them in the press. Subsequently, he became their patron, propagandizer in print, financial backer, agent, and would-be instructor. Ruskin traveled to Switzerland and Italy with landscape artists John Brett and John W. Inchbold, guiding them to create paintings according to his principles. In the 1850s he eulogized Millais's exhibited works in his *Academy Notes*, even after a disastrous trip with the Millais family to Scotland in 1853, which resulted not only in a great Millais

John Ruskin, 1866 (wood-engraving, as published in M. H. Spielmann's John Ruskin, *1900)*

painting (a portrait of Ruskin at a waterfall) but in Millais's eventual marriage to Ruskin's then-wife, Effie.

Rossetti became Ruskin's enthusiasm from the mid-1850s—Ruskin secured patrons for him, bought his works, and even lent him money to go to Europe with Elizabeth Siddal. A trip with Ruskin to Italy was instrumental in Burne-Jones's adopting elements of Renaissance painting in his work. Ruskin called Arthur Hughes's early Pre-Raphaelite painting *April Love* (1855–56) "exquisite in every way" and Holman Hunt's *The Triumph of the Innocents* (1876–87) "the greatest religious painting of our time"—two assessments decades apart with which it is hard to disagree. Yet, Ruskin with typical inconsistency never mentioned Brown or Sandys in his writings.

Ruskin was a member of the Pre-Raphaelites' Hogarth Club; he was himself a fine watercolorist, draughtsman, and etcher. Strangely, for someone who praised the prints of Holbein and Dürer—whose "every line . . . is as good as can be"—Ruskin was not a fan of

wood-engraving, which he considered by its nature too "formal" to reproduce thin, sketchy lines well; steel-engraving was preferred for fine lines (John Ruskin, *Ariadne Florentina*, 1890, pp. 125, 188, 78–82). In *The Art of England* (1883, from a lecture at Oxford), Ruskin says that "while no entirely beautiful thing can be represented in a woodcut, every form of vulgarity or unpleasantness can be given to the life . . . nor can any woodcut represent [the beauty] . . . of a nobly bred human form" (pp. 115–16). That the Pre-Raphaelites created wood-engravings not sketchy but linearly reminiscent of Dürer seemed to matter little to Ruskin, who would have preferred that Rossetti's Moxon designs were engraved on copper (*English Print*, p. 125).

Although Ruskin's juvenile fantasy, the famous *King of the Golden River*, was published in 1851 with wood-engravings by Richard Doyle, many of his other books are amply illustrated with engravings (including aquatints and mezzotints) after his sketches, or with his own etched plates. Ruskin's drawings are always precise, detailed, and characterized by a lively realism and special attention to effects of light and shade. These are the works of a fine draughtsman and are among the best Victorian architectural and landscape drawings. His most ambitious and successful prints in this manner may be found in the last three volumes of *Modern Painters* and the three volumes of *The Stones of Venice*.

Catalogue

The following books are all written and illustrated by John Ruskin; only Ruskin's illustrations are listed

Aratra Pentelici (Orpington, Kent/London: Allen, 3d ed., 1890)
¶ 21 illustrations
• 1st edition is 1872, with 9 illustrations

Art Journal
Vol. 46 [new ser., vol. 23], 1884:

¶ **"Mr. Ruskin on 'The Storm Cloud,'"** 5 illustrations* (pp. 105, 106 [2 illus.], 107, 108; J. D. Cooper)

Deucalion (Orpington, Kent: Allen, 1875)
¶ *Frontispiece:* **First Conditions of Accumulation and Fusion** (part 1; steel-engraving, G. Allen)
¶ *Frontispiece:* **The Progress of Modern Science in Glacier Survey** (part 2; steel-engraving, G. Allen)

The Elements of Drawing (Smith, Elder, 1857)
¶ 48 illustrations: wood-engravings in text plus a few full pages; diagrams and drawings mostly by Ruskin

Hortus Inclusus (Orpington, Kent: Allen, 1887)
¶ 1 illustration

The Laws of Fésole (Orpington, Kent: Allen, 1879)
¶ 10 illustrations (steel-engravings, G. Allen)
• Also issued in a large-paper edition with extra copies of the plates
• First issued in 4 parts, 1877–78

Lectures on Architecture and Painting (Smith, Elder, 1854)
¶ 23 illustrations of architectural and botanical details on 15 plates: 14 wood-engraved plates plus *frontispiece* (steel-engraving, T. Lupton) with 2 images

Love's Meinie (Lecture 2) (Keston, Kent: Allen, 1873)
¶ 11 illustrations of birds

Modern Painters (Smith, Elder, 5 vols., 1843, 1846, 1856, 1860)
¶ Vols. 1 and 2 (1843, 1846) have no illustrations; vols. 3, 4, and 5 contain numerous full-page plates (steel-engraved and mezzotint illustrations after and by Ruskin) and wood-engraved text illustrations after Ruskin and others. Ruskin's contributions (with his own etchings listed separately) are as follows:
¶ Vol. 3 (1856): 8 text wood-engravings, mostly after Ruskin sketches; 12 steel-engravings/mezzotints after Ruskin (R. P. Cuff, T. Lupton, J. C. Armytage); plus 1 other: • **The Shores of Wharfe** (etching, Ruskin; after Turner; see information below [§])
¶ Vol. 4 (1856): 116 text wood-engravings, mostly after Ruskin sketches; 23 engravings/mezzotints/etchings after Ruskin (J. C. Armytage, J. H. Le Keux, R. P. Cuff); plus 5 others: • **Pass of Faida: Simple Topography** (etching, Ruskin) • **Pass of Faida: Turnerian Topography** (etching, Ruskin) • **Cleavage of Aiguille Bouchard** (etching, Ruskin) • **Crests of La Côte and Taconay** (etching, Ruskin) • **Crests of the Slaty Crystallines** (etching, Ruskin; after Turner) (see information below [§])
¶ Vol. 5 (1860): 100 text wood-engravings (including 8 full pages), mostly after Ruskin sketches; 22 steel-engravings/etchings after Ruskin (J. C. Armytage, Holl, J. Emslie, R. P. Cuff, J. H. Le Keux); plus 3 others: • **Loire Side** (etching, Ruskin; after Turner) • **The Millstream** (etching, Ruskin; after Turner; 2 images) • **Quivi Trovammo** (etching, Ruskin; after Turner) (see information below [§])

"Our Fathers Have Told Us" (Orpington, Kent: Allen, 1880)
¶ *Frontispiece:* **St. Mary** (steel-engraving, W. Roffé; after Cimabue)
¶ **Dynasties of France** (photo-engraving)
¶ **Amiens, Northern Porch** (photogravure)
¶ **Amiens, Jour des Trépassés** (photogravure)

The Poetry of Architecture (Orpington, Kent: Allen, 1893)
¶ 15 illustrations: 14 photogravures plus *frontispiece* (color lithograph after Ruskin)

Praeterita (Orpington, Kent: Allen, 2 vols., 1886–87)
¶ *Frontispiece* engraving on india paper in each volume
• Also issued in a large-paper edition in 28 parts, 1885–88

Prosperina (Orpington, Kent: Allen, 2 vols. [10 parts], 1875–79)
¶ 8 "engravings" and several text wood-engravings (vol. 1)
¶ 13 "engravings" (lithographs) plus numerous text wood-engravings of flowers (vol. 2)

[Ruskin] *The Poems of John Ruskin* (W. G. Collingwood, ed.; Orpington, Kent: Allen, 2 vols., 1891)
¶ 11 illustrations (vol. 1; photo-engravings)
¶ 12 illustrations (vol. 2; photo-engravings)
• Also issued in a large-paper edition with india-paper proofs

The Seven Lamps of Architecture (Smith, Elder, 1849)
¶ 14 illustrations (etchings, Ruskin; see information below [§])

The Stones of Venice (Smith, Elder, 3 vols., 1851–53)
¶ 53 illustrations (aquatints, mezzotints, steel-engravings, wood-engravings, lithographs), including 7 in color: • Vol. 1 (1851): 21 illustrations (T. Boys, T. Lupton) • Vol. 2 (1853): 20 illustrations (J. C. Armytage, J. H. Le Keux, R. P. Cuff, Dickes) • Vol. 3 (1853): 12 illustrations (J. H. Le Keux, T. Lupton, R. P. Cuff)
¶ Companion volume: *Examples, Etc., Illustrative of the Stones of Venice* (1851): 16 illustrations (etchings, lithographs, mezzotints; T. Boys, T. Lupton)
• Also issued in a large-paper edition, 1894

Studies in Both Arts (Orpington, Kent: Allen, 1895)
¶ 10 illustrations (photogravures)
• Plus cover design by Edward Burne-Jones

The Two Paths (Smith, Elder, 1859)
¶ **The Grass of the Field** (steel-engraving, J. C. Armytage)

Verona and Other Lectures (Orpington, Kent: Allen, 1894)

¶ ***Frontispiece*** (color photo-engraving)
¶ 9 illustrations (photogravures)

§ Etchings executed by Ruskin for *Modern Painters*:
¶ Vol. 3 (1856): • **The Shores of Wharfe** (2 colors, 1855; 8 1/4 x 5; signed and dated in plate; after Turner)
¶ Vol. 4 (1856): • **Pass of Faida: Simple Topography** (1855; 4 7/8 x 7 1/8, signed and dated in plate) • **Pass of Faida: Turnerian Topography** (1856; 4 3/8 x 6 3/4, signed and dated in plate) • **Cleavage of Aiguille Bouchard** (1855; 5 1/8 x 8 3/8, signed and dated in plate) • **Crests of La Côte and Taconay** (1856; 5 3/4 x 7 7/8, signed and dated in plate) • **Crests of the Slaty Crystallines** (1856; 5 1/8 x 8 1/4, signed and dated in plate; after Turner)
¶ Vol. 5 (1860): • **Loire Side** (4 3/4 x 7 1/8; after Turner) • **The Millstream** (2 images on one plate, total 7 1/8 x 4 1/2; after Turner) • **Quivi Trovammo** (5 1/4 x 7 3/4; after Turner)

§ For *The Seven Lamps of Architecture* Ruskin drew and etched 14 illustrations (each signed with initials; page size: 6 3/4 x 9 3/4)

An Old Fashioned Sunset: Herne Hill
(wood-engraving, J. D. Cooper; 3 3/8 x 4 7/8; Art Journal, vol. 46 [new ser., vol. 23], 1884, p. 105)

Thomas Seddon

(1821–1856)

Sons of a cabinet-maker, Thomas Seddon and his brother, the architect John P. Seddon, became members of the Pre-Raphaelite circle. Thomas painted landscapes in 1850 at Barbizon and for a few years afterward in Wales and Brittany, and exhibited a handful of paintings at the Royal Academy (1852–56). In 1850 he established a drawing school for workers and artisans in London, aided by his good friend Ford Madox Brown.

In 1853 Seddon traveled with William Holman Hunt to Palestine to paint and benefit from Hunt's exceptional technique. Hunt grew impatient with Seddon, stating in his memoir: "My travelling companion had, I confess, sometimes tried my patience by his propensity to make fun when it did not altogether seem the time to laugh" (*Pre-Raphaelitism*, vol. 1, p. 391). William Michael Rossetti in *Some Reminiscences* confirms that Seddon "had very high spirits, with a keen eye for the sunny side of things. . . . [He was] a general favourite with all sorts of people" (vol. 1, p. 143). This trip to the Holy Land produced Seddon's most famous work, *Jerusalem and the Valley of Jehoshaphat* (1854), which took five months to paint and was exhibited in London after Seddon's return to England.

Three paintings from the journey were exhibited at the Royal Academy in 1856, including *Sunset Behind the Pyramids*. On a return trip to the Middle East, Seddon became ill of dysentery and died in Cairo.

Despite the influential John Ruskin's praise for his paintings, *Jerusalem* is rather shrill in color and overwrought in detail, not quite the equal of the Pre-Raphaelite landscapes of John Inchbold and John Brett.

Some of Seddon's drawings, all detailed but unexceptional landscapes, were engraved on wood by the Dalziels for two books, *Lays of the Holy Land* and *Land of Promise*, both 1858.

Catalogue

Land of Promise (Horatius Bonar; Nisbet, 1858)
 ¶ **A Scene in the South of Palestine** (Dalziels)
 ¶ **A Well Near Bethany** (Dalziels)
 ¶ **Bethany** (Dalziels)

Lays of the Holy Land (Nisbet, 1858)
 ¶ **A Desert Scene** (Dalziels; a.k.a **The Desert Journey**)

[Seddon] *Memoirs and Letters of the Late Thomas Seddon, Artist* (John P. Seddon; Nisbet, 1858)
 ¶ 18 illustrations (after drawings)

James Smetham

(1821~1889)

James Smetham was a minor artist and writer but a significant, highly original member of the Pre-Raphaelite circle as a friend of Dante Gabriel Rossetti. Clearly influenced by William Blake and Samuel Palmer—and Rossetti—he concentrated on small watercolors and drawings of a poetic nature, often with personal symbolism and religious themes (he was the son of a minister and extremely religious throughout his life). One of his most characteristic and best-known works is the pen-and-ink-and-wash drawing, *The Eve of St. Agnes* (1858), from a favored Pre-Raphaelite source, the poetry of John Keats. He painted *Naboth's Vineyard* in 1856, and exhibited perhaps nine paintings in all at the Royal Academy (1851–69), among them *The Enchanted Princess* and *The Death of Earl Siward* (also the subject of an etching).

Smetham's essay on William Blake, first published in 1868 in the *Quarterly Review*, was an early understanding of Blake's importance and was reprinted as an appendix to the second edition (1880) of Gilchrist's *The Life of William Blake*, whose first edition of 1863 Dante Rossetti helped finish. Rossetti, writing to Mrs. Anne Gilchrist in an undated letter, refers to Smetham as "a very dear & intimate friend of mine, & his relation to Blake in his art I shall have occasion to refer to in the concluding chapter" (Princeton University Library, Troxell Collection).

Ruskin admired Smetham's work and particularly singled out for praise his *The Last Sleep*—which is contained in a portfolio of twelve etchings, *Studies from a Sketch Book*,

published in 1862. This book is a fascinating collection of the work of a poetic miniaturist, and the quality of the best pieces—*The Days of Noah*, *The Death of Earl Siward*, *The Last Sleep*, and a few others—shows the imaginative and compositional power and overwrought Romantic quirkiness that characterized early Pre-Raphaelitism, especially of the Rossetti school.

This series of twelve etchings constitutes Smetham's main contribution to published graphics. According to William Davies, "In 1859 he sought to make his way into book illustration, but without much success. . . . His want of any decided success here led him to conceive the idea of etching his own designs at a cheap rate, and of issuing them quarterly to subscribers." With six hundred subscribers, he continued his plan for three years ("Memoir of James Smetham," in Sarah Smetham and William Davies, ed., *Letters of James Smetham*, 1891, p. 22).

In the *Sketch Book*, several etchings seem to have employed a mechanical ruling device for even, parallel lines—a strangely lazy solution given that Smetham's graphic art rests mostly on linear technique. This approach produced the least successful images: figures with boring, detailless backgrounds (*Lord of the Sabbath*, *Resurrection of the Daisy*, *Hugh Miller*, and *Midsummer*). The remainder, however, have much to recommend them.

Mr. Robert Levett, for which Samuel Johnson's poem is printed on the plate (most of the etchings have texts attached), depicts Johnson's departed friend and his family, with

Snow-bound *(wood-engraving proof, Dalziels; 5 1/16 x 3 5/8; for the* **frontispiece** *for* Snow-bound in Cleeberrie Grange: A Christmas Story, *1861; courtesy British Museum, Department of Prints and Drawings: Dalziel Collection, vol. 14, 1861, no. 1208)*

As uneven as these etchings are in inspiration and quality, the *Art Journal* obviously thought highly enough of the project to review it in 1862, calling *Studies from a Sketch Book* "a series of small figure-subjects, designed by an artist possessed of true poetical feeling, and who handles the etching needle with much delicacy. Among the eight or ten subjects he has published, are three or four gems. *The Last Sleep*, a design admirably adapted for monumental sculpture; *Hugh Miller Watching for His Father's Vessel* is full of spirit and expression; *Midsummer*, a boy basking in the sun, as he lies, face upward, in an open common, with his young sister seated upon him, is natural in composition, and clever in execution; *The Lord of the Sabbath*, in a corn-field, is a work of no ordinary merit. Mr. Smetham's name is unknown to us as an artist, but he has evidently some of the right metal in him: only let him beware of modern pre-Raffaellism, towards which he seems to have a bias" (vol. 24 [new ser., vol. 1], p. 164).

The Death of Earl Siward *(etching, Smetham; 8 3/4 x 6 3/4; Studies from a Sketch Book, [1862])*

Johnson, a book in his pocket, looking on; it's very Rossettian in the poses, heads, groupings, and props. *The Days of Noah* includes biblical quotes on the plate and offers beautiful mouse-line details (like Ford Madox Brown's "The Prisoner of Chillon"); and although certain faces seem caricatured, there are some Pre-Raphaelite faces and poses and massed figures, all nicely modeled. *The Last Sleep*, with its dead lovers laying in parallel and quirky poses, is archaically rendered but richly worked and etched.

In *The Death of Earl Siward*, two hand-held staffs emerge from either side of the frame; there's a terrific Pre-Raphaelite woman with flowing hair, a Millais-type face, and a decorative dress. The subject is a Saxon earl who, feeling the approach of death, desired to be clothed in his armor and set upon his feet so he wouldn't die—as the poem states—"crouching like a cow."

Finally, "Snow-bound" (for G. E. Roberts's

Snow-bound in Cleeberrie Grange, 1861), engraved by the Dalziels, is a neglected masterpiece of Pre-Raphaelite graphics. Smetham's major published wood-engraving is one of the most characteristic and least-known Pre-Raphaelite illustrations, a cross in style between Palmer and Dürer, quite claustrophobic and shallow-spaced, with intriguing figures and nicely detailed decorative qualities.

Filled with religious angst and despair over personal failures, Smetham suffered from mental illness during the last twelve years of his life, and Rossetti and Frederic Shields were actively engaged in helping his family through the sale of his works.

Catalogue

Snow-bound in Cleeberrie Grange: A Christmas Story (George Edwin Roberts; n.p., 1861)
    ¶ *Frontispiece:* **Snow-bound*** (Dalziels)

Studies from a Sketch Book (James Smetham; Williams and Lloyd, [1862])
    ¶ **Forsake Not the Law of Thy Mother** (oval, 2 15/16 x 4)
       ¶ **The Last Sleep*** (2 1/8 x 4 1/4)
       ¶ **The Days of Noah*** (5 1/2 x 4 1/4)
       ¶ **Hugh Miller** (2 7/8 x 6 3/8)

¶ **Midsummer** (4 5/16 x 6 7/16)
¶ **Mr. Robert Levett*** (4 x 4 1/8)
¶ **The Lord of the Sabbath*** (4 3/8 x 6 3/4)
¶ **The Resurrection of the Daisy*** (4 x 5 7/8)
¶ **The Death of Earl Siward*** (8 3/4 x 6 3/4)
¶ **The Morland Edge** (6 7/8 x 9)
¶ **The Dell** (4 3/8 x 3 7/8)
¶ **The Water Lily** (7 x 8 7/8)
• Etchings by Smetham, dated 1860–61

§ William Michael Rossetti states that Smetham also contributed to the Moxon's Popular Poets series, which includes the edition of *Byron's Poetical Works* (1870) illustrated by Ford Madox Brown: "James Smetham was the artist who did the delicate little head and tail pieces to the earlier volumes of the series, of landscape-glimpses, foliage, etc.; he did not do any of the regular illustrations" (*Rossetti: His Family-Letters*, vol. 2, p. 199, n.)

The Days of Noah *(etching, Smetham; 5 1/2 x 4 1/4;* Studies from a Sketch Book, *[1862])*

Mr. Robert Levett *(etching, Smetham; 4 x 4 1/8;* Studies from a Sketch Book, *[1862])*

Thomas Woolner

(1825-1892)

Thomas Woolner was one of the main practitioners of Pre-Raphaelitism in the field of sculpture. Woolner met Dante Gabriel Rossetti at the Royal Academy Schools, and Rossetti sponsored him for membership in the Brotherhood. In those early days Woolner introduced two important poets into the Pre-Raphaelite circle: Coventry Patmore and William Allingham. For the *Germ* in 1850, Woolner provided a number of poems, including "My Beautiful Lady" and "Of My Lady in Death," which were illustrated by a William Holman Hunt etching.

Woolner emigrated to Australia in 1852—an event immortalized in Ford Madox Brown's masterful painting *The Last of England* (exhibited 1856). After he returned to London from this ill-fated gold-prospecting adventure, he wrote to William Bell Scott on October 23, 1854: "You see I am back to England and civilisation. . . . But one were better poor than rich at the price I have seen paid for it in Australia . . ." (Princeton University Library, Troxell Collection). He restarted his sculptor's career, beginning a lively correspondence and friendship with the Tennysons, earning success especially through his statues and relief-medallion portraits of notable Victorians: Alfred Tennyson, John Henry Newman, Robert Browning, Prince Albert, Queen Victoria. Woolner's attraction to the literary was partly based on his own inclinations to poetry; he maintained a friendship with poet-painters Rossetti and Scott and wrote five books of poetry, including *My Beautiful Lady* (1863),

Pygmalion (1881), and *Silenus* (1884).

Rather than through any major illustrations, Woolner expressed his Pre-Raphaelite tendencies in figural sculptures that exhibit the movement's rebellious spirit through unconventional treatment—in representing

Thomas Woolner in his studio, c. 1880s (photograph; photo-engraving, as published in Amy Woolner's Thomas Woolner, R.A., His Life and Letters, *1917)*

realistic emotions and gestures and unusual poses. His four pulpit relief panels (1858) at the restored Llandaff Cathedral are interesting Pre-Raphaelite figures (*Moses* and *St. John*

The Crucifixion (plaster model for marble reredos, St. John the Evangelist, Liverpool, 1876; photo-engraving, as published in Amy Woolner's Thomas Woolner, R.A., His Life and Letters, *1917)*

seem like Madox Brown drawings made three-dimensional), and a similar spirit informs his *Crucifixion* (1876) for St. John the Evangelist, Liverpool. *Heavenly Welcome* (1867) for Wrexham Church, North Wales, and *The Lord's Prayer* (for Sir Walter Trevelyan of Wallington Hall, 1867) are Pre-Raphaelite illustrations come alive, of Victorian women and children—real people in realistic poses, with clutched hands and lovely Germanic garments. Woolner also sculpted such Arthurian/Tennysonian subjects as *Guinevere* (1872) and *Enid* (1881). *The Housemaid*, an 1892 life-size bronze statue of a working woman on her knees with a bucket, is pure poetic social realism.

Woolner's graphic-arts contribution consists mainly of a few titlepage vignettes engraved on steel. Of course, the Moxon *Tennyson*, with the engravings of his Pre-Raphaelite brothers Hunt, Rossetti, and John Everett Millais, is also adorned by a steel-engraved frontispiece of his Tennyson portrait medallion. For the Macmillan Golden Treasury Series, Woolner made three titlepage designs, all engraved on steel by C. H. Jeens. For Palgrave's *The Golden Treasury* (1861) there is a "Piping Shepherd" vignette (reprinted endlessly afterward)—very slight, especially when one sees the original drawing for it.

For the same series, an engraving of an existing statue accents *Bacon's Essays*. Woolner wrote to Macmillan on this subject and his next project, the drawing for *The Book of Praise* (1862), on June 14, 1862: "Jeens has made a most beautiful engraving of the Bacon; it seems to me one of the prettiest little bits of work I have seen for a long while, and he has taken endless pains to make the best job he could of it. . . . [I] have taken him the drawing for the *Book of Praise*. . . . Palgrave thinks it will make a remarkably [?] nice vignette" (New York Public Library, Berg Collection). Indeed, this exemplary steel-engraving of King David is a powerful image in a small space—the work of a master draughtsman, a subject and treatment that might have well suited *Dalziels' Bible Gallery*. For *The Children's Garland* (1871) by Woolner's friend Coventry Patmore, the sculptor designed a sharply detailed, Pre-Raphaelite–looking vignette of a knight and two children outside a castle wall.

Catalogue

The Book of Praise (Roundell Palmer; Macmillan Golden Treasury Series, 1862)
   ¶ ***Titlepage illustration*** (steel-engraving, C. H. Jeens)

The Children's Garland (Coventry Patmore, ed.; Macmillan Golden Treasury Series, 1871)
   ¶ ***Titlepage illustration*** (steel-engraving; C. H. Jeens)

English Art in 1884 (Henry Blackburn; New York: Appleton, 1885)
   ¶ **The Water Lily** (drawing by the artist [?] after his sculpture; photo-engraving)

The Golden Treasury (Francis Turner Palgrave, ed.;

Macmillan Golden Treasury Series, 1861)
¶ ***Titlepage illustration*** (steel-engraving, C. H. Jeens)

[Tennyson] *Poems by Alfred Tennyson* (Moxon, 1857)
¶ ***Frontispiece*** (steel-engraving after the artist's sculpted portrait medallion of Tennyson)

Titlepage illustration for The Children's Garland, *1871 (steel-engraving, C. H. Jeens; 3 x 2 3/4)*

Titlepage illustration for The Book of Praise, *1862 (steel-engraving, C. H. Jeens; 3 x 2 5/8)*

• Reprinted in *Enoch Arden* (Alfred Tennyson; Moxon, 1866)

§ Woolner's own books of poetry, with gilt vignette designs on the front covers, include: *My Beautiful Lady* (Macmillan, 1863), *Pygmalion* (Macmillan, 1881), *Silenus* (Macmillan, 1884), *Tiresias* (Bell, 1886), and *Poems* (Bell, 1887)

Frederick R. Pickersgill

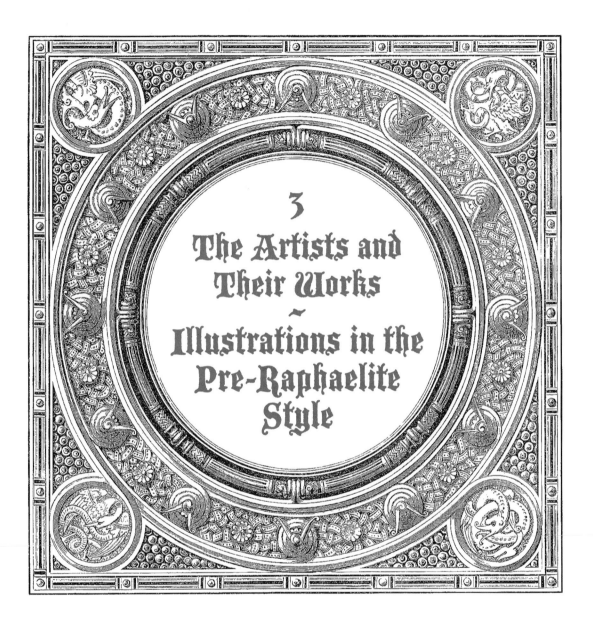

3

The Artists and
Their Works
~
Illustrations in the
Pre-Raphaelite
Style

John R. Clayton

(c. 1820s–c. 1900s)

J. R. Clayton was one of the major illustrators for wood-engraved books in the 1850s. Not much is known about Clayton's life other than a few details of his career and works. Yet one can extrapolate his dates with some conviction through references to him by the Dalziels and William Holman Hunt in their books. Since he was alive at the publication of the Dalziels' memoir in 1901 and had been a friend of theirs "for over fifty years" (*Brothers Dalziel*, p. 19), we can assume he was in the area of seventy-five years old in 1901—to

The Way to Conquer *[#1] (wood-engraving, Dalziels; 3 5/8 x 3 1/8; Dramatic Scenes and Other Poems, 1857)*

which we can add at least four more years, since Holman Hunt in his 1905 book gives this message: "In going to press I receive the following information [about early Pre-Raphaelite enthusiasm for Tennyson] from my friend Mr. John R. Clayton" (*Pre-Raphaelitism*, vol. 1, p. 223, n. 1). Clayton was an early acquaintance of Hunt and Dante Gabriel Rossetti, was first a sculptor (he designed a monument to illustrator William Harvey) and then devoted much of his energies to stained-glass design—according to the Dalziel firm's memoir, which also states, "Although not really one of the P.R.B., he was of them, and with them in all their ways and works" (*Brothers Dalziel*, pp. 19, 114–16).

This Pre-Raphaelite connection has not always been easy to see; in discussions of the period's illustration, Clayton's work has often been ignored or placed in the old school of 1850s illustrators. Yet, Clayton's style is austere and Romantic, and his drawings for the block often feature angular figures in quirky poses, although they do not always stress the fidelity to realistic models and natural detail that characterizes much of authentic Pre-Raphaelite illustration. Clayton anticipated the graphic work of the Pre-Raphaelite illustrators (he always seemed to be *anticipating*, rather than fully diving in, even in his 1860s work) and was certainly influenced by the simplification of the early-Italian style of painting in the 1840s and 1850s of William Dyce, John Rogers Herbert, John Everett Millais, and Hunt and by the woodcuts of Albrecht Dürer, Alfred Rethel, and Julius Schnorr von

Carolsfeld. Rossetti is known to have consulted Clayton about drawing for the wood-block (in relation to *The Music Master*), and Clayton was one of the members of that famous late 1850s organization of Pre-Raphaelite–circle artists, the Hogarth Club.

Throughout the mid-1850s Clayton was in full view as a respected illustrator for several books. The *Art Journal* in 1854 reproduced three of his illustrations as examples of good art in children's books, for *The Parables of Krummacher*, engraved by the Dalziels ("Illustrated Juvenile Literature," vol. 16, p. 48). These works are examples of the "early–Pre-Raphaelite" style of the artist—open and angular elements; large figures in the foreground; heads bowed and almost awkward; arms intertwined, with the best "eccentric realism" effects.

Two Clayton samples from *The Poetical Works of George Herbert* accompany the review of that book in the *Art Journal* in 1856 (vol. 18, p. 32): "Vanitie" and "Faith," also engraved by the Dalziels, feature large figures, their hands holding their heads, and details and shapes of objects that are distinctly Pre-Raphaelite. As in *Herbert*, Clayton joined other artists—and produced even better and more detailed work—for three Dalziel books: *Lays of the Holy Land* (1858), *Dramatic Scenes and Other Poems* (1857), and *The Poets of the*

The Way to Conquer *[#2] (wood-engraving, Dalziels; 3 5/8 x 3 1/8;* Dramatic Scenes and Other Poems, *1857)*

Nineteenth Century (1857). In the latter book, Clayton's illustrations approach the tonality effects and denseness of massed figures of the works of Millais and Tenniel, and of Marks and Armstead in *English Sacred Poetry* (1862); particularly fine are the contemporary-dress subjects "Our Wee White Rose" and "A Good Villager" in *Poets* and the two very Pre-Raphaelite wood-engravings for "Juan" in *Dramatic Scenes*.

Catalogue

The Course of Time (Robert Pollok; Edinburgh/ London: Blackwood, 1857)
¶ Among 19 illustrations (Dalziels): **Jesus, Son of God, The Christian Still Was Mocked, The Prison House, Like Beauty Newly Dead, He Journeyed Forth, The Old Man Lay**, and **Did He Not Die**

Dramatic Scenes and Other Poems (Barry Cornwall [Bryan Weller Procter]; Chapman and Hall, 1857)
¶ Among 12 illustrations (Dalziels): 2 for **"The Way to Conquer"** and 2 for **"Juan"**

A Mother's Love *(etching, Clayton; 2 3/8 x 3 1/2;* Passages from Modern English Poets, *[1862])*

The Christian Still Was Mocked (*wood-engraving, Dalziels; 4 x 3 3/8;* The Course of Time, *1857*)

The Home Affections [*Pourtrayed*] *by the Poets* (Charles Mackay, ed.; Routledge, 1858)
  ¶ **The Dying Boy** (Dalziels)

Lays of the Holy Land (Nisbet, 1858)
  ¶ **On Wheels of Light** (Dalziels)

¶ **A Mother's Love** (etching, Clayton; 2 3/8 x 3 1/2; a.k.a. **A Family Group**)

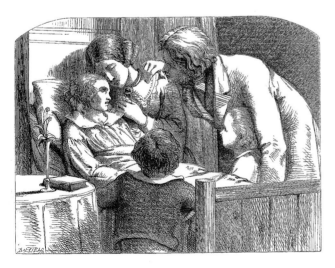

• Published in *Passages from Modern English Poets* (Day, [1862])

The Parables of Frederick Adolphus Krummacher (Cooke, 1854)
  ¶ Among 40 illustrations (Dalziels): **The Canary-Bird**, **Life and Death**, and **David and Saul**
    • Reissued by Bohn in 1858

The Poets of the Nineteenth Century (Rev. Robert Aris Willmott, ed.; Routledge, 1857)
  ¶ Among 6 illustrations: **A Good Villager** (J. Andrew), **Artvelde in Ghent** (J. Andrew?), and **Our Wee White Rose** (J. Andrew)

Juan [*#2*] (*wood-engraving, Dalziels; 3 7/8 x 3 3/8;* Dramatic Scenes and Other Poems, *1857*)

The Dying Boy (*wood-engraving, Dalziels; 3 x 4;* The Home Affections, *1858*)

Walter Crane

(1845–1915)

Walter Crane, working with the color printer/engraver Edmund Evans, revolutionized children's books, with color woodcut designs for such ambitiously decorated "toy" books as *Sing a Song of Sixpence* (c. 1866); *Old Mother Hubbard* (c. 1872); the trio of *The Baby's Opera* (1877), *The Baby's Bouquet* (1878), and *The Baby's Own Aesop* (1887); and a series of flower-themed books (*Flora's Feast*, 1889). Crane's dedication to the socialist movement involved bringing art into the lives of everyone; he helped found the Art Worker's Guild and was a member of William Morris's Socialist Guild.

Crane was concerned with creating books that were well-designed works of art in their entirety. While much of black-and-white book art of the 1850s through 1870s served as self-sufficient additions to a text, Crane's books were fully integrated works where pictures, type, layout, endpapers, and often calligraphy all blended into a harmonious whole. His Evans color

The Sleeping Beauty *(wood-engraving, Swain; 6 7/8 x 4 1/4;* **frontispiece** *for* Household Stories, *1882)*

illustrations can be described as stemming from all the currents of the Pre-Raphaelite movement refined into its Aesthetic phase—decoration for its own sake, medieval and fantastic subjects, Morris-style decorative and repetitive elements, female figures as elastic, elegant designs under the influence of Edward Burne-Jones, John Spencer-Stanhope, Albert Moore, and Frederic Leighton.

Through his populist approach (owing somewhat to the wood-engraver W. J. Linton, with whom he apprenticed), Crane exerted more influence on illustration and book design than William Morris at the end of the nineteenth century. Crane wrote an important book, *Of the Decorative Illustration of Books Old and New* (1896), that submits the history of illustration to his total-design cause. He also contributed to Morris's Kelmscott Press—*The Story of the Glittering Plain*. For this 1894 book, Crane's black-and-white illustrations were cut on

Treasure Trove (wood-engraving, Dalziels; 7 1/4 x 4 5/8;
Good Words, *vol. 4, 1863, p. 796)*

wood in the best thick-lined, decoratively
detailed, but unshaded manner of Burne-
Jones, Charles Gere, and Arthur Gaskin—all
derived from the art of Dürer and early
Renaissance woodcuts.

Crane was first and foremost an illustrator,
who sometimes exhibited (his best-known
painting is *The Laidly Worm*, 1881). When he
began his career as an illustrator in the 1860s,
he was a fairly steady contributor of work in
a competent, realistic style to periodicals
(first *London Society* in 1862, then *Good Words*,
Once a Week, the *Argosy*, and others). Among
his wood-engraved black-and-white books
are Hawthorne's *Transformation* (1865),
Roberts's *Legendary Ballads of England and*

Scotland (1868), H. and A. Mayhew's *The
Magic of Kindness* (1869), Zschokke's *Labour
Stands on Golden Feet* (1870), and a formida-
ble series of the works of Mrs. Molesworth
(*Tell Me a Story*, 1875; *Grandmother Dear*,
1878; *A Christmas Child*, 1880; et al.).

The Pre-Raphaelite influences on Crane's
style outlined above characterize his wood-
engraved illustrations in various degrees; as
in his Evans-cut color art, he could be loose-
lined and woodenly "realistic" or Rethel-like in
his tight, naturalistically modeled, carefully
composed designs. In the latter style are two
fine Pre-Raphaelite illustrations, similar to
Edward Poynter's fastidious engravings:
"Treasure Trove" (*Good Words*, 1863) and
"Castle of Mont Orgueil" (*Once a Week*, 1863).
In his ensuing black-and-white work he often
reverted to nonrealistic "types" for his figures
and faces and adopted a somewhat looser, but
still German-woodcut–influenced, style. For
Living English Poets (1883), however, he contributed a Pre-Raphaelite frontispiece of
detailed foliage and massed figures, depicting
such poets as Morris, Matthew Arnold, Alfred
Tennyson, and Algernon Charles Swinburne.
This recalls Crane's approach the previous
decade in his two elaborately realistic but
densely decorative Pre-Raphaelite images for
Labour Stands on Golden Feet.

A similar drawing, on a grander scale, is
"The Triumph of Labour"—a broadsheet to
commemorate International Labor Day, May 1,
1891—published in Crane's *Cartoons for the
Cause* (1896). The large horizontal image is a
late Pre-Raphaelite composition in the artist's
best detailed, woodcutty style; the shallow
space is unflinchingly covered with tightly
compacted realistic and allegorical figures
and objects—a socialist procession, reminiscent of William Blake's famous *Canterbury
Pilgrims* engraving of 1810.

Many consider Crane's work on the
Grimms' *Household Stories* (1882) to be his
finest black-and-white achievement. It is an
interesting example of realistic Pre-Raphaelite

illustration just at the brink of pure Aesthetic decoration—a pre-Kelmscott book filled to the brim with, in addition to the full-page bordered and lettered images, head- and tail-pieces and pictorial initials. The illustration for "The Sleeping Beauty" perhaps comes closest to Pre-Raphaelitism in spirit and execution.

*The Travelling Tinker (wood-engraving, 5 x 3 1/4; **frontispiece** for* Labour Stands on Golden Feet, *1870)*

Catalogue

Argosy
Vol. 5, 1868:
   ¶ ***Frontispiece:*** **Out in the Wood**
   ¶ **Margaret** (p. 281)

Cartoons for the Cause, 1886–1896 (Walter Crane; Twentieth-Century, 1896)
   ¶ Among 14 illustrations: **The Triumph of Labour** (H. Schell)

Good Words
Vol. 4, 1863:
   ¶ **Treasure Trove** (p. 796, Dalziels; a.k.a. **The Islanders Fell Back from Them**)

Household Stories (Grimm Brothers; Macmillan, 1882)
   ¶ Among 12 illustrations (Swain): ***Frontispiece:*** **The Sleeping Beauty**
   • Plus ***titlepage illustration*** and numerous ***pictorial initials***, ***headpieces***, and ***tailpieces***

Veit and Ida (wood-engraving, 5 x 3 1/4; Labour Stands on Golden Feet, *1870)*

Labour Stands on Golden Feet (Heinrich Zschokke; Cassell, Petter, and Galpin, 3d ed., rev., 1870)
¶ *Frontispiece:* **The Travelling Tinker**
¶ **Veit and Ida**
• Plus numerous *pictorial initials*, *head-pieces*, and *tailpieces*

Castle of Mont Orgueil *(wood-engraving, Swain; 6 1/4 x 4 5/8; Once a Week, vol. 9, 1863, p. 713)*

Legendary Ballads of England and Scotland (John S. Roberts, ed.; Warne, 1868)
¶ Among 3 illustrations: **Thomas of Ercildoune** (E. Evans)

Living English Poets, 1882 (Paul, Trench, 1883)
¶ *Frontispiece* (Swain?)

The Magic of Kindness (H. and A. Mayhew; Cassell, Petter, and Galpin, [1869])
¶ Among 8 illustrations (D. J. Anderson): *Frontispiece:* **Defeat of the Hostile Army, Huan**

Frontispiece *for* ***Living English Poets, 1882****, 1883 (wood-engraving, Swain?; 5 1/4 x 3 5/8)*

Leading Anthy to the Palace, and **Departure of Huan and Anthy**

Once a Week
Vol. 9, 1863:
¶ **Castle of Mont Orgueil** (p. 713, Swain)

Stories of the Olden Time (M. Jones, comp.; Cassell, Petter, and Galpin, 1870)
¶ **Queen Philippa's Appeal**
¶ **Wat Tyler's Insurrection**
• Plus numerous *pictorial initials*, *head-pieces*, and *tailpieces*

Transformation [*The Marble Faun*] (Nathaniel Hawthorne; Smith, Elder, 1865)
¶ Among 5 illustrations: *Titlepage illustration* (W. J. Linton)

George Du Maurier

(1834-1896)

George Du Maurier was part of the continental-trained group of Victorian artists who studied together at Gleyre's Paris atelier in the late 1850s—among them Edward Poynter, James McNeill Whistler, and Val Prinsep; Frederic Leighton too was in the city, already famed for his *Cimabue* of 1855. Born in Paris, Du Maurier first studied chemistry in London,

A Legend of Camelot: Part 1 *(wood-engraving, Swain; 5 1/4 x 6 7/8;* Punch, *vol. 50, 1866, p. 94;* A Legend of Camelot*)*

then art in Paris and Antwerp. With the use of only one eye (an affliction he shared with fellow illustrator Arthur Boyd Houghton), he decided to concentrate on black-and-white drawing for publication.

When Du Maurier returned to London in 1860, his extraordinary skills and speed at illustrating (talents that he also shared with Houghton) got him work at the periodicals

Punch, Illustrated London News, and *Once a Week*. In 1864 he succeeded John Leech as *Punch*'s main cartoonist of fashionable society, becoming a fixture there through the 1890s. With his public status as a satiric commentator on the Victorian social scene, Du Maurier was able to produce three successful novels (which he illustrated): *Peter Ibbetson* (1891), *Trilby* (1894), and *The Martian* (1896), inspired by his Parisian and English art circles. Among other books with his illustrations are Douglas Jerrold's *The Story of a Feather* (1866); Owen Meredith's *Lucile* (1868); and Wilkie Collins's *Poor Miss Finch* (1872), *The New Magdalen* (1873), and *The Frozen Deep* (1875).

Over the years Du Maurier's work took on

A Legend of Camelot: Part 2 *(wood-engraving, Swain; 5 1/2 x 6 7/8;* Punch, *vol. 50, 1866, p. 97;* A Legend of Camelot*)*

Top: ***A Legend of Camelot: Part 3*** *(wood-engraving, Swain; 5 x 6 3/4; Punch, vol. 50, 1866, p. 109;* A Legend of Camelot*)*

Middle: ***A Legend of Camelot: Part 4*** *(wood-engraving, Swain; 8 1/2 x 4 3/8; Punch, vol. 50, 1866, p. 128;* A Legend of Camelot*)*

(*Wives and Daughters, Cousin Phillis, Cranford*, and others, 1863–65), as well as several by Mrs. Oliphant in the 1870s. His popularity was such that books devoted solely to his illustrations were issued, collecting his *Punch* cartoons: *English Society at Home* (1880) and *A Legend of Camelot* (1898, with its appropriately over-detailed, mock-medieval parodies of Pre-Raphaelites and their female "types").

Three of Du Maurier's early illustrations are most representative of Pre-Raphaelite influence: "A Time to Dance" (*Good Words*, 1861), "On Her Death-Bed" (*Once a Week*, 1861), and "The Cilician Pirates" (*Cornhill Magazine*, 1863). These high-quality compositions are marked by a control of decorative line; realistically treated objects, backgrounds,

a slickness and breezy sketchiness, well suited to his journalistic and humorous aims. But in the 1860s, his illustrations were often exceptional—with a decorative understanding of blacks and whites, superb in their use of line, and exciting compositionally, frequently showing a Pre-Raphaelite quality both in spirit and in the emphasis on realistic detail. His specialty became novels of manners and society: for the *Cornhill Magazine* alone he illustrated eight serial novels by Mrs. Gaskell

A Legend of Camelot: Part 5 (wood-engraving, Swain; 5 5/8 x 6 7/8; Punch, vol. 50, 1866, p. 131; A Legend of Camelot)

The Cilician Pirates
(wood-engraving,
Swain; 4 x 6 1/4;
Cornhill Magazine,
vol. 7, 1863, p. 530;
The Cornhill Gallery)

and figures;
meandering,
angular garments;
and masterful
effects of light
and shade. These
works display a
clear reverence
for the woodcut
designs of
Albrecht Dürer,
Frederick Sandys,
and Alfred
Rethel—whose famous print of Death appears on the wall in Du Maurier's wood-engraving "Der Tod als Freund," for the *English Illustrated Magazine* (vol. 1, 1883–84).

Der Tod als Freund (wood-engraving, J. D. Cooper; 7 3/4 [max.] x 5; English Illustrated Magazine, *vol. 1, 1883–84, p. 542)

A Time to Dance *(wood-engraving, Dalziels; 5 5/8 x 4 1/4;* Good Words, *vol. 2, 1861, p. 579)*

Catalogue

Cornhill Magazine
Vol. 7, 1863:
 ¶ **The Cilician Pirates** (p. 530, Swain; reprinted in *The Cornhill Gallery*)
Vol. 10, 1864:
 ¶ **Molley's New Bonnet** (for **"Wives and Daughters"** by Mrs. [Elizabeth] Gaskell; p. 129)
Vol. 16, 1867:
 ¶ **Joan of Arc** (p. 584, Swain)

English Illustrated Magazine
Vol. 1, 1883–84:
 ¶ **Der Tod als Freund** (p. 542, J. D. Cooper)

Good Words
Vol. 2, 1861:
 ¶ **A Time to Dance** (p. 579, Dalziels)

The Ingoldsby Legends (Thomas Ingoldsby [R. H. Barham]; Bentley, 2 vols., 1866)
 ¶ Among 5 illustrations (Dalziels): **The Grey Dolphin** [#1]

Once a Week
Vol. 4, 1861:
 ¶ **On Her Death-Bed** (p. 603)
Vol. 6, 1862:
 ¶ **Hotel Garden** (p. 24)
 ¶ **Metempsychosis** (p. 294, Swain; 2 images)
Vol. 7, 1862:
 ¶ **"Santa; or, A Woman's Tragedy,"** 4 illustrations (pp. 225, 253, 281, 309; Swain)

On Her Death-Bed *(wood-engraving, 4 1/2 x 5;* Once a Week, *vol. 4, 1861, p. 603)*

Punch
Vol. 50, 1866:
 ¶ **"A Legend of Camelot,"** 5 illustrations (in 5 parts; pp. 94, 97, 109, 128, 131; Swain; reprinted, along with many of the artist's other illustrations from *Punch*, in Du Maurier's *A Legend of Camelot* [Bradbury, Agnew, 1898])

Arthur Boyd Houghton

(1836–1875)

Like many of the Victorian artists who made their livings primarily from illustration, Arthur Boyd Houghton exhibited paintings at the Royal Academy (e.g., *Volunteers*, a sunlit street scene with animated, realistic, even quirky adults and—the artist's specialty—children). Houghton is, however, chiefly remembered today as probably the best black-and-white English *illustrator* of the second half of the nineteenth century—this despite having sight in only one eye. During

The Two Sisters (*wood-engraving, Dalziels; 4 7/8 x 4;* Ballad Stories of the Affections, *[1866]*)

his short career he contributed a huge amount of drawings to books and periodicals. Perhaps his best-known project is "Graphic America," a then-controversial series of journalistic impressions of life in the United States, published in the *Graphic* in the early 1870s.

Although Houghton's Sixties drawings are his finest—and most Pre-Raphaelite—his uncanny draughtsmanship never deteriorated into the slick sketchiness that marks the later illustrations of George Du Maurier and John Everett Millais. His treatment of lines, their swirling tendrils seemingly alive with energy but also well conceived in terms of placement and direction and relation, was not equaled until Aubrey Beardsley's pure-line art in the Art Nouveau style of the 1890s.

According to Laurence Housman in his perceptive 1896 monograph on the artist, Houghton's reliance on one eye caused it to gradually weaken and became painful, and he'd have to stop drawing for days at a time. "In consequence of this," states Housman, "his work seems for the most part to have been done at desperate speed to make up for lost time. It was his habit to draw his illustrations straight upon the wood without any preliminary sketches and any study from the model was, I have been told, made actually on the block, a wonderful accomplishment in view of the elaborate character of many of his compositions." Houghton was clearly indebted to the Pre-Raphaelites, who "had created or revived a school of intellectual as well as passionate expression: and in regard to these qualities Houghton and those who worked with him were its followers." Further, says Housman, "Houghton, in spite of all differences, is to be reckoned as a direct descendant and disciple of those whom one may call the pre-Raphaelite Fathers. With the two giants who are his forerunners, Millais and Rossetti, I do not seek to compare him: but next to them I can find no greater man, no master of invention or of technique, so large, so sudden, and so accomplished in his ideas and in his achievement." Like all good Pre-Raphaelite work, Houghton's illustrations are not repetitions of some passage in the text "but something new with further appeals and fresh charms for the imagination" (*Arthur Boyd Houghton*, pp. 27, 14, 16, 22).

My Treasure *(wood-engraving, Dalziels; 6 5/8 x 4 3/4;* Good Words, *vol. 3, 1862, p. 504;* Touches of Nature*)*

Houghton had a wonderful affinity for the world of children, and the Rethel-like, highly detailed, well-designed, claustrophobic, and eccentric compositions of these juvenile subjects in the periodical *Good Words* ("My Treasure," "True or False?", and "About Toys" in 1862, "Childhood" in 1863) and the book *Home Thoughts and Home Scenes* (1865) are some of his finest work, in an engaging Pre-Raphaelite spirit and style. In the *Art Journal*'s 1864 review of *Home Thoughts*, the praise was effusive, the writer considering it a sumptuous volume not necessarily to be handled by children: "Neither pen nor pencil ever produced truer phrases of child-life than are found

here. . . . Such are some of the scenes presented by Mr. Houghton's vigorous pencil, the truth of which, however peculiarly used, and his designs are undoubtedly peculiar, must be universally admitted, even with its exaggerations, and occasionally with its redundancy of matter" (vol. 26 [new ser., vol. 3], p. 376). These scenes of contemporary life, with their brilliant effects of shade and light and perfectly realized Germanic-woodcut technique, are among the great works of 1860s illustration.

Mention should also be made of similarly Pre-Raphaelite "adult" contemporary scenes for "St. Elmo" and "A Missionary Cheer" (both *Good Words*, 1863) and "Finding a Relic" (*London Society*, 1862). Among the most dramatic in composition and lighting of Houghton's works in this style are those he did for Wilkie Collins's *After Dark* (1862).

In *Golden Thoughts from Golden Fountains* (1867), a Dalziel production in which the thirteen full-page illustrations are printed over a tan color leaving highlight areas in white, Houghton appears to be the star, since his work takes up almost all of the art-allocated full pages. Other significant books where he joined fellow artists are *Dalziels' Illustrated Arabian Nights' Entertainments* (1865), *A Round of Days* (1866), *Poems by Jean Ingelow* (1867), and *North Coast and Other Poems* (1868). *Adventures of Don Quixote de La Mancha* (1866) has 101 illustrations, all by Houghton.

As can be seen by the drawings and other material in the Hartley Collection in Boston (Museum of Fine Arts), for the *Arabian Nights* Houghton prepared numerous pencil studies—reporterlike sketches—and returned to

The Scramble for Sugarplums *(wood-engraving, Dalziels; 6 1/2 x 5;* Home Thoughts and Home Scenes, *1865)*

Noah's Ark *(wood-engraving, Dalziels; 7 x 5 3/8;* Home Thoughts and Home Scenes, *1865)*

the Dalziels lots of touched-up proofs for corrections. Photographs of his drawings on the blocks before they were cut show well-thought-out designs, with thick, uniform, and flowing lines.

Catalogue

After Dark (Wilkie Collins; Smith, Elder, 1862)
¶ *Frontispiece:* **Sister Rose**
¶ **The Yellow Mask**
¶ **Gabriel's Marriage**
¶ **Lady of Glenwith Grange**
• Eng. Dalziels

Art Pictures from the Old Testament (Aley Fox, text; Society for Promoting Christian Knowledge, 1894)
¶ **Gathering of Manna** (Dalziels)
¶ **The Chronicles Being Read to the King** (Dalziels; reprinted from *Dalziels' Bible Gallery*)

Ballad Stories of the Affections (Robert Buchanan; Routledge, [1866])
¶ Among 9 illustrations (Dalziels): **The Two Sisters**

Good Words
Vol. 3, 1862:
¶ **My Treasure** (p. 504, Dalziels; reprinted in *Touches of Nature*)
¶ **True or False?** (p. 721, Dalziels)
¶ **About Toys** (p. 753, Dalziels)

Vol. 4, 1863:
¶ **St. Elmo** (p. 64, Dalziels)
¶ **A Missionary Cheer** (p. 548, Dalziels)
¶ **Childhood** (p. 637, Dalziels)

Home Thoughts and Home Scenes (Jean Ingelow, ed.; Routledge, 1865)
¶ Among 35 illustrations (Dalziels): **Noah's Ark, Age and Youth, A Story by the Fire, The Chair Railway, At School, Snapdragon, Grandmother Nodding,** and **The Scramble for Sugarplums**
• Reissued in 1868

[Ingelow] *Poems by Jean Ingelow* (Longmans, Green, Reader, and Dyer, 1867)
¶ Among 16 illustrations (Dalziels): **Seven Times One: Exultation; Seven Times Seven: Love;** and **Seven Times Five: Widowhood**

St. Elmo (wood-engraving, Dalziels; 7 1/2 x 4 3/4; Good Words, vol. 4, 1863, p. 64)

London Society
Vol. 2, 1862:
¶ **Finding a Relic** (p. 89, Dalziels)

North Coast and Other Poems (Robert Buchanan; Routledge, 1868)
¶ Among 13 illustrations (Dalziels): **Closer Still She Crept** and **And Fell upon the Sands** for "Meg Blaine" and **Lad and Lass, To-night Beware!** for "The Northern Wooing"

Sunday Magazine
Vol. 3, 1866–77 [1867]:
¶ **The Martyr** (p. 345, Dalziels)
Vol. 7, 1870–71 [1871]:
¶ **The Woman That Was a Sinner** (p. 104, Dalziels)

***True or False?** (wood-engraving, Dalziels; 6 1/2 x 4 3/4; Good Words, vol. 3, 1862, p. 721)*

§ Paul Goldman (*Victorian Illustration*, p. 325) notes a reprinting of 30 of the engravings from *Home Thoughts and Home Scenes* in H. W. Dulcken's *Happy-Day Stories for the Young* (Routledge, Warne, and Routledge, 1874)

§ For an excellent collection of Houghton illustrations see Laurence Housman's *Arthur Boyd Houghton: A Selection from His Work in Black and White* (Paul, Trench, Trubner, 1896): 89 illustrations, 84 of which are printed from original woodblocks

Childhood *(wood-engraving, Dalziels; 6 5/8 x 4 3/4; Good Words, vol. 4, 1863, p. 637)*

John Lawson
(fl. 1865–1909)

John Lawson, like J. R. Clayton, remains a bit of a shadowy figure in the world of Victorian publishing. Of the three Lawsons who worked as illustrators at the time (the others were Cecil Gordon Lawson and Francis Wilfrid Lawson, to whom John was not related), it was he who most often showed that spark of distinction that would occasionally tilt his art into the Pre-Raphaelite sphere.

Lawson worked mostly in Scotland, exhibiting paintings at the Royal Scottish Academy. He contributed significantly in the latter half of the 1860s to numerous periodicals, including *Once a Week, Sunday Magazine*, the *Quiver*, the *Shilling Magazine*, and the *Argosy*. Two especially fine pieces are "Ariadne" (*Once a Week*, 1866), an every-inch-covered composition of the Greek hero Theseus, a storm at sea, and figures contorted and cropped off in all directions; and "Murtoch Is Dead, Man!" (a.k.a. "Ancient Clan Dirge," *Once a Week*, 1866), whose woodcut style and image of warriors carrying a dead body recall the work of Joseph Noel Paton in *Lays of the Scottish Cavaliers* (1863). Lawson's style in these, and in many other

drawings, is similar to that of Paton, Frederick Sandys, Frederic Shields, and Edward Poynter—large figures, exactingly placed lines, the Dürer/Rethel woodcut school.

Among the notable books that contain Lawson illustrations are *Ballad Stories of the Affections* (1866), *Golden Thoughts from Golden Fountains* (1867), *Roses and Holly* (1867), *The Fiery Cross* (1875), and *The World Well Lost* (1877). Some of Lawson's finest illustrations from *Once a Week* are reprinted in that quintessential collection of Sixties wood-engravings, *Historical and Legendary Ballads and Songs* (1876), under the new titles: "Norse Battle-Song," "The Death of King Warwolf" [#2], and "The Wood Echo," among a total of nine.

"Murtoch Is Dead, Man!" (*wood-engraving, Swain; 4 1/2 x 7 3/8;* Once a Week, *new ser. [ser. 2], vol. 1, 1866, p. 491*)

Catalogue

Ballad Stories of the Affections (Robert Buchanan; Routledge, [1866])

¶ Among 7 illustrations (Dalziels): **With Eight Red Wounds upon His Breast** and **So Sweet Walborg in Cloister Dwelt** (reprinted as **Bowed Down Beneath a Load of Sin** in *The Spirit of Praise* [Warne, 1867]) for **"Axel and Walborg"**

Once a Week
Vol. 13, 1865:

¶ **The Epitaph of Adonis** (p. 687, Swain; reprinted as **The Gibbet Tree** in *Historical and Legendary Ballads and Songs* [Walter Thornbury;

Chatto and Windus, 1876])
New ser. [ser. 2], vol. 1, 1866:

¶ **Pan Pipes** (p. 211, Swain; reprinted as **The Wood Echo** in *Historical and Legendary Ballads and Songs*)

¶ **"Murtoch Is Dead, Man!"** (p. 491, Swain; a.k.a. **Ancient Clan Dirge**)
New ser. [ser. 2], vol. 2, 1866:

¶ **Ariadne** (p. 127, Swain; reprinted as **The Death of King Warwolf** [#2] in *Historical and Legendary Ballads and Songs*)
New ser. [ser. 2], vol. 3, 1867:

¶ **Sir Ralph de Blanc-Minster** (p. 188, Swain)

Quiver
New ser. [ser. 2], vol. 2, 1865:

¶ **July** (p. 343, R. Paterson)

Ariadne (wood-engraving, Swain; 5 1/4 x 5 1/16; Once a Week, new ser. [ser. 2], vol. 2, 1866, p. 127; Historical and Legendary Ballads and Songs*)*

Thomas Morten

(1836~1866)

Thomas Morten, who studied drawing for wood-engraving at Leigh's school in London, was primarily an illustrator whose short career was marked by work in a highly distinct and almost wildly sloppy style. Nevertheless, he was influenced by and associated with the Pre-Raphaelites. Concerning an exhibition of drawings by that circle's Hogarth Club (c. 1858–61), William Michael Rossetti states, "Mr. Morten was a young painter who had sent a picture which was not generally liked (I myself saw no serious objection to it), and he had been persuaded to withdraw it" (*Ruskin: Rossetti: PreRaphaelitism,* p. 214). This says much about the artist's work, for it was often strange and haphazard, while at the same time full of stylistic and compositional borrowings from his friends (even a monogram could succumb, as witness the *TM* in "The Christmas Child" in *Good Words*, 1862, which adopts the characteristic initial-lettering of both John Tenniel and John Everett Millais)—and somehow all very personal and memorable.

It is easy to see why Morten has been frequently placed in the Pre-Raphaelite group. His best work of the 1860s exhibits a clear observation of reality, a lively contrast of blacks and whites (marked by striking lighting effects), the massing of details, claustrophobic compositions, and eccentric poses. They also bear his own unique stamp, which combines the solidity and Dürer-like elements of Frederick Sandys with the expressive, scrawling linework of later Millais or Arthur Boyd Houghton. Morten's lines, however, often

appear out of control, their frenzy (and sloppiness) marring and sometimes working against their otherwise brilliant images ("The Bell-Ringer's Christmas Story" in *Churchman's*

The Bell-Ringer's Christmas Story (*wood-engraving, Dalziels; 7 x 4 1/2; Churchman's Family Magazine, vol. 2, 1864, p. 481;* Pictures of Society)

Family Magazine, 1864, and "The Curse of the Gudmunds" in *Once a Week*, 1866).

The wild, swirling lines of "What Hester Durham Lived For" (a.k.a. "They Clung Around Hester," *Good Words*, 1863) might have driven the Dalziels crazy, but in this case the composition works beautifully in balancing tones and contours. Morten is a bit more controlled in "The Christmas Child," a lovely, atmospheric contemporary scene, with a subtle shadow of the chair-back thrown against the woman's dress. "The Dying Viking" (*Once a Week*, 1867) seems quite the spectacular Pre-Raphaelite piece, every historical inch covered with figures and details—until we realize that it's pretty much a ripoff of Sandys's "Rosamund, Queen of the Lombards" from the same magazine of 1861, down to the foreground brazier.

In addition to the above-mentioned periodicals, Morten contributed to *Entertaining*

The Dying Viking (*wood-engraving, Swain; 6 5/8 x 4 3/4; Once a Week, new ser. [ser. 2], vol. 3, 1867, p. 239; Historical and Legendary Ballads and Songs*)

The Christmas Child (*wood-engraving, Dalziels; 4 x 3 7/8; Good Words, vol. 3, 1862, p. 56*)

Things, London Society, the *Quiver*, the *Welcome Guest, Aunt Judy's Magazine*, and *Cassell's Family Paper*, as well as to the books *The Laird's Return* (1861), *A Round of Days* (1865), and *Dalziels' Illustrated Arabian Nights' Entertainments* (1865). Morten's best-known book, completely illustrated by him, is Swift's *Gulliver's Travels* (1865). Several of his *Once a Week* illustrations were reprinted in *Historical and Legendary Ballads and Songs* of 1876. But by then the artist was dead, a probable suicide due to financial difficulties. The *Art Journal* noted his passing with regret ("Thomas Morten," vol. 28 [new ser., vol. 5], 1866, p. 364), writing that he excelled as a draughtsman and contributed to nearly every illustrated periodical and to other works, "many of which have had favourable notice in our columns; especially we may notice his illustrations of *Gulliver's Travels*, not a few of which remind us much of Gustave Doré in their wild grotesqueness."

What Hester Durham Lived For (*wood-engraving, Dalziels; 7 1/4 x 4 9/16; Good Words, vol. 4, 1863, p. 492*)

Catalogue

Churchman's Family Magazine
Vol. 1, 1863:
  ¶ **Black Peter's Little Passenger** (p. 243, Swain)
  ¶ **The Moment of Danger** (p. 531, Swain)
Vol. 2, 1864:
  ¶ **The Bell-Ringer's Christmas Story** (p. 481, Dalziels; reprinted as **The Story of the Bells** [a.k.a. **In the Belfry**] in *Pictures of Society* [Low, Son, and Marston, 1866])
Vol. 3, 1865:
  ¶ **The Twilight Hour** (p. 553, Dalziels)

Good Words
Vol. 3, 1862:
  ¶ **The Christmas Child** (p. 56, Dalziels)
  ¶ **The Carrier-Pigeon** (p. 121, Dalziels; reprinted in *Touches of Nature* [Strahan, 1867])
Vol. 4, 1863:
  ¶ **What Hester Durham Lived For** (p. 492, Dalziels; a.k.a. **They Clung Around Hester**)

London Society
Vol. 1, 1861:
  ¶ **The Widow's Wail** (p. 125, Dalziels)
Vol. 3, 1863:
  ¶ **Ruth Grey's Trial** (p. 59, H. Harral)

Once a Week
New ser. [ser. 2], vol. 2, 1866:
  ¶ **The Curse of the Gudmunds** (p. 155, Swain; reprinted as **Castle Clare** in *Historical and Legendary Ballads and Songs* [Walter Thornbury; Chatto and Windus, 1876])
New ser. [ser. 2], vol. 3, 1867:
  ¶ **The Dying Viking** (p. 239, Swain; reprinted [same title] in *Historical and Legendary Ballads and Songs*)

Frederick R. Pickersgill

(1820-1900)

Frederick Pickersgill is part of the transitional 1850s group of illustrators whose established styles incorporated, or gradually came to exhibit, Pre-Raphaelite elements. He was also an important painter (his uncle was the well-known artist Henry William Pickersgill) who had studied in the Royal Academy Schools, first exhibiting at the Academy in 1839 and becoming a full Academician in 1857. He was one of the prize winners in the Houses of Parliament fresco competitions of 1843 and 1847.

Like J. R. Clayton, Pickersgill in his early works displays a kind of proto–Pre-Raphaelitism. His seven illustrations for "Hengist and Mey" in *The Book of British Ballads* (1844), for example, are very slight and lack detail, in the sketchy manner of pre-1850s illustration; but their convoluted poses mark them as unlike anything else in the volume.

Pickersgill was associated with the Dalziels from their earliest wood-engraved Fine Art Books. The Dalziel brothers later recalled: "Our connection with Pickersgill—one of the kindest and best of men—soon ripened into a close friendship, and it was to him that we gave the first commission at our own cost for a set of drawings to illustrate *The Life of Christ* [1850], desiring to follow the example of Alfred Rethel's *Dance of Death*, which had just been published in Germany at a very small price" (*Brothers Dalziel*, p. 52). Pickersgill's illustrations for this project show his early influences—a tendency to Romantic, dramatic gestures; large, solid figures; and an austere

Nazarene style that owes something to Dürer. As the 1850s progressed Pickersgill's art grew more Germanically modeled and less outliney, the poses and garments more realistic and quirky, exactly paralleling Clayton's similar progress in reflecting Pre-Raphaelite style.

Pickersgill's overly simplified sculptural figures that seem to stretch across the entire picture surface often make for bland illustrations. Nearly as often, however, he struck just

The People Presenting Gifts to Moses (*wood-engraving, Dalziels; 8 1/2 x 7; Art Pictures from the Old Testament, 1894*)

Korah Swallowed Up *(wood-engraving, Dalziels; 8 5/8 x 7 1/8;* Dalziels' Bible Gallery, *1881;* Art Pictures from the Old Testament*)*

the right note of inspiration and strangeness to go with his basic method. He produced his best, most Pre-Raphaelite, work for three Dalziel projects, *The Home Affections by the Poets* (1858), *English Sacred Poetry* (1862), and *Dalziels' Bible Gallery* (1881; with six of the eight illustrations that were eventually published in *Art Pictures from the Old Testament*, 1894). For *Home Affections*, "Oriana" and "Hero and Leander" possess a true poetry and revel in dramatic lovers' tragedies and convoluted poses. For *English Sacred Poetry*, "The Destruction of Sennacherib" has a Huntish oddness about the figures, over whose twisted bodies a strange, dark angel hovers. In the *Bible Gallery* one can easily "pick out" Pickersgill, for his is any drawing in which huge figures of sturdy and unmoving three-dimensionality take up an entire picture area. Nevertheless, an image like "The People Presenting Gifts to Moses" has a fine German-

woodcut feel, especially in the light-and-shade contrasts, the solidity of clothing material, and the very precise draughtsmanship and lines.

Pickersgill also provided illustrations for *Proverbial Philosophy* (1854), *The Poets of the Nineteenth Century* (1857), *The Poetical Works of Edgar Poe* (1858), *Lays of the Holy Land* (1858), *The Poetical Works of James Montgomery* (1860), and *The Lord's Prayer* (1870).

Catalogue

Art Pictures from the Old Testament (Aley Fox, text; Society for Promoting Christian Knowledge, 1894)
- **Jacob Blessing Ephraim and Manasseh**
- **Moses' Hands Held Up**
- **The People Presenting Gifts to Moses**
- **The Rebels Swallowed Up**
- **The Brazen Serpent**

The Destruction of Sennacherib *(wood-engraving, Dalziels; 6 x 4 1/2;* English Sacred Poetry, *1862)*

¶ **The Daughters of Zelophehad**
¶ **Rahab and the Spies**
¶ **The Passage of the Jordan**
• Eng. Dalziels
• 6 illustrations are reprinted from *Dalziels'*
Bible Gallery (Routledge, 1881); two are original to
Art Pictures (**The Brazen Serpent** and **The People**
Presenting Gifts to Moses); **The Rebels**
Swallowed Up is titled **Korah Swallowed Up** in the
Bible Gallery

English Sacred Poetry (Rev. Robert Aris Willmott,
ed.; Routledge, Warne, and Routledge, 1862)
¶ **The Destruction of Sennacherib** (Dalziels)

The Home Affections [*Pourtrayed*] *by the Poets*
(Charles Mackay, ed.; Routledge, 1858)
¶ **Oriana**
¶ **The Sculptor**
¶ **The Hermit**
¶ **Good Night in the Porch**
¶ **Familiar Love**
¶ **Hero and Leander**
• Eng. Dalziels

London Society
Vol. 1, 1862:
¶ **Private Theatricals** (p. 193, E. Evans)
Vol. 2, Christmas Number, 1862:
¶ **The Wishing Well** (p. 28, E. Evans; reprinted
in *Pictures of Society* [Low, Son, and Marston,
1866])

Oriana *(wood-engraving, Dalziels; 5 3/4 x 4 1/2;* The
Home Affections, *1858)*

[Poe] *The Poetical Works of Edgar Poe* (Low, 1858)
¶ Among 13 illustrations (W. J. Linton,
Hammond, E. Evans): **Dream-Land** (W. J. Linton)

The Poets of the Nineteenth Century (Rev. Robert
Aris Willmott, ed.; Routledge, 1857)
¶ **The Water-Nymph Appearing to the Shepherd**
(Dalziels)

Hero and Leander *(wood-engraving,*
Dalziels; 4 7/8 x 3 5/8; The Home
Affections, *1858)*

George John Pinwell

(1842–1875)

One of the premier illustrators of the 1860s, George Pinwell has been categorized as belonging to the rustic-naturalistic school, along with Fred Walker, J. W. North, Arthur Boyd Houghton, George Du Maurier, and William Small. All of these men stood apart from the Pre-Raphaelite movement; but they were artists with distinctive styles, and in

The Saturnalia *(wood-engraving, Swain; 6 1/2 x 4 1/2;* Once a Week, *vol. 8, 1863, p. 154)*

many cases their earliest wood-block drawings are indebted to John Everett Millais, Edward Poynter, and Frederick Sandys. While not as well known as Houghton, Pinwell is possibly the most original of the group, his unique style characterized by unusual figural arrangements, framings, and vantage points.

Pinwell had designed for an embroiderer and silversmith and studied at Heatherley's Academy; he exhibited at the Dudley Gallery and Old Water Colour Society from 1865 through 1875. Like Walker, Morten, and Lawless, Pinwell died at the height of his powers; yet he still produced a significant body of work whose quality nearly matches that of Sandys's relatively small oeuvre.

Pinwell began his illustration career as a protégé of the Dalziels, drawing for their periodicals *Fun* and *Good Words* and for whom he illustrated his masterpiece, *Dalziels' Illustrated Goldsmith* (1864), with a hundred drawings. The Dalziel brothers had a high opinion of his paintings—many of which they purchased. He also contributed to a number of their other books: *Dalziels' Illustrated Arabian Nights' Entertainments* (1865), *Poems by Jean Ingelow* (1867), and the *Bible Gallery* (his one illustration published only in *Art Pictures from the Old Testament*, 1894).

For *Wayside Posies* (1867), Pinwell joined fellow Dalziel illustrators North and Walker and produced eighteen amazing cuts, boasting unique compositions and angles, interesting lighting and tonal effects, and mysterious characters—yet these are also realistic

The Spies Bringing the Grapes *(wood-engraving, Dalziels; 6 7/8 x 6 1/2;* Art Pictures from the Old Testament, *1894)*

excellent draughtsmanship in the large figures of the couple, all seen from Pinwell's trademark low vantage point; "The Sirens," in which two naked women with flowing hair, positioned low against a high horizon—and with a symbolic skull in the foreground—lure a ship through the firmly controlled swirling

Young Axelvold *[#2] (wood-engraving, Dalziels; 5 x 4;* Ballad Stories of the Affections, *[1866])*

scenes, detailed observations of rustic countrysides, objects, and buildings. Many of the engravings are close to Pre-Raphaelitism—especially several "bird" pictures: "By the Dove-cot," "The Swallows," and "Winter Song." For the Dalziels' *Ballad Stories of the Affections* (1866), alongside works by Houghton, William Small, and John D. Watson are four of Pinwell's most Pre-Raphaelite illustrations: "Maid Mettelil," a medieval scene with a female figure, reminiscent of Armstead and Poynter; "Sir Morten of Fogelson"; and two for "Young Axelvold"—the second of which could be a missing link between a typical multiplied-female Pre-Raphaelite work and the Aesthetic lounging-women arrangements of Frederic Leighton and Albert Moore.

Pinwell drew for the major magazines, including *London Society*, *Sunday Magazine*, the *Cornhill Magazine*, the *Graphic*, and *Punch*. For *Once a Week* in 1863 he produced three memorable Pre-Raphaelite works: "Seasonable Wooing," a nice blend of decorative swirls and shapes, detailed realism, and

lines of a rushing sea; and "The Saturnalia," weirdly Pre-Raphaelite in its evocation of ancient ritual, with visions of nude women in smoke and a monkey waving a peacock feather. Thornbury's *Historical and Legendary Ballads and Songs* of 1876 reprints eight of Pinwell's *Once a Week* designs.

Maid Mettelil (wood-engraving, Dalziels; 5 1/8 x 4 1/8;
Ballad Stories of the Affections, [1866])

Catalogue

Art Pictures from the Old Testament (Aley Fox,
text; Society for Promoting Christian Knowledge,
1894)
¶ **The Spies Bringing the Grapes** (Dalziels)

Ballad Stories of the Affections (Robert Buchanan;
Routledge, [1866])
¶ **"Young Axelvold,"** 2 illustrations (Dalziels)
¶ **Maid Mettelil** (Dalziels)
¶ **Sir Morten of Fogelsong** (Dalziels)

Good Words
Vol. 11, 1870:
¶ **Two Margarets** (p. 280)

[Ingelow] *Poems by Jean Ingelow* (Longmans,
Green, Reader, and Dyer, 1867)
¶ Among 20 illustrations (Dalziels): **"Cusha!
Cusha! Cusha!" Calling** and **The Waters Laid
Thee at His Doore** for **"The High Tide on the

Coast of Lincolnshire"** and **"Good Mercer, Be the
Ships Come Up?"** for **"Winstanley"**

Once a Week
Vol. 8, 1863:
¶ **The Saturnalia** (p. 154, Swain)
¶ **Seasonable Wooing** (p. 322, Swain)
Vol. 9, 1863:
¶ **The Sirens** (p. 616, Swain)
Vol. 10, 1864:
¶ **Hero** (p. 350, Swain)

Wayside Posies (Robert Buchanan; Routledge,
1867)
¶ Among 18 illustrations (Dalziels): **By the
Dove-cot**, **The Swallows**, and **Winter Song**

§ An important illustrated survey of Pinwell's art is
George C. Williamson's *George J. Pinwell and His
Works* (Bell, 1900)

The Sirens (wood-engraving, Swain; 6 1/8 x 4 5/8; Once
a Week, vol. 9, 1863, p. 616)

William Small

(1843–1929)

Born in Edinburgh, William Small attended the Royal Scottish Academy Schools and worked in the art department of a publisher. He exhibited at the Royal Academy and Grosvenor Gallery, but he was known above all as a prodigious illustrator. Small's work spanned the classic facsimile reproductions of wood-engravings of the 1860s through the tonal re-creations of the new school of engraving (as emphasized by the *Graphic* in the 1870s and 1880s) through the photo-mechanical reproductions of the late century. Small's later art was always a cut above the average, but seldom unique or outstanding. He was extremely well paid for his *Graphic* work, which was executed in wash, establishing the norm for the newer generation of illustrators.

In the 1860s, Small drew for the *Shilling Magazine*, *Once a Week*, *Good Words*, the *Quiver*, the *Argosy*, and *Sunday Magazine*, among others, and he contributed to some of the most important books of the period: *Ballad Stories of the Affections* (1866), *Poems by Jean Ingelow* (1867), *Two Centuries of Song* (1867), *Golden Thoughts from Golden Fountains* (1867), *The Spirit of Praise* (1867), *North Coast and Other Poems* (1868), and even *Dalziels' Bible Gallery* (1881). In this last work, his pictures done in 1876 in his tonal *Graphic* style and cut by the Dalziels in the new white-line manner seem so out of place as to pale beside so many wood-engraved masterpieces.

In most of this work, Small is of the contemporary-realistic, quick-sketch school of Arthur Boyd Houghton, George Du Maurier, and Fred Walker. Small's figures are solidly

modeled and composed of fluid, intelligent lines. In the best and most Pre-Raphaelite of his illustrations, these qualities are enhanced by unusual compositions, dramatic uses of light and shade, oddly positioned figures, and much attention to natural details. Especially

Lilies (wood-engraving, Dalziels; 6 1/2 x 4 1/2; **frontispiece** *for* Good Words, *vol. 7, 1866)*

Philip's Mission *(wood-engraving, Swain; 6 1/4 x 4 1/2;* Sunday Magazine, *vol. 3, 1866–67 [1867], p. 752)*

individualistic is Small's "Between the Cliffs," reprinted in *Idyllic Pictures* (1867) from a previous incarnation in the *Quiver* magazine. Here, a woman with flowing hair lies on the rocks, across the full picture surface, and the contours of her body and the natural shapes seem united; she is here "dead and alone, / By the trysting-stone," sobbing and prostrate, on a boulder in the brook between "the cold, grey cliffs"—and by poem's end will of course throw herself into the river after being abandoned by her lover. Small did a number of exceptional drawings for the story *Griffith Gaunt* in the *Argosy* (1866), including "Miss Peyton Relapsed into the Transcendental," a hunting scene with an elaborate background and figures and horses near and far that softly curve and interlock in the manner of Ford Madox Brown's later compositions. "Philip's

Mission," a biblical image for *Sunday Magazine* (1867), is realistic and decorative—and would have been more at home stylistically (if not thematically) in the *Bible Gallery* than are Small's late-date contributions.

Catalogue

Argosy
Vol. 1, 1866:
     ¶ **Miss Peyton Relapsed into the Transcendental** (for **"Griffith Gaunt"** by Charles Reade; p. 4, Swain)

A Workman Sang for ***"Scholar and Carpenter"*** *(wood-engraving, Dalziels; 5 x 4;* Poems by Jean Ingelow, *1867)*

Good Words
Vol. 7, 1866:
     ¶ ***Frontispiece:*** **Lilies** (Dalziels)
     ¶ **Deliverance** (p. 663, Dalziels)

[Ingelow] *Poems by Jean Ingelow* (Longmans, Green, Reader, and Dyer, 1867)

¶ Among 4 illustrations (Dalziels): **I Picked Up Such a Flute** for **"Honours"** and **A Workman Sang** for **"Scholar and Carpenter"**

The Child Leans on Its Mother's Breast
(wood-engraving, Dalziels; 4 3/4 x 3 3/8;
The Spirit of Praise, *[1867])*

Ode on the Morning of Christ's Nativity (John Milton; Warne, [1867])

¶ Among 5 illustrations: **And Sullen Muloch Fled** (W. J. Palmer)

Once a Week
New ser. [ser. 2], vol. 2, 1866:
¶ **The Gift of Clunnog Vawr** (p. 463, Swain)

Quiver
New ser. [ser. 2], vol. 2, 1865:
¶ **An Old Story** (p. 174, J. D. Cooper; reprinted in *Idyllic Pictures* [Cassell, Petter, and Galpin, 1867])
Ser. 3, vol. 1, 1866 [1865–66]:
¶ **Between the Cliffs** (p. 152, Williamson; reprinted in *Idyllic Pictures*)
¶ **East by East** (p. 217, Williamson)

The Spirit of Praise (Warne, [1867])
¶ Among 4 illustrations (Dalziels): **The Child Leans on Its Mother's Breast**
• Reissued in 1871

Sunday Magazine
Vol. 2, 1865–66 [1866]:
¶ **"Wind Me a Summer Crown," She Said** (p. 657, Dalziels)
Vol. 3, 1866–67 [1867]:
¶ **Philip's Mission** (p. 752, Swain)

Frederick Smallfield

(1829–1915)

Frederick Smallfield was an etcher and painter (primarily of watercolors) who often exhibited genre scenes at the Royal Academy (1849–86), as well as at the British Institution, Grosvenor Gallery, and above all, at the Royal Institute of Painters in Watercolours, where he showed about four hundred works.

Though his illustrations are few, his etchings for the Junior Etching Club's books show a strong Pre-Raphaelite spirit, in moodiness, lighting, myriad details, and realism. Three etchings for *Passages from the Poems of Thomas Hood* (1858) are firmly in this school. In *Ode to the Moon* a man kneels—somewhat contorted—on a bed, looking out an attic window at the moon; the image reminds one of Frederick Sandys's and John D. Watson's darkroom, window-light illustrations and Henry Wallis's Pre-Raphaelite painting *The Death of Chatterton* (1856). In *Ballad: Sigh On, Sad Heart*, full of etched detail and tightly worked "wood-engraving" lines, a woman's whole figure, lit evocatively by a church's open door, takes up most of the picture surface, with lots of other heads and figures crammed into the space behind her. *Ballad: It Was Not in the Winter* is a typical Pre-Raphaelite

romantic scene of two lovers, reminiscent of Arthur Hughes's work; a Gothic arch frames the image of the oddly but realistically posed couple, who are surrounded by masses of sharply drawn botanical elements. Smallfield's very Pre-Raphaelite painting *First Love* of 1858 is based on a poem of Thomas Hood—it

Ballad: Sigh On, Sad Heart *(etching, Smallfield; 6 1/8 x 4 5/8;* Passages from the Poems of Thomas Hood, *1858)*

being, of course, the same composition as his *Winter* etching.

Smallfield also contributed one wood-engraved illustration each to *English Sacred Poetry* (1862)—nice—and *The Spirit of Praise* (1867)—indifferent.

Ode to the Moon *(etching, Smallfield; 3 x 4 5/8; Passages from the Poems of Thomas Hood, 1858)*

Catalogue

¶ **Ballad: It Was Not in the Winter** (etching, Smallfield; 5 5/8 x 3 1/4)
 • Published in *Passages from the Poems of Thomas Hood* (Junior Etching Club; Gambart, 1858)

Supping on Horrors *(etching, Smallfield; 3 5/8 x 5;* Passages from Modern English Poets, *[1862])*

¶ **Ballad: Sigh On, Sad Heart** (etching, Smallfield; 6 1/8 x 4 5/8; signed with initials and dated in plate)
 • Published in *Passages from the Poems of Thomas Hood* (Junior Etching Club; Gambart, 1858)

¶ **Ode to the Moon** (etching, Smallfield; 3 x 4 5/8)
 • Published in *Passages from the Poems of Thomas Hood* (Junior Etching Club; Gambart, 1858)

¶ **Supping on Horrors** (etching, Smallfield; 3 5/8 x 5)
 • Published in *Passages from Modern English Poets* (Junior Etching Club; Day, [1862]); reissued by Tegg in 1874 and, with the etchings transferred to stone for lithographic prints, in 1875

John Tenniel

(1820~1914)

John Tenniel was and is perhaps the most recognizable of all Victorian illustrators. He briefly attended the Royal Academy Schools and exhibited at the Royal Academy and the New Water Colour Society. But it was his popular illustrations in *Punch* and for Lewis Carroll's *Alice* books that earned him a knighthood in 1893, and enduring fame.

The Book of British Ballads (1842, 1844) contains some early Tenniel work, nine pedestrian illustrations, well of their time. His first book success was an edition of *Aesop's Fables* (1848), and soon Mark Lemon, editor of

Punch, hired him as a main cartoonist; Tenniel became principal cartoonist in 1864 and over the next half-century drew more than two thousand *Punch* cartoons (collaborating with his favorite engraver, Swain), most of a political nature. Tenniel also illustrated for *Once a Week* from its first volume in 1859 through much of the 1860s (he did twenty-eight in the fourth volume alone). Among his Junior Etching Club plates are *The Elm Tree* for *Passages from the Poems of Thomas Hood* (1858) and *War and Glory* for *Passages from Modern English Poets* (1862).

Tenniel's most successful book commissions were for Lewis Carroll's *Alice's Adventures in Wonderland* (1865) and *Through the Looking-Glass and What Alice Found There* (1871), both cut by the Dalziels. According to George and Edward Dalziel, Tenniel wished to drop out of the second project, and Carroll had chosen as *Looking-Glass* illustrator Joseph Noel Paton—who declined, saying to the author, "Tenniel is the man" (*Brothers Dalziel*, p. 126). These books and their drawings have been reprinted constantly since, and even in film or television productions of the stories it is Tenniel's vision that is invariably replicated. The Dalziels used Tenniel for a number of their Fine Art Books, including *Proverbial Philosophy* (1854), *Dramatic Scenes and Other Poems* (1857), *The Course of Time* (1857), *The Poets of the Nineteenth Century* (1857), *The Home Affections by the Poets* (1858), and *Lalla Rookh* (1861).

Tenniel is known to have made all his drawings on wood with a fine-pointed lead

The Raven *[#1] (wood-engraving, J. D. Cooper; 4 3/8 x 3 3/4; The Poetical Works of Edgar Poe, 1858)*

pencil and to seldom have used models for figures, clothing, or backgrounds—certainly not a very Pre-Raphaelite approach. Nevertheless, when he wasn't being cartoony or whimsical, Tenniel effectively used lines

The Smuggler's Leap [#1] (wood-engraving, Dalziels; 4 7/8 x 3 7/8; The Ingoldsby Legends, *1864)*

and built up tones and treated cloth like a typical Rethelian Pre-Raphaelite, filling every inch of space with detail. And though his figures and faces may not always have had a specific model as their basis, they often are true to life and have an emotional intensity.

In a sea of always admirable work that often has a slight comicality in the facial expressions, Tenniel occasionally produced works so rich in line, texture, and tone and so dramatically compelling and compositionally striking that they fit neatly into the Pre-Raphaelite school. In *The Ingoldsby Legends* (1864/1867), in the midst of thirty-one stan-

dard Tenniel drawings are two really startling works for "The Smuggler's Leap"—moody, unforgettable nighttime chase scenes, pulsating with speeding horses, one of which is a glowing ghost. In his four drawings for "The Raven," engraved by J. D. Cooper in *The Poetical Works of Edgar Poe* (1858), Tenniel establishes a serious and poetically realistic mood, especially in the first image, with the figure seated and reading, in a dark study illuminated from various directions and light sources. It's certainly hard to believe that all these exceptional works were created without recourse to models.

Tenniel's book masterpiece is Thomas Moore's *Lalla Rookh*, for which he designed sixty-nine "Arabian Nights"–type drawings, full of Middle Eastern decorative motifs in costume and architecture. While all the drawings show masterful draughtsmanship and controlled linework, there are some extraordinary ones that seem to have been done by the artist on more inspired days. These illustra-

The Smuggler's Leap [#2] (wood-engraving, Dalziels; 4 1/2 x 3 7/8; The Ingoldsby Legends, *1864)*

And They Beheld an Orb *for* ***"The Veiled Prophet of Khorassan"*** *(wood-engraving, Dalziels; 4 5/8 x 3 7/8;* Lalla Rookh, *1861)*

tions also give the impression of being more carefully based on life models: "He Raised His Veil," "And They Beheld an Orb," "'There, Ye Wise Saints,'" "Then Swift His Haggard Brow He Turn'd," "As Mute They Pass'd Before the Flame," and "'Now, Freedom's God!'" All of these have in common (as in the *Ingoldsby* drawings) a more thoroughly rendered scene giving equal weight to background and figures; tonal effects that bring light out of darkness; people that are passionate, emotional, strongly posed; an element of terror; Germanic and exceptionally realistic treatment of cloth, often of uncanny sheerness; and the lack of distinct faces. It almost seems that freed from a need to show full faces—his weakest and most caricatured element—Tenniel was able to invest these scenes with a naturalism and seriousness lacking elsewhere.

The *Art Journal* in reviewing *Lalla Rookh*

took note of Tenniel's artistic influences: "But the designs of this artist, whatever he undertakes to illustrate, . . . [have a] Pre-Raffaellite tendency, which, in some way or other, seems to have influenced these Eastern subjects also. . . . These are powerful designs" (vol. 22, 1860, p. 379). Tenniel was certainly not a Pre-Raphaelite, but he could, when the occasion moved him, create masterful works tantalizingly suggestive of their principles.

"There, Ye Wise Saints" *for* ***"The Veiled Prophet of Khorassan"*** *(wood-engraving, Dalziels; 4 5/8 x 3 7/8;* Lalla Rookh, *1861)*

Catalogue

The Home Affections [Pourtrayed] by the Poets (Charles Mackay, ed.; Routledge, 1858)
 ¶ **The Braes of Yarrow** (Dalziels)
 ¶ **Fair Ines** (Dalziels)

The Ingoldsby Legends (Thomas Ingoldsby [R. H. Barham]; Bentley, 1864)
¶ Among 31 illustrations: **"The Smuggler's Leap,"** 2 illustrations (Dalziels)

Lalla Rookh (Thomas Moore; Longmans, Green, Longmans, and Roberts, 1861)
¶ Among 69 illustrations (Dalziels): **He Raised His Veil**, **And They Beheld an Orb**, and **"There, Ye Wise Saints"** for **"The Veiled Prophet of Khorassan"**; **The Glorious Angel**, **Then Swift His Haggard Brow He Turn'd**, and **And Now—Behold Him Kneeling There** for **"Paradise and the Peri"**; and **His Chiefs Stood Round**, **As Mute They Pass'd Before the Flame**, and **"Now, Freedom's God!"** for **"The Fire-Worshippers"**

Legends and Lyrics (Adelaide Proctor; Bell and Daldy, 1866)
¶ **A Legend of Bregenz** (H. Harral)

[Poe] *The Poetical Works of Edgar Poe* (Low, 1858)
¶ **"The Raven,"** 4 illustrations (J. D. Cooper)

¶ **War and Glory** (etching, Tenniel; 3 1/2 x 5 1/4; signed with monogram in plate)
• Published in *Passages from Modern English Poets* (Junior Etching Club; Day, [1862]); reissued by Tegg in 1874 and, with the etchings transferred to stone for lithographic prints, in 1875

***Then Swift His Haggard Brow He Turn'd** for "Paradise and the Peri" (wood-engraving, Dalziels; 4 1/2 x 3 3/4; Lalla Rookh, 1861)*

Henry J. Townsend

(1810-1890)

Henry Townsend was educated as a surgeon, but he transferred his allegiance to art, becoming a painter of historical, literary, landscape, and genre scenes and a teacher at the Government School of Design, Somerset (1839–66). He exhibited at the Royal Academy and British Institution, and was among those who won prizes at the 1843 Houses of Parliament fresco competition.

In his illustrations, most of which were done while he was a member of the Etching Club (which he helped to found in 1838), Townsend was a proto–Pre-Raphaelite, filling his spaces with sharply rendered and unusual figures in atmospheric, congested compositions—a tendency that increased as Pre-Raphaelitism emerged. Already in 1842, Townsend's illustrations for *The Book of British Ballads* show a care to create realistic scenes of solid, intriguingly posed figures and well-conceived backgrounds that places him well above the book's other artists, including Joseph Noel Paton, William Bell Scott, and John Tenniel. While his six drawings for "Lord Thomas and Fair Annet" are excellent, Townsend's ten illustrations for "Glenfinlas" are haunting and mysterious, apparently influenced by William Blake and Henry Fuseli, with twisting figures and Romantic/realistic gestures, and with a forceful command of tonal and lighting effects.

Townsend devoted most of his talent in the graphic arts to creating plates for numerous Etching Club books, including: Goldsmith's *The Deserted Village* (1841), *Etch'd Thoughts* (1844), Gray's *Elegy Written in a Country Churchyard* (1847), Milton's *L'Allegro* (1849), *Songs and Ballads of Shakespeare* (1853), and *Etchings for the Art Union of London* (1857). In collections that mostly include work by Charles W. Cope, J. C. Horsley, Thomas Creswick, Richard Redgrave, and other older academic artists, Townsend's etchings stand out. In his profusely detailed, almost decorative compositions with realistically rendered figures, Townsend recalls Edward Calvert and Samuel Palmer (Palmer contributed to *Shakespeare* and other

The Wood-breakers *(etching, Townsend, 1856; 4 3/16 x 5 7/8; Etchings for the Art Union of London, 1857)*

Etching Club books). Especially with *L'Allegro*, he anticipates the illustrations of the Pre-Raphaelites, who had been painting for nearly ten years before they revolutionized English illustration in the Moxon *Tennyson* of 1857.

For *L'Allegro* Townsend etched five illustrations, each looking as out of place among the other stilted-figure and academically composed pictures as Dante Gabriel Rossetti's, John Everett Millais's, and William Holman Hunt's drawings do in relation to the old school's illustrations in the Moxon *Tennyson*. Townsend's figures crackle with vitality and emotional interest, and he surrounds them with multiples of themselves, or landscape/interior details that cover every inch of space. For *And the Milkmaid Singeth Blithe*, the three figures, occupied in a natural way—not classically posed—with singing and working, are encased in the myriad details of the decorative landscape (like Holman Hunt's picture surface, among many other Pre-Raphaelite examples, in his *The Day in the Country* etching). With *Wood-breakers* (*Etchings for the Art Union of London*), Townsend's Pre-Raphaelitism becomes truly of the movement: in the unusual composition of assembled details and awkward poses, sheep decorate the background, while playing children and working men are huddled together in a small space in the foreground.

Catalogue

¶ **And the Milkmaid Singeth Blithe** (etching, Townsend; 3 3/8 x 4 5/8; signed in plate)
• Published in *L'Allegro* (John Milton; Etching Club; Cundall, 1849)
• Reissued by Low in 1859 in a wood-engraved edition (W. J. Linton)

¶ **And Then in Haste Her Bowre She Leaves** (etching, Townsend, 1848; 3 1/8 x 4 7/8; signed and dated in plate)
• Published in *L'Allegro* (John Milton; Etching Club; Cundall, 1849)

¶ **Haste Thee Nymph, and Bring with Thee** (etching, Townsend, 1848; 5 1/4 x 6; signed and dated in plate)
• Published in *L'Allegro* (John Milton; Etching Club; Cundall, 1849)

¶ **The Shepherd** (etching, Townsend, 1850; 4 x 3 1/2; signed and dated in plate)
• Published in *Etchings for the Art Union of London* (Etching Club; Cundall, 1857)

¶ **The Wood-breakers** (etching, Townsend, 1856; 4 3/16 x 5 7/8)
• Published in *Etchings for the Art Union of London* (Etching Club; Cundall, 1857)

And the Milkmaid Singeth Blithe (etching, Townsend, 1848; 3 3/8 x 4 5/8; L'Allegro, 1849)

John D. Watson

(1832–1892)

J. D. Watson was one of the most prolific of the Sixties illustrators and a favorite of the Dalziels. He attended the Manchester School of Art (1847) and the Royal Academy Schools in 1851, and returned to Manchester to exhibit, making the acquaintance of Ford Madox Brown. Back in London, he came further under the influence of John Everett Millais and Pre-Raphaelitism and began receiving commissions for illustrative work. He exhibited hundreds of works (mostly genre) in oil and watercolor from the early 1850s through 1890 (Royal Academy, British Institution, Old Water Colour Society, Grosvenor Gallery). His subjects were often children in domestic and outdoor settings, of which the painting *Children at Play* (1856), with its carefully painted ivy and tree stump, crisply delineated group of seven youngsters, and bright Pre-Raphaelite colors, is a fine example.

The Dalziels played a major role in Watson's career and in their memoir acknowledge their professional respect for him as well as his friendship. Seeing a few of Watson's other illustrations of about 1860, they immediately commissioned him to do the 110 drawings for their new Fine Art gift book, *Pilgrim's Progress* (1861)—"this edition of Bunyan's immortal work being, in a pecuniary sense, among the most successful of the many Fine Art Books issued by the Messrs. Routledge," they explained. "Immediately on the publication and instant success of this work, we were instructed to secure Watson's services in illustrating Defoe's *Robinson Crusoe* with a like number of pictures. This he readily undertook

Places of Worship *(wood-engraving, Dalziels; 4 x 3 1/2;* English Sacred Poetry, *1862)*

to do. . . ." Through the Dalziels, Watson developed a lifelong friendship with fellow illustrator Birket Foster—who (true to the web of relationships within the artistic community) married Watson's sister. The Dalziels also gave an interesting characterization by the artist of his sometimes too facile ability: "In the early days of our connection with him he often spoke of what he called his 'fatal facility,' and no doubt that gift told to his detriment. His art was no trouble to him; and this was the root of a certain indolence shown in his later productions which, generally speaking, were far inferior to what might have been expected from his natural powers—though his work was at all times full of tender refinement, beauty, and sympathetic feeling" (*Brothers Dalziel*, pp. 170–72, 174).

Still, Watson was as concerned as anyone about the results of his efforts, remarking on his white-corrected burnished proof of "Too Late" ("In the *Times*" in *London Society*, 1862): "Take away the black which looks like the nostril—which would not be visible in this view of the head" (Museum of Fine Arts, Boston, Hartley Collection).

The *Art Journal* in its review had no qualms about the quality of the art in *Pilgrim's Progress*. "[Watson's] illustrations are exceedingly good—sound and bold in design: no attempt has been made to allegorise the figures. . . . We realise them as creatures of the earth.... The name of the artist is new to us: it will not be long so, for he is undoubtedly a man of genius . . ." (vol. 23, 1861, p. 31).

Watson's drawings for *Pilgrim's Progress* are uniformly excellent, most exhibiting his trademark of one or several large figures close up against the picture plane and very solidly and sturdily portrayed, with tightly controlled lines. But some of his other works emphasize these elements even more, plus experiment with composition, concentrate on decorative details, and achieve greater "German-woodcut" effects. There's no better place to find these excellent Watson pieces than in *English Sacred Poetry* (1862), a book that brought out the best in many illustrators, notably H. S. Marks and Watson. Here there are several drawings of the latter's specialty, children in contemporary settings, plus three especially fine historical images, "Vanity of Learning," "Employment," and "Time and the Year." There's not a hesitant line in the bunch.

Watson also did exceptional work for the periodicals, often filling his space with one or

two poignant female figures realistically and lovingly drawn: "Sunday Evening" and "Her Arms Are Wound About the Tree" (both *Churchman's Family Magazine*, 1863) and "The Duet" (*London Society*, 1864), for example. "The Toad" in *Good Words* (1861) has more

Ash Wednesday *(wood-engraving, Dalziels; 4 5/8 x 7 1/2;* London Society, *vol. 1, 1862, p. 150;* Pictures of Society*)*

children and just basically looks strange—perhaps why some have seen it as his most Pre-Raphaelite work, which it is not necessarily. *Pictures of Society* (1866) has a nice selection (ten) of Watson reprints from publisher Sampson Low's *Churchman's Family Magazine* and *London Society*.

Catalogue

Churchman's Family Magazine
Vol. 1, 1863:
¶ **Her Arms Are Wound About the Tree** (p. 346, Dalziels)
¶ **Sunday Evening** (p. 113, Dalziels; reprinted as **Thinking of Heaven** in *Pictures of Society* [Low, Son, and Marston, 1866])
¶ **The Spirit of Christianity: The Hermit** (p. 260, Dalziels)

English Sacred Poetry (Rev. Robert Aris Willmott, ed.; Routledge, 1862)
¶ Among 28 illustrations (Dalziels): **Time and the Year**, **Vanity of Learning**, **Employment**, **Scene**

in a Scottish Cottage, **Sunday in the Fields**, **Places of Worship**, **Moonlight**, **A Mother's Grief**, and **Last Words**

Good Words
Vol. 2, 1861:
¶ **The Toad** (p. 33, Dalziels; reprinted in *Touches of Nature* [Strahan, 1867; full edition only])

London Society
Vol. 1, 1862:
¶ **Ash Wednesday** (p. 150, Dalziels; reprinted as **Prayer** in *Pictures of Society*)
Vol. 5, 1864:
¶ **The Duet** (*frontispiece* to March issue; Dalziels)

Pilgrim's Progress (John Bunyan; Routledge, 1861)
¶ Among 110 illustrations (Dalziels): **Christian Flies for Destruction**, **Giant Pope**, and **Mercy Left Without the Gate**

Time and the Year (*wood-engraving, Dalziels; 5 1/2 x 4 1/2; English Sacred Poetry, 1862*)

Employment (*wood-engraving, Dalziels; 4 x 3 1/2;* English Sacred Poetry, *1862)*

Sunday in the Fields (*wood-engraving, Dalziels; 3 1/4 x 4;* English Sacred Poetry, *1862)*

Some Occasional
Pre-Raphaelites

At the end of our extended group of Pre-Raphaelites, there still can be added some more names—those artists who produced a few pieces of graphic art somewhat Pre-Raphaelite in style despite careers not always

Charles West Cope: **Christmas at Sunnymeade Hall** *(wood-engraving, 6 7/8 x 4 1/2;* London Society, *vol. 4, Christmas Number, 1863, p. 48)*

in sympathy with the movement.

The historical, literary, biblical, and genre painter **Charles West Cope** (1811–1890) won a prize in the Houses of Parliament fresco competition, became a member of the Royal Academy in 1848, and was among the founders of the Etching Club. In addition to prints for many of the Club's books, he also drew for the wood-block, contributing to Moore's *Irish Melodies* (1856) and Adams's *Sacred Allegories* (1858). Verging on Pre-Raphaelitism are his interesting composition "Christmas Eve and Morn" in *Churchman's Family Magazine* (frontispiece, 1863), with its ominous figure swaying backwards in the snow, and "Christmas at Sunnymeade Hall" in *London Society* (1863), a tightly drawn and modeled contemporary figural composition. Among Cope's best etchings, whose moods, poses, realistically solid figures, and fussy penwork engage the spirit of Pre-Raphaelitism, are *Milton's Dream of His Deceased Wife* and *The Stolen Kiss* (*Etchings for the Art Union of London*, 1857) and *The Spring Flood* (*A Selection of Etchings by the Etching Club*, 1865).

James C. Hook (1819–1907) was another notable Royal Academician and prize-winner in the Houses of Parliament competition. He was an important painter of genre, landscapes, and portraits, specializing in coastal/seascape pictures, which were praised by Ruskin for their rich colors. Like Henry Townsend and C. W. Cope, Hook was instrumental in the founding of the Etching Club and contributed to many of its publications;

these etchings constitute his slight contribution to Pre-Raphaelite illustration. Three of his plates for *Etchings for the Art Union of London* (1857) are exceptional: *Colin Thou Ken'st the Southern Shepherd Boy*, *A Few Minutes Before Dinner Time*, and *The Fisherman's "Good Night."* *Gathering Eggs from the Cliff* (*A Selection of Etchings by the Etching Club*, 1865) is a beautifully tonal drawing with a variety of dotted, crosshatched, and linear textures, just like a Dalziel wood-engraving. *Sea-Urchins* (*Etchings from the Art Union of London*, 1872) has two children on a rock in the bay in semi–Pre-Raphaelite poses.

Arthur Murch, a shadowy artist known to have worked in Italy in the early 1870s, did two incredible designs for *Dalziels' Bible Gallery*—"The Arrow of Deliverance" and "The Flight of Adrammelech." The latter drawing, with its shadows and lighting, effects of incense smoke, perfectly rendered running figures, and Assyrian architectural elements, is one of the more outstanding pieces in the book.

Henry Wallis (1830–1916), the Pre-Raphaelite painter of two famous works, *The Death of Chatterton* (1856) and *The Stonebreaker* (1857), wrote a number of books in his later years on his favorite subject, historic ceramic design—volumes that he illustrated (*Egyptian Ceramic Art*, 1898; *Persian Lustre Vases*, 1899; *The Oriental Influence on Italian Ceramic Art*, 1900; et al.). An extraordinary Pre-Raphaelite illustration in the British Museum's Dalziel Collection (vol. 17, 1863, no. 34) of a bending angel holding the hand of a woman at a gate—for an unknown publication—may be his.

Fred Walker (1840–1875) was a successful painter and illustrator in the naturalistic-pastoral school. (*The Lost Path*, 1863, is among his many paintings based on previous illustrations, and *Autumn*, 1864, is a female-figure-enveloped-by-flowers picture in the best Rossetti/Sandys tradition.) Walker had apprenticed to the wood-engraver Josiah Whymper and was a friend of Swain's manager, W. H. Hooper. During his short career he

Arthur Murch: **The Flight of Adrammelech** *(wood-engraving, Dalziels; 8 3/8 x 6 3/4; Dalziels' Bible Gallery, 1881; Art Pictures from the Old Testament)*

was a prolific illustrator especially for periodicals (from 1860 for *Once a Week*, the *Cornhill Magazine*, and *Good Words*); notable for their sturdy realism are his illustrations for Thackeray's *The Adventures of Philip* in the *Cornhill Magazine* (1861–62). The quality of Walker's work is so high that it would almost be a shame not to include him here; fortunately, he created a famous work that smacks of Pre-Raphaelitism and points to the Aesthetic movement. For Wilkie Collins's play *The Woman in White*, Walker produced a striking composition of a woman rhythmically walking away from the viewer, her face turned to look back, the white of her garments against a black background with stars; this ground-breaking illustrated poster was cut on a 7-by-4-foot composite wood-block by Hooper.

Frederick Sandys

Selected Bibliography and References

Allingham, H., and E. Baumer, eds. *Letters to William Allingham*. London: Longmans, Green, 1911.

Andrews, Keith. *The Nazarenes*. Oxford: Clarendon, 1964.

Art Journal. "Reviews" [Books]. Vols. 15–23 [n.s., 1–10] (1853–71).

Atkinson, J. Beavington. "English Painters of the Present Day: Frederic Leighton, R.A." *Portfolio* 1 (1870), pp. 161–66.

———. "English Painters of the Present Day: H. S. Marks." *Portfolio* 1 (1870), pp. 129–34.

Baker, Charles, ed. *Bibliography of British Book Illustrators, 1860 to 1900*. Birmingham Book Shop, 1978.

Baldry, A. L. "Drawings by Frederick Sandys." *Art Journal* 71 [n.s., 48] (1909), pp. 149–51.

Barrington, Mrs. Russell. *Life, Letters, and Work of Frederic Leighton*. 2 vols. London: Allen, 1906.

Bate, Percy H. *The English Pre-Raphaelite Painters, Their Associates and Successors*. London: Bell, 1899.

———. "The Late Frederick Sandys: A Retrospect." *Studio* 30 (1904), pp. 3–17.

Bickley, Francis. *The Pre-Raphaelite Comedy*. New York: Holt, 1944.

Birmingham Museum and Art Gallery. *Catalogue of the Collection of Drawings and Studies by Sir Edward Burne-Jones, Dante Gabriel Rossetti, Sir J. E. Millais, Ford Madox Brown, Frederick Sandys, John Ruskin, and Others.* 1913.

Bishop, Marchand, and Edward Malins. *James Smetham and Francis Danby*. London: Stevens, 1974.

Blackburn, Henry. *English Art in 1884*. New York: Appleton, 1885.

Bland, David. *A History of Book Illustration*. London: Faber and Faber, 1969.

Bliss, Douglas Percy. *A History of Wood-Engraving*. London: Dent, 1928.

Bodkin, Thomas. "James Collinson." *Apollo* 31 (1940), pp. 128–33.

Brighton Museum and Art Gallery. Catalogue: *Frederick Sandys, 1829–1904*. Betty O'Looney, ed. 1974.

"British Artists: Their Style and Character, No. 7: F. R. Pickersgill, A.R.A.," *Art Journal* 17 (1855), pp. 233–36.

"British Artists: Their Style and Character, No. 12: James Clarke Hook, A.R.A," *Art Journal* 18 (1856), pp. 41–45.

British Painters. New York: Appleton, 1881.

Bryan, Michael. *Bryan's Dictionary of Painters and Engravers*. 5 vols. London: Bell, 1903.

Burne-Jones, Georgiana. *Memorials of Edward Burne-Jones*. 2 vols. London: Macmillan, 1904.

Caine, T. Hall. *Recollections of Dante Gabriel Rossetti*. London: Stock, 1882.

[Calvert, Samuel.] *A Memoir of Edward Calvert*. London: Low, 1893.

Campbell, Robin, and Joanna Drew. *The Paintings, Graphics, and Decorative Work by Edward Burne-Jones, 1831–1898*. London: Arts Council of Great Britain, 1975.

Carpenter, J. "Concerning the Graphotype." *Once a Week*, n.s. [ser. 2], 3 (1867), pp. 181–84.

Cary, Elisabeth Luther. "Frederick Sandys." *Print-Collector's Quarterly* 7, no. 2 (1917), pp. 201–16.

———, ed. *Poems by Dante Gabriel Rossetti*. 2 vols. New York/London: Putnam's, 1903.

Casteras, Susan P. *Pocket Cathedrals: Pre-Raphaelite Book Illustration*. New Haven/London: Yale Center for British Art, 1991.

Castle, Egerton. *English Book-plates*. London/New York: Bell, 1893.

Chamberlain, Arthur B. "Works by Frederick Sandys in the Birmingham Art Gallery." *Apollo* 2 (1925), pp. 258–63.

Chatto, William Andrew, and John Jackson. *A Treatise on Wood-Engraving*. 2d edition. Henry G. Bohn, additional text. London: Chatto and Windus, 1861.

Colvin, Sidney. "English Painters of the Present Day: Edward Burne-Jones." *Portfolio* 1 (1870), pp. 17–22.

———. "English Painters of the Present Day: E. J. Poynter, A.R.A." *Portfolio* 1 (1870), pp. 1–4.

———. "English Painters of the Present Day: Ford Madox Brown." *Portfolio* 1 (1870), pp. 81–86.

———. "English Painters of the Present Day: Simeon Solomon." *Portfolio* 1 (1870), pp. 33–35.

Concise Dictionary of National Biography. Oxford University Press, 1969.

"Contemporary Portraits, New Series, No. 7: E. J. Poynter, R.A." *Dublin University Magazine* 92 (1878), pp. 24–32.

Crane, Walter. *An Artist's Reminiscences.* London: Methuen, 1907.

———. *Of the Decorative Illustration of Books Old and New.* New York: Bell, 1896.

"Criticisms on Contemporaries, No. 7. The Rossettis, Part 2: Dante Gabriel Rossetti." *Tinsley's Magazine* 5 (1869–70), pp. 142–51.

Crombie, Theodore. "Macmillan's Eminent Victorians: A Portrait Gallery by Frederick Sandys." *Apollo* 85 (1967), pp. 45–47.

———. "Some Portraits by Frederick Sandys." *Apollo* 82 (1965), pp. 398–400.

Dale, William. "A Portrait by Frederick Sandys." *Burlington Magazine* 152 (1965), pp. 250–53.

Dalziel, George and Edward. *The Brothers Dalziel: A Record of Fifty Years' Work, 1840–1890.* London: Methuen, 1901.

Dalziel, Gilbert. "Wood Engraving in the Sixties and Some Criticisms of Today." *Print-Collector's Quarterly* 15, no. 1 (1928), pp. 81–84.

Daniels, Morna. *Victorian Book Illustration.* London: British Library, 1988.

Delaware Art Museum. Catalogue: *The Pre-Raphaelite Era, 1848–1914.* Rowland and Betty Elzea, text. Wilmington, 1976.

De Maré, Eric. *The Victorian Woodblock Illustrators.* London: Fraser, 1980.

Doughty, Oswald. *A Victorian Romantic: Dante Gabriel Rossetti.* New Haven: Yale University Press, 1949.

———, ed. *Dante Gabriel Rossetti: Letters to His Publisher, F. S. Ellis.* London: Scholartis, 1928.

Doughty, Oswald, and J. R. Wahl, eds. *The Letters of Dante Gabriel Rossetti.* 4 vols. Oxford: Clarendon, 1965–67.

Du Maurier, George. *The Martian.* New York: Harper, 1897.

Dunlap, Joseph. *The Book That Never Was.* New York: Oriole Editions, 1971.

Earland, Ada. *Ruskin and His Circle.* New York: Putnam's, 1910.

Engen, Rodney. *Dictionary of Victorian Engravers, Print Publishers, and Their Works.* Cambridge: Chadwick-Healy, 1979.

———. *Dictionary of Victorian Wood Engravers.* Cambridge: Chadwick-Healy, 1985.

———. *Pre-Raphaelite Prints.* London: Humphries, 1995.

Esdaile, Katherine. "English Book Illustration in the Eighteenth Century." *Bibliophile* 2 (1909), pp. 114–23, 305–17.

Ewart, Henry, ed. *Toilers in Art.* London: Isbister, 1891.

"Examples of German Artists [Bible Illustrations by German Artists]." *Art Journal* 16 (1854), pp. 16, 41, 104, 201, 328, 360.

Fagan, Louis. *The History of Engraving in England.* London: Low, 1893.

Fairholt, F. W. "Albert Dürer: His Works, His Compatriots, and His Times." *Art Journal* 17 (1855), pp. 1–5, 61–63, 82–84, 122–24.

Falk, Bernard. *Five Years Dead.* London: Book Club, 1938.

Faxon, Alicia Craig. *Dante Gabriel Rossetti.* New York: Abbeville, 1989.

Fenn, W. W. "Our Living Artists: Henry Stacy Marks, R.A." *Magazine of Art* 2 (1879), pp. 97–100.

Fincham, H. W. *The Artists and Engravers of British and American Book Plates.* London: Paul, Trench, Trubner, 1897.

Fitzgerald, Penelope. *Edward Burne-Jones: A Biography.* London: Joseph, 1975.

Ford, Julia Ellsworth. *Simeon Solomon: An Appreciation.* New York: Sherman, 1908.

Fredeman, William E. *Pre-Raphaelitism: A Bibliocritical Study.* Cambridge, Mass.: Harvard University Press, 1965.

———, ed. *A Pre-Raphaelite Gazette: The Penkill Letters of Arthur Hughes to William Bell Scott and Alice Boyd, 1886–97.* Manchester: John Rylands Library, 1967.

Friedrich, Walther. *Alfred Rethel.* Mainz, 1907.

Gaunt, William. *The Pre-Raphaelite Tragedy.* London: Cape, 1942.

———. *Victorian Olympus.* New York: Oxford University Press, 1952.

The Germ. Reprint. Portland, Maine: Mosher, 1898.

Gibson, Robin. "Arthur Hughes: Arthurian and Related Subjects of the Early 1860s." *Burlington Magazine* 112 (1970), pp. 51–56.

Gissing, A. C. *William Holman Hunt: A Biography.* London: Duckworth, 1936.

Glynn, Jennifer. *Prince of Publishers.* New York/London: Allison and Busby, 1986.

Godefrey, Richard T. *Printmaking in Britain.* Oxford: Phaidon, 1978.

Goldman, Paul. *Victorian Illustrated Books, 1850–1870.* Boston: Godine, 1994.

———. *Victorian Illustration.* Aldershot: Scolar, 1996.

Grant, Colonel M. H. *A Dictionary of British Etchers.* London: Rockliff, 1952.

Graves, Algernon. *A Dictionary of Artists Who Have Exhibited Works in the Principal London Exhibitions from 1790 to 1893.* Bath: Kingsmead, 1970.

Gray, Basil. *The English Print.* London: Black, 1937.

Gray, J. M. "Frederick Sandys and the Woodcut Designers of Thirty Years Ago." *Century Guild Hobby Horse* 3 (1888), pp. 147–57.

Grieve, Alastair. "Rossetti's Applied Art Designs 2: Book Bindings." *Apollo* 115 (1973), pp. 79–84.

Guichard, Kenneth H. *British Etchers, 1850–1940.* London: Garton, 1981.

Guise, Hilary. *Great Victorian Engravings: A Collector's Guide.* London: Astragal, 1980.

Hall, John N. *Trollope and His Illustrators.* New York: St. Martin's, 1980.

Hamerton, P. G. "Edward J. Poynter, R.A." *Portfolio* 8 (1877), pp. 11–14.

Hands, Lydia. *Golden Threads from an Ancient Loom: Das Nibelungenlied.* With Fourteen Wood Engravings by Julius Schnorr, of Carolsfeld. London: Griffith and Farran / New York: Dutton, 1880.

Hardie, Martin. "The Moxon *Tennyson.*" *Book-Lover's Magazine* 7 (1908), pp. 45–51.

Harris, Jack. "The Pre-Raphaelites and the Moxon *Tennyson.*" *Journal of Pre-Raphaelite Studies* 3, no. 2 (1983), pp. 26–37.

Harrison, Martin, and Bill Waters. *Burne-Jones.* New York: Putnam, 1973.

Hartnoll and Eyre. Catalogue: *Pre-Raphaelite Graphics.* London, 1974.

Henderson, Marina. *Dante Gabriel Rossetti.* Susan Miller, intro. New York: St. Martin's, 1973.

Hill, George Birbeck, ed. *Letters of Dante Gabriel Rossetti to William Allingham, 1854–1870.* London: Unwin, 1897.

Hogarth, Paul. *Arthur Boyd Houghton.* London: Fraser, 1981.

Holbein, Hans. *Dance of Death.* London: Bohn, 1858.

Holme, Geoffrey, ed. *British Book Illustration Yesterday and Today.* Malcolm Salaman, text. London: *Studio* Special Number, 1923.

Houfe, Simon. *Dictionary of British Book Illustrators and Caricaturists.* Woodbridge, Suffolk: Antique Collectors' Club, [1981].

Housman, Laurence. *Arthur Boyd Houghton.* London: Paul, Trench, Trubner, 1896.

———. "The Illustrations of Arthur Hughes." *Bibliophile* 1, no. 5 (1908), pp. 231–37.

Hubbard, Hesketh. *Some Victorian Draughtsmen.* Cambridge: Cambridge University Press, 1944.

Hueffer, Ford Madox, ed. *Ford Madox Brown: A Record of His Life and Work.* London: Longmans, Green, 1896.

Hunnisett, Basil. *A Dictionary of British Steel Engravers.* Leigh-on-Sea: Lewis, 1980.

———. *Steel-Engraved Book Illustration in England.* London: Scolar, 1980.

Hunt, Diana Holman. *My Grandfather, His Wives and Loves.* London: Hamilton, 1969.

Hunt, William Holman. *Pre-Raphaelitism and the Pre-Raphaelite Brotherhood.* 2 vols. London/New York: Macmillan, 1905–06.

Husni, Samira. "The Relation Between Dante Gabriel Rossetti and William Allingham." *Journal of Pre-Raphaelite Studies* 3, no. 2 (1983), pp. 102–10.

Huxley, Leonard. *The House of Smith, Elder.* London: Clowes, 1923.

"Illustrations of the Parables." *Art Journal* 26 [n.s., 3] (1864), pp. 106–07.

Incorporated Printsellers' Association of London Alphabetical Listing of Engravings. Catalogues of Registered Engravings. London, 1847–75, 1892, 1894, 1912.

Ironside, Robin, intro. *Pre-Raphaelite Painters.* John Gere, descriptive catalogue. New York: Oxford University Press / Phaidon, 1948.

Jackson, F. Hamilton. "The Work of Sir E. J. Poynter, P.R.A." *Architectural Review* 2 (1897), pp. 2–13, 51–63, 118–30, 155–66, 224–31.

James, Philip. *English Book Illustration, 1800–1900.* London / New York: King Penguin, 1947.

"James Smetham and C. Allston Collins." *Art Journal* 66 [n.s., 43] (1904), pp. 281–84.

Lago, Mary, ed. *Burne-Jones Talking: His Conversations, 1895–1898.* Preserved by His Studio Assistant Thomas Rooke. London: Murray, 1982.

Laver, James. *A History of British and American Etching.* New York: Dodd, 1929.

[Lawless] "Mr. M. J. Lawless." Obituary. *Art Journal* 26 [n.s., 3] (1864), p. 290.

Layard, George Somes. "Millais and *Once a Week.*" *Good Words* 34 (1893), pp. 552–58.

———. *Tennyson and His Pre-Raphaelite Illustrators.* London: Stock, 1894.

Lee, Brian North. *British Bookplates.* London: David and Clark, 1979.

Lindley, Keith. *The Woodblock Engravers.* London: Abbot, 1970.

Linton, W. J. *Engravings on Wood.* Scrapbook, presented by Linton to Mrs. A.N.S. Anthony, 1902. Print Room, New York Public Library, Humanities and Social Sciences Library.

———. *The Masters of Wood-Engraving.* New Haven: Chiswick, 1889.

———. *Some Practical Hints on Wood-Engraving.* Boston: Lee and Shepard / New York: Dillingham, 1879.

———. *Thirty Pictures by Deceased British Artists.* Engraved Expressly for the Art-Union of London by W. J. Linton, 1860. Together with pasted-in proofs inscribed by Linton to Samuel P. Avery, 1894. Print Room, New York Public Library, Humanities and Social Sciences Library.

———. *Wood-Engraving.* Scrapbook. Print Room, New York Public Library, Humanities and Social Sciences Library.

Lutyens, Mary, intro. *John Everett Millais's Illustrated Edition of The Parables of Our Lord.* New York: Dover, 1975.

Maas, Jeremy. *Victorian Painters.* London: Barrie and Rockliff, 1969.

MacColl, D. S. *Nineteenth Century Art.* Glasgow: Maclehose, 1902.

Macmillan and Company. *Bibliocritical Catalogue of Macmillan and Company's Publications from 1843 to 1889.* London: Macmillan, 1891.

Marks, Henry Stacy. *Pen and Pencil Sketches by H. S. Marks.* 2 vols. London: Chatto and Windus, 1894.

Massé, Gertrude. *A Bibliography of First Editions of Books Illustrated by Walter Crane.* London: Chelsea, 1923.

Masters in Art: Leighton. Boston: Bates and Guild, 1908.

Masters in Art: Millais. Boston: Bates and Guild, 1908.

[Mendez] Christopher Mendez Gallery and Ian Hodgkins and Company. Catalogue: *Exhibition of Proof Wood Engravings, 1840–1880.* Rodney Engen, intro.: "The Triumph of Wood." The Vatch, Slad, Gloucestershire, 1986.

Merrill, Linda. *The Peacock Room: A Cultural Biography.* Washington, D.C.: Freer Gallery of Art / New Haven and London: Yale University Press, 1998.

Meynell, Wilfred. "Val Prinsep, A.R.A.: Painter and Dramatist." *Magazine of Art* 6 (1883), pp. 405–09.

Millais, John Guille. *The Life and Letters of Sir John Everett Millais.* 2 vols. New York: Stokes, 1899.

Mills, Ernestine, ed. *The Life and Letters of Frederic Shields.* London: Longmans, Green, 1912.

Morris, William: "Death the Avenger and Death the Friend." In *Churches of Northern France.* Portland, Maine: Mosher, 1901.

[Morten] "Thomas Morten." Obituary. *Art Journal* 28 [n.s., 5] (1866), p. 364.

Muir, Percy. *Victorian Illustrated Books.* New York: Praeger, 1971.

National Gallery, Millbank. Catalogue: *Book Illustration of the Sixties.* Harold Hartley, intro. 1923.

National Museums and Galleries on Merseyside, Liverpool. Catalogue of Works in the Walker Art Gallery, Lady Lever Art Gallery, and Sudley Art Gallery. *Artists of the Pre-Raphaelite Circle: The First Generation.* Mary Bennett, text. London: Humphries, 1988.

Neve, Christopher. "The Woman-Goddess as Seen by Frederick Sandys." *Country Life* 155 (1974), pp. 1268–69.

Nicoll, John. *Dante Gabriel Rossetti.* New York: Macmillan, 1975.

———. *The Pre-Raphaelites.* London: Studio Vista, 1970.

Noel-Paton, M. H., and J. P. Campbell. *Noel Paton, 1821–1901.* Edinburgh: Ramsay Head, 1990.

Ormond, R. L. "Another Bulwer Portrait by Sandys." *Burlington Magazine* 108 (1966), pp. 194–97.

Packer, Lona Mosk, ed. *The Rossetti-Macmillan Letters.* Berkeley / Los Angeles: University of California Press, 1963.

Palmer, A. H. "James Clarke Hook, R.A." *Portfolio* 19 (1888), pp. 35–43.

Pennell, Joseph. "An English Illustrator." *Quarto,* no. 1 (1896), pp. 33–37.

———. "A Golden Decade in English Art." *Savoy,* no. 1 (1896), pp. 112–24.

———. "John Everett Millais, Painter and Illustrator." *Fortnightly Review* 66 [n.s., 60] (1896), pp. 443–50.

———. *Modern Illustration.* London / New York: Bell, 1895.

———. *"Once a Week:* A Great Art Magazine." *Bibliographica* 3 (1897), pp. 60–82.

———. *Pen Drawing and Pen Draughtsmen.* London: Unwin, 1921.

———, ed. *Some Poems by Alfred, Lord Tennyson.*

William Holman Hunt, intro. New York: New Amsterdam, 1903 [London: Freemantle, 1901].

Phelps, Sarah Hamilton. "The Hartley Collection of Victorian Illustration." *Boston Museum Bulletin* 71, no. 360 (1973), pp. 52–67.

Pierpont Morgan Library. *William Morris and the Art of the Book.* Paul Needham, Joseph Dunlap, John Dreyfus, and John M. Crawford, Jr., text. New York, 1976.

Portfolio. Vol. 3, 1872 [Samuel Palmer etching: *Sunrise* (a.k.a. *Sunset*)].

"Potentia Silentii: Being a Further Selection of Passages from the Letters and Papers of James Smetham." *Century Guild Hobby Horse* 3 (1888), pp. 8–12.

"A Pre-Raphaelite Exhibition." *Saturday Review* 4 (1857), pp. 11–12.

Pre-Raphaelite Illustrations from Moxon's Tennyson. London: Academy, 1978.

Prinsep, Val. "A Chapter from a Painter's Reminiscence. The Oxford Circle: Rossetti, Burne-Jones, and William Morris." *Magazine of Art*, n.s., 2 (1904), pp. 167–72, 281–86.

Rabin, Lucy. *Ford Madox Brown and the Pre-Raphaelite History Picture.* New York / London: Garland, 1978.

Ray, Gordon. *The Illustrator and the Book in England from 1790 to 1914.* New York: Pierpont Morgan Library, 1976.

Read, Benedict. *Victorian Sculpture.* New Haven / London: Yale University Press, 1982.

Read, Benedict, and Joanna Barnes, eds. *Pre-Raphaelite Sculpture.* London: Humphries, 1991.

Reid, Forrest. *The Illustrators of the Sixties.* London: Faber, 1928.

Rethel, Alfred. *Ein Todtentanz aus dem Jahre.* Leipzig: Wigland, 1848.

Review of *Relics of Albert Dürer, Dedicated to His Admirers. Foreign Quarterly Review* 11 (1833), pp. 73–89.

Reynolds, Simon. *The Vision of Simeon Solomon.* Gloucestershire: Catalpa, 1984.

Rhys, Ernest. *Frederic, Lord Leighton.* London: Bell, 1900.

Roberts, Leonard. *Arthur Hughes: His Life and Work.* Catalogue raisonné. Stephen Wildman, intro. Woodbridge, Suffolk: Antique Collectors' Club, 1997.

Ross, Robert. "Simeon Solomon: A Biography." *Bibelot* 17 (1911), pp. 139–51.

"Rossetti: Some Extracts from His Letters to Mr. Frederic Shields." *Century Guild Hobby Horse,* no. 15 (1889), pp. 82–96.

Rossetti, William Michael. "English Painters of the Present Day: A. Hughes, Windus, Miss Spartali, the Younger Madox Brown." *Portfolio* 1 (1870), pp. 113–19.

———. "The Pre-Raphaelite Brotherhood." *Magazine of Art* 4 (1881), pp. 434–37.

———. *Some Reminiscences of William Michael Rossetti.* 2 vols. New York: Scribner's, 1906.

———, ed. *Dante Gabriel Rossetti: His Family-Letters.* 2 vols. Boston: Roberts, 1895.

———, ed. *The Family Letters of Christina Georgina Rossetti.* London: Brown, Langham, 1908.

———, ed. *Praeraphaelite Diaries and Letters.* London: Hurst and Blackett, 1900.

———, ed. *Ruskin: Rossetti: PreRaphaelitism: Papers 1854 to 1862.* London: Allen / New York: Dodd, Mead, 1899.

Rowley, Charles. *Fifty Years of Work Without Wages.* London: Hodder and Stoughton, [1912].

Ruskin, John. *Ariadne Florentina.* Six Lectures on Wood and Metal Engraving Given Before the University of Oxford, 1872. London: Allen, 1890.

———. *The Art of England.* Sunnyside, Kent: Allen, 1883.

———. *Modern Painters.* 5 vols. Smith, Elder, 1843–60.

———. *Notes on Some of the Principal Pictures Exhibited in the Rooms of the Royal Academy.* Nos. 1–5. London: Smith, Elder, 1855–59.

———. *Pre-Raphaelitism.* London: Smith, Elder, 1851.

[Sandys] "Frederick Sandys." *Art Journal* 46 [n.s., 23] (1884), pp. 73–78.

Schnorr's Bible Pictures. London: Williams and Norgate, 2d ser., 1857.

Scott, William Bell. *Autobiographical Notes of the Life of William Bell Scott.* W. Minto, ed. 2 vols. New York: Harper, 1892.

Seddon, John P. *Memoir and Letters of the Late Thomas Seddon, Artist.* London: Nisbet, 1858.

[Seddon] "Mr. Thomas Seddon." Obituary. *Art Journal* 19 (1857), p. 62.

Shaberman, R. B., comp. *George MacDonald's Books for Children: A Bibliography of First Editions.* London: Privately printed, 1979.

Sharp, William. *Dante Gabriel Rossetti: A Record and a Study.* London: Macmillan, 1882.

Shaw-Sparrow, W. *A Book of British Etching.* London: Lane, Bodley Head, 1926.

Shields, Frederic. "An Autobiography." *Good Words* 30 (1889), pp. 821–27.

Smetham, Sarah, and William Davies, eds. *Letters*

of *James Smetham.* Davies: "Memoir of James Smetham," pp. 1–50. London/New York: Macmillan, 1891.

Smith, Janet Adam. *Children's Illustrated Books.* Britain in Pictures series. London: Collins, 1948.

Smyser, William E. "Romanticism in Tennyson and His Pre-Raphaelite Illustrators." *North American Review* 192 (1910), pp. 504–15.

Sotheby, Wilkinson, and Hodge. *Catalogue of the Choice Collection of Engravings and Etchings Formed by W. B. Scott, Esq.* London: Dryden, 1885.

Spencer, Isobel. *Walter Crane.* London: Studio Vista, 1975.

Spielmann, M. H. *John Ruskin.* Philadelphia: Lippincott, 1900.

———. *Millais and His Works.* Edinburgh: Blackwood, 1898.

Staley, Allen. *The Pre-Raphaelite Landscape.* Oxford: Clarendon, 1973.

Stephens, F. G. "Edward Burne-Jones, A.R.A." *Portfolio* 16 (1885), pp. 220–25, 227–32.

———. "Frederick John Shields and His Work." *Portfolio* 15 (1884), pp. 134–36.

———. "Mr. Rossetti's Pictures." *Athenaeum* (Oct. 21, 1865), pp. 545–46.

Story, Alfred. *Sir Joseph Noel Paton, His Life and Work.* Art Journal Annual (1895), pp. 97–128.

Sullivan, Edmund J. *The Art of Illustration.* London: Chapman and Hall, 1921.

Surtees, Virginia. *Dante Gabriel Rossetti: 1828–1882.* 2 vols. London: Oxford University Press, 1971.

———, ed. *The Diary of Ford Madox Brown.* New Haven/London: Yale University Press, 1981.

Swinburne, Algernon C. "Simeon Solomon: Notes on His 'Vision of Love' and Other Studies." *Dark Blue* 1, no. 5 (1871), pp. 568–77.

Symons, Arthur. "Studies in Seven Arts: Simeon Solomon." *Bibelot* 12 (1906), pp. 152–58.

Tanis, James, and John Dooley, eds. *Lewis Carroll's The Hunting of the Snark, Illustrated by Henry Holiday.* Martin Gardner, Charles Mitchell, and Selwyn H. Goodacre, text. Los Altos, Cal.: Kaufman, 1981.

Tate Gallery. *Catalogue of a Loan Exhibition of Drawings, Engravings, and Artist's Proofs of Book Illustration of the 1860s.* London, 1923.

Victoria and Albert Museum. *Catalogue of the Loan Exhibition of British Engravings and Etchings.* London, 1903.

———. *Catalogue of the Loan Exhibition of Modern Illustration.* London, 1901.

———. *Catalogue of Modern Wood Engravings in the Victoria and Albert Museum.* London, 1906.

———. *Catalogue of Prints: 2. Modern Etchings and Aquatints of the British and American Schools in the National Art Library.* 2 vols. London, 1906.

———. *Catalogue of Prints and Wood Engravings After Sir John Everett Millais in the Victoria and Albert Museum.* London, 1908.

———. *Handbook of the Department of Prints and Drawings.* London, 1964.

Wakeman, Geoffrey. *Aspects of Victorian Lithography, Anastatic Printing, and Photozincography.* Wymondham: Brewhouse, 1970.

Walker Art Gallery and Victoria and Albert Museum. *William Holman Hunt.* Mary Bennett, text. Liverpool/London, 1969.

[Wallach] Miriam and Ira D. Wallach Art Gallery, Columbia University in the City of New York. *The Post–Pre-Raphaelite Print.* Allen Staley, Martha M. Evans, Pamela M. Fletcher, Yael Ksander, Lisa R. Leavitt, Jason M. Rosenfeld, and Paul Tabor, text. New York, 1995.

Manuscript and Art Collections Consulted

Ashmolean Museum, Oxford. Department of Western Art.

Beinecke Rare Book and Manuscript Library, Yale University Library, New Haven.

Birmingham Museums and Art Gallery. Art Department.

Boston Public Library. Print Department; Rare Books.

British Museum, London. Department of Prints and Drawings (Dalziel Collection).

Castle Museum, Norwich.

Delaware Art Museum, Wilmington.

Fitzwilliam Museum, Cambridge. Prints Division.

Fogg Art Museum, Harvard University, Cambridge, Mass. Rare Books; Prints and Drawings departments.

Glasgow Museums, Art Gallery and Museum. Department of Art.

Houghton Library, Harvard University, Cambridge, Mass.

Hunterian Museum and Art Gallery, University of Glasgow.

Library of Congress, Washington, D.C. Rare Book Collection; Prints and Photographs Division.

Manchester City Art Galleries. Fine Art Department.

Museum of Fine Arts, Boston. Department of Prints, Drawings, and Photographs (Hartley Collection).

National Gallery of Scotland, Edinburgh. Prints and Drawings.

New York Public Library, Humanities and Social Sciences Library. Henry W. and Albert A. Berg Collection of English and American Literature (Macmillan Papers); Print Room.

Newark [N.J.] Public Library. Special Collections.

Norfolk and Norwich Central Library.

Paton, Joseph Noel. Letter to Berlin Photographic Company, 1898. Manuscript, author's collection.

Perth Museum and Art Gallery.

Pierpont Morgan Library, New York. Autographs: English Miscellaneous Manuscripts (Millais Papers); Print Room.

Princeton University Library. Department of Rare Books and Special Collections (Janet Camp Troxell Collection of Rossetti Manuscripts;

Metzdorf Collection; Parrish Collection).

Rutgers University Libraries, New Brunswick, N.J. Early British Periodicals and English Literary Periodicals microform collections.

Sandys, Frederick. Letter to Dalziel Brothers, n.d. Manuscript, author's collection.

Victoria and Albert Museum, London. Department of Prints, Drawings, and Paintings.

Walker Art Gallery, National Museums and Galleries on Merseyside, Liverpool. Fine Art Department.

Whitworth Art Gallery, University of Manchester.

William Morris Gallery, London Borough of Waltham Forest.

Yale Center for British Art, New Haven. Department of Prints and Drawings; Rare Books.

William Holman Hunt

Frederick Sandys

Index

Joseph Noel Paton